Collins

WATERWAYS GUIDE 5

North West & the Pennines

CONTENTS

Map showing the waterways of Britain	4
Key to map pages	6
General information for waterways users	8
Aire & Calder Navigation: Leeds to Wakefield	15
Bridgewater Canal	27
Calder & Hebble Navigation	46
Huddersfield Narrow Canal	56
Huddersfield Broad Canal	65
Lancaster Canal	69
Leeds & Liverpool Canal	85
Macclesfield Canal	141
Manchester Bolton & Bury Canal	156
Peak Forest and Ashton Canals	167
Rochdale Canal	179
Sankey Canal	198
Trent & Mersey Canal: Hardings Wood to Dutton	207
Index	220

Map data

Published by Nicholson
An imprint of HarperCollins Publishers
Westerhill Road, Bishopbriggs, Glasgow G64 2QT
www.harpercollins.co.uk

River Thames Guide first published by Nicholson 1969
Waterways guides 1 South, 2 Midlands and 3 North first published by Nicholson 1971
This edition first published by Nicholson and Ordnance Survey 1997
New edition published by Nicholson 2000, 2003, 2006, 2009, 2012, 2015

Wildlife text from *Collins Complete Guide to British Wildlife* and *Collins Wild Guide*.

This product uses map data licensed from Ordnance Survey © Crown copyright and database rights (1999, 2014) Ordnance Survey (100018598)

The representation in this publication of a road, track or path is no evidence of the existence of a right of way.

Researched and written by Jonathan Mosse.

The publishers gratefully acknowledge the assistance given by Canal & River Trust and their staff in the preparation of this guide. Grateful thanks are also due to the Environment Agency, members of the Inland Waterways Association, and CAMRA representatives and branch members.

All photographs reproduced by kind permission of Derek Pratt Photography, apart from:
Jonathan Mosse pp14, 47, 156–165, 157, 160, 163, 178, 193, 198–205, 200;
Shutterstock: p22 Gordon Ball LRPS; p27–45 Paul Reid, p68 Andrei Nekrassov, p69–83 Kevin Eaves,
p76 (Green Woodpecker) Borislav Borisov, p151 (Great Tit) Marcin Perkowski, p192 Areipa.lt, p217 Karel Gallas;
Paul Huggins (www.paulhugginsphotography.com) pp42, 43, 72, 76 (Grey Heron).

A catalogue record for this book is available from the British Library

Printed in China

ISBN 978-0-00-810160-2

10 9 8 7 6 5 4 3 2

MIX
Paper from
responsible sources
FSC
www.fsc.org **FSC™ C007454**

FSC™ is a non-profit international organisation established to promote the responsible management of the world's forests. Products carrying the FSC label are independently certified to assure consumers that they come from forests that are managed to meet the social, economic and ecological needs of present and future generations, and other controlled sources.

Find out more about HarperCollins and the environment at
www.harpercollins.co.uk/green

Wending their quiet way through town and country, the inland navigations of Britain offer boaters, walkers and cyclists a unique insight into a fascinating, but once almost lost, world. When built this was the province of the boatmen and their families, who lived a mainly itinerant lifestyle: often colourful, to our eyes picturesque but, for them, remarkably harsh. Transporting the nation's goods during the late 1700s and early 1800s, negotiating locks, traversing aqueducts and passing through long narrow tunnels, canals were the arteries of trade during the initial part of the industrial revolution.

Then the railways came: the waterways were eclipsed in a remarkably short time by a faster and more flexible transport system, and a steady decline began. In a desperate fight for survival canal tolls were cut, crews toiled for longer hours and worked the boats with their whole family living aboard. Canal companies merged, totally uneconomic waterways were abandoned, some were modernised but it was all to no avail. Large scale commercial carrying on inland waterways had reached the finale of its short life.

At the end of World War II a few enthusiasts roamed this hidden world and harboured a vision of what it could become: a living transport museum which stretched the length and breadth of the country; a place where people could spend their leisure time and, on just a few of the wider waterways, a still modestly viable transport system.

The restoration struggle began and, from modest beginnings, Britain's inland waterways are now seen as an irreplaceable part of the fabric of the nation. Long-abandoned waterways, once seen as an eyesore and a danger, are recognised for the valuable contribution they make to our quality of life, and restoration schemes are integrating them back into the network. Let us hope that the country's network of inland waterways continues to be cherished and well-used, maintained and developed as we move through the 21st century.

If you would like to comment on any aspect of the guides, please write to Nicholson Waterways Guides, Collins, Westerhill Road, Bishopbriggs, Glasgow G64 2QT or email nicholson@harpercollins.co.uk.

Also available:

Collins NICHOLSON

Waterways guides and map

1   **Grand Union, Oxford & the South East**
2   **Severn, Avon & Birmingham**
3   **Birmingham & the Heart of England**
4   **Four Counties & the Welsh Canals**
6   **Nottingham, York & the North East**
7   **River Thames & the Southern Waterways**
Norfolk Broads
Inland Waterways Map of Great Britain

The Waterways of Britain

KEY Waterways featured in:

Guide 1 Grand Union, Oxford & the South East
Guide 2 Severn, Avon & Birmingham
Guide 3 Birmingham & the Heart of England
Guide 4 Four Counties & the Welsh Canals
Guide 5 North West & the Pennines
Guide 6 Nottingham, York & the North East
Guide 7 River Thames & the Southern Waterways

Norfolk Broads

·············· Unnavigable section

Kingston upon Hull

R Humber

Lincoln
Fossdyke & Witham Navigations
Kyme Eau
South Kyme
Boston

King's Lynn
Wisbech
R Nene
Peterborough

River Ant
River Thurne
River Bure
Norwich
River Yare
River Chet
Beccles
River Waveney
Great Yarmouth
Lowestoft

R Great Ouse
R Cam
Cambridge

R Great Ouse

Bishop's Stortford
River Stort
Hertford
Chelmer & Blackwater Navigation
Hemel Hempstead
River Lee
Watford
Chelmsford
Maldon
Slough
London
R Thames

River Wey
Guildford
Godalming

Chatham
River Medway
Maidstone
Tonbridge
Dover

Brighton

English Channel

The Inland Waterways Map of Great Britain covers the canal and river navigations of England, Scotland and Wales.

Mapping for the canal between the two markers can be found on the pages shown

Lock (symbol points uphill)
Tunnel
90-91
Aqueduct
Flight of locks (5=number of locks)

Acworth Moor Top
Navigation
Failing
Wakefield
Calder & Hebble Navigation
48-49
Thornhill
50-51
Huddersfield Broad Canal
66
Aspley Basin
64
Huddersfield Narrow Canal
Huddersfield
62-63
20
Marsden
Standedge Tunnel 5698yds

Barnsley
Holmfirth
Holmfirth
Rotherham
SHEFFIELD
Sheffield City
Chesterfield

Dearne
Derwent Reservoir
Ladybower Reservoir
Glossop
Woodley Tunnel 176 yds
Hyde Bank Tunnel 308 yds

New Mills
Buxworth Basins
Whaley Bridge
168-169
Peak Forest Canal
172
Marple Junction
Buxton
Leek
Cheddleton

Littleborough
188
Milnrow
Rochdale
186-187
61
Oldham
Stalybridge
Ashton-under-Lyne
58-59
Portland Basin
Hyde
175
Hazel Grove
Stockport
155
Bollington
Bollington Aqueduct
149
153
Macclesfield Canal
147
Bosley
144-145
Biddulph
142
Poole Aqueduct
Congleton Wharf
208-209
Kidsgrove

185
Bury
164-165
158-159
Manchester Bolton & Bury Canal
180-181
Hunts Bank
Salford
Mode Wheel
176-177
Ashton Canal
36-37
Waters Meeting Junc.
34-35
MANCHESTER
Manchester
Wilmslow
Macclesfield
Sandbach
210-211
Wheelock
Alsager
Thurlwood
10
Newcastle-under-Lyme

Johnson's Hill
Chorley
109
Adlington
106
21
Coal Railway
162
161
Nob End
Bolton
40-41
44-45
Bridgewater Canal Leigh Branch
Leigh
Altrincham
Sale
32-33
Lymm
Bridgewater Canal
Knutsford
Saltersford Tunnel 424 yds
Barnton Tunnel 572 yds
Anderton Lift
Croxton Aqueduct
214-215
Trent & Mersey Canal
212-213
Middlewich
Kings
Northwich
Winsford
Crewe
Nantwich

101
Rufford
98-99
96-97
Burscough
Appleby
Ormskirk
Skelmersdale
Ell Meadow
Wigan Pier
102-103
104-105
Leeds & Liverpool Canal
Wigan
Prestbolt
204-205
Warrington
30-31
Stockton Heath
Preston Brook Tunnel 1239 yds
218-219
Dutton
Saltersford
River Weaver
Tarvin
Chester

Southport
95
Maghull
Lydiate
Crosby
Formby
93
Kirkby
Aintree
Bootle
Birkenhead
87
LIVERPOOL
Liverpool Dock
Stanley Dock
St Helens
Sankey Canal
Sankey Bridges
200-201
202
Huyton
Widnes
Widnes Lock
28-29
Runcorn
Mersey
Gowy
Ellesmere Port
Queensferry
Wrexham
Chester

GENERAL INFORMATION FOR WATERWAYS USERS

INTRODUCTION

Boaters, walkers, fishermen, cyclists and gongoozlers (on-lookers) all share in the enjoyment of our quite amazing waterway heritage. Canal & River Trust (CRT) and the Environment Agency, along with other navigation authorities, are empowered to develop, maintain and control this resource. It is to this end that a series of guides, codes, and regulations have come into existence over the years, evolving to match a burgeoning – and occasionally conflicting – demand. Set out in this section are key points as they relate to everyone wishing to enjoy the waterways.

The *Boater's Handbook* is available from all navigation authorities. It contains a complete range of safety information, boat-handling know-how, warning symbols and illustrations, and can be downloaded from www.canalrivertrust.org.uk/boating/navigating-the-waterways/boaters-handbook.

CONSIDERATE BOATING

Considerate Boating gives advice and guidance to all waterway users on how to enjoy the inland waterways safely and can be downloaded from www.canalrivertrust.org.uk/boating/navigating-the-waterways/considerate-boating. It is also well worth visiting www.considerateboater.com. These publications are also available from the Customer Services Team which is staffed *Mon – Fri, 08.00 – 18.00.* The helpful staff will answer general enquiries and provide information about boat licensing, mooring, boating holidays and general activities on the waterways. They can be contacted on 0303 040 4040; customer.services@canalrivertrust.org.uk; Canal & River Trust, Head Office, First Floor North, Station House, 500 Elder Gate, Milton Keynes MK9 1BB. Visit www.canalrivertrust.org.uk for up to date information on almost every aspect of the inland waterways from news and events to moorings.

Emergency Helpline Available from Canal & River Trust outside normal office hours on weekdays and throughout weekends. If lives or property are at risk or there is danger of serious environmental contamination then contact 0800 47 999 47 immediately for emergency help.

ENVIRONMENT AGENCY

The Environment Agency (EA) manages around 600 miles of the country's rivers, including the Thames and the River Medway. For general enquiries or to obtain a copy of the *Boater's Handbook*, contact EA Customer Services on 03708 506 506; enquiries@environment-agency.gov.uk. To find out about their work nationally (or to download a copy of the *Handbook)* and for lots of other useful information, visit www.gov.uk/government/organisations/environment-agency. The website www.visitthames.co.uk provides lots on information on boating, walking, fishing and events on the river.

Incident Hotline The EA maintain an Incident Hotline. To report damage or danger to the natural environment, damage to structures or water escaping, telephone 0800 80 70 60.

LICENSING – BOATS

The majority of the navigations covered in this book are controlled by CRT and the EA and are managed on a day-to-day basis by local Waterway Offices (you will find details of these in the introductions to each waterway). All craft using the inland waterways must be licenced and charges are based on the dimensions of the craft. In a few cases, these include reciprocal agreements with other waterway authorities (as indicated in the text). CRT and the EA offer an optional Gold Licence which covers unlimited navigation on the waterways of both authorities. Permits for permanent mooring on CRT waterways are issued by CRT.

Contact Canal & River Trust Boat Licensing Team on 0303 040 4040; www.canalrivertrust.org.uk/boating/licensing; Canal & River Trust Licensing Team, PO Box 162, Leeds LS9 1AX.

For the Thames and River Medway contact the EA. River Thames: 0118 953 5650; www.gov.uk/government/organisations/environment-agency; Environment Agency, PO Box 214, Reading RG1 8HQ. River Medway: 01732 223222 or visit the website.

BOAT SAFETY SCHEME

CRT and the EA operate the Boat Safety Scheme – boat construction standards and regular tests required by all licence holders on CRT and EA waterways. A Boat Safety Certificate (for new boats, a Declaration of Conformity), is necessary to obtain a craft licence. CRT also requires proof of insurance for Third Party Liability for a minimum of £1,000,000 for powered boats. The scheme is gradually being adopted by other waterway authorities. Contact details are: 0333 202 1000; www.boatsafetyscheme.org; Boat Safety Scheme, First Floor North, Station House, 500 Elder Gate, Milton Keynes MK9 1BB. The website offers useful advice on preventing fires and avoiding carbon monoxide poisoning.

TRAINING
The Royal Yachting Association (RYA) runs one and two day courses leading to the Inland Waters Helmsman's Certificate, specifically designed for novices and experienced boaters wishing to cruise the inland waterways. For details of RYA schools, telephone 023 8060 4100 or visit www.rya.org.uk. The practical course notes are available to buy. Contact your local boat clubs, too. The National Community Boats Association (NCBA) run courses on boat-handling and safety on the water. Telephone 0845 0510649 or visit www.national-cba.co.uk.

LICENSING - CYCLISTS
You no longer require a permit to cycle on those waterways under the control of Canal & River Trust. However, you are asked to abide by the ten point Greenway Code for Towpaths available at www.canalrivertrust.org.uk/see-and-do/cycling which also provides a wide range of advice on cycling beside the waterways. Cycling along the Thames towpath is generally accepted, although landowners have the right to request that you do not cycle. Some sections of the riverside path, however, are designated and clearly marked as official cycle ways. No permits are required but cyclists must follow London's Towpath Code on Conduct at all times.

TOWPATHS
Few, if any, artificial cuts or canals in this country are without an intact towpath accessible to the walker at least and the Thames is the only river in the country with a designated National Trail along its path from source to sea (for more information visit www.nationaltrail.co.uk). However, on some other river navigations, towpaths have on occasion fallen into disuse or, sometimes, been lost to erosion. The indication of a towpath in this guide does not necessarily imply a public right of way or mean that a right to cycle along it exists. Horse riding and motorcycling are forbidden on all towpaths.

INDIVIDUAL WATERWAY GUIDES
No national guide can cover the minutiae of detail concerning every waterway, and some CRT Waterway Managers produce guides to specific navigations under their charge. Copies of individual guides (where available) can be obtained from the relevant CRT Waterway Office or downloaded from www.waterscape.com/things-to-do/boating/guides. Please note that times – such as operating times of bridges and locks – do change year by year and from winter to summer. For free copies of a range of helpful leaflets for all users of the River Thames – visit www.visitthames.co.uk/about-the-river/publications.

STOPPAGES
CRT and the EA both publish winter stoppage programmes which are sent out to all licence holders, boatyards and hire companies. Inevitably, emergencies occur necessitating the unexpected closure of a waterway, perhaps during the peak season. You can check for stoppages on individual waterways between specific dates on www.canalrivertrust.org.uk/notices/winter, lockside noticeboards or by telephoning 0303 040 4040; for stoppages and river conditions on the Thames, visit www.gov.uk/river-thames-conditions-closures-restrictions-and-lock-closures or telephone 0845 988 1188.

NAVIGATION AUTHORITIES AND WATERWAYS SOCIETIES
Most inland navigations are managed by CRT or the EA, but there are several other navigation authorities. For details of these, contact the Association of Inland Navigation Authorities on 0113 243 3125 or visit www.aina.org.uk. The boater, conditioned perhaps by the uniformity of our national road network, should be sensitive to the need to observe different codes and operating practices.

The Canal & River Trust is a charity set up to care for England and Wales' legacy of 200-year-old waterways, holding them in trust for the nation forever, and is linked with an ombudsman. CRT has a comprehensive complaints procedure and a free explanatory leaflet is available from Customer Services. Problems and complaints should be addressed to the local Waterway Manager in the first instance. For more information, visit their website.

The EA is the national body, sponsored by the Department for Environment, Food and Rural Affairs, to manage the quality of air, land and water in England and Wales. For more information, visit its website.

The Inland Waterways Association (IWA) campaigns for the use, maintenance and restoration of Britain's inland waterways, through branches all over the country. For more information, contact them on 01494 783453; iwa@waterways.org.uk; www.waterways.org.uk; The Inland Waterways Association, Island House, Moor Road, Chesham HP5 1WA. Their website has a huge amount of information of interest to boaters, including comprehensive details of the many and varied waterways societies.

STARTING OUT

Extensive information and advice on booking a boating holiday is available from the Inland Waterways Association, www.visitthames.co.uk and www.canalrivertrust.org.uk/boating/boat-trips-and-holidays. Please book a waterway holiday from a licensed operator – this way you can be sure that you have proper insurance cover, service and support during your holiday. It is illegal for private boat owners to hire out their craft. If you are hiring a holiday craft for the first time, the boatyard will brief you thoroughly. Take notes, follow their instructions and do ask if there is anything you do not understand. CRT have produced a 40 min DVD which is essential viewing for newcomers to canal or river boating. Available to view free at www.canalrivertrust.org.uk/boatersdvd or obtainable (charge) from the CRT Customer Service Centre 0303 040 4040; www.canalrivertrust.org.uk/shop.

PLACES TO VISIT ALONG THE WAY

This guide contains a wealth of information, not just about the canals and rivers and navigating on them, but also on the visitor attractions and places to eat and drink close to the waterways. Opening and closing times, and other details often change; establishments close and new ones open. If you are making special plans to eat in a particular pub, or visit a certain museum it is always advisable to check in advance.

MORE INFORMATION

An internet search will reveal many websites on the inland waterways. Those listed below are just a small sample:

National Community Boats Association is a national charity and training provider, supporting community boat projects and encouraging more people to access the inland waterways. Telephone 0845 0510649; www.national-cba.co.uk.
National Association of Boat Owners is dedicated to promoting the interests of private boaters on Britain's canals and rivers. Visit www.nabo.org.uk.
www.canalplan.org.uk is an online journey-planner and gazetteer for the inland waterways.
www.canals.com is a valuable source of information for cruising the canals, with loads of links to canal and waterways related websites.
www.associationofcontinuouscruisers.org.uk is the independent organisation supporting continuous cruisers. As well as providing support and advice to its members, the Association is an advocate for the interests of all actively cruising boaters.
www.ukcanals.net lists services and useful information for all waterways users.

GENERAL CRUISING NOTES

Most canals and rivers are saucer shaped, being deepest at the middle. Few canals have more than 3-4ft of water and many have much less. Keep to the centre of the channel except on bends, where the deepest water is on the outside of the bend. When you meet another boat, keep to the right, slow down and aim to miss the approaching craft by a couple of yards. If you meet a loaded commercial boat keep right out of the way and be prepared to follow his instructions. Do not assume that you should pass on the right. If you meet a boat being towed from the bank, pass it on the outside. When overtaking, keep the other boat on your right side.

Some CRT and EA facilities are operated by pre-paid cards, obtainable from CRT and EA regional and local waterways offices, lock keepers and boatyards. Weekend visitors should purchase cards in advance. A handcuff/anti-vandal key is commonly used on locks where vandalism is a problem. A watermate/sanitary key opens sanitary stations, waterpoints and some bridges and locks. Both keys and pre-paid cards can be obtained via CRT Customer Service Centre.

Safety

Boating is a safe pastime. However, it makes sense to take simple safety precautions, particularly if you have children aboard.

- Never drink and drive a boat – it may travel slowly, but it weighs many tons.
- Be careful with naked flames and never leave the boat with the hob or oven lit. Familiarise yourself and your crew with the location and operation of the fire extinguishers.
- Never block ventilation grills. Boats are enclosed spaces and levels of carbon monoxide can build up from faulty appliances or just from using the cooker.
- Be careful along the bank and around locks. Slipping from the bank might only give you a cold-water soaking, but falling from the side of, or into a lock is more dangerous. Beware of slippery or rough ground.
- Remember that fingers and toes are precious! If a major collision is imminent, never try to fend off with your hands or feet; and always keep hands and arms inside the boat.
- Weil's disease is a particularly dangerous infection present in water which can attack the central nervous system and major organs. It is caused by bacteria entering the bloodstream through cuts and broken skin, and the eyes, nose and mouth. The flu-like symptoms occur two-four weeks after exposure. Always wash your hands thoroughly after contact with the water. Visit www.leptospirosis.org for details.

Speed

There is a general speed limit of 4 mph on most CRT canals and 5 mph on the Thames. There is no need to go any faster – the faster you go, the bigger a wave the boat creates: if your wash is breaking against the bank, causing large waves or throwing moored boats around, slow down. Slow down also when passing engineering works and anglers; when there is a lot of floating rubbish on the water (try to drift over obvious obstructions in neutral); when approaching blind corners, narrow bridges and junctions.

Mooring

Generally you may moor where you wish on CRT property, as long as you are *not causing an obstruction*. Do not moor in a winding hole or junction, the approaches to a lock or tunnel, or at a water point or sanitary station. On the Thames, generally you have a right to anchor for 24 hours in one place provided no obstruction is caused, however you will need explicit permission from the land owner to moor. There are official mooring sites along the length of the river; those

provided by the EA are free, the others you will need to pay for. Your boat should carry metal mooring stakes, and these should be driven firmly into the ground with a mallet if there are no mooring rings. Do not stretch mooring lines across the towpath and take account of anyone who may walk past. Always consider the security of your boat when there is no one aboard. On tideways and commercial waterways it is advisable to moor only at recognised sites, and allow for any rise or fall of the tide.

Bridges

On narrow canals slow down well in advance and aim to miss one side (usually the towpath side) by about 9 inches. *Keep everyone inboard when passing under bridges and ensure there is nothing on the roof of the boat that will hit the bridge.* If a boat is coming the other way, the craft nearest to the bridge has priority. Take special care with moveable structures – the crew member operating the bridge should be strong and heavy enough to hold it steady as the boat passes through.

Going aground

You can sometimes go aground if the water level on a canal has dropped or you are on a particularly shallow stretch. If it does happen, try reversing *gently*, or pushing off with the boat hook. Another method is to get your crew to rock the boat from side to side using the boat hook, or move all crew to the end opposite to that which is aground. Or, have all crew leave the boat, except the helmsman, and it will often float off quite easily.

Tunnels

Again, ensure that everyone is inboard. Make sure the tunnel is clear before you enter, and use your headlight. Follow any instructions given on notice boards by the entrance.

Fuel

Hire craft usually carry fuel sufficient for the rental period.

Water

It is advisable to top up daily.

Lavatories

Hire craft usually have pump out toilets. Have these emptied *before* things become critical. Keep the receipt and your boatyard will usually reimburse you. The Green Blue, an organisation providing environmental advice for boating and watersports, has produced a series of maps locating pump out facilities within the UK. Visit www.thegreenblue.org.uk/youandyourboat for these and other advice.

Boatyards
Hire fleets are usually turned around at a weekend, making this a bad time to call in for services.

VHF Radio
The IWA recommends that all pleasure craft navigating the larger waterways used by freight carrying vessels, or any tidal navigation, should carry marine-band VHF radio and have a qualified radio operator on board. In some cases the navigation authority requires craft to carry radio and maintain a listening watch. Two examples of this are for boats on the tidal River Ouse wishing to enter Goole Docks and the Aire & Calder Navigation, and for boats on the tidal Thames, over 45ft, navigating between Teddington Lock and Limehouse Basin. VHF radio users must have a current operator's certificate. The training is not expensive and will present no problem to the average inland waterways boater. Contact the RYA (see Training) for details.

PLANNING A CRUISE
Don't try to go too far too fast. Go slowly, don't be too ambitious, and enjoy the experience. Mileages indicated on the maps are for guidance only. A *rough* calculation of time taken to cover the ground is the lock-miles system:

Add the number of *miles* to the number of *locks* on your proposed journey, and divide the resulting figure by three. This will give you an approximate guide to the number of *hours* your travel will take.

TIDAL WATERWAYS
The typical steel narrow boat found on the inland waterways is totally unsuitable for cruising on tidal estuaries. However, the adventurous will inevitably wish to add additional 'ring cruises' to the more predictable circuits of inland Britain. Passage is possible in most estuaries if careful consideration is given to the key factors of weather conditions, tides, crew experience, the condition of the boat and its equipment and, perhaps of overriding

importance, the need to take expert advice. In many cases it will be prudent to employ the skilled services of a local pilot. Within the text, where inland navigations connect with a tidal waterway, details are given of sources of advice and pilotage. It is also essential to inform your insurance company of your intention to navigate on tidal waterways as they may very well have special requirements or wish to levy an additional premium. This guide is to the inland waterways of Britain and therefore recognizes that tideways – and especially estuaries – require a different approach and many additional skills. We do not hesitate to draw the boater's attention to the appropriate source material.

LOCKS AND THEIR USE
A lock is a simple and ingenious device for transporting your craft from one water level to another. When both sets of gates are closed it may be filled or emptied using gates, or ground paddles, at the top or bottom of the lock. These are operated with a windlass. On the Thames, the locks are manned all year round, with longer hours from April to October. You may operate the locks yourself at any time.

If a lock is empty, or 'set' for you, the crew open the gates and you drive the boat in. If the lock is full of water, the crew should check first to see if any boat is waiting or coming in the other direction. If a boat is in sight, you must let them through first: do not empty or 'turn' the lock against them. This is not only discourteous, and against the rules, but wastes precious water.

In the diagrams the *plan* shows how the gates point uphill, the water pressure forcing them together. Water is flooding into the lock through the underground culverts that are operated by the ground paddles: when the lock is 'full', the top gates (on the left of the drawing) can be opened. One may imagine a boat entering, the crew closing the gates and paddles after it.

In the *elevation*, the bottom paddles have been raised (opened) so that the lock empties. A boat will, of course, float down with the water. When the lock is 'empty' the bottom gates can be opened and the descending boat can leave.

Remember that when going *up* a lock, a boat should be tied up to prevent it being thrown about by the the rush of incoming water; but when going *down* a lock, a boat should never be tied up or it will be left high and dry.

Balance beam

Culvert

Pivot

Upper level → Head → Cill → Lock chamber → Cill → Lower level

Tail

Ground paddles open. Water fills the chamber through the culverts.

Gate paddles closed, retaining water in the lock chamber.

A plan of a lock filling.

Ground paddle

Gate paddle mechanism

Cill

Culvert

Cill

Ground paddles closed preventing water from the upper level filling the chamber.

Gate paddles open. Water flows from the chamber to the lower level.

An elevation of a lock emptying.

Crew prepares to open ground paddles after lower gates and paddles have been closed by departing crew.

Boat leaves lock to lower level – crew begins to close lower gates and then to close gate paddles so the chamber may refill.

Windlass

Rack and pinion

Balance beam

Boat waiting to enter from upper level after chamber has been refilled.

Lock gate with paddle mechanism.

- Make safety your prime concern. *Keep a close eye on young children.*
- Always take your time, and do not leap about.
- Never open the paddles at one end without ensuring those at the other end are closed.
- Keep to the landward side of the balance beam when opening and closing gates.
- Never leave your windlass slotted onto the paddle spindle – it will be dangerous should anything slip.

- Keep your boat away from the top and bottom gates to prevent it getting caught on the gate or the lock cill.
- Never drop the paddles – always wind them down.
- Be wary of fierce *top gate* paddles, especially in wide locks. Operate them slowly, and close them if there is *any* adverse effect.
- Always follow the navigation authority's instructions, where given on notices or by their staff.

13

Branford Barges' Fossdale H approaches Bulholme Lock loaded (see page 21)

MAXIMUM DIMENSIONS

River Lock to tail of Leeds Lock
Length: 141' 0"
Beam: 17' 9"
Headroom: 11' 9"
Draught: 7' 7"

Leeds Lock to Castleford
Length: 200' 0"
Beam: 20' 0"
Headroom: 11' 9"
Draught: 8' 2"

Castleford to Wakefield
Length: 141' 0"
Beam: 17' 9"
Headroom: 11' 10"
Draught: 7' 7"

MANAGER

0303 040 4040;
enquiries.northeast@canalrivertrust.org.uk

MILEAGE

LEEDS to
Castleford: 10 miles, 5 locks
Wakefield: 17½ miles, 10 locks including Fall Ing

SAFETY NOTES

CRT produce an excellent set of *Cruising Notes* for pleasure boaters using this navigation, obtainable by contacting the Waterway Unit Manager's office above, or downloadable from www.waterscape.com/boatersguides. This is both a commercial waterway and one developed from a river navigation: both pose their own disciplines highlighted in the notes.
Each lock on the waterway has a set of traffic lights both upstream and downstream of the lock chamber. The purpose of these lights is to convey instructions and advice to approaching craft.

Red light
Stop and moor up on the lock approach. The lock is currently in use.

Amber light *(between the red and green lights)*
The lock keeper is not on duty. You will need to self-operate.

Green light
Proceed into lock.

Red & green lights together
The lock is available for use. The lock keeper will prepare and operate the lock for you.

Flashing red light
Flood conditions – unsafe for navigation.

Most lock approach moorings are immediately upstream and downstream of the lock chamber. However, **please note:**

1   Knostrop Lock downstream approach mooring is located alongside the lock bullnose.

2   Locks at Leeds, Lemonroyd, Castleford, Woodnook and Broadreach allow access to river sections of the navigation. For interpretation of river level gauge boards *see* Safety Notes in the introduction to the Calder & Hebble Navigation on page 46.

3   There is a safe haven mooring immediately upstream of Lemonroyd Lock.

All locks between Leeds and Wakefield (except Fall Ing Lock) are equipped with VHF Marine Band Radio. They monitor and operate on channel 74. In an emergency non-VHF users contact the manager's office or out of office hours telephone 0800 47 999 47.

The River Aire was first made navigable to Leeds in 1700, and rapidly became a great commercial success, taking coal out of the Yorkshire coalfield and bringing back raw wool, corn and agricultural produce. Improvements were then made to the difficult lower reaches, with first Selby and later Goole becoming Yorkshire's principal inland port. The opening of the New Junction Canal in 1905 further secured its suitability for commercial traffic, which until recently amounted to some 2 million tonnes a year, mainly coal, sand and petroleum. With the completion of coal extraction at the St Aidens opencast site, together with the unacceptably high sulphur content of the material from Kellingley colliery, coal carrying came to an abrupt halt. With the amalgamation of the two aggregate giants – Lafarge and Tarmac – a similar fate met the long established sand and gravel freight from Besthorpe to Whitwood, when Tarmac (now responsible for all quarrying operations within the group) elected to move aggregate required in the Leeds area by road from their pit near Ripon.

Leeds

The great Aire & Calder
Navigation joins the Leeds &
Liverpool Canal at River Lock, in
the centre of Leeds by the City's
station. The area above the lock has
undergone extensive redevelopment,
effectively separating the waterway from the
railway. Heading east, the waterway passes under
three substantial bridges, generally hemmed in by tall
buildings and warehouses with much new building and
development, particularly housing. Industry predominates
below Leeds Lock, although the lock itself is quite handsomely
situated – overlooked by tall Victorian warehouses and the Royal
Armouries Museum. Keep right to avoid the weir at Leeds Lock. Boaters
should take the centre channel at Knostrop Flood Lock, through the
gates which are usually open (they are closed when the river level rises after
prolonged heavy rain, effectively closing the navigation), avoiding the river and a
weir to the left, and the disused basin of Leeds Oil Terminal to the right. Passing the
old bonded warehouses and container terminal the navigation enters an artificial channel,
with the River Aire to the north, which is to persist for a little over 7 miles until the river is
rejoined below Lemonroyd Lock. Beyond the Thwaite Mills Industrial Museum a no-man's-land
of closed collieries and landscaped spoil heaps is entered. Below the museum boaters should brace
themselves for loud detonations emanating from a factory on the south bank of the navigation.
These are caused by the destructive testing of gas bottles. The towpath is diverted at Fishpond Lock,
a lonely outpost, to avoid a small wooded area now maintained as a local nature reserve.

WALKING & CYCLING
The towpath from Leeds to Mickletown is now part of the Trans Pennine Trail (National Cycle Route 67) and
is well used by walkers and cyclists alike. There are two excellent interpretation boards between Victoria and
Crown Point Bridges – entitled 'Eye on the Aire' – depicting local activity in times gone by.

NAVIGATIONAL NOTES

1   All the locks on the Aire & Calder operate mechanically. Lock keepers move from lock to lock, primarily to operate them for commercial traffic. They will assist boaters through locks whenever possible but all locks can now be self-operated. Obey the traffic light signals.

2   Remember that this is a river navigation. Many of the locks are accompanied by large weirs, so keep a sharp lookout for the signs which direct you safely into the locks.

3   When the river level rises after prolonged heavy rain, the flood gates will be closed. Pleasure craft should stay put until they are advised by a lock keeper that it is safe to proceed.

4   This is still a commercial waterway capable of carrying 600-tonne barges. Keep a lookout for them, and give them a clear passage. Moor carefully, using bollards or fixed rings rather than mooring stakes, since the wash from these craft can be substantial.

5   Leeds Rowing Club run regular training sessions between Knostrop and Fishponds Locks *Apr-Oct, Mon-Fri 06.00-08.00 & 16.00-21.00; additional Wed session 12.00-16.00. Also Sat-Sun 08.00-16.00*. Be prepared to slow down and give way.

> **BOAT TRIPS**
> *Kirkstall Flyboat* 26 Canal Wharf, Holbeck, Leeds LS11 5PS (0113 245 6195; www.tripboat.co.uk) is a restaurant boat seating up to 44 persons. Licensed bar and food available. Café open *Mon-Fri 08.00-14.00*. Yorkshire Hire Cruisers also operate a free water taxi service *daily* between the new southern station exit and Leeds Dock.

Boatyards

Ⓑ**Leeds Dock** Armouries Drive, Leeds LS10 1LE (0113 281 6800). Beside the Royal Armouries Museum. 🚻🚿 🛢 Overnight mooring, long-term mooring, pump out, showers, toilets, disabled facilities.

Leeds

W. Yorks. All services. A vast industrial city that was a wool centre in the Middle Ages and has continued to grow to prosperity under the textile and clothing trades; indeed Marks & Spencer started business here with a stall in the market. Montague Burton also became established in the city, building what was to become, by 1921, the largest clothing factory in the world. However the last few years have brought substantial changes, with old industries being replaced by new, and the atmosphere is one of growth and prosperity. The great town hall in Victoria Square (walk north from Victoria Bridge and turn left at Great George Street) stands as a magnificent monument to Victorian civic pride. It was designed by Cuthbert Brodrick and opened in 1858. Looking at the Corinthian columns on all sides and the clock tower some 255ft high, it is hard to believe that Brodrick was only 29 years old when he submitted his plans. As a measure of this man's self-confidence, note that he also designed the organ, installed in 1859, which itself weighs almost 70 tonnes, has 6,500 pipes and stands 50ft high. The light and airy Corn Exchange (north of Leeds Bridge along Call Lane and now a shopping arcade) built in 1861 is also Brodrick's work. Always the cultural centre of Yorkshire, the city hosts an international concert season and an international piano competition. It has several splendid theatres, including The Grand in Briggate, modelled on La Scala, Milan; the City Varieties, the oldest surviving music hall in the country; and the Leeds Playhouse Repertory Theatre. Also impressive is the way, perhaps unique in the development of northern industrial towns, that contemporary and Victorian buildings stand harmoniously side by side. There are several splendid parks and rich museums, and excellent shopping facilities, including the ornate Victorian Queens and County arcades. Headingley, the home of Yorkshire cricket and a test match venue, attracts an enthusiastic following in the area, and of course the city's association with football and rugby teams is known worldwide. Boaters should try to spend a day here if they possibly can - there are good moorings on the Leeds & Liverpool Canal by Office Lock, or above Leeds Lock. *See also* page 135 (Leeds & Liverpool Canal) for information on Leeds Industrial Museum and Abbey House Museum.

Metro. The area is well served by an excellent, cheap bus and train service which offers a variety of Day Rover tickets. Telephone 0113 245 7676 or www.wymetro.com for details.

Tourist Information Centre Leeds Railway Station, New Station Street, Leeds LS1 1PL (0113 242 5242; www.visitleeds.co.uk). The usual mine of information concerning places to visit and accommodation. *Open Tue-Sat 09.00-17.30, Sun 10.00-16.00 & Mon 10.00-17.30.*

Henry Moore Institute 74 The Headrow, Leeds LS1 3AH (0113 246 7467; www.henry-moore.org). Walk north from Victoria Bridge. Award-winning institute housing four galleries showing temporary sculpture exhibitions of all periods and nationalities. Shop. *Open Tue-Sun 11.00-17.30.* Information line 0113 234 3158. Free.

City Art Gallery The Headrow, Leeds LS1 3AA (0113 247 8256; www.leeds.gov.uk/artgallery). Fine collections of paintings, watercolours, sculpture and 20th-C British Art. Collections include Victorian paintings, British watercolours, French Post-Impressionist paintings and British sculpture. *Open Mon-Sat 10.00-17.00 (Wed from 12.00) and Sun 13.00-17.00.* Disabled facilities. Free.

Leeds-Settle-Carlisle Line From Leeds City Station LS1 4DT (www.settle-carlisle.co.uk). The 70 miles from Settle to Carlisle is said to be one of the most memorable rail journeys in the world, so this would make an excellent day trip away from the boat. There is a *daily* passenger service between Leeds and Carlisle with no need to book. *Every Sat and Sun, May-Oct* there are free guided walks from trains on the line. Coach tours around the Yorkshire Dales also connect. Details from leaflets at the station or Tourist Information Centre.

Middleton Railway The Station, Moor Road, Hunslet, Leeds LS10 2JQ (0113 271 0320; 0845 680 1758; www.middletonrailway.org.uk). Built in 1758 to link Leeds with the Middleton Colliery, this is considered to be the world's oldest railway. It operates at *weekends Easter-end of year* from the industrial suburb of Hunslet, where steam engines were once built. Charge.

Royal Armouries Armouries Drive, Leeds LS10 1LT (0113 220 1999; www.royalarmouries.org/leeds). Beside Leeds Lock with moorings in Clarence Dock, adjacent to the complex. The emphasis is on participation in this massive, interactive museum reputed to be Britain's largest post-war leisure development. Five themed galleries unfold stories of weapons, battles, tournaments, falconry and the Wild West. See, touch, smell and handle before retiring to watch the skills of an armourer or experience the tranquillity of a Japanese tea garden. *Open daily 10.00-17.00. Closed 24-26th Dec.* Two cafés and a bistro. Free.

Thackray Medical Museum 141 Beckett Street, Leeds LS9 7LN (0113 244 4343; www.thackraymedicalmuseum.co.uk). A hands-on experience covering the history of medicine from Victorian times to the present day. This award-winning museum introduces you to Sherlock Bones and his tour of the Giant Gut, allows you to experience surgery without anaesthetics in 'Pain, Pus and Blood' and lets you assist Mrs Hirst with her 12th child. A truly participative establishment. Shop and café. *Open daily 10.00-17.00 - allow 3 hours for your visit.* Bus Nos 4, 4C, 22, 42, 50, 50A, 88. Information hotline 0113 245 7084. Charge (tickets valid for 12 months).

Leeds Town Hall The Headrow, Leeds LS1 3AD (0113 224 3801; www.leedstownhall.co.uk). Built in 1858, Queen Victoria performed the official opening. Today it is a venue for concerts of all types of music and light entertainment.

Leeds Corn Exchange 42 Call Lane, Leeds LS1 6DT (0113 234 0363; www.cornx.net; www.leedscornexchange.co.uk). A Grade 1 listed Victorian building, restored to its original splendour. There are plans to turn the building into a focus for food, with a restaurant and food and drink retailers, as well as cookware and kitchen appliances.

The Grand Theatre 46 New Briggate, Leeds LS1 6NZ (0844 848 2700; www.leedsgrandtheatre.

com) Theatre and opera house, showing ballet as well as all types of shows. Also workshops and special events.

The City Varieties Music Hall Swan Street, Leeds LS1 6LG (0845 644 1881; www.cityvarieties. co.uk). Pantomine and all kinds of variety shows in a grade II listed building where variety shows have been held since 1865.

Headingley Carnegie Stadium St Michael's Lane, Headingley, Leeds LS6 3BR (0844 248 6651; www.therhinos.co.uk). Home to theYorkshire County Cricket Club since 1891.

Thwaite Mills Watermill Thwaite Lane, Stourton, Leeds LS10 1RP (0113 378 2983; www.leeds.gov.uk/thwaitemills). A canalside flint and china stone-grinding mill built in 1872 and powered by two waterwheels until 1975, when they were washed away, bringing closure a year later. Telephone to confirm opening.

Tropical World and Roundhay Park Roundhay, Leeds LS8 1DF (0113 395 7400; www.roundhaypark. org.uk). A wide selection of buses from the city centre serves this tropical paradise featuring butterflies, exotic blooms and colourful fish. This is also one of Europe's largest parks, with woodland walks, scented gardens (including National Collections), canal gardens, waterfalls and a ruined castle. *Open 10.00–18.00 (16.00 in winter) daily except Christmas.* Charge.

- **Woodlesford**
W. Yorks. PO, tel, stores, butcher, baker, fish & chips, takeaways, garage, library, station. Good moorings above the lock and nearby pubs make this a popular stopping place for boaters. There is a very popular bird hide adjacent to the canal. *Gas* is available at Woodlesford Motor Spares in the centre of the village.

Pubs and Restaurants

A fine city such as Leeds has many pubs and restaurants. The following is a selection of those fairly close to the navigation.

Hansa's Gujarati Vegetarian Restaurant 72–74 North Street, Leeds LS2 7PN (0113 244 4408; www.hansasrestaurant.com). Worth seeking out for excellent, home-cooked dishes with an Indian flavour. A unique establishment serving Indian vegetarian cuisine from the State of Gujarat in a split-level restaurant with an elegant, homely atmosphere. Families warmly welcomed. *Open Tue-Fri L and E; Sat E & Sun L.*

The Grove Back Row, Leeds LS11 5PL (0113 243 9254; www.thegroveinn.com). South of Victoria Bridge. Small traditional ale house dispensing an excellent selection of real ales (four regulars and four rotating guests) and inexpensive bar snacks *L & early E (not Sat and Sun)*. Home-made steak pie and hot beef and onion rolls are specialities. Children welcome *until 21.00*; dogs at all hours. Traditional pub games, open fires and real cider. *Open all day from 12.00.*

Mr Foleys Cask Ale House 159 The Headrow, Leeds LS1 5RG (0113 242 9674; www.york-brewery. co.uk/Pubs/Mr-Foley-s-Cask-Ale-House). ¼ mile north of the railway station. Situated in a splendid Grade II listed building, this hostelry serves up to 10 real ales together with a wide range of continental bottled beers, lagers and malt whiskies. Food is available *daily 11.00-19.00 (Sun 17.00)*.

The Adelphi Hotel 3-5 Hunslet Road, Leeds LS10 1JQ (0113 245 6377; www.theadelphileeds. co.uk). South of Leeds Bridge. A superbly restored and very grand Victorian pub, with lots of etched glass and mahogany. Listed inside and out. Real ale and appetising food *daily 12.00-22.00 (Sun 21.00)*. Children welcome, dogs in taproom only. Outside seating. *Regular* entertainment. Wi-Fi.

Whitelock's Ale House 4 Turks Yard, Briggate, Leeds LS1 6HB (0113 245 3950; www. whitelocksleeds.com). North of Leeds Bridge.

An unspoilt Edwardian pub, one of the first buildings to have electricity. Reputedly the oldest pub in the city (its first licence was granted in 1715) and described by John Betjeman as 'the very heart of Leeds', this hostelry serves up to eight real ales and has a floral-hung beer garden set in an alleyway. Excellent, freshly prepared traditional English food is available, both in the bar and restaurant *daily 12.00-21.00 (Sun 20.00)*. Children welcome in restaurant. *Open from 11.00.*

Duck & Drake 43 Kirkgate, Leeds LS2 7DR (0113 245 5432; www.duckndrake.co.uk). North of Crown Point Bridge, near the church. Real ales and music are the focus of this Victorian pub. Bar snacks available *L only*. Beer garden. *Regular* live music and jam nights. No children.

The Palace Kirkgate, Leeds LS2 7DJ (0113 244 5882; www.nicholsonspubs.co.uk/ thepalacekirkgateleeds). Straightforward, no-frills pub dispensing 12 changing real ales, *open all day*. Food is available *daily 10.00-22.00* including excellent breakfasts. Children welcome *at mealtimes*; dogs *other than at mealtimes*. Outside seating and pub games.

The Two Pointers 69 Church Street, Woodlesford, Leeds LS26 8RE (0113 282 1884; www. thetwopointerspub.co.uk). Up the hill from the lock. A smart and friendly village pub. Real ale. *Regular* live music and large-screen TV. Quiz *Sun*. Outside seating; dogs and children welcome. Wi-Fi. *Open from 15.00 (Sat-Sun 12.00)*.

The Midland Hotel 97 Aberford Road, Woodlesford, Leeds LS26 8LQ (0113 282 2357; www. themidlandleeds.com). South west of Swillington Bridge, beyond the station. Friendly establishment serving real ales and food *Mon-Fri 07.00-20.00 (Sat 08.30-20.00 & Sun 08.30-15.00)*. Children and dogs welcome; outside seating. Large-screen TV, quiz *Tue* and disco *Thu*. Traditional pub games. Wi-Fi. B&B. Adjacent **Coffee Shop**.

Castleford

The navigation continues along its straight course with the River Aire just to the north, its meanderings having endowed it with a series of oxbow lakes. All around are the remains of disused coal workings, some landscaped into smooth grassy banks, others a gaunt pale grey. At Woodlesford a path up from the lock leads to *two pubs, a post office, and shops.* There is also a *supermarket and off-licence.*

Just before Fleet Bridge an arm branches off to the north. A disused lock here once used to

NAVIGATIONAL NOTES

1 Boaters must on *no account* take the river course towards the weir at Castleford Junction. Make sure you are clear about where to go *before* you get there.
2 The Lafarge Tarmac sand and gravel wharf, just below the old Fairies Hill Lock, used to receive regular barge deliveries. At the time of writing this traffic has finished and the intention is to remove the wharfage.

WALKING & CYCLING

It is possible – during the summer months – for pedestrians to follow a path on the north side of the navigation, from Caroline Bridge to Allerton Bywater, with waymarked deviations around the lake near Woodend and through Allerton Bywater. Otherwise see notes on page 23.

connect with the river. Enclosed within the arm is an oil terminal – notice how the storage tanks have been colonised by house martins. The facility is not currently serviced by tanker barges but this situation could change, so be on the look out for loaded craft manoeuvring above Fleet Bridge. The river by Fleet Lock was the site of a disastrous breach which occurred in March 1988, when the ground separating it from the adjacent St Aidens open-cast mine collapsed and the water poured in. Apparently the river below the breach flowed backwards for half a day, such was the volume of water consumed, and the workforce only just managed to rescue the two large draglines. There are *visitor and long-term moorings* available in the marina above the new Lemonroyd Lock (combining the old Lemonroyd Lock with the now-vanished Kippax Lock). Rejoining the river at Lemonroyd Lock, the mining village of Allerton Bywater appears at the end of the newly constructed section of waterway. There is a welcome waterside pub here but mooring outside has become difficult. Should you stop, make sure you moor securely, since passing commercial craft cause a considerable wash. There is a waterways 'crossroads' at Castleford. Navigators heading towards Sowerby Bridge should turn right here and must on no account go straight across – since that way leads to

continued in Book 6

the huge Castleford Weir. To the left, through the Flood Lock, are a *sanitary station*, *showers* and good *moorings*, beyond which lies the route to Sheffield (*see* Book 6), Goole, Hull, York, the River Trent and ultimately the North Sea. Large commercial craft may still emerge from here, so boats travelling downstream on either the rivers Aire or Calder, though not entering the flood lock, must still observe the traffic signals to avoid collision with vessels leaving the lock. Entering the River Calder, navigators will notice that its course here has been straightened, as the oxbow lakes either side will testify. After ducking under a large road bridge and two railway bridges, a path which gives access to the New Wheatsheaf pub can be seen heading east from the aggregate wharf. Your nose will also tell you there is a large sewage works here. Pressing on, the large, deep mechanised Woodnook Lock is reached. This replaced the earlier Fairies and Altofts locks (now disused) to the south. By comparing the sizes of the locks, an impression of the improvements carried out on the navigation during the last 100 years can be gained. Beyond the large motorway bridge is King's Road Lock (also mechanised) and paths from here lead to Altofts, although there is little reason to walk the 1/2 mile or so, except for supplies.

- **Temple Newsam House and Garden**
Temple Newsam Road, off Selby Road,
Leeds LS15 0AE (0113 336 7560; www.
leeds.gov.uk/museumsandgalleries/Pages/
templenewsamhouse). Walk north from Swillington
Bridge, fork left after the river – 2 miles. A superb
Tudor/Jacobean house in 900 acres of parkland.
Magnificent Georgian and Regency interiors. Walks
in park and woods, magnificent displays of roses
and rhododendrons in gardens. Regular events and
activities. *House open: Nov–Mar Tue–Sun, and B Hol
Mon, 10.30–16.00; Apr–Oct Tue–Sun 10.30–17.00.*
Charge. *Park and gardens open all year. Free.*
Temple Newsam Farm A working rare breeds
farm – home to 400 animals. Sheep, pigs, goats,
chickens, ducks and largest Vaynol herd in the
world. Three-hundred-year-old Great Barn
and other traditional farm buildings housing a
collection of old agricultural tools and machinery.
Open Tue–Sun 10.00–17.00 (16.00 winter). Shop and
café. Charge.
- **Mickletown**
*W. Yorks. PO, tel, stores, hardware, fish & chips,
takeaway.* Claimed by the locals to be the second
largest village in England – it is suggested that
Wroxham in Norfolk is the largest – Mickletown
has clearly had its problems since the neighbouring
colliery closed. The next-door village of Wood Row
is close by, and the *pub, store and PO* there can be
easily reached via a path from Caroline Bridge. The
stores are *open 08.00–21.00 daily.*
- **Allerton Bywater**
*W. Yorks. PO, tel, stores, butcher, cheesemonger, off-
licence, chemist.* A mining village, but the pit is now
closed. Coal was once loaded from wagons onto
barges from a small staithe here.
- **Castleford**
W. Yorks. All services. Once the Roman settlement
of *Lagentium*, now a busy industrial town which has
grown up at this important waterways junction, it is
also the birth place of the sculptor Henry Moore.
Castleford Museum Carlton Street, Castleford
WF10 1BB (01977 722740; www.experiencewakefield.
co.uk/thedms.aspx?dms=3&venue=2192828). In
the library. Recently refurbished and extended,
the museum presents the history of Castleford
from the Bronze Age to the present day. There are
objects from when the settlement was an important
Roman town, not forgetting marbles, rugby, mining,
pottery and glass. The early life of Henry Moore is
also depicted. *Open Mon, Tue & Fri 09.30-17.30; Thu
09.30-19.00 and Sat 09.30-16.00.* Free.
Diggerland Willowbridge Lane, Whitwood,
Castleford WF10 5NW (0871 227 7007; www.
diggerland.com). Approximately 1 mile south east
of Whitwood Wharf, on A655, opposite Castleford
Rugby Union Football ground. The ultimate
adventure for children old and young –
everything from mini-tractors and digger driving
through to dumper truck racing – with some
fairground rides thrown in for good measure! *Open
daily 10.00-17.00.* Charge.
- **Altofts**
W. Yorks. PO, tel, stores, delicatessen, fish & chips.
Originally a mining village and now a suburb of
Wakefield. There was once a pub by the river, but it
is now a private house. There are still three pubs in
the village. The stores are open *05.30-23.00.*

Approaching the aqueducts at Stanley Ferry (see page 25)

Pubs and Restaurants

The Commercial 12 Main Street, Mickletown LS26 9JE. Busy, two-roomed local serving real ale and food *L and E Thu-Sun (not Sun E)*. Dogs and children welcome. Sports TV and Wi-Fi. Garden. Quiz *Thu* and live music *Fri. Open from 12.00*.

The Boat Inn Boat Lane, Allerton Bywater, Castleford WF102BX (01977 552646). An attractive riverside pub where once a ferry operated carrying miners and boat horses across the river. Real ales. Food is available *daily 12.00-21.00*. Family-friendly with riverside seating. Children's room and outdoor play area. Quiz *Thu and Sun*. Take care when mooring here, as passing commercial craft can create a sizeable wash.

The Anchor Victoria Street, Allerton Bywater, Castleford WF10 2DF (01977 603119). Friendly two-roomed local serving real ale, *open from 11.00*. Family friendly with a garden. Large-screen TV and Wi-Fi.

The Victoria Hotel Main Street, Allerton Bywater, Castleford WF10 2BZ (01977 516438). Friendly, modernised local dispensing real ale and good cheer. Children and dogs welcome. Pool and sports TV. Garden and Wi-Fi. *Open from 15.00 (14.00 Fri & Sat & 12.00 Sun)*.

The Griffin Lock Lane, Castleford WF10 2LB (01977 557551). Friendly local serving real ale and food *L*. Children welcome and outside seating. Traditional pub games. *Open from 14.00 (12.00 Fri & Sat & 11.00 Sun)*.

The Junction 109 Carlton Street, Castleford WF10 1EE (01977 278867; www.

thejunctionpubcastleford.com). A warm, friendly welcome awaits the visitor to this community pub that takes its real ale seriously, serving beer from the wood. Entertainment comes in the form of bar billiards, conversation and general banter. Dogs and children welcome. Real fires and traditional pub games. Quiz *Wed. Open Mon-Thu 14.00 & Fri-Sun 12.00 (closes 20.30 Mon-Tue)*.

The New Wheatsheaf Altofts Lane, Whitwood, Castleford WF10 5QB (01977 553052; www.wheatsheaf.com). Large, brightly decorated traditional pub, where someone clearly takes a great pride in their flower arrangements. Real ales, and a wide range of interesting and appetising food served *Mon-Sat L and E and Sun all day*. Children welcome. *Open from 10.00 (Sun 12.00)*.

The Miners Arms 169 Church Road, Altofts WF6 2QR. ½ mile south of Nordens Bridge, along Lock Lane. Friendly community pub serving real ale. Garden. *Open from 16.00 (Sun 13.00)*.

The Poplar Inn 151 Church Road, Altofts WF6 2QN (01924 893416). Almost opposite the Miners Arms. Lively village local serving real ale and with barbecues *in summer*. Large garden and children's play area. *Open Sat-Sun 12.00 and Mon-Fri mid afternoon*.

The Horse & Jockey 47 Church Road, Altofts WF6 2NU (01924 892994). ½ mile south of Foxhills Lane Bridge, turning right along Church Road. Village local serving real ales and food *L and E*. Outdoor drinking area. *Regular* live music. *Open from 10.00 (Sun 11.00)*.

WALKING & CYCLING

Currently there is no continuous towpath from Caroline Bridge to Castleford so walkers and cyclists wishing to follow the navigation are presented with two choices:

1 Leave the towpath ½ mile east of Shan Bridge and follow the Trans Pennine Trail signs onto Mickletown Road and thence to the junction of Savile Road and Church Road. Turn left along Savile Road and right along Pinfold Lane at the T junction. At the main road (Barnsdale Road) turn left and follow this road – along the pavement – round a sharp right-hand bend (ignore the left-hand turning here into Micklefield) and then south to Methley Bridge over the Wakefield Branch of the Aire & Calder Canal. Join the towpath here and follow it east into Castlefield. For those following this diversion in reverse (i.e. from Castleford) leave the navigation at Barnsdale Road Bridge and head south, over the river and turn right along Savile Road. Immediately past the roundabout look for a Public Footpath sign leading you back onto the river bank.

2 Follow the directions above to Methley Bridge where, by turning west along the towpath, it is possible to reach Wakefield and, with the assistance of the excellent Metro bus/rail system (0113 245 7676; www.wymetro.com) complete a circular walk/ride that might have commenced in Leeds. N.B. A section of the towpath Methley Bridge to Wakefield is only cyclable with care and at the cyclist's own risk!

3 A third option is to make use of the Trans Pennine Trail throughout its route in the Leeds area. Starting at Crown Point Bridge (*see page 16* near the city centre, it follows the canal to Mickletown (*see* 1 above) where, by following the excellent waymarking west along a minor road and a disused railway line, it heads into Wakefield making use of a further section of canal (the Aire & Calder Wakefield Branch) at Stanley Ferry. This is part of Euro-route E8 (ultimately running from the west coast of Ireland to Istanbul). For further information (free) and detailed guides (charge) contact the Trans Pennine Trail Officer on 01226 772574 or visit www.transpenninetrail.org.uk.

Wakefield

Birkwood Lock was for a long time the last mechanised lock when travelling upstream. At Stanley Ferry the canal is diverted over the new aqueduct, which stands alongside the original and was opened in 1981. The original aqueduct was thought to be at risk from the large craft which can now navigate here. There is a Canal & River Trust repair yard and lock gate building workshop immediately before the aqueduct, and *a marina with a pub* beyond. This has been built in a defunct loading basin beside the splendid, stone wharf office. It was here that empty 'Tom Puddings' were hauled onto railway wagons and, after loading at the nearby colliery, re-launched en route for Goole. After Ramsden's Swing Bridge (*sanitary station, pump out and showers*) the navigation continues in a dead straight line, passing Broadreach Flood Lock and Heath Old Hall before turning west to join the Calder & Hebble at Fall Ing Lock. There are craft moored here by an old loading chute, a *picnic area* and convenient *pub*. Below Wakefield Flood Lock the river is navigable for a short distance towards the weir, although much cluttered by large craft undergoing refurbishment at the boatyard here. Leaving Wakefield you pass under a splendid curving brick railway viaduct known locally as 'the 99 arches'. A careful count will reveal only 95.

Stanley Ferry Aqueduct

It is a good idea to moor at Stanley Ferry Marina and walk to the road bridge for a full view of this fine structure – a trough suspended from a two-pin cast iron arch – built on the same principle as the Sydney Harbour Bridge, which it predates by 100 years. Nearly 7000 tons of Bramley Fall stone and 1000 tons of cast iron were used in its construction. The first boat to pass across it was the *James*, a schooner of 160 tons drawn by three grey horses, on 8 August 1839. The 700 men who worked on it were fed at the nearby public houses, one of which, The Ship, still stands. Designed by George Leather, the strength of the structure was severely tested when, soon after opening, the largest flood for 20 years caused the river below actually to flow into the trough. The towpath is carried on a separate steel girder structure designed to protect the aqueducts during such floods. The concrete aqueduct was built in 1981, and the original, by its side, is still in water.

NAVIGATIONAL NOTES

1 Take heed of the notices and flood indicator boards at the locks. Pleasure craft should only proceed if the water level is in the *green* or *amber* sectors. Amber indicates that the river is above normal levels and that boaters should proceed with caution to and THROUGH the next lock.

2 Most locks on the Calder & Hebble have a unique type of paddle gear, consisting of a small perforated wheel which is turned using a 'handspike'. These are obtainable from boatyards on the navigation. Or a piece of 3" x 2" hardwood, 3ft long (and planed down to size), will do just as well.

3 When coming downstream (from Sowerby Bridge direction) keep a sharp lookout for the entrance to Wakefield Flood Lock. There is a large weir on the river, a short distance beyond the boatyard, by the bridge.

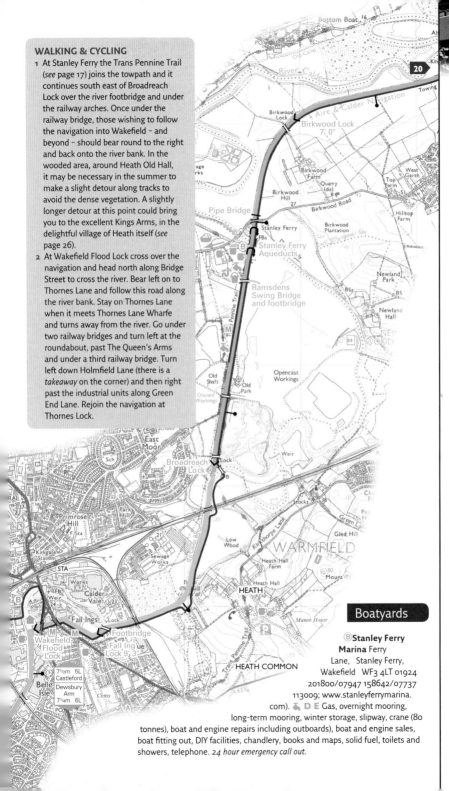

WALKING & CYCLING

1 At Stanley Ferry the Trans Pennine Trail (*see* page 17) joins the towpath and it continues south east of Broadreach Lock over the river footbridge and under the railway arches. Once under the railway bridge, those wishing to follow the navigation into Wakefield – and beyond – should bear round to the right and back onto the river bank. In the wooded area, around Heath Old Hall, it may be necessary in the summer to make a slight detour along tracks to avoid the dense vegetation. A slightly longer detour at this point could bring you to the excellent Kings Arms, in the delightful village of Heath itself (*see* page 26).

2 At Wakefield Flood Lock cross over the navigation and head north along Bridge Street to cross the river. Bear left on to Thornes Lane and follow this road along the river bank. Stay on Thornes Lane when it meets Thornes Lane Wharfe and turns away from the river. Go under two railway bridges and turn left at the roundabout, past The Queen's Arms and under a third railway bridge. Turn left down Holmfield Lane (there is a *takeaway* on the corner) and then right past the industrial units along Green End Lane. Rejoin the navigation at Thornes Lock.

Boatyards

B Stanley Ferry Marina Ferry Lane, Stanley Ferry, Wakefield WF3 4LT 01924 201800/07947 158642/07737 113009; www.stanleyferrymarina. com). 🛢 D E Gas, overnight mooring, long-term mooring, winter storage, slipway, crane (80 tonnes), boat and engine repairs including outboards), boat and engine sales, boat fitting out, DIY facilities, chandlery, books and maps, solid fuel, toilets and showers, telephone. *24 hour emergency call out.*

Wakefield

W. Yorks. All services. The city centre is north of the navigation. The regional capital of West Yorkshire, it gained city status in 1888 when the cathedral was granted its charter. Mainly 15th-C Perpendicular in style, the cathedral's 247ft spire is a landmark for miles around. On a much smaller scale, but perhaps of equal interest, is the Chantry Chapel of St Mary, a rare 14th-C example of a bridge chapel, just a short walk north of Fall Ing, by the weir. Industrial pollution has meant that the entire front of the building has had to be replaced twice in the last two centuries: the original now graces the entrance to a boathouse at Kettlethorpe. The city itself is set on a hill, and still contains some quiet streets and dignified Georgian houses, notably those in St John's Square, with its delightful church and handsome council buildings. Wakefield's prosperity was founded on the textile and engineering industries, both of which have taken a battering in recent years. However, the city has been successful in attracting new industry, such as Coca Cola/Schweppes; and the vast and spectacular Ridings shopping complex has created many new jobs.

The Hepworth Wakefield Gallery Walk, Wakefield WF1 5AW (01924 247360; www.hepworthwakefield. org). Contemporary art gallery and museum, including work from Wakefield's art collection and works by Barbara Hepworth. Café, shop, regular events and nearby children's play area. *Open Tue-Sun 10.00-17.00 (also B Hol and School Hol Mon).*

The Theatre Royal & Opera House 12 Drury Lane, Wakefield WF1 2TE (01924 211311; www. theatreroyalwakefield.co.uk). Provides a lively and varied programme of entertainment.

Yorkshire Sculpture Park at Bretton Hall, West Bretton WF4 4LG (01924 832631; www.ysp.co.uk). displays some important works by Barbara Hepworth and Henry Moore, both local artists. *Open daily 10.00-17.00.* Free.

Wakefield Museum Burton Street, Wakefield WF1 2DD (01924 305356; www.wakefield.gov.uk). Local history and archaeology, excavations from Sandal Castle, and the Waterton collection of exotic birds and animals. The building, designed in 1820, was originally a music saloon. *Open Mon-Tue 09.00-18.00; Wed 09.00-20.00; Thu-Fri 09.00-19.00 & Sat 09.00-17.00.* Free.

Tourist Information Centre The Bull Ring, Wakefield WF1 1HB (0345 601 8353; www.experiencewakefield. co.uk). *Open Mon-Fri 09.00-16.30 (Wed closes 15.45), Sat 10.00-15.00.*

Heath Village 2 miles east of Wakefield. A beautifully preserved village with some 18th-C merchants' houses amongst other substantial buildings. Heath Hall is a fine Georgian house by John Carr (1753) with carved woodwork and moulded plaster ceilings. The gas-lit King's Arms pub is a gem (*see below*).

Pubs and Restaurants

▶✕**The Stanley Ferry** Ferry Lane, Stanley Ferry, Wakefield WF3 4LT (01924 290596; www.fayre-square.com/pub/stanley-ferry-stanley-wakefield/m7438). One of the old converted wharf-side buildings. Restaurant with bar serving food all day, everyday. Varied menu and two-for-one offers. Wacky Warehouse soft play area for the children. Patio and canalside seating. Wi-Fi. *Open 11.00-23.00 - food available from 12.00 (Sun 11.30).*

▶✕**The King's Arms** Heath Village, near Wakefield WF1 5SL (01924 377527; www.thekingsarmsheath. co.uk). Overlooking the common, originally built as houses in the 18th C and converted into a pub in 1841. A wide choice of real ale is served in an exceptional setting with a gas-lit, wood-panelled bar, a range of different rooms, stone-flagged floors, and full of antiques. Open fire, excellent bar and restaurant food *Mon-Thu L and E; Fri-Sat all day until 19.00 & Sun 12.00-17.00.* Children welcome. Two walled gardens and a lawn in front. *Open from 12.00.*

▶**Fernandes Brewery Tap** 5 Avison Yard, Kirkgate, Wakefield WF1 1UA (01924 291709). Once a malt store and conditioning room for Beverley Brewery – and a malt kiln before that – this pub resurrects the original brewer's name and now dispenses both the present incumbent's own beers and that of guests. A dearth of electronic machines; brewery memorabilia and an open fire *in winter* making this popular hostelry a real ale drinker's dream. Pets welcome and *Sun afternoon* live music. Real cider. *Open from 16.00 Mon-Thu & Sun; 12.00 Fri-Sat.*

▶**Henry Boon's** 130 Westgate, Wakefield WF2 9SR (01924 378126). West of the cathedral, next to the prison. Fine traditional brewery tap for Clark's Brewery, also serving other real ales in an enthusiast's pub, with live music *Sat.* Outside pavement seating. *Open from 11.00 (Sun 12.00).*

▶**The Redoubt Inn** 28 Horbury Road, Wakefield WF2 8TS (01924 377085). Little changed in 150 years, this heritage pub dispenses real ales *all day, every day.* Pub games, its own football team and outside seating. A 'bring your own food' regime operates in lieu of more immediate provision. Family friendly.

▶**The Wagon** 45 Westgate End, Wakefield WF2 9RQ (01924 372478). Near the railway station. A selection of real ales served in this popular, friendly local with outside seating and bar games. Small garden with play area. Quiz *Sun.*

▶**Harry's Bar** 107B Westgate, Wakefield WF1 1EL (01924 373773). Tucked away down a narrow passage, this one-roomed hostelry serves an interested variety of real ales together with real cider. Real fires and pub games. Outdoor drinking area and live music *Wed. Open from 17.00 (Sun 12.00).*

▶✕**The Wharfside** 46 Thornes Lane Wharf, Wakefield WF1 5RL (01924 360772). Opposite Wakefield Flood Lock and across the bridge from the Hepworth Wakefield gallery. Formerly the Jolly Sailor, this pub restaurant has been extensively refurbished.

BRIDGEWATER CANAL

MAXIMUM DIMENSIONS

Length: 70'
Beam: 14' 9"
Headroom: 8'
Draught: 2' 6"

LICENCES

The Bridgewater Canal Company Limited,
Peel Dome, Intu Trafford Centre,
Manchester M17 8PL
Enquiries: 0161 629 8266/8432;
www.bridgewatercanal.co.uk.

All craft using the canal must be licensed. They must also be insured against third party risks which should include the cost of salvage and removal of wreck. Any boat holding a Canal & River Trust canal and river licence may cruise on the Bridgewater Canal for seven consecutive days free of charge.

MILEAGE

PRESTON BROOK to:
Lymm: 10½ miles
Waters Meeting, junction with
Leigh Branch: 22 miles

CASTLEFIELD JUNCTION, start of
Rochdale Canal: 23½ miles
No locks

DUCIE STREET JUNCTION, start of
Ashton Canal: 25 miles (Rochdale Canal, 9 locks)
Preston Brook to Runcorn: 4¾ miles, no locks
Leigh Branch: 10¾ miles, no locks

The Bridgewater Canal received Royal Assent on 23 March 1759, four years after the Sankey Brook, or St Helens, Canal and 18 years after the Newry Canal (once known as Black Pig's Dyke), which linked Lough Neagh to the sea below Newry, in Northern Ireland, and was probably the first 'modern' canal in the British Isles. The Bridgewater was built by Francis Egerton, third Duke of Bridgewater, to enable coal from his mines at Worsley to be transported to Manchester and sold cheaply. His agent was John Gilbert and his engineer was James Brindley, who designed a lockless contour canal which crossed the River Irwell on a stone aqueduct – a revolutionary concept and one that was ridiculed by many sceptics. However, the line was open to Castlefield by the end of 1765.

While the canal was under construction, there began the excavation of a remarkable system of underground canals to serve the Duke's mines, reached through two entrances at Worsley Delph. Eventually 46 miles of underground canal were built, some on different levels and linked by an ingenious inclined plane built along a fault in the sandstone. The craft used in the mines were known as 'starvationers', double-ended tub boats which could carry up to 12 tons of coal. This whole system remained in use until the late 19th C.

In 1762 the Duke received sanction to extend his canal to the Liverpool tideway at Runcorn – this was later amended in order to connect with the new Trent & Mersey Canal at Preston Brook. The route between Liverpool and Manchester was opened in 1776, although Brindley did not live to see its completion. In 1795 the Duke, then 60 years old, received the Royal Assent for the final part of the network, which linked Worsley to the Leeds & Liverpool Canal at Leigh.

The coming of the railways did not initially affect the prosperity of the canal. In 1872 the newly formed Bridgewater Navigation Company purchased the canal for £1,120,000, and they in turn sold it to the Manchester Ship Canal Company in 1885. When the building of the new Ship Canal meant that Brindley's original stone aqueduct over the River Irwell was replaced, its successor, the Barton Swing Aqueduct, was no less outstanding than the original, being a steel trough closed by gates at each end, pivoting on an island in the Ship Canal.

The Bridgewater Canal is a tribute to its builders in that it continued to carry commercial traffic until 1974 – indeed its wide gauge, lock-free course and frequent use of aqueducts makes many later canals seem retrograde. It is now an oasis of tranquillity amidst the burgeoning new industry of Manchester.

Preston Brook

Although the main line of the Bridgewater once locked down to the Mersey in Runcorn, this is now a dead end, with the locks being closed in 1966. It does, however, still make an interesting diversion – there is a *supermarket* and *PO* south of bridge 74. What is now the main canal route to Manchester bears to the right immediately after the big M56 motorway bridge, and its direct course to the south of the Mersey affords good views of the Manchester Ship Canal. The canal frontage at Moore is attractive, with moored boats, a *PO, shop and off-licence*, and a *telephone box* right by the canal.

Boatyards

Ⓑ**Claymoore Canal Holidays** The Wharf, Preston Brook WA4 4BA (01928 717273; www.claymoore.co.uk). 🎁📚 D Pump out, gas, narrowboat and day-hire craft (2–10 berth boats), overnight mooring, boat repairs, engine repairs, toilets, books, maps, gifts.

Ⓑ**Preston Brook Marina** Preston Brook WA7 3AF (01928 719081). 🎁📚 Secure long-term mooring, slipways, toilets, showers.

Ⓑ**Boat and Butty Company** Ockleston's Wharf, Ringway Road, Runcorn WA7 5QN (07976 303696). 🎁📚 Pump out, gas, long-term mooring, winter storage, DIY facilities.

- **Preston Brook Tunnel**
1239yds long and forbidden to unpowered craft. *A notice indicates when you may enter – see page 202.*
- **Preston Brook**
Cheshire. PO, tel, stores, delicatessen. A village which grew to serve the canal, where goods were transshipped from wide beam craft of the north west to narrowboats of the Midlands. Unfortunately, little remains as evidence of this activity, and the M56 dominates.
Norton Priory Museum and Garden Tudor Road, Manor Park, Runcorn WA7 1SX (01928 569895; www.nortonpriory.org). Access from mooring north east of bridge 75. Only the undercroft survives from the 12th C. A recorded commentary describes points of interest. Walled garden, pleasant woodland and sculpture gardens. Regular events and hands-on activities for children. Seasonal fruit and vegetables for sale. *Apr-Oct Museum open 10.00–17.00 & Walled Garden open 12.00–16.00 daily. Nov-Mar Museum open 12.00–16.00, Garden closed.* Charge.
- **Runcorn**
Cheshire. All services. The old town is to be found down by the docks, where the elegant curved 1092ft single span of the steel road bridge (built 1961), with the railway beside, leaps over the Ship Canal and the Mersey. The massive

flight of 10 double locks which connected the Bridgewater Canal to the Mersey was abandoned in 1966 and filled in, much to the dismay of industrial archaeologists and canal enthusiasts. Since 1964 Runcorn has been a 'new town', its rapid growth being carefully planned.
Tourist Information Centre 6 Church Street, Runcorn WA7 1LT (0151 907 0303; www.touruk.co.uk/cheshire/Runcorn.htm). *Open Mon-Fri, 09.00–17.30, and Sat 09.00–13.00.*
- **Daresbury**
Cheshire. PO box, tel. Half-a-mile up the road from Keckwick Bridge, this was the birthplace of Charles Lutwidge Dodgson, better known as Lewis Carroll. The church of All Saints (WA4 4AE; www.daresburycofe.org.uk) has a pretty Lewis Carroll memorial window in the Daniell Chapel, where he is shown with characters from *Alice in Wonderland:* the Dormouse, the Mad Hatter and the Cheshire Cat. This window was designed by Geoffrey Webb, and was dedicated in 1934. The original church on this site dates from the 12thC, and was a daughter house of nearby Norton Priory (*see above*). The present tower dates from around 1550, with the rest of the church being rebuilt in the 1870s. The fine oak pulpit, dating from 1625, and the rood screen incorporated into the panelling behind the altar, are both worth a look. *The church is open daily.*

Pubs and Restaurants

⬛✕**The Ring O' Bells** Old Chester Road, Daresbury, Warrington WA4 4AJ (01925 740256; www.ringobells-daresbury.co.uk). There has been an ale house here since 1641, although this building dates from 1841. The adjoining stables are older than the pub: to the other side the old Petty Sessions room has been incorporated. Pleasantly busy, with a relaxed atmosphere and open fires. Real ale, and good food, including fresh fish specials *12.00–22.00 (21.30 Sun)*. Children are welcome *until 21.00 when dining*. Outside seating. *Open from 12.00.*

⬛**The Red Lion** 119 Runcorn Road, Moore, Warrington WA4 6UD (01925 740205; www.theredlionmoore.co.uk). A friendly and traditional pub just a few minutes' walk west of bridge 7. Real ale, and meals, with an excellent choice *12.00–21.00 (Sun 20.00)*. Family-friendly and Wi-Fi. Garden, darts and pool.

There are plenty of pubs in Runcorn, including:

⬛**The Lion** 100 Greenway Road, Runcorn WA7 5AG (01928 574129). Close to the station, and enjoying a new lease of life, this pub serves an ever-changing choice of real ale. Family-friendly. *Open Mon-Fri E from 17.00 & Sat-Sun all day from 12.00.*

⬛**The Ferry Boat** 10 Church Street, Runcorn WA7 1LR (01928 583380; www.jdwetherspoon.co.uk/home/pubs/the-ferry-boat). Celebrating the ferry service, that used to cross the Mersey between Runcorn and Widnes, this one-time cinema lies in the centre of the old town and serves real ale and cider, together with food *daily 08.00–22.00*. Children welcome. Outside seating and Wi-Fi. Sports TV.

WALKING & CYCLING

The towpath is in good condition throughout, but is only open to walkers. The towpath on the main line forms part of the Cheshire Ring Canal Walk, which makes a circuit with the Ashton, Peak Forest, Macclesfield and Trent & Mersey canals. Leaflets giving details of cycle routes in Runcorn can be downloaded from www2.halton.gov.uk. A Cyclists Map and Guide to Runcorn can be obtained from www.cycling.org.uk. The Trans Pennine Trail is a 350-mile national route which crosses Runcorn on its way from Liverpool to Warrington. Maps and an Official Accommodation and Visitor Guide are available from www.transpenninetrail.org.uk, www.sustrans.gov.uk or Barnsley Metropolitan Borough Council, Central Offices, Kendray Street, Barnsley, South Yorkshire, S70 2TN (01226 772574; www.barnsley.gov.uk).

Stockton Heath

A short rural stretch is interrupted by the estate village of Higher Walton, which can be seen among trees, and this is followed by a secluded tree-lined length in a shallow cutting before the outskirts of Stockton Heath are approached. The building occupied by Thorn Marine was once a fodder store, stables and staff house for the packet boats (more

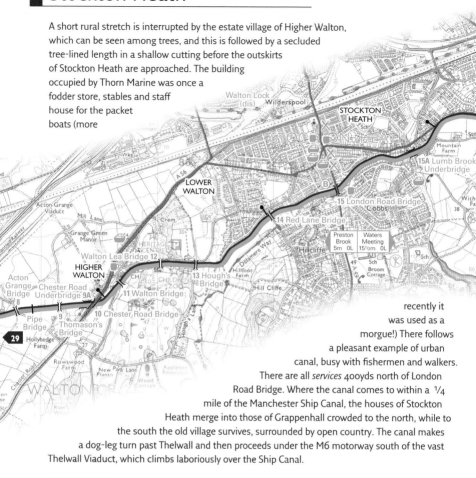

recently it was used as a morgue!) There follows a pleasant example of urban canal, busy with fishermen and walkers. There are all *services* 400yds north of London Road Bridge. Where the canal comes to within a ¼ mile of the Manchester Ship Canal, the houses of Stockton Heath merge into those of Grappenhall crowded to the north, while to the south the old village survives, surrounded by open country. The canal makes a dog-leg turn past Thelwall and then proceeds under the M6 motorway south of the vast Thelwall Viaduct, which climbs laboriously over the Ship Canal.

Boatyards

ⓑ **Thorn Marine** London Road, Stockton Heath, Warrington WA4 6LE (01925 265129; www.thornmarine.co.uk). 🛏🛢 D Pump out, gas, day-boat hire, boat safety examiner, Gas

Safe registered, boat and engine repairs, chandlery, toilets, books, maps and gifts, solid fuels. Public telephone and shopping centre *nearby*.

● **Higher Walton**
Cheshire. *PO box, tel.* A pretty, late-Victorian estate village among trees.
Walton Hall Walton Lea Road, Higher Walton, Warrington WA4 6SN (01925 262908; www. warrington.gov.uk/waltonhall). Thirty two acres of parkland and gardens *open from dawn to dusk.* Facilities include children's zoo, outdoor games, heritage centre, play area, café and Ranger Service organising activities for the public and groups. Café *(open from 11.00)*. Zoo open 10.30-17.00 (winter 16.00). Free entry – charge for parking only.

● **Stockton Heath**
Cheshire. *PO, tel, stores, banks, chemists, fish & chips, off-licence, takeaways, library.* A useful selection of shops and services north of London Road Bridge 15. An outer suburb of Warrington, England's centre for vodka distilling and a useful place for supplies.
Stockton Quay London Bridge 15. The terminus of the canal from 1771 to 1776, before the Duke of Bridgewater completed his route from Manchester to Runcorn, and consequently a major transshipment point with stables, yards, wharves, warehouses and

WALKING & CYCLING
The Delamere Way parallels the canal near Red Lane Bridge. This is a 21-mile route following rights of way and quiet roads, from Frodsham to Warrington via Delamere Forest. A leaflet describing the entire route is published by the Mid Cheshire Footpath Society and is available from local shops, or details from www.mcfs.org.uk.

a canal company office. Passenger packet boat services also ran from here from 1771 to the mid 1880s, one of the craft being the renowned *Duchess-Countess*.

● **Grappenhall**
Cheshire. PO, tel, stores, library. A fine group of buildings on cobbled streets survive around the church of St Wilfred, where the village stocks remain. There are two excellent pubs, which makes a stop here very worthwhile.

● **Thelwall**
Cheshire. PO box, tel. A pretty village with its name now indelibly linked with a motorway viaduct.

Pubs and Restaurants

The Walton Arms 148 Old Chester Road, Higher Walton, Warrington WA4 6TG (01925 262659; www.greatbritishcarvery.co.uk). North of bridge 11. Real ale in a comfortable 'Country Carvery'. Traditional food *all day, every day*. Children welcome if eating. Outside seating. Wi-Fi.

The London Bridge Inn 163 London Road, Appleton, Warrington WA4 5BG (01925 267904; www.londonbridgeinn.co.uk). Beside Bridge 15. A homely and welcoming pub with a canalside terrace, offering real ale and food *daily 12.00-21.00*. Beer garden and family-friendly. Quiz *Tue and Sun*. Real fires. Wi-Fi.

The Rams Head Church Lane, Grappenhall, Warrington WA4 3EP (01925 262814; www.ramshead-inn.co.uk). A comfortable old-fashioned pub on a cobbled street in a conservation village, where *Sherlock Holmes* was filmed. Appetising food is served *Mon-Thu L and E and Fri-Sun all day until 22.00 (Sun 20.00)*. Child- and dog-friendly. Wi-Fi and outside seating. Live music *Thu*. B&B.

The Parr Arms Grappenhall Lane, Grappenhall, Warrington WA4 3EP (01925 212120; www. theparrarms.co.uk). A comfortable and homely pub on the cobbled street, right beside the church,

serving real ale. Good food available *daily 12.00-21.00 (Sun 20.30)*. Children welcome *until 20.30*. Outside seating.

Little Manor Bell Lane, Thelwall, WA4 2SX (01925 212070; www.brunningandprice. co.uk/littlemanor). ¼ north of Bridge 19A, along Bell Lane. Set in large, pleasant grounds – and originally built for the Percival family in 1660 – this fine building now dispenses real ales and excellent food *daily 12.00-22.00 (Sun 21.30)*. Well-behaved dogs and children welcome. Open fires and Wi-Fi.

The Pickering Arms 1 Bell Lane, Thelwall WA4 2SU (01925 861262; www.pickeringarms.co.uk). ¼ north of Bridge 19A, along Bell Lane. This Grade II listed building exudes an understated elegance, dispensing real ales and appetising, good value food *daily from 12.00-20.00*. Family- and dog-friendly. Garden and open fires. Traditional pub games and Wi-Fi.

Penny Ferry Inn 271 Thelwell Lane, Latchford, Warrington WA4 1NF (01925 558870; www.pennyferry.co.uk). You can have a snack and a pint here while you wait for the ferry. Children are welcome, and there is a garden and a play park next door. Free wifi and sport TV.

31

Lymm

There are fine views of the distant Pennines to the north before the canal makes a very pleasing passage through the heart of Lymm, where the streets come right down to the water's edge. There are convenient

24 hour moorings here. The canal then passes the village of Oughtrington *(boater facilities include laundry, coal, gas, toilets and showers)* to the north before entering surroundings which are surprisingly rural. Rows of moored boats, some in an advanced state of decay, announce the presence of three useful boatyards and a fine pub, with a free ferry for towpath walkers (hit the clanger!) The fields then gently fall away into the valley of the River Bollin, which the Bridgewater crosses on a large embankment, with expansive views of the Manchester Ship Canal and Dunham Park. Dunham Underbridge is a new concrete and steel construction, built to replace the original stone trough which breached disastrously in August 1971 and resulted in a two-year closure and repairs amounting to £250,000 at the time. There are good moorings by Dunham Town Bridge.

● **Lymm**
Cheshire. PO, tel, stores, banks, chemists, butcher, baker, fish & chips, takeaways, delicatessen, library. The 17th-C Lymm Cross stands just a few yards from the canal in the centre of this hilly and attractive little town. The dam at the back of the town was built to carry the turnpike road over a sharp ravine, thus creating a pleasant lake in the process.

● **Bollington**
Cheshire. A compact and attractive village, with a fine old pub and a converted mill.

Dunham Massey Hall NT Altrincham WA14 4SJ (0161 941 1025; www.nationaltrust.org.uk). Once the seat of the Earl of Stamford, this beautiful 18th-C house by John Norris stands in a wooded and well-stocked deer park, landscaped by George Booth, the Second Earl of Warrington, and now considered to be one of the north west's great plantsman's gardens. A sumptuous interior contains collections of Huguenot silver, paintings and walnut furniture. There is also an 18th-C orangery, an Elizabethan

mount and a well-house. Concerts are staged in the gallery; exhibitions, fairs and services are held in the house and chapel; and there is a short programme of interesting conducted walks. Access is via Bollington, over the footbridge near the Swan with Two Nicks pub. House and garden *open all year,* telephone or check website for times. Admission charge. Restaurant and shop.

● **Dunham Town**
Cheshire.PO box, tel, stores. A small, scattered, farming village with a pub. The shop is *open Mon-Fri 08.30-12.30 & Sat-Sun 09.00-12.00.*

Boatyards

Ⓑ**Hesford Marine** Warrington Lane, Lymm WA13 0SW (01925 754639; www.hesfordmarine.com). Ⓓ Gas, long-term mooring, winter storage, slipway, crane (35 ton), covered hard standing, shot blasting, boat sales and repairs, engine repairs, chandlery, toilets, small selection of books, maps and gifts, DIY facilities.

Ⓑ**Lymm Marina Boat Sales** Warrington Lane, Lymm WA13 0SW (01925 752945 or 07798 752945; www.lmbs.co.uk). New boat sales – sailaway and fully fitted, long-term mooring, winter storage, 20-ton boat lift. *Open Fri and Sat.*

Pubs and Restaurants

⬛**The Golden Fleece** 41 The Cross, Lymm WA13 0HR (01925 755538; www.goldenfleecelymm.co.uk). Beside Bridge 23. A picturesque canalside pub, serving real ale. Food is available *daily 11.30-21.00 (Sun 20.00).* Dog- and family-friendly. Garden, traditional pub games and sports TV. Wi-Fi.

⬛**The Bull's Head** 32 The Cross, Lymm WA13 0HU (01925 752831). By bridge 23. A cosy traditional village local serving real ale. Dogs and children welcome. Open fires, traditional pub games and Wi-Fi. *Open from 12.00.*

⬛✕**The Spread Eagle** 47 Eagle Brow, Lymm WA13 0AG (01925 757467; www.spreadeaglehotel. co.uk). Traditional local serving real ale and home-cooked food *daily 12.00-21.00 (Sun 19.00).* Child- and dog-friendly. Garden. Open fires, large screen TV, traditional pub games and Wi-Fi.

⬛**The Brewery Tap** 18 Bridgewater Street, Lymm WA13 0AB (01925 755451; www.lymmbrewing.co.uk). Established in the old post office, this friendly hostelry serves a range of real ales from its own microbrewery in the cellar. No food but you can bring pies etc in from the next-door delicatessen. Dog- and child-friendly *(the latter until 18.30).* Open fires, newspapers and Wi-Fi. *Open 12.00.*

✕☐**Trattoria Baci** 18 The Cross, Lymm WA13 0HU (01925 756067). Smart Italian restaurant offering fresh authentic Italian pizza, as well as all other main Italian dishes. *Open Thu-Sun from 12.00 and Mon-Wed from 17.00.*

⬛✕**Barn Owl Inn** Agden Wharf, Warrington Lane, Lymm WA13 0SW (01925 752020; www.

thebarnowlinn. co.uk). Between bridges 25 and 26. A friendly pub in a converted boatyard building, with fine views and serving a variety of real ales. Food *Mon-Fri L and E & Sat-Sun all day.* Children welcome and canalside garden. Traditional pub games.

⬛**Ye Olde No. 3** Lymm Road, Little Bollington, Altrincham WA14 4TA (01925 757222). Near Bollington Underbridge. An attractive former coaching inn with no less than three ghosts, which now serves a good selection of real ales. Food is available *daily 12.00-20.00* and there is a canalside garden with play area. Open fires, sports TV and traditional pub games.

⬛✕**The Swan With Two Nicks** Park Lane, Little Bollington, Altrincham WA14 4TJ (0161 928 2914; www. swanwithtwonicks.co.uk). By Bollington Underbridge (26A), and just a few minutes' walk into the village. A very fine, comfortable and cosy pub with a friendly atmosphere, serving real ale. Extensive menu for upmarket bar food and à la carte *daily 12.00-21.00 (Sun 20.00).* Gluten-free options available. Dog- and family-friendly. Open fires and garden. *Afternoon* tea is served *Mon-Fri 14.30-17.30. May close early on quiet winter evenings* so it is advisable to telephone to check.

⬛**The Axe and Cleaver Hotel** School Lane, Dunham Massey, Altrincham WA14 4SE (0161 928 3391; www. chefandbrewer.com). Chain pub serving real ales and food *daily 12.00-22.00 (Sun 21.30).* Family-friendly with a garden. Open fires, newspapers and Wi-Fi. *Open 11.00.*

⬛**The Vine Inn** Barns Lane, Dunham Massey WA14 5RU (0161 928 3275). ¼ mile west of Dunham Woodhouse Underbridge 26B. Very inexpensive real ale dispensed in a relaxed, friendly atmosphere together with food *L.* Large garden, open fires and traditional pub games. *Open 12.00.*

⬛✕**The Rope & Anchor** Paddock Lane, Dunham Massey, Altrincham WA14 5RP (0161 927 7901; www. theropeandanchor.co.uk). ½ mile west of Dunham Town Bridge 27. Large pub with extensive gardens and play area, serving real ale and food *daily 12.00-21.00 (Sun 20.00).* Open fires, newspapers and Wi-Fi. *Open 11.00.*

Sale

Beyond Seamon's Moss Bridge 29, where a *PO, chemist, stores and a takeaway* will be found to the south, buildings close in upon the canal, and the countryside rapidly disappears from view. Among the many industrial buildings, both old and new, stands the superb Victorian Linotype Factory, dated 1897, where metal printing type was manufactured. The Metrolink tramway closes in from the south east and escorts the canal all the way through Sale and on into Stretford. At Sale Bridge the area around the imposing Town Hall has been rebuilt, and a couple of pubs and a restaurant, along with The Robert Bolt Theatre and The Waterside Arts Centre, take full advantage of their canal frontage. There is another canalside pub before the waterway is crossed by the M60 motorway, which then crosses the River Mersey. A large expanse of graves opposite the Watch House Cruising Club heralds the entrance to Stretford.

Pubs and Restaurants

The Bay Malton Hotel Seamon's Road, Dunham Massey, Altrincham WR14 5RA (0161 928 0655). Beside Seamon's Moss Bridge 29. A friendly community pub, offering real ale together with Thai, Chinese and British food *L and E*. Family-friendly with a large beer garden. Traditional pub games, sports TV and Wi-Fi. *Open Mon-Fri 17.00 & Sat-Sun 12.00.*

The Old Packet House 1 Navigation Road, Broadheath WA14 1LW (0161 929 1331). Just south of Broadheath Bridge 30. An excellent choice of real ales, together with good value food (*L daily and E Tue-Fri)* is served in this low-beamed hostelry, which is both family- and dog-friendly. Beer garden and Wi-Fi. Real fires, traditional pub games and sports TV. *Open 12.00 (Sat 11.00).*

The Waterside 7 Waterside Plaza, Sale M33 7BS (0161 969 8966). Beside Sale Bridge 35. Smart modern bar, with dress code stating no sportswear or three-quarter length trousers. Bar meals are served *all day, including breakfast until 12.00.* Patio seating overlooking the canal. Family-friendly and Wi-Fi. *Open 10.00 (Sun 11.00).*

✕♀**Vao** Waterside Plaza, Sale M33 7BS (0161 962 6666; www.vao-restaurants.co.uk). Beside Sale Bridge 35. Modern and stylish Italian restaurant serving traditional and gourmet pizzas alongside some great pasta dishes. *Open Mon-Sat 11.30-23.00, and Sun 12.00-22.30.*

The King's Ransom Brittania Road, off Northenden Road, Sale M33 2AB (0161 969 6006; www.gkpubs.co.uk/pubs-in-sale/kings-ransom-pub). Beside Sale Bridge 35. In fine converted canalside brick buildings, which were at one time part of a coal yard. They extend under the railway, so the pub is larger than you might think. Real ale is served, and food is available *daily 11.00-21.00.* Family-friendly. Canalside seating on a floating pontoon. Wi-Fi.

The Bridge Inn Dane Road, Sale M33 7QH (0161 969 7536). Beside Whites Bridge 36. Comfortable canalside pub offering an ever-changing range of real ales, along with bar meals *L and E Mon-Thu & all day Fri-Sun.* Dog- and family-friendly with a garden. Traditional pub games and sports TV. Mooring. *Open 12.00.*

STRETFORD

● **Altrincham**

Gt Manchester. All services. A few black and white half-timbered buildings remain in the market square of what was once a small market town. Later in the 18th C it became a textile manufacturing centre, and is now, inevitably, a dormitory town for Manchester. **Silver Blades Ice Rink** Oakfield Road, Station Site, Altrincham WA15 8EW (08700 852929; www.silver-blades.co.uk). A wide variety of different skating sessions are available to suit all budgets – telephone or visit the website for further details. Charge.

● **Sale**

Gt Manchester. All services. A residential suburb of Manchester, transformed from a farming community by the building in 1849 of the Altrincham to Manchester Railway – hence most of its buildings are Victorian or later. St Martin's Church is, however, 18th-C and has a hammerbeam roof. The clock tower of the town hall, built in 1914, is a prominent landmark. Look for the plaque in the wall commemorating the work of James Prescott Joule, who was born in Salford and calculated the mathematical relationship between heat and electrical energy. The northern part of Sale merges without boundary into Ashton upon Mersey, which is unremarkable except as the birthplace of Stanley Houghton (1881–1913) who wrote *The Dear Departed* in 1908 and *Hindle Wakes* in 1912. The area around Sale Bridge has been imaginatively redeveloped. **Waterside Arts Centre & Robert Bolt Theatre** Waterside Plaza, Sale M33 7ZF (0161 912 5616; www.watersideartscentre.co.uk). Music, drama and exhibitions. Robert Bolt (1924–1995) was a dramatist and screenwriter, born in Sale.

ARTERIES OF INDUSTRY

A growing economy demands transport and power. The Romans recognised these needs and built the Caer-dyke, a part of which still survives as the Fossdyke Navigation, to the west of Lincoln. They realised a horse can pull only 2 tons on a good road, but up to 100 tons on a waterway.

Edward the Confessor ordered improvements on the Thames, Severn, Trent and Yorkshire Ouse, and it was about this time that an artificial cut, a revolutionary idea at the time, was made to improve navigation on the Itchen. The development of the 'flash' lock, where a weir was used to build up a head of water which was then released to propel craft over an obstruction, was eventually superseded by the 'pound' lock, still in use today.

But it was the Newry Canal, the Sankey Brook and the Bridgewater Canal, which was built to serve the Duke's mines at Worsley and was still in commercial use until the 1970s, which heralded the start of the Canal Age.

Waters Meeting

At Waters Meeting, marked with a fine vortex sculpture hidden amongst the bushes, the original main line of the canal is joined – to the north west is Barton, Leigh and the connection with the Leeds & Liverpool Canal; to the east is the centre of Manchester and the Rochdale Canal, which once again crosses the hills to Rochdale, having now been restored. The Bridgewater's route passes close to Manchester United football ground, where the new stand of this famous club towers above the canal, and the magnificent Salford Quays. Old Trafford cricket ground, the home of Lancashire Cricket Club and a Test Match venue, is a little further south. Near bridge 95 there is a fine mural, painted in 1993 by Walter Kershaw, depicting transport and industry. More empty docks are passed following the well-painted Throstle Nest Footbridge. The Manchester Ship Canal is now very close – indeed just across the towpath – with good views of the City Park buildings and the distant city centre. The new Metrolink towers above, before crossing high above Pomona Lock – the connection with the Ship Canal. Have a look on the towpath side for the circular overflow weir by bridge 97, and notice the disused basins beyond the towpath. These are followed by a railway bridge, more overgrown basins and the remains of the Hulme Lock Branch – the original junction with the Ship Canal. The excitingly restored Castlefield Junction is then reached. It is well worth stopping here to explore the basins under the railway bridge, and to visit the pubs and restaurants. Moor on the stretch below Grocers Warehouse (*laundrette* facilities are available at the YHA on the Staffordshire Arm). The first of the nine wide locks of the Rochdale Canal is right beside the restored Merchants' Warehouse. The gear is anti-vandal locked, so you will need to use a Watermate key. The canal now passes between the backs of tall buildings and beneath elaborate railway arches, all of which have a certain faded grandeur. Tantalising glimpses of Victorian buildings invite exploration, but be wary of mooring away from Castlefield. You then pass the gay village, adjacent to Chorlton Street Lock, before finally the canal crawls under an 18-storey office block where you will find the top lock amidst concrete pillars. Ahead lies the Rochdale Canal (see page 179). Sharp right and left turns bring you to the start of the Ashton Canal, and the climb to Fairfield Junction (see page 167).

NAVIGATIONAL NOTES

See Navigational Notes on page 177 if you intend to proceed up the Rochdale 9 – Locks 92-84.

Boatyards

See page 185, for details of
Ⓑ **New Islington Marina** at Ducie Street Junction.

BOAT TRIPS

City Centre Cruises Contact Liverpool Road, Manchester M3 4JN (0161 902 0222; www.citycentrecruises.co.uk). Based at Castlefield (opposite Castlefield Hotel M3 4JR), *L.S. Lowry and Emmeline Pankhurst* provides state-of-the-art restaurant and hospitality facilities on a wide-beamed boat. An unusual cruising venue for any occasion ranging from private functions to business meetings and corporate entertainment. Its spacious interior allows for a variety of settings and layouts for up to 50 diners. Licensed bar, and also available for private charter.

● **Manchester**
All services. One of Britain's finest Victorian cities, a monument to 19th-C commerce and the textile boom, its size increasing remorselessly with the building of the canals, and later railways. Unfortunately virtually no early buildings survived the city's rapid growth, although there

is an incredible wealth of Victorian architecture surviving, in spite of redevelopment. The town hall and surrounding streets are a particularly rich area (north of Oxford Street Bridge). St Peter's Square, by the town hall, was the site of the 'Peterloo Massacre' in 1819, when a meeting demanding political reform was brutally dispersed by troops

37

carrying drawn sabres. Eleven people were killed and many more were injured. The Free Trade Hall, once the home of the Hallé Orchestra, is a little further along the road. Built in 1856, it was badly damaged in World War II, but was subsequently re-built to its original Palladian design. There is theatre, ballet and cinema, art galleries, and a wealth of interesting buildings, Victorian shopping arcades, many pubs with a choice of good beer and a variety of restaurants just a short walk from the canal. Sporting facilities are excellent, partly as a consequence of Manchester being the venue for the 2002 Commonwealth Games. The new developments at Salford Quays, on the Manchester Ship Canal, are quite breathtaking, and the building work continues elsewhere. See page 182 for details of attractions to be found in the city.

Imperial War Museum North Quay West, Trafford Wharf Road, Manchester M17 1TZ (0161 836 4000; www.iwm.org.uk/visits/iwm-north). Right beside the Ship Canal, in a stunning building by Daniel Libeskind, clad in shimmering aluminium and representing a world shattered by war. Visitors enter through the 55-metres-high air shaft, giving fine views over the city. Exhibitions depict weapons, aircraft, the experience of war, science and war, interactive collections and a spectacular audio-visual display. *Open daily, 10.00–17.00.* Free.

Metrolink The new electric 'supertram'. G-Mex is a station close to the canal (G-Mex, Deansgate Railway Station, Manchester, M3 4LG), near to the second lock, if you fancy a ride. Information on 0161 205 2000; www.metrolink.co.uk.

Manchester Visitor Information Centre Piccadilly Plaza, Portland Street, Manchester M1 4BT (0871 222 8223; www.visitmanchester.com). *Open 10.00–17.30 (Sun and B Hols 16.30).*

● **Manchester Ship Canal**
The Harbour Master, Manchester Ship Canal Company, Eastham Locks, Queen Elizabeth II Dock, Eastham (0151 327 1461; www.shipcanal.co.uk). The canal was opened in 1894 at a cost of £15½ million and carries ships up to 15,000 tons displacement. It is 36 miles long and connects the tidal Mersey at Eastham to Manchester. The Weaver Navigation, the Bridgewater Canal and the Shropshire Union Canal connect with it. All craft using the canal must be licensed. They must also be insured against third party risks which should include the cost of salvage and removal of wreck. There is a charge for the use of Pomona Lock, and advance notice is required – telephone 0161 629 8266. Any boat holding a Canal & River Trust canal and river licence may cruise on the Bridgewater Canal for seven consecutive days free of charge.

Pubs and Restaurants

There are many fine pubs in Manchester. Those close to the canal include:

●**Dukes 92** 18 Castle Street, Castlefield, Manchester M3 4LZ (0161 839 3522; www. dukes92.com). Serving real ale, this very popular modern bar was once a stable for the nearby Merchant's Warehouse. Bar and restaurant meals, together with speciality cheese and paté *all day.* Canalside terrace and balcony overlooking the canal basin. Children welcome.

●✕**The Wharf** 6 Slate Wharf, Manchester M15 4ST (0161 220 2960; www.brunningandprice. co.uk/thewharf). Housed in a purpose-built building beside Castlefield Basin, this busy pub serves a wide range of real ales, together with real cider, wines and malt whiskies. Food is available *12.00–22.00 (Sun 21.30)* and there is extensive outside seating. Well-behave children and dogs welcome. Real fires, traditional pub games and a family room. *Open 11.00.*

●**The Knott Bar** 374 Deansgate, Manchester M3 4LY (0161 839 9229; www.knottbar.co.uk). Close to Deansgate railway station. A deservedly popular pub serving a wide and ever changing range of real ales. Also real cider, lagers and bottled beers. Excellent food is available (with a children's menu and vegan options) *daily 12.00–20.00* and children are welcome *until 20.00.* Outdoor drinking area. *Open 12.00 (weekends 11.30).*

●**The Rising Sun** 22 Queen Street, Manchester M2 5HX (0161 834 1193). ½ mile north of Deansgate Tunnel, just off Deansgate itself. Traditional city pub, offering visitors a warm welcome, serving a wide range of real ales and a real cider. Food available *L Mon-Fri. Open 12.00 (Sun 13.00).*

●**Joshua Brooks** 106 Princess Street, Manchester M1 6NG (0161 273 7336; www.joshuabrooks.co.uk). 300yds south of Princess Street Bridge. Popular city-centre venue, which is a pub by day and a club by night, serving a good selection of real ales and cider, together with food *until 19.00 (17.00 at weekends).* Outside seating area. *Open 12.00 (11.00 at weekends).*

●**The Waterhouse** 67-71 Princess St, Manchester, Lancashire M2 4EG (0161 200 5380; www. jdwetherspoon.co.uk/home/pubs/the-waterhouse). ¼ mile north of Princess Street Bridge. This former row of Georgian cottages now dispenses a range of beers, including those from local microbreweries. Also real cider. Food is available *throughout the day, starting with breakfast.* Children welcome, large-screen TV, Wi-Fi and an outdoor drinking area. *Open 08.00–23.00.*

●**Jolly Angler** Ducie Street, Ancoats, Manchester M1 2JW (0161 236 5307). Near the junction. A small, plain and friendly pub offering real ale and snacks *at all times* (or you can eat your own sandwiches!). Café nearby. Regular live music sessions. Children welcome. Moorings nearby, but don't leave your boat here overnight.

See also **Pubs and Restaurants** on page 181.

NAVIGATIONAL NOTES

MANCHESTER SHIP CANAL

Harbour Master, Queen Elizabeth II Dock, Eastham, Wirral (0151 327 1461; www.shipcanal. co.uk). The ship canal currently carries an increasing annual tonnage of approximately 2,500 vessel movements per year. A great deal of it is hazardous, petro-chemical traffic and therefore a no smoking régime is enforced. The canal company is happy to allow pleasure boats use on the understanding that certain conditions are adhered to. It is not a navigation for the novice boater and should be viewed as a daytime transit corridor for the experienced boat owner (not hire boater) to access the River Weaver, the River Mersey and the Shropshire Union Canal. In essence the company's requirements are as follows:

1　The boat must carrying at least £3 million third party insurance cover.
2　The boat is subject to an annual Certificate of Seaworthiness carried out by an MSC approved surveyor (listed in the Pleasure Craft Transit Notes). This is not required for the passage from Pomona Lock east to The Manchester, Bolton & Bury Canal.
3　The appropriate fee is paid by cheque, currently set at £29 Weston Marsh Lock to Ellesmere Port and £143 Manchester to Ellesmere Port. Transit through Pomona Lock is £25 each way.
4　The boater must contact the harbourmaster at least 48hrs in advance of passage to obtain copies of:
a)　Pleasure Craft Transit Notes (or visit www.waterways.org.uk and search on 'Manchester Ship Canal').
b)　Port of Manchester Navigation By-laws.
At this juncture boaters can discuss appropriate times of arrival and departure to coincide with scheduled shipping movements.
5　At all times the boater is required to act in a responsible manner and be aware that this is a *daytime* transit route only, with no lay-by facilities. Boaters should familiarise themselves with the geography of the canal before setting out. A schematic map of the canal is appended to the Pleasure Craft Transit Notes.
6　VHF radio equipment is desirable (the Manchester Ship Canal Company call on channel 14 in the canal; channel 7 in the River Mersey and operate on channels 14 and 20) and if not available a mobile phone should be considered essential. (Eastham VTS – 0151 327 1242; Latchford Locks – 01925 635249).

The above synopsis is a brief note of the essential requirements and should be read in conjunction with **The Transit Notes** and **Navigation Bylaws** referred to in 4 above. Also available from the MSC at Peel Dome are notes for the transit of Pomona Lock and 'The Upper Reach', for which a Certificate of Seaworthiness is NOT required.

Weston Marsh Lock For access to the River Weaver, through Weston Marsh Lock, you must give *48 hours prior notice* to the Northwich office (0303 040 4040; enquiries. northwalesborders@canalrivertrust.org.uk). Please note these locks are only operated *during office hours Mon-Fri*. All necessary paperwork MUST be in place for the Manchester Ship Canal *prior to passage*. During the summer season (*from approximately mid Mar to end of Oct)* Weston Marsh Lock is also available for passage once in any *weekend period* subject to prior notice being given to the Northwich office *before 16:30pm on the previous Thu*. The passage is based on a first come first served basis and will normally mean the lock is available for a *4-hour period*. VHF channel for the River Weaver is 74.

Ellesmere Port Bottom Lock Entry into the Manchester Ship Canal from the Shropshire Union is restricted by a swing bridge over the first lock (adjacent to the Holiday Inn) which is not under the control of CRT. Boaters wishing to enter the canal must first contact Ellesmere Port & Neston Borough Council (0151 356 6543) to make arrangements for the bridge to be swung. They require *eight hours* notice and will make a charge for weekend operation. Any difficulties in obtaining assistance should be referred to CRT at Northwich (0303 040 4040; enquiries.northwalesborders@canalrivertrust.org.uk).

Bridgewater and Rochdale Canals Waters Meeting

Worsley

This is a surprisingly interesting section of waterway, well worth visiting for its own sake and a useful link with the Leeds & Liverpool Canal. What was the original line of the Bridgewater Canal leaves Waters Meeting through the vast Trafford Park Industrial Estate to cross the Manchester Ship Canal on the impressive Barton Swing Aqueduct, after passing an incongruous landscaped pagoda, and an even more incongruous 'lighthouse' at Parrin Lane Bridge. Curving through the suburbs of Salford and the leafy expanse of Broadoak Park, the navigation reaches the village of Worsley and what was the entrance to the underground mines which provided its *raison d'être*. It is well worth stopping to take a look around the Delph, to see at first hand what brought about the canals' construction, and a sturdy brick fountain built in 1905 to commemorate the Third Duke of Bridgewater in the park to the east of bridge 51. You will also notice that dissolved iron ore colours the canal bright ochre around here. After Worsley the M60 motorway and its attendant slip roads cross the canal as the Bridgewater then heads west through open country now only hinting at its industrial past. There is, however, more solid evidence of the area's mining connections at Astley, where it's worth stopping for a short while to visit the Colliery Museum. You will see the pit-head gear as you approach. North of Bridge 54, west along A572, there is a useful selection of shops including a *PO, chemist, library and supermarket*. There are also *fish & chips* 100yds north of Bridge 58.

Boatyards

Ⓑ**Worsley Dry Docks** The Boatyard, Worsley Road, Worsley M28 2WN (0161 793 6767). **D** Gas, hull surveys, Boat Safety Certification, dry docks, overnight & short-term mooring, winter mooring, hull blacking, chandlery, emergency docking, anodes supplied and fitted, breakdown advice.
Ⓑ**Bridgewater Marina** 14 Quayside Close, Boothstown, Worsley M28 1YB (0161 702

8622//07713 098032; www.bridgewatermarina. co.uk). By bridge 54. 🛏🚿♿ **D** Pump out, gas, day-boat hire and holiday hire with disabled access, overnight and long-term mooring, winter storage, boat sales and repairs, boat building, engine repairs, chandlery, toilets, showers, solid fuel, DIY facilities. *Emergency call out.*

Salford

Gt Manchester.
All services.
Although now
merged with
Manchester,
Salford was granted
its charter in 1230,
71 years before that
of its now larger
neighbour. It has a
fine new university,
built in 1967 and a
Roman Catholic cathedral
consecrated in 1848. It is,
however, most widely known
as being the subject of many
paintings by the artist L.S. Lowry
(1887–1976). What is less widely
known is that he gained his
inspiration by walking the streets
of Salford for many years as a rent
collector, only painting in the evenings
and at weekends – a fact to which he
would never willingly admit. His work is
exhibited at The Lowry Pier, Salford Quays
(*see page 158*).

Salford Art Gallery and Museum Peel Park,
The Crescent, Salford M5 4WU (0161 778 0800; www.
salfordcommunityleisure.co.uk). In the centre of Salford
University Campus. Stroll down a Victorian Street, admire
the Landau Carriages and discover a Victorian heritage. Test your
strength or listen to the Victorian Top 20. Experience the sights and
sounds of Victorian Salford with original shop fronts and fascinating interiors.
Victorian Gallery with paintings, pottery and fine art. Temporary exhibition
programme, from hands-on activities to modern art. *Open all year, Mon-Fri 10.00–
16.45, Sat-Sun 12.00-16.00.* Coffee Shop. Free.

Barton upon Irwell

Gt Manchester. Tel, stores, garage. In an interesting position overlooking the two canals. The richly
decorated Catholic Church of the City of Mary Immaculate is by Pugin, 1867, and is considered to be one of
his best works. Indeed the architect can be found featured in a painting on the south wall of the chancel.

41

- **Barton Aqueduct**
One of the wonders of the waterways, it carries the Bridgewater Canal over the Manchester Ship Canal. Designed by Sir Edward Leader Williams, it was built in the early 1890s in a bold style comparable to contemporary railway engineering. Gates seal off the 235ft-long 1450-ton section that swings at right angles to the Ship Canal over a central island. It replaced Brindley's earlier aqueduct, built in 1761 and which carried the canal in a trough over 660ft long and 39ft above the Irwell, truly a wonder in its day. The aqueduct operates *summer, daily, 09.15–21.00; winter, daily 09.15–16.30*. The aqueduct is usually *closed for maintenance during the last two weeks of March* – telephone 0161 629 8200 for details.

- **Patricroft**
Gt Manchester. All services. Here are the Bridgewater Mills, established in 1836 by Nasmyth, who invented the steam hammer.

- **Eccles**
Gt Manchester. All services. The town peaked as a cotton and silk weaving centre between 1870–90, and little has happened since, although its name will always be remembered in connection with the famous cakes – round pastry filled with currants. The Church of St Mary has its origins in the 10th C, although the present sandstone building dates from the late 15th C.

- **Worsley**
Gt Manchester. PO box, tel, stores, garage (distant). There are more facilities approximately 1 mile to the north east. An attractive estate village dating from the 18th–19th C, and widely recognised as the place which triggered the 'canal age', in spite of the fact that the Bridgewater was not the first modern canal in the British Isles. Coal had been mined in Worsley since the 14th C, originally from the surface, and later by sinking shafts. It is thought that a drainage sough, common in underground workings, may have provided the germ of the idea for an underground canal network which could be used to bring the coal out. John Gilbert, the Duke of Bridgewater's agent, probably designed the system, which included an inclined plane on a 1 in 4 gradient 453ft long and 60ft wide. Work started at the same time on the building of the canal to Manchester, and eventually

46 miles of tunnels were hewn out. A particular kind of simple double-ended tub boat was used underground, called a 'starvationer'. These carried up to 12 tons of coal. The old canal basin at Worsley Delph, with its entrance tunnels to the mines, is still intact, and information boards help to explain its workings. On the canal, look out for the Boathouse, built by Lord Ellesmere to house the royal barge, prepared for Queen Victoria's visit in 1851, and Duke's Wharf, an old oil store. Close by is Worsley Old Hall, the half-timbered Court House and The Old Reading Room, which was originally a nailers shop, shown on a plan of 1785 and painted on a Wedgwood dinner service presented to Queen Catherine II of Russia. The church, by George Gilbert Scott, 1846, has a spire decorated with crockets and gargoyles – inside there is a rich collection of monuments to the Dukes of Bridgewater.

- **Astley Green**
Gt Manchester. Tel. Canalside mining village dominated by a gaunt red-brick Victorian church.
Astley Green Colliery Museum Higher Green Lane, Astley Green, Tyldesley M29 7JB (01942 708969; www.agcm.org.uk). To the north of the canal, perched on the edge of Chat Moss. The colliery was originally owned by the Pilkington Colliery Company, a branch of the Clifton and Kearsley Coal Company, which commenced the sinking of the first of two shafts in 1908. There are various pit relics to explore, plus a superb engine house containing a 3,300 HP twin tandem compound engine by Yates & Thom of Blackburn. This once wound the 8 ton lift which transported the miners to their work 873yds underground, at a maximum speed of 82ft per second (55mph!). Astley Green Colliery is situated in an area that was once full of collieries, but over the years they have all been closed, and demolished. There is now only one headgear and engine house left in Lancashire – this one, which ceased commercial activity in 1970. Being restored by the Red Rose Steam Society, it remains as a valuable reminder of life and work in this area in the recent past. *Open Sun, Tue and Thu 13.30–17.00. The site can also be visited at any other time by prior arrangement by school parties and groups. No fixed charge, just give as you wish.*

WALKING & CYCLING
Broadoak Park, to the north of Parrin Lane Bridge (50), contains some pleasant paths, suitable for a short walk. Bridgewater Park, Boothstown, has a few paths which can be enjoyed, while to the south of the canal is an area known as Chat Moss, a surprisingly remote area about 7,000 years old, and which was not reclaimed until the late 18th C. Close to the canal it consists mainly of reclaimed open-cast mine workings. A path from bridge 56 gives restricted access.

BIRD LIFE
Mallard ducks are widespread and familiar. The colourful male has a yellow bill and a green, shiny head and neck, separated from the chestnut breast by a white collar. Its plumage is otherwise grey-brown except for a black stern and white tail. The female has an orange bill and mottled brown plumage. In flight both sexes have blue and white speculum (patch on trailing edge of inner wing).

WILDLIFE

As water quality has improved, many different species of wildlife are being spotted in the Manchester Ship Canal (*see* page 38), including the *Grey Seal*. This large mammal is streamlined in water, but extremely cumbersome on land. It is frequently seen 'bottling', with its head and neck clear of the water. The coat colour is extremely variable, but usually some shade of blue-grey; the background colour of the male is generally darker than that of the female. Both sexes show an irregular and individually unique pattern of blotches and spots on their coats.

Pubs and Restaurants

Crompton's at the Waterside 1 Parrin Lane, Monton M30 8AN (0161 788 8788; www.watersidebarrestaurant.com). Restaurant/ bar offering a varied menu. Children welcome. Large garden. *Open Tue–Sun from 12.00 (closed Mon except B Hols).*

The Barton Arms 2 Stableford, Barton Road, Worsley M28 2ED (0161 728 6157; www.emberinns.co.uk/the-barton-arms-worsley). An excellent selection of real ale is served in this modern pub, which majors on food available *daily 11.30-22.00 (Sun 12.00)*. Child- and dog-friendly. Open fires and Wi-Fi.

The Bridgewater Arms 23 Barton Road, Worsley M28 2PD (0161 728 6206; www.fayre-square.com/pub/bridgewater-worsley-manchester/p0915). By Bridge 51. Large comfortable pub serving real ale and food *11.00-21.00 daily*. Family-friendly with outside seating. Garden, open fires and Wi-Fi. Nearby .

Tung Fong 2 Worsley Road, Worsley M28 2NL (0161 794 5331; www.tung-fong.co.uk). Smart Chinese restaurant, with interesting décor. *Open daily from 18.00.*

George's Dining Room & Bar 17-21 Barton Road, Worsley M28 2PD (0161 794 5444; www.georgesworsley.co.uk). Named after the famous Victorian architect, Sir George Gilbert Scott (who designed St Marks – the village church) this contemporary restaurant serves a modern British menu together with an array of cocktails and fine wines. Food is available *10.00-22.00 –* drinks *until 23.00.*

The Moorings 2 Quayside Close, Boothstown, Manchester M28 1YB (0161 703 8895; www.fayre-square.com/pub/moorings-boothstown-worsley/p1595). By Bridge 54. In a lovely spot overlooking open country and the canal, on the corner of the Bridgewater Park Nature Reserve. Serving real ale and food available *daily 12.00-22.00 (Sun 21.30).* Family-friendly with canalside seating. Mooring and Wi-Fi. *Open 11.00 (Sun 12.00).*

The Old Boathouse Inn 164 Higher Green Lane, Astley, Tyldesley M29 7JB (01942 883300). By bridge 58. A comfortable canalside pub with a garden, serving real ale and food *L and E, daily.* Children welcome, mooring. Traditional pub games, open fires and Wi-Fi. *Regular weekend live music.*

The Bull's Head 504 Manchester Road, Astley, Tyldesley M29 7BP (01942 887109; www.emberinns.co.uk/the-bulls-head-astley). ¾ mile north of Bridge 58, across A580. A large, comfortable establishment serving real ale (you can try before you buy!), real cider and food *daily 12.00-10.00.* There are large gardens and patio areas and quizzes *Sun, Mon & Wed.* Family-friendly and Wi-Fi.

CHAT MOSS DESCRIBED

From hence [Warrington], on the road to Manchester, we passed the great bog or waste called Chatmos, the first of that kind that we see in England, from any of the south parts hither. It extends on the left-hand of the road for five or six miles east and west, and they told us it was, in some places, seven or eight miles from north to south. The nature of these mosses, for we found there are many of them in this country, is this, and you will take this for a description of all the rest. The surface, at a distance, looks black and dirty, and is indeed frightful to think of, for it will bear neither horse or man, unless in an exceedingly dry season, and then not so as to be passable, or that any one should travel over them. What nature meant by such a useless production, 'tis hard to imagine; but the land is entirely waste, except for the poor cottager's fuel, and the quantity used for that is very small.

Daniel Defoe, around 1720.

Leigh

After the excitement and interest of Barton, Worsley and Astley Green, the canal now passes through pleasant open country and reclaimed land towards the mill town of Leigh, where it transforms into the Leeds & Liverpool Canal, continuing the route to Wigan. Raised canal banks reveal past problems of subsidence in this area, caused by old mine workings. At Leigh the canal passes a sturdy warehouse by bridge 66 before it becomes the Leeds & Liverpool – the familiar stop plank cranes of the Bridgewater finish here, and signs announce you are back in Canal & River Trust territory. Wigan is 7¼ miles away (*see* page 102).

(*see* page 102)

● **Leigh**
Gt Manchester. All services. Once the archetypal mill town, most of the tall buildings and chimneys have now been demolished to be replaced with ubiquitous new developments. However, in the market place you can see the fine Edwardian baroque town hall, built 1904-7, facing the battlemented church of St Mary.

Pubs and Restaurants

🍺**The Waterside Inn** Twist Lane, Leigh WN7 4DB (01942 605005; www.gkpubs.co.uk/pubs-in-leigh/waterside-inn-pub). This pub is contained within very handsome grade II listed canalside buildings, one a two-storey stone warehouse dated 1821, the other a brick warehouse dated 1894. A distinctive wooden tower adjoins. Real ale is served, and food is available *daily 11.00-21.00.* Open fires, a garden, moorings and family-friendly. *Weekend discos 'til late.*
🍺**The White Lion** 6A Leigh Road, Leigh WN7 1QL (07814 575883; www.allgatesbrewery.com/our_pubs/the-white-lion-leigh). ¼ mile north of Leigh Bridge 11. Situated opposite Leigh's historic parish church, this friendly All Gates Brewery pub serves a range of their own (and guest) real ales, real cider and bar snacks. Quiz and food *Thu.* Traditional pub games. *Open Sun-Thu 12.00 & Fri-Sat 11.00.*
🍺**The Thomas Burke** 20A Leigh Road, Leigh WN7 1QR (01942 685640; www.jdwetherspoon.co.uk/home/pubs/the-thomas-burke). Named in honour of a famous local tenor – the 'Lancashire Caruso' – this striking pub serves a large range of real ales and food *all day from breakfast onwards.* Large screen TV and Wi-Fi. Children welcome and outside drinking area. *Open from 08.00.*

WALKING & CYCLING

Pennington Flash is a 200ha country park, centred on a 70ha lake or 'flash', with a variety of well-maintained paths suitable for both walkers and cyclists. Over 230 bird species have been recorded in the park, and there is a wide variety of butterflies, dragonflies and damselflies. There is a small Information Centre.

NAVIGATIONAL NOTE

Plank Lane Swing Bridge 8 is now boater operated and requires a Watermate Key. It is available for use at all times outside the periods *Mon-Fri 08.00-09.30 & 16.00-18.00*. Any difficulties contact CRT (0303 040 4040; enquiries.northwest@canalrivertrust.org.uk).

A VISIT TO THE MINES AT WORSLEY

'Arrived at Worsley, passing athwart the river Irwell, over which the canal runs, being raised on arches not less than fifty feet in height above that stream. Sent compliments to Mr Gilbert, the steward, asking the favour of seeing the duke's underground works, which was granted, and we stepped into the boat, passing into an archway partly of brick and partly cut through the stone, of about three and a half feet high; we received at entering six lighted candles. This archway, called a funnel, runs into the body of the mountain almost in a direct line three thousand feet, its medium depth beneath the surface about eighty feet; we were half an hour passing that distance. Here begins the first underground road to the pits, ascending to the wagon road, so called, about four feet above the water, being a highway for wagons, containing about a ton weight of the form of a mill-hopper, running on wheels, to convey the coals to the boats.

Arrived at the coal mine, which appearing about five feet through the roof, was supported by many posts, the area being about twenty feet square and the height scarce four. A hundred men are daily employed, and each turns out a ton a day; the miners' wages two shillings, and the laborers' about one shilling.'

Samuel Curwen, *Journal and Letters*, 7 June 1777.

CALDER & HEBBLE NAVIGATION

CALDER & HEBBLE NAVIGATION

Wakefield to Broad Cut
Length: 120'
Beam: 17' 6"
Headroom: 11' 10"
Draught: 6' 6"

Broad Cut to Sowerby Bridge
Length: 57' 6" (or 60' narrowboat)
Beam: 14' 2"
Headroom: 9' 4"
Draught: 3' 6"

HUDDERSFIELD BROAD CANAL

Length: 57' 6" (or 60' narrowboat)
Beam: 14' 2"
Headroom: 9' 6"
Draught: 2' 6"

MANAGER

0303 040 4040;
enquiries.northeast@canalrivertrust.org.uk

MILEAGE

WAKEFIELD to
Cooper Bridge: 13 miles, 13 locks
Sowerby Bridge: 23½ miles, 27 locks including Fall Ing
Huddersfield Broad Canal: 3¾ miles, 9 locks

SAFETY NOTES

Where locks give access onto river sections of the
navigation, river level gauge boards are located at
each lock chamber indicating conditions as follows:

Green band – Normal river levels safe for navigation.

Amber band – River levels are above normal.
If you wish to navigate the river section you are
advised to proceed on to and through the next lock.

Red band – Flood conditions unsafe for navigation.
Lock closed.

In an emergency telephone the manager's office or
out of office hours telephone 0800 47 999 47.

The construction of the Aire & Calder resulted in pressure to improve the Calder above Wakefield. After much opposition, the Calder & Hebble was built, with boats finally reaching Sowerby Bridge in the 1770s. The first survey had been made in 1740 and the Bill to implement it defeated by partisan landowners and millers. Sixteen years later John Smeaton produced a survey that was more acceptable and a Bill was finally passed in 1758. Construction was slow and conflict amongst the overseeing commissioners was rife. In 1765 Brindley was called upon to advise and Smeaton was dismissed. Three years later the position was reversed after serious flooding had damaged the recently completed navigation at Salterhebble. Further monies were raised to fund repairs and the waterway finally re-opened throughout in 1770.

From then on it was a case of continuous improvement and development with the addition of branch canals to profit from local pockets of trade. As always there were conflicts over water with mill owners, which curtailed some of the company's more ambitious plans to canalize large sections of the navigation but wherever possible the mills themselves were bought up. During the first half of 19th C, in line with developments on the Aire & Calder, further improvements were made (which included the cut at Horbury) but burgeoning railway competition severely blunted their impact. As a result the navigation was first leased to the Manchester & Leeds Railway and subsequently to the Aire & Calder. This second association led to a programme of lock enlargement under W.H. Bartholomew, which was of particular benefit to the section between Fall Ing Lock and Broad Cut Top Lock, above which the prevailing gauge remained consistent with the dimensions of the 57'x14' Yorkshire Keel. In 1885, on the expiry of the Aire & Calder's lease, the Calder and Hebble turned their attention to rebuilding their overbridges and establishing a carrying company: the Calder Carrying Co.

Beyond this there was little further investment, although the company continued to pay a dividend right through to Nationalization in 1948; often financed by the sale of assets. Never as successful as the Aire & Calder, it did, however, benefit from trade coming in from the Huddersfield Broad Canal and later, in 1811, from the Huddersfield Narrow. Commercial traffic ended in 1981, when the last coal barges unloaded at Thornhill Power Station. Becoming increasingly popular and yet still uncrowded, this waterway has much to offer, with great industrial interest and, in many places, considerable charm.

WALKING & CYCLING

The Calder & Hebble, as its name suggests, is largely a river navigation and it incorporates a series of lock cuts where weirs have been constructed to maintain a navigable depth. This approach, whilst excellent for boaters, can pose problems for those following the waterway along the towpath. These problems are twofold: erosion of the river bank during times of flood and the need to cross the river at either the head or tail of a lock cut in order to remain with the navigation. When boats relied upon horse power, before the invention of the internal combustion engine, both towpaths and horse bridges were maintained in a usable condition. Subsequently both have suffered from the ravages of time and the vagaries of flood – hence the need to come up with some 'creative alternatives' as detailed below.

1 At Thornes Flood Lock (*see* page 49) follow the river south west and under the motorway bridge. Strike off west across the mown sward through the clumps of trees at almost any point before reaching Broad Cut Low Lock and head west to meet the railway line where it intersects the north bank of the river. The bridge here incorporates an enclosed walkway accessible to walkers and cyclists and, in conjunction with a lane running south, returns you to Broad Cut beside the Navigation pub.

2 At Ledgard Bridge 17 (*see* page 50) cross over the navigation, go under the railway and over the river and turn right. At Chadwick Lane fork right and go through the industrial estate with Ledgard Boats on your right. Pass Navigation Garage on the left and as the road swings left, take the stone path on the right back towards the river, to the left of the PFS Factory Unit.

3 Due to severe bank erosion, only a small section of the towpath between Cooper Bridge and Brighouse (*see* page 52) remains, therefore walkers and cyclists should leave the navigation at Cooper Bridge, briefly heading south west along the A6107, before turning right at the garage along Lower Quarry Road. Cross the railway bridge and fork right down a track under the line signposted to Bradley Hall Farm. Just before the farm turn right and rejoin the waterway at bridge 11, below Kirklees Top Lock.

Salterhebble Locks (see page 52)

Horbury Bridge

At Thornes Lock only one of the two chambers is now in use – you will need a Calder & Hebble handspike to operate this, and subsequent locks. Here the navigation enters a short cut and rejoins the River Calder at Thornes Flood Lock, before passing under the M1 motorway. Ahead is the tall spike of Elmley Moor television transmitter. The beautifully kept Broad Cut Low Lock marks the start of a 5-mile-long canal section with 8 locks. There was regular trade on this stretch until 1981, when West Country barges took coal from the British Oak Colliery to Thornhill Power Station. Remains of loading staithes can be seen opposite the Navigation Inn. There are good moorings at Horbury Bridge, *and a shop and post office* are close by. A short. A short arm here used to connect with the river and this has now become an attractive long-term mooring with *showers* and the usual *facilities*. Beyond the bridge a tree-lined cutting leads to Figure of Three Locks. There are two locks on the navigation with another now disused which used to connect with the river. Is it this, or the fact that the river here makes the shape of a '3', which gives these locks their unusual name? Experts seem unable to agree. The towpath from Broad Cut to Dewsbury is good, having been improved in 1986-7. After Mill Bank look out for a milestone marked 'from FALL ING 7 miles' on the towpath side, by the next bridge. Thornhill Double Locks mark the junction with the Dewsbury Arm, which branches off to Savile Town Basin. Climbing Thornhill Double Locks (good *moorings* here) the navigation enters a deep, secluded cutting spanned by tall bridges.

NAVIGATIONAL NOTES

1 The Calder & Hebble joins the Aire & Calder Navigation (Wakefield branch) at Fall Ings Lock, outside Wakefield. Details of the last stretch, and information on Wakefield, *appear on page 18 in the Aire & Calder section.*
2 When ascending Broad Cut Low Lock both ground paddle and gate paddle outlets may be above the water level. Exercise caution when opening to avoid flooding your boat.
3 Take care when ascending locks, especially Kirklees Low Lock, to avoid trapping your tiller below the platform which extends over the locks, suspended from the lower gates.

Boatyards

Ⓑ**Broadcut Marine** The Yard, Broadcut Road, Calder Grove, Wakefield WF4 3DS (01924 270070/07855 930051; www.broadcutmarine. co.uk). Marine engineering, boat repairs and restoration.

Ⓑ**Calder Valley Marine** Savile Town Wharf, Mill Street East, Dewsbury WF12 9BD (01924 467976; www. cvmarine.co.uk). Gas, pump out, overnight mooring, long-term mooring, slipway, winter storage, boat and engine repairs, boat sales, books and maps, showers, laundry, toilets, solid fuel.

Pubs and Restaurants

The Navigation Inn Broad Cut Road, Calder Grove, Wakefield WF4 3DS (01924 274361). Broad Cut Top Lock, by the railway viaduct. A well-placed canalside pub serving real ales and inexpensive bar snacks and meals *all day, every day*. Children welcome; dogs outside only. Children's room and indoor ball pool. Massive garden and play area. Good moorings here; *PO and fish & chips* just a short distance to the south.

The Bingley Arms 221 Bridge Road, Horbury, Wakefield WF4 5NL (01924 272838). A warm friendly establishment in another fine-looking pub serving real ales and food *L Fri-Sun*. Children and dogs welcome. Garden with swings. Regular quiz and karaoke. Pub games and pool.

The Horse & Jockey Inn Bridge Road, Horbury Bridge WF4 5PP (01924 650321). Friendly pub serving real ale and food *Sun L* from a carvery. Children welcome. Traditional pub games and *regular* live music. *Open Mon-Thu 16.00 & Fri-Sun 12.00.*

Capri Bistro 223 Bridge Road, Horbury WF4 5QA (01924 263090; www.caprirestaurant. co.uk). Italian restaurant and wine bar serving a range of pasta dishes, pizzas and appetising deserts. Children welcome. There is also a takeaway service (01924 277666) operating *from 16.30*, together with a café (01924 270065) offering breakfast, lunch and snacks. Bistro *open Mon-Fri 18.00; Sat 17.30 & Sun12.00.*

The Leggers' Inn Savile Town Wharf, 66 Mill Street East, Dewsbury WF12 9BD (01924 502846; www.saviletownwharf.co.uk). Real ale and real cider are available in this converted stables together with *Sun L* and bar snacks *daily until 20.00*. Open fires, outside drinking area and traditional pub games. *Open 10.30.*

The Nelson Inn 145 Slaithwaite Road, Thornhill Lees, Dewsbury WF12 9DW (01924 461685). Walk up the path west of Brewery Bridge. Real ales served in a 17th-C pub atop the canal. Food available *daily 12.00-20.00*. Dog- and family-friendly. Sports TV, a garden and traditional pub games. Newspapers and Wi-Fi. There is a *chemist* opposite.

Try also: **The Cricketers Arms** Cluntergate, Horbury WF4 5AG (01924 267032; www. thecricketershorbury.co.uk). Approximately 1 mile up the hill in Horbury itself.

● **Horbury Bridge**
W. Yorks. PO, tel, stores, off-licence, takeaway, garage. A useful selection of shops, pubs and a restaurant close to the canal. A mile or so up the hill, to the north east, is the small town of Horbury itself. The Hymn 'Onward Christian Soldiers' was written and first sung here by the Reverend S. Baring-Gould as a marching song for children.
National Coal Mining Museum for England Caphouse Colliery, New Road, Overton, Wakefield WF4 4RH (01924 848806; www.ncm.org.uk). On the A642, 2 miles south west of Horbury Bridge (bus service) and accessible by bus 263 from Huddersfield and Wakefield. Go 450ft underground to visit old- and new-style coalfaces. Audio-visual show, café, shop, picnic area. Wear warm clothes; not suitable for children under 5. *Open daily 10.00–17.00*. Free – but donations very welcome.

● **Dewsbury**
W. Yorks. All services, station. The compact and attractive town centre is 1 mile away from Savile Town Basin.
Dewsbury Arm WF12 9BB Extending for 3/4 mile to Savile Town Basin.

Cooper Bridge

Before long the deep cutting gives way to an open industrial wasteland (for which there are large-scale redevelopment plans) around the site of Thornhill Power Station, where barges once used to unload coal. Between Thornhill Flood Lock and Greenwood Lock a short, wide, river section intervenes before the navigation enters another artificial channel to the south of Mirfield. Landscaping and pretty waterside gardens make this a pleasant spot. At Greenwood Flood Gates the river is briefly rejoined on a sweeping bend, before the navigation enters another artificial cut.

● **Thornhill**
W. Yorks. PO, tel, stores, fish & chips.
This old stone-built mining village up on a hill above the canal offers fine views across the valley and an excellent pub. Best approached up Hall Lane from Bridge 29. Closer to the canal is Thornhill Lees, just north east of Brewery Bridge. There is a *PO, stores, chemist, takeaways and an off-licence* here.

● **Mirfield**
W. Yorks. All services. A useful place for supplies.
Kirklees Park Mirfield. In the grounds are the modest ruins of a priory founded in the 12th C for Cistercian nuns. Most of the stones were incorporated in the construction of Kirklees Hall during the late 16th C. It is believed that Robin Hood died whilst at the priory but before so doing he shot two arrows from the window to mark his burial place. One landed in the River Calder and floated away, the other landed in the grounds of the park. A tablet marks the spot thought to be his grave.

NAVIGATIONAL NOTES

1 When coming downstream, look out for the entrance to Ledgard Bridge Flood Lock. A large weir awaits those who miss it. This warning applies equally to boaters leaving Shepley Bridge Lock and approaching Greenwood Flood Gates.
2 There are landing stages below the locks which you can use, as well as ladders in virtually all the locks.

Boatyards

▬**Shepley Bridge Marina** Huddersfield Road, Mirfield WF14 9HR (01924 491872). 🛢🏠🔧 Pump out, gas, overnight mooring, long-term mooring, winter storage, slipway, boat sales, engine repairs, books, maps and gifts, toilets, dry dock, wet dock.

The towpath is generally good on the canal sections, less so, or indeed non-existent, on the river sections (*see* note on page 47). At Battyeford there is a short canal section which rejoins the river opposite a large sewage works. A fine display of roses suggests they are not short of fertilizer! Cooper Bridge marks the junction of the Calder & Hebble with the Huddersfield Broad Canal (*see* page 64), which branches off to the south below the flood gates, overlooked by the tall chimney of Bottomley & Sons. Kirklees Park lies on a hillside to the north before the navigation passes under the M62 motorway.

Pubs and Restaurants

Savile Arms 12 Church Lane, Thornhill, Dewsbury WF12 0JZ (01924 463738). South east of Thornhill Lees – best approached by walking from Bridge 29 up Hall Lane. A genuine old village local that rather surprisingly shares consecrated ground with the nearby church, hence its other name – Church House. It dispenses an excellent range of real ales and totally eschews noisy machines. Traditional pub games and large garden – children welcome in the garden. *Open Mon-Thu 17.00; Fri 16.00 and Sat-Sun L and E.* Homemade food available for groups with *advanced notice.*

The Ship Inn Steanard Lane, Shepley Bridge, Mirfield WF14 8HB (01924 493364; www.hungryhorse.co.uk/pubs/ship-inn-mirfield). East of Shepley Bridge Lock. Large, smart and comfortable pub dispensing real ale. A carvery restaurant serves food *all day until 21.00, every day.* Children welcome. Garden, indoor and outdoor play area. Traditional pub games, pool and Wi-Fi. Dogs welcome. *Open Mon-Fri 11.00 & Sat-Sun 10.00.* Breakfast available *from 10.00 at weekend.*

The Navigation Tavern 6 Station Road, Mirfield WF14 8NL(01924 492476). Canalside near Shepley

Bridge Flood Lock. An excellent selection of real ales and real cider is dispensed in this canalside pub. There is a garden and limited moorings. Large screen TV, traditional pub games and Wi-Fi. B&B. *Open 11.30 (Sun 12.00).*

The White Stag 212 Huddersfield Road, Mirfield WF14 9PX (01924 480868). North of bridge 17. *Mon-Wed & Sun 12.00-17.00 (Wed 19.00) and Thu-Sat L and E.* Dog- and family-friendly. Garden and large-screen TV. Open fires, traditional pub games and Wi-Fi. *Open 11.30 (Sun 12.00).*

The Flowerpot 65 Calder Road, Mirfield WF14 8NN (01924 496939). South of Bull Bridge 18, over the river. Newly refurbished, this pub dispenses real cider, eight real ales – many from local breweries – from a central bar with a tiled flowerpot as its focal point. Pie and peas are available *Mon-Fri L* and there is a riverside garden. Dog- and family-friendly, open fires and traditional pub games. *Open 12.00.*

The Old Colonial Dunbottle Lane, Mirfield WF14 9JJ (01924 496920; www.theoldcolonial.webplus.net). 1 mile north of Shepley Bridge Lock, up Dunbottle Lane. Once a club and now an excellent venue to enjoy a selection of real ales. Food available *Thu-Sun L and E (not Sun E).* Sun roasts are particular popular. Children welcome. Open fires, a garden and Wi-Fi. *Open Mon-Thu 17.00 & Fri-Sun 12.00.*

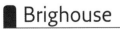

Brighouse

Leaving the river the navigation enters an artificial cut on its approach to Brighouse, completely enclosed by factories. There are good *moorings* between the two Brighouse Locks, and the passage through the town is pleasant, with gardens, seats and willow trees. At Brookfoot Lock there is evidence of a connection with the river giving some idea of how the navigation has evolved as canalised sections were progressively constructed.

Flooded gravel pits nearby are used for waterskiing. A milestone right by Park Nook Lock reveals that you are now 18 miles from Fall Ing, with just a short distance to travel to Sowerby Bridge. Elland Basin, with its tastefully restored buildings and gardens, is worth more than a fleeting glance, however, and makes a good stopping place en route. There are several pubs close by. Have a look at the fine converted warehouse with its covered dock, before pressing on to the three superbly kept and picturesque Salterhebble Locks. The bottom lock here has an electrically-powered guillotine gate operated with a Watermate key. This was installed when the road was widened in the 1930s. The towpath passes separately through its own narrow tunnel. Immediately after this first lock the canal passes over a small aqueduct before climbing the top two. To the right is the Salterhebble Branch (where the old Salterhebble Basin has been restored providing visitor and long-term *moorings* and a range of boater *facilities*), to the left the route to Sowerby Bridge. The towpath improves above Brighouse.

● **Brighouse**
W. Yorks. All services, station. A woollen textile producing village transformed into an important canal port with the building of the Calder & Hebble Navigation. In the 19th C silk and cotton were also spun here. Now there seems to be plenty of thriving new industry. The canal bisects the town, passing very close to the market place. A large Victorian church at the top of the hill is surrounded by trees and flowers.
Smith Art Gallery Halifax Road, Brighouse HD6 2AF (01484 288065; www.calderdale.gov.uk; www.museums. calderdale.gov.uk/visit/smith-art-gallery). Permanent display of 19th-C art works and touring exhibitions. *Open Mon & Fri 10.00-17.00; Tue & Thu 10.00-18.00 and Sat 10.00-15.30. Free.*

● **Elland**
W. Yorks. PO, tel, stores, banks, chemists, butcher, hardware, fish & chips, takeaways, delicatessen, off-licence.
Elland has an enviable position on the steep south side of the Calder Valley, its narrow streets discourage through traffic, and its handsome church and terraces of stone houses give an air of tranquillity. The well-restored canal basin makes an excellent stopping point.

WALKING & CYCLING
At Anchor Pit Flood Lock follow the track around the outside of the river bend and join the straight road running north west through the industrial estate. Turn left at the T junction with Calder Street and right at its junction with Birds Royd Lane. At the junction with Huddersfield Road again turn right and rejoin the navigation at bridge 10.

Pubs and Restaurants

✕♀**Prego** Huddersfield Road, Brighouse HD6 1JZ (01484 715566; www.waterfrontlodge. co.uk/Prego-Restaurant). Beside Bridge 10. Italian and continental cuisine served in a sophisticated contemporary setting *Open Mon-Sat E and Sun 12.00–19.00.* Children welcome; play area *Sun 12.00–18.00.*

🍺**The Richard Oastler** Bethel Street, Brighouse HD6 1JN (01484 401756; www.jdwetherspoon. co.uk/home/pubs/the-richard-oastler). Housed in a former Grade II listed Methodist chapel, this establishment now serves real ciders and an excellent range of real ales, including a selection from local microbreweries. Children welcome, outside seating, large-screen TV and Wi-Fi. *Open 08.00* with food available *all day.*

🍺**The Red Rooster**, 123 Elland Road, Brookfoot, Brighouse HD6 2QR (01484 713737). ¼ mile north of Ganny Lock. Purpose-built around 1900 to serve the local colliery wharf, this welcoming hostelry now dispenses an excellent selection of real ales. Dog-friendly with an outside seating area. Traditional pub games and Wi-Fi. *Open Sun-Thu 16.00 & Fri-Sat 12.00.*

🍺**The Colliers Arms** 66 Park Road, Elland HX5 9HZ (01422 372007). Between Elland and Park Nook locks. Traditional canalside pub offering real ale. Children and dogs welcome. Canalside garden and open fires. *Open 12.00.*

🍺**The Barge & Barrel** 10-12 Park Road, Elland HX5 9HP (01422 371770; www.ellandbrewery. co.uk). An interesting choice of real ales from their own Barge & Barrel Brewery Co range together with guest beers in a comfortable Victorian-style pub. Inexpensive, home-cooked food *L.* Children welcome *until 20.00.* Canalside seating, open fires and traditional pub games. Quiz *Thu* and Wi-Fi. *Open 12.00.*

🍺✕**The Watermill** Huddersfield Road, Salterhebble, Halifax HX3 0QT (01422 347700; www.premierinn.com). Pub and hotel at the terminus of the Salterhebble Branch. Real ales served in this relaxed, family-orientated establishment. Food is available *daily from 12.00.* Outside seating and play area. Mooring. B&B. *Open 11.00 (Sun 12.00).*

Sowerby Bridge

The canal, now relatively narrow, clings to the side of a wooded hill, its clean water alive with small fish. A conspicuous building to the north is Wainhouse Tower, built in 1875 as a 253ft dyeworks chimney (but never used as such) and converted into a viewing tower. A superb example of stonemasonry, it is *open on Bank Holidays* (400 steps to the top). The buildings close in as the navigation approaches the basins at Sowerby Bridge, where the Rochdale Canal once again branches off to cross the Pennines. Now restored throughout its entire length, a third Pennine crossing has been made available offering the opportunity for two dramatic northern cruising rings. The towpath throughout this section is excellent.

Boatyards

Ⓑ**Shire Cruisers** The Wharf, Sowerby Bridge, Halifax HX6 2AG (01422 832712; www. shirecruisers.co.uk). Facilities either here or in the basin. 🏠🛎️🛒 D Gas, pump out, narrowboat hire, overnight mooring, long-term mooring, winter storage, slipway, crane, boat sales & repairs, chandlery, books, maps and gifts, boat fitting out, engine sales and repairs, toilets, DIY facilities, Gas Safe registered.

● **Halifax**
W. Yorks. All services. Well known as the home of the Halifax Building Society, founded in 1853, which now has ultra-modern offices in Portland Place; it is worth the journey north from the canal to visit this industrial town. Town. The splendid **Piece Hall** (www.thepiecehall.co.uk) is currently undergoing an extensive restoration and due to re-open in 2016, housing a variety of retail outlets. Previously rebuilt in 1779, it is the last remaining manufacturers' hall in the country. Here weavers traded their products, the continuation of an industry that dates back to 1275 in Halifax. Now restored, the hall houses arts and craft shops, a museum, art gallery, restaurant and the **Tourist Information Centre** (01422 368725). The parish church of St John the Baptist is Perpendicular in style, battlemented and with a mass of pinnacles, parapets and gargoyles.
Bankfield Museum Akroyd Park, Boothtown Road, Halifax HX3 6HG (01422 352334; www.museums. calderdale.gov.uk/visit/bankfield-museum). Magnificent 19th-C mill owner's residence housing a fascinating range of costumes from around the world, displayed in exotic surroundings. *Open Mon-Sat 10.00-16.00.* Free.
Eureka Museum for Children Discovery Road, Halifax HX1 2NE (01422 330069; www.eureka.org. uk). Hands-on museum designed for children to touch, listen and smell. Three main exhibition areas: Me and my body, Living and working together, and Invent, create, communicate. *Open during term time Tue-Fri 10.00-16.00 & Sat-Sun 10.00-17.00. During school holidays & B Hols daily 10.00-17.00.* Charge.
Shibden Hall Folk Museum Lister's Road, Halifax HX3 6XG (01422 352246; www.museums.calderdale. gov.uk/visit/shibden-hall). A 15th-C building with 17th-C furniture and extensive folk Exhibits. Also a miniature railway, boating lake, play area, restored gardens, woodland and café. *Open Sat-Thu 10.00-17.00.* Charge.

Wainhouse Tower Wakefield Gate, Halifax HX2 7EN (01422 288001; www.calderdale.gov.uk/leisure/ localhistory/wainhouse-tower). *Open B Hols and Father's Day 11.00-16.00 (last ascent 15.30).* Charge. Private parties catered for. The *Aug B Hol opening* is in conjunction with Calderdale Heritage Walks who offer a selection of around 90 conducted walks in the area (www.calderdaleheritagewalks.org.uk). Charge.
Tourist Information Centre Halifax Visitor Centre, Halifax Library, Northgate, Halifax HX1 1UN (01422368725; www.visitcalderdale.com). *Open Mon, Tue, Thu & Fri 09.30-19.00 and Sat 09.30-17.00.*
● **Sowerby Bridge**
W. Yorks. All services. Although this is an industrial town, the scale and grandeur of the surrounding landscape dominate the mill chimneys and factory roofs that are dotted about. This rare subservience to nature makes the town human and attractive. The 19th-C classical church is in a good position, overlooking the restored deep lock and tunnel.
● **Sowerby Bridge Basin**
This great canal centre is a classic example of the functional tradition in industrial architecture, and has thankfully survived to be given a new life in restoration, while many other such examples have disappeared. The Rochdale Canal was built to accommodate vessels up to 72ft in length, so goods had to be transshipped here into the shorter Calder & Hebble craft before they could continue their journey; hence this important centre grew in stature.
● **Rochdale Canal**
One of three canal routes across the Pennines, its 92 wide locks over a distance of 33 miles virtually guaranteed its ultimate commercial failure. With the new tunnel and deep lock out of the basin open, it is once again possible to cruise across the Pennines to Manchester: hard work but the effort is amply rewarded.

Boatman and
son statue
at Sowerby
Bridge Basin

Pubs and Restaurants

🍺**Navigation Inn** 47 Chapel Lane, Sowerby Bridge,
Halifax HX6 3LF (01422 316073;
www.thenavigationpub.co.uk). By bridge 1. Friendly
canalside pub dating back to 15th C complete with
inglenook fireplace and Victorian cast iron range.
Four rotating guest real ales, and an extensive bar
menu *Mon-Sat L and E & Sun 12.00-18.00*. Children
welcome; there are two gardens and *regular*
entertainment. *Open Tue-Thu L and E & Fri-Sun all
day. Closed Mon except B Hols.*

🍺✕**The Moorings** No 1 Warehouse, Canal Basin,
Sowerby Bridge, Halifax HX6 2AG (01422 833940;
www.themooringspub.co.uk). A good choice of bar
food is served together with real ale in this attractive
coversion. Food is available *Mon-Sat 12.00-21.00
(Mon 20.30) and Sun 12.00-18.00. (Last food orders
15 mins before finish)*. Children welcome in dining
area. Quiz Mon. *Open 12.00.*

✕**Tenujin** No 1 Warehouse, Canal Basin, Sowerby
Bridge, Halifax HX6 2AG (01422 835500; www.

temujinrestaurant.co.uk). Specialists in Mongolian
barbecues. Children welcome. *Open Fri-Sun L & E
daily (Sun until 20.00)*. Inexpensive Early Bird menus
available – telephone for *stipulated daily* arrival times.

✕**Java Village Restaurant** Wharf Street, Sowerby
Bridge, Halifax HX6 2AF (01422 831654; www.
javavillagerestaurant.co.uk). By the basin. A restaurant
specialising in Indonesian and Indian food. Children
welcome. *Open daily 17.00-00.00.*

🍺**The Commercial Inn** The Wharf, 31 Wharf Street,
Sowerby Bridge HX6 2LA (01422 317350; www.
jdwetherspoon.co.uk/home/pubs/the-commercial-
inn). Modern pub, sitting atop Tuel Lane Tunnel,
serving a wide range of real ales and inexpensive food
daily from 08.00. Children welcome, outside seating
and Wi-Fi.

See also Pubs and Restaurants on page 197

HUDDERSFIELD NARROW CANAL

MAXIMUM DIMENSIONS

Length: 70'
Beam: 6' 10"
Headroom: 6' 2"
Draught: 3' 3"

MANAGER

0303 040 4040;
www.manchesterpennine@
canalrivertrust.org.uk

MILEAGE

ASHTON-UNDER-LYNE
Junction with Peak Forest Canal to
Stalybridge: 2 miles
Mossley: 6 miles
Diggle: 8½ miles
Marsden: 12 miles
Linthaite: 16 miles
HUDDERSFIELD
Junction with Huddersfield Broad Canal: 19½ miles

Passage through Standedge Tunnel is on a chaperoned basis, allowing the helmsman to steer his vessel through the tunnel, accompanied by a member of the Canal & River Trust Tunnel Team. Transit is available *from late Mar to early Nov on Mon, Wed & Fri*. Bookings must be made *in advance* by telephoning 0303 040 4040 and the Standedge Customer Guidelines can be downloaded in pdf form from www.canalrivertrust.org.uk/canals-and-rivers/huddersfield-narrow-canal#Standedge. This provides full details of the transit, including a diagram setting out the limiting dimensions for craft wishing to undertake the passage.

Boats may travel no further than Lock 32E or 24W without having first made a booking.

One of three transPennine canals, and by far the shortest route, this waterway was conceived in 1793, at the height of 'Canal Mania' (the bulk of canal construction was concentrated into the 1790s), and encouraged by the success of the Ashton and Huddersfield Broad canals. Benjamin Outram was retained as engineer and he reported in favour of a narrow canal (in the interest of cost saving) following the route of the present navigation. There was the inevitable conflict with local mill owners over water supply and a total reservoir capacity of 20,000 locks full of water was provided by way of appeasement.

As always optimism was in far greater supply than the capital raised from the initial share issue following the enabling Act passed on 4 April 1794. The estimated cost was some £183,000, of which nearly one-third was allocated to the construction of a 3-mile tunnel under the Pennines. As work progressed the canal was opened in sections to generate income; the first section opened in March 1797 between Huddersfield and Slaithwaite and two more, linking Slaithwaite to Marsden and Ashton to Greenfield, were completed late in the following year. It was not until 12 years later that the first boat passed through the completed Standedge Tunnel.

From the outset the waterway was dogged by shoddy workmanship and flood damage. In its 436ft rise to the eastern tunnel portal at Marsden, the canal follows the Colne Valley, whilst from the west end of the summit pound – 645ft above sea level – it follows the Tame Valley, dropping 334ft in 8½ miles to Ashton-under-Lyne. Damage extended along 16 miles of canal after flooding during the winter of 1799 and Robert Whitworth, called in to report during Outram's absence through illness, observed that the masonry and earthworks along the navigation 'were the worst executed of any he had seen'. Benjamin Outram resigned in 1801 and he was not replaced, although subsequently, five years later, Thomas Telford was asked to survey the work to date and advise on its completion. Two further Acts were passed to raise more capital before the navigation was officially opened on 4 April 1811 at a final cost of over £300,000. However, this was only after another disastrous flood occasioned after Swellands Reservoir (recommended by Telford as an addition to Outram's design) burst its banks and inundated large areas of the Colne Valley. Six people were drowned and many factories and mills severely damaged.

High tolls, in conjunction with an additional charge levied on boats using the tunnel, suppressed use of the waterway and although individual communities along the route expanded and thrived, within the climate of industrial prosperity brought by the canal, profits were disappointing. With the reduction of dues in the 1830s, trade was greatly stimulated, only to fall in the face of the inevitable railway competition which came with the completion of the Leeds and Manchester Railway in 1841. Three years later the Huddersfield and Manchester Railway Company was formed with the aim of building a line closely following the route of the navigation, which it acquired in 1845. The existing canal tunnel at Standedge was linked at intervals by cross adits to the infant railway tunnel during construction, thereby greatly reducing time and expense. Subsequent railway tunnels, built as traffic increased, also benefited immensely from the existence of the canal tunnel.

Much trade was surrendered to the railways over the years and by the time of its official abandonment in 1944, regular cargoes were limited to coal and iron ore. The last end-to-end voyage was made by Robert Aickman and fellow IWA members, in *Ailsa Craig*, during 1948.

WALKING & CYCLING

There is an interesting interpretation board beside the Roaches Lock pub (*see* page 61) detailing the industrial history of the area and setting out a short walk that takes in significant local features. The Oldham Way is a 40-mile trail, linking the newly opened Huddersfield Narrow and Rochdale canals, split up into seven more easily manageable sections. Visit the TIC for further details. The Medlock Valley Way leads walkers from the remote uplands of Saddleworth Moor above Oldham into the heart of Manchester linking meadows, rivers, moors, woodlands and canals along a trail of great diversity. Further information from local TICs. The Public Art Sculpture Trail links a number of pieces installed along the section of the canal running through Oldham. These images reflect life on the canal; they have been inspired by the geography of the area, by a local school and, in many cases, make use of recycled and reclaimed materials. Further details from local TICs and Brownhill Visitor Centre – *see* page 60. The Tameside Trail is a 40-mile circular walk that intersects with the canal at Division Bridge and broadly follows the Tameside boundary linking river valleys, country parks and other places of interest. Further details from Tameside Countryside Service (0161 330 9613; www.tameside.gov.uk/countryside). A section of the 268-mile-long Pennine Way runs through wild country along the eastern edge of Saddleworth Moor. *See* Leeds & Liverpool Canal, page 124 for further details.

To negotiate Standedge Tunnel, walkers and cyclists can make use of one of the several waymarked routes over the Pennines, commencing beside the Diggle Hotel. Walkers can also take a bus from Uppermill or a boat trip through the tunnel. Charge. See above for booking details.

The Colne Valley Circular Walk is 12 miles long and majors on the contrasts of impressive industrial buildings set against a backdrop of a striking river valley. Details from Huddersfield TIC (*see* page 66). The Kirklees Way beats the bounds of this eponymous district, totalling a demanding 72 miles. Again contrast abounds: landscape versus history, scenery versus industry. Details from Huddersfield TIC. The Marsden and Tunnel End Trail is a 'hands on' version of much that is depicted in The Old Goods Yard (*see* page 63 under Marsden Moor Estate) and as such is a fascinating insight into the area. There is a regular series of walks and events based on Marsden Moor Estate's 5,685 acres of unenclosed moorland. For a programme and copies of the trail detailed above, visit The Old Goods Yard or www.nationaltrust.org.uk/marsdenmoor, or telephone 01484 847016.

Apart from the range of walks detailed above, the presence of the transPennine railway line close to the waterway throughout makes planning expeditions along the canal straightforward. Trains run at frequent intervals, some stopping at all stations and some only at major stations. All trains carry bicycles free of charge although space is limited on First Transpennine Express services and it is advisable to book in advance during busy periods. Telephone 08457 48 49 50 for details.

To avoid the somewhat daunting trek over the top of Standedge Tunnel *see* note on page 63.

Stalybridge

The canal follows the River Tame east out of Portland Basin, crossing it just over 1 mile later to arrive at the first newly constructed lock in Stalybridge. In 1947 the section from here through the town was culverted and the enthusiasm for the recently exhumed navigation, ascending a series of locks amidst busy streets, is universal. Replacing a forgotten drain, there is now a vibrant waterway, a bustle of activity made colourful with boats: a scene reminiscent of a Dutch town, the canal its central focus, roads subservient. Good moorings are plentiful, well distributed between locks 4W and 8W. The Pennines beckon over the rooftops of Stalybridge, as the waterway continues on its steady climb towards Scout Tunnel, ducking directly between the legs of an unfortunately sited electricity pylon, more recently placed in its path. There are *showers and toilets* beside Grove Road bridge. The climb is unremitting, though largely through leafy glades with just the occasional glimpses of open hill views, punctuated with the dereliction of past industry – largely coal mining. Throughout its ascent, the waterway remains discrete, almost shunning the outside world, winding through woods and passing several attractively sited, waterside picnic areas. Whilst road crossings do briefly intrude, it is the transPennine railway that keeps constant company with the waterway: a not altogether unwelcome diversion bringing a source of well-ordered activity and flashes of colour on a dull day.

- **Stalybridge**
  Cheshire. PO, tel, stores, banks, chemist, hardware, butcher, baker, greengrocer, delicatessen, fish & chips, takeaways, library, station. With the first mill completed in 1776, this was one of the original centres of textile production during the Industrial Revolution. 19th-C prosperity went on to transform a series of small, scattered rural communities into a prosperous industrial town, which the effects of the past 50 years of decline appear well on the way to reversing. See also page 174.

Pubs and Restaurants

■The Station Buffet Bar Rassbottom Street, Stalybridge SK15 1TB (0161 303 0007; www.stalybridgebuffetbar.co.uk). The original station buffet, decorated with old railway photographs and memorabilia, and now dispensing an excellent range of real ales, cider and food *daily 11.00-18.30*. Children and dogs welcome (dogs' water bowl provided). Open fires *in winter*. No electronic machines – just the rattle of passing trains. *Open all day.*

■Q Inn 3 Market Street, Stalybridge SK15 2AL (0161 303 9157; www.our-pub.co.uk/Pubs/QBar.php). In the *Guinness Book of Records* as the pub with the shortest name in the UK. Pool and darts. *Regular* live music. Real ale and food *daily*. Large beer garden. *Open 12.00.*

■The White House 1 Water Street, Stalybridge SK15 2AG (0161 303 2154; www.hydesbrewery.com). Exposed brickwork, tiled floors and old cast iron radiators create the atmosphere in a pub serving real ales and real cider. *Sun L served 12.00-18.00*. Traditional pub games. Quiz *Sun*, live music *Fri*, and a Folk night on *Thu*. *Open 12.00*.

■The Society Rooms 49-51 Grosvenor Street, Stalybridge SK15 2JN (0161 338 9740; www.jdwetherspoon.co.uk/home/pubs/the-society-rooms-stalybridge). Occupying the old Co-op store, this friendly pub now purveys real ale and inexpensive food available *all day from 08.00*. Children welcome, large-screen TV, outside seating and Wi-Fi.

✕♀ The Bistro 57 Grosvenor Street, Stalybridge SK15 2JN (0161 303 9991). Specialising in traditional Malay-style cooking, this bistro offers the chance to taste the delights of one of Asia's most exotic countries. *Open Tue-Fri 10.00-15.00; Sat 09.00-15.00 & Thu-Sat 18.00-22.00*. *All day* breakfasts, coffee and takeaway service.

See also **Pubs and Restaurants** on page 175.

Saddleworth

The Pennines rear up ahead, although their full impact is softened by the fringe of woodland accompanying the navigation up the valley. To the west the imposingly situated building of Quickwood church, with its needle-like spire, oversees the bustle of road, rail and waterway activity below. Impressive mills, now sadly decaying, line the canal as it winds its tortuous path towards Uppermill, where it is greeted by what appears to be a castle keep, complete with portcullis. Closer inspection reveals a somewhat elaborate stone facing, topped with iron railings and employed to disguise a concrete box culvert, with further embellishment to hide a vertical gas main! By now the scale of the textile industry is subdued by the imposing bulk of Saddleworth Moor, while the sprawling conurbation of Manchester gives way to a straggle of attractive villages, constructed in the local gritstone and strewn randomly over the surrounding hillsides. Looking back towards the smoking chimneys below, there are wide open views now appearing over the high ground that had seemed to pose such a formidable obstacle when viewed from Stalybridge. Beyond the striking Wool Road Transhipment Warehouse *(all facilities including toilets)* the waterway, still climbing relentlessly, breaks out alongside the railway and together they both pick their way across heathered moorland towards their interlaced passage, deep beneath the Pennines.

● **Mossley**
Gt Manchester. PO, tel, stores, chemist, takeaways, station. A small agricultural hamlet of 1,200 souls in 1821, Mossley had grown into a prosperous cotton town by 1885 with a population of 15,000. The shops, PO etc are all close to the station as are several additional pubs.
Mossley Industrial Heritage Centre Longlands Mill, Queen Street, Mossley OL5 9AH (01457 832813; www. emmausmossley.org.uk/heritage-centre). Memories abound and are brought to life in an old cotton spinning mill now owned by Emmaus, a charitable organisation which provides work and a home for people who would otherwise be homeless. The Centre now seeks to answer questions about past times in a boom era of cotton and woollen manufacture. Shop and café. Heritage Centre *open Wed-Sat 14.00-16.00*; Emmaus shop *open Mon-Sat 09.00-17.00 (Mon 10.00)*. Café *open Mon-Sat 10.00-16.00*.

● **Greenfield**
Gt Manchester. PO, tel, stores, chemist, butcher, off-licence, library, station. Another cotton community attempting to adjust to the demise of a past prosperity. The nearest station to Uppermill is here and there is a useful coal merchant – The Saddleworth Coal Hut (01457 871267/0777 5801413).

● **Uppermill**
Gt Manchester. PO, tel, stores, bank, chemists, butchers, baker, fish & chips, hardware, takeaways, library, garage. A traditional Pennine village and once the centre of the local cotton and cottage weaving industry, it has become a focus for the tourist trade that has long supplanted all such activity. Now the largest settlement in Saddleworth, it only gained its supremacy in the late 18th C with the coming of the canal and turnpike road, ousting nearby Dobcross.
Saddleworth Museum & Art Gallery High Street, Uppermill, Oldham OL3 6HS (01457 874093; www. saddleworthmuseum.co.uk). By Wade Lock.

A family-friendly museum full of intriguing objects from the past telling the story of the people who have created Saddleworth's landscape and character. Gallery with changing exhibitions, many of local interest. Shop. *Open daily 13.00-16.00*. Charge. There is also a **Visitor Information Centre** and **Boat Trips** aboard Pennine *Moonraker Sat & Sun and daily during school holidays*.
Visitor Information Centre Saddleworth Museum & Art Gallery, High Street, Uppermill, Oldham OL3 6HS (01457 870336/874093). *Open Mon-Sat 10.00-16.00, Sun 12.00-16.00*.

● **Dobcross**
Gt Manchester. PO, tel, stores, off-licence. A delightful village, quintessentially Pennine, every building and winding narrow street a gem, the whole presided over by the charming Saddleworth Bank – now fulfilling a more homely role.
Brownhill Countryside Centre Wool Road, Dobcross, Oldham OL3 5PB (0161 770 5888; www. visitoldham.com/attractions/brownhill-countryside-centre-p84811). Wildlife and historical interpretation centre for the area with changing exhibitions and displays, a woodland 'crawly tunnel' for children, shop, café, toilets and a picnic area. *Open daily 09.00-19.00*.

● **Diggle**
Gt Manchester. PO, tel, off-licence, takeaway, fish & chips. Together with its neighbours Dobcross and Delph, Diggle lay at the heart of local hand-weaving until, in the late 18th C, the Industrial Revolution spawned mills as the centres of production, sited further down the valley for easier access.

Pubs and Restaurants

■ **The Roaches Lock** 387 Manchester Road, Mossley OL5 9BB (01457 837151; www.roacheslockinn.co.uk). Canal-oriented pub serving real ales and food *L and E*. Children welcome. Bar games, canalside patio and an interesting selection of reading matter. *Open 12.00*.

■ **The Tollemache Arms** 415 Manchester Road, Mossley OL5 9BG (01457 834555; www.tollemachearmsmossley. robinsonsbrewery.com). This pub serves a selection of real ales. Children welcome and there is outside seating overlooking the canal. *Open 12.00*.

■ **The King William VI** 134 Chew Valley Road, Greenfield Oldham OL3 7DD (01457 873933). East of the canal in the village centre. A cosy village local that welcomes families and serves a good selection of real ales. Traditional bar meals *available all day, every day*. Pub games and outside seating.

■ **The Railway** 11 Shaw Hall, Bank Road, Greenfield, Saddleworth OL3 7JZ (01457 872307). West of the canal, opposite the station. Photographs of old Saddleworth adorn the bar in a local that serves a variety of real ales. Pub games and open fires. Beer garden and camping. Live music *Thu, Fri & Sun*. Real cider. *Open 12.00*.

■ **The Granby Arms** 28 High Street, Uppermill, Oldham OL3 6HR (01457 873028). Real ale and traditional pub food *served daily 12.00–18.00* in this traditional village local. Children welcome.

■✕ **The Waggon** 34 High Street, Uppermill, Oldham OL3 6HR (01457 879106; www.thewagoninn.com). Cosy village local dispensing real ale and food *daily L and E (not Sun E)*. Family-friendly, traditional pub games, garden and Wi-Fi. B&B. *Open 12.00*.

■ **The Navigation Inn** 21-23 Wool Road, Dobcross, Oldham OL3 5NS (01457 872418). West of Wool Road Bridge 71. This traditional pub welcomes walkers, families and dogs and serves real ale and food *daily L and E*. Garden and B&B. *Open Mon-Fri L and E & Sat-Sun all day from 12.00*.

■ **The Swan Inn** 1 The Square, Dobcross, Oldham OL3 5AA (01457 873451; www. theswandobcross.com). Also known locally as The Top House, this 18th-C hostelry serves real ale and home-cooked food *Mon-Sat L and E (not Mon L) & Sun 12.30-18.00*. A garden, Wi-Fi and real fires. Quiz *Thu*.

■ **The Diggle Hotel** Station Houses, Diggle, Saddleworth OL3 5JZ (01457 872741; www.digglehotel. com). Close to the western tunnel portals (both canal and railway) this one time merchant's house went on to become a store, and then a pub, and now dispenses real ale and home-made food *daily 12.00-20.30 (Sun 19.30)*. Children welcome, large garden with play centre and Wi-Fi. B&B.

Try also:

■ **The Commercial** 58 Manchester Road, Mossley OL5 9AD (0871 261 1098); ■ **The Britannia Inn** 217 Manchester Road, Mossley OL5 9AJ (01457 832799; www.britanniamossley.co.uk); ■ **The Kingfisher** Chew Valley Road, Greenfield OL3 7AE (01457 872295; www.kingfisherpubsaddleworth.co.uk) and ■ **The Hanging Gate** 217 Huddersfield Road, Diggle OL3 5PQ (01457 876411).

Marsden

It comes as almost something of a relief to leave the activity centred around the tunnel mouth and start the long steady descent into Huddersfield. Lock operation is no less arduous going downhill and there is a feeling akin to anti-climax as the waterway drops rapidly through a profusion of trees and almost into Sparth Reservoir. In places the hills lining the Colne Valley step back a little, leaving level grazing and fields for hay and silage making. The infant river is never far away and in places is separated only by a narrow band of trees. From time to time the landscape is punctuated by the gaunt remains of a splendid old mill as views open out briefly before the often tree-lined hills close in once again. *Gas* is available beside Shuttle Lock 24E. The railway shadows the canal into Slaithwaite where once again the harmony wrought by its focal position amidst shops and streets is most satisfactory.

Pubs and Restaurants

The Railway 34 Station Road, Marsden HD7 6DH (01484 841541). Beside Dirker Lock. Real ale is served in this traditional English pub. Home-made food is available *daily 12.00-21.00*. Dog- and child-friendly. Garden, Wi-Fi, traditional pub games and large-screen TV. *Open 11.00.*

The Shakespeare 33 Peel Street, Marsden HD7 6BW (01484 844818). Village centre local serving real ale and showing sport on large-screen TVs. Dog- and family-friendly. Garden and traditional pub games. Wi-Fi. *Open Mon-Thu 16.00; Fri 15.00 & Sat-Sun 12.00.*

The Riverhead Brewery Tap 2 Peel Street Marsden HD7 6BR (01484 841270; www. theriverheadmarsden.co.uk). This lively brew-pub now dispenses real ciders and an excellent range of its own real ales, which mostly carry the names of local reservoirs. Good quality restaurant upstairs serving food *Mon-Thu L and E & Fri-Sun all day from 12.00*. Outside drinking area overlooking the river. Real cider. Quiz *Tue.*

The New Inn Manchester Road, Marsden HD7 6EZ (01484 841917; www.newinnmarsden. co.uk). Traditional local's pub offering real ale, together with home-made food *Mon-Fri L and E & Sat-Sun (and B Hols) from 08.30*. Children and dogs welcome. Traditional pub games, beer garden and Wi-Fi. B&B.

● **Marsden**
W. Yorks. PO, tel, stores, chemist, greengrocer, baker, off-licence, takeaways, fish & chips, library, garage, station. Situated at an important transPennine crossing point, Marsden has always been a focus for the weaving industry and is associated with the Luddite riots. Enoch Taylor, pivotal figure in this industrial unrest, is buried beside the fine church and there is a set of stocks nearby. Its popularity as a location for TV soaps now make a different set of dramatic demands upon its environs.

Marsden Information Point Marsden Library, Peel Street, Marsden HD7 6BW (01484 222555; www.kirklees.gov.uk). More than just a TIC – a fund of information and a community lifeline. *Open Tue and Thu-Sat 09.30-12.30 & 13.30-17.00 (Sat 16.00); Wed 13.30-19.00.*

Marsden Mechanics Institute Peel Street, Marsden HD7 6BW (01484 844587; www.marsdenmechanics.co.uk). A striking stone building with a colourful wooden tower (the foundations of the main structure were considered inadequate to bear the weight of anything heavier) erected in 1861 to provide education for the betterment of the working man. Now the library and community hall. Also home to the evergreen Mikron Theatre Company (when not touring the waterways on their boat *Tysley*) who can be contacted on 01484 843701; www.mikron.org.uk.

Marsden Moor Estate The Old Goods Yard, Station Road, Marsden HD7 6DH (01484 847016; www.nationaltrust.org.uk/marsdenmoor). Over 5,000 acres of moorland in the hands of the NT and accessible through a series of walks and trails. The exhibition in the Old Goods Yard, beside the towpath at Marsden Railway Station, uses a series of excellent displays to provide a wealth of information about every aspect of the area, from natural phenomena through to the relatively recent industrial impact of weaving, water, canal and railway. Free.

Standedge Tunnels At first sight there appears to be an indecently large number of tunnels connecting Diggle with Marsden. The canal tunnel came first, completed in 1811, followed by the single bore of the Huddersfield and Manchester Railway dating from 1845. Two years later this railway company was taken over by the LNWR who built a second single – and parallel – track to cope with increasing demand. In 1894 the present double track tunnel was constructed to cope with the burgeoning traffic. In all instances the canal tunnel, now owned by the railway company and connected to its tunnels by cross-adits, proved invaluable for spoil removal during construction.

Standedge Tunnel Visitor Centre Waters Road, Marsden HD7 6NQ (01484 844298; www.canalrivertrust.org.uk/standedge-tunnel). All the superlatives marshalled within the confines of one extremely long tunnel: highest, longest and deepest in Britain and largely hewn out of solid rock. The centre offers the opportunity to get to grips with all the facts, figures and dates. *Open Mon-Fri 11.00-16.00 & Sat-Sun and B Hols 10.30-17.00.* Café and boat trips: *daily 30 min* trips into the tunnel and occasional through trips – telephone for details. Park at Marsden Railway Station and walk west along the towpath. A water taxi service operates at weekends (01457 871800; www.huddersfieldcanal.com/#boat-trips).

BOAT TRIPS
Thirty-minute trips into Standedge Tunnel operate when the Visitor Centre (see above) is open starting at *12.00 Mon-Fri & 11.00 Sat-Sun.* Also rides on the *Marsden Shuttle* water taxi service as above - see website for timetable.

63

Slaithwaite

The railway, as enthusiastic a companion to the navigation as ever, shadows the canal into Slaithwaite where once again the harmony wrought by its focal position amidst shops and streets is most satisfactory. It is a matter of intense speculation as to why it has taken so long to replace a secret subterranean trickle with this overtly delightful scene. East of the settlement the waterway settles into a broader valley bottom and the hills become a little more submissive. Attractive tree-lined glades alternate with views of a still bold landscape and everywhere there are the gaunt remains of mills: reminders of this area's supremacy as a textile producer and the canal's real purpose. The descent into Huddersfield is steady and not without contrast – pretty stone bridges vie with an imposing railway viaduct and many of the locks (although still in need of more use) appear in attractive settings.

● **Slaithwaite**
W. Yorks. PO, tel, stores, bank, chemist, greengrocer, butcher, off-licence, takeaways, fish & chips, laundrette, garage, station. Another settlement founded on the woollen and cotton industries with a fine Georgian church and the 16th-C Slaithwaite Hall. The juxtaposition of canal with the village streets is very pleasing.

● **Linthwaite**
W. Yorks. Tel. Although strung out and somewhat detached from the waterway, this village is not without charm and is home to several very striking (and very derelict) mills which tell of its former glory as a textile producer. Happily several of these structures are now undergoing renovation to fit them for their new rôle as appartments.

NAVIGATIONAL NOTES

See p67.

Pubs and Restaurants

✗**Moonraker Floating Tearooms** Commercial Mills, Slaithwaite HD7 5HB (01484 846370). A boat-based tearoom, moored above Dartmouth Lock 23E, serving home-made meals, snacks, cakes, scones, sandwiches, salads, hot and cold drinks of all kinds and ices. *Open Apr–Sep, Tue–Sun 09.00–18.00 (Sun 10.00); Oct–Mar, Wed–Sun 09.00–16.00 (Sun 10.00). Also all B Hols except 25–26 Dec.*

●**The Shoulder of Mutton** 9 Church Street, Slaithwaite HD7 5AS (01484 844661). Traditional pub serving real ale and food *daily 12.00–18.00.* Dogs and children welcome. Traditional pub games and Wi-Fi. Real cider.

●**The Commercial Hotel** 1 Carr Lane, Slaithwaite HD7 5AN (01484 846258; www.commercial-slaithwaite. co.uk). Traditional pub, with a strong community focus, dispensing real cider and a wide range of real ales. Dog-friendly with an outdoor drinking area and traditional pub games. Bar snacks available *Fri–Sun. Open 12.00.*

✗**The Captain's Table** 15 Carr Lane, Slaithwaite HD7 5AN (01484 841068). Fresh fish and chips with a difference. Eat in or take away.

✗**Penny's Pantry** 39 Bridge Street, Slaithwaite HD7 5JN (01484 844646). Hot and cold meals to eat in or take out; a range of cakes and sticky buns; hot and cold drinks. Dog-friendly.

HUDDERSFIELD BROAD CANAL

MAXIMUM DIMENSIONS

Length: 57' 6"
Beam: 14' 2"
Headroom: 9' 6"
Draught: 2' 6"

MANAGER

0303 040 4040;
enquiries.northeast@canalrivertrust.org.uk

MILEAGE

ASPLEY BASIN, HUDDERSFIELD to:
Cooper Bridge: 3¾ miles
Locks: 9

Travel through Standedge Tunnel is on a chaperoned basis, allowing the helmsman to steer his vessel through the tunnel, accompanied by a member of the Canal & River Trust Tunnel Team. Transit is available *from late Mar to early Nov on Mon, Wed & Fri*. Bookings must be made *in advance* by telephoning 0303 040 4040 and the Standedge Customer Guidelines can be downloaded in pdf form from www.canalrivertrust.org.uk/canals-and-rivers/huddersfield-narrow-canal#Standedge. This provides full details of the transit, including a diagram setting out the limiting dimensions for craft wishing to undertake the passage.

Boats may travel no further than Lock 32E or 24W without having first made a booking.

The Huddersfield Broad Canal was built to serve the rapidly expanding woollen industry of the 18th C. Known also as Sir John Ramsden's Canal, it was authorised in 1774 and completed in 1780. Costing £12,000, the waterway gave local textile manufacturers access to markets throughout Yorkshire as well as coal to feed the steam-driven mills. Despite the inevitable amalgamation with the competing railway company (the London and North Western Railway in 1847) the waterway remained a profitable concern until the late 1940s. It was conceived as a broad gauge canal to accommodate square-rigged, sailing keels or 'Yorkshire craft' – 58' 0" in length and 14' 0" beam. Due to the navigation's low bridges these had to be de-rigged at Cooper Bridge and bow hauled the remaining 3¾ miles. The Huddersfield Narrow Canal, completed some 30 years later, was built as a narrow gauge waterway unable to accept traffic from the Broad Canal; consequently warehousing and transshipment facilities were developed at Aspley Basin. The problem was partially overcome with the introduction of the West Riding narrowboat: a specially shortened craft able to negotiate locks on both systems. Immediately south west of Aspley Basin is a warehouse built prior to 1778 which is probably the oldest surviving example of such a building, demonstrating an early stage in the development of the large multi-storey warehouses of the 19th C. The crane beside it dates from the early 19th C.

Huddersfield

The two factory tunnels (now reduced to one) were an ingenious solution to recent building on the old canal line and, in conjunction with the re-siting of the locks, represent the very best in Northern pragmatism! However, it is with some relief that you leave the stygian gloom of the remaining tunnel – the towpath employs an above-ground and altogether less elegant solution to the blockage – and, winding between university buildings, arrive at Apsley Basin. Beyond is the remarkable Turnbridge Loco Liftbridge dating from 1865; you will need a Watermate key to unlock it. The outskirts of Huddersfield present a mix of industry, a new waste incineration plant and by way

of relief, a vast expanse of green sports fields. The nine locks appear with a steady regularity and, passing through Cooper Bridge Lock, the canal finally enters a river section of the Calder & Hebble Navigation (*see page 50*). Before leaving this lock, boaters should be quite clear of the layout of the junction and of their intended passage.

Boatyards

⒝**Aspley Wharf Marina** Aspley Basin, Huddersfield HD1 6SD (01484 514123; www.aspleywharfmarina.co.uk). 🛒🎁🛠D Pump out, gas, overnight mooring, long-term mooring, slipway, chandlery, books, maps and gifts, solid fuel, boat sales, engine repairs (including outboards), boat repairs, telephone, toilets, showers, laundrette.

NAVIGATIONAL NOTES

1 When leaving or joining the Huddersfield Broad Canal at Cooper Bridge, take care to avoid the weir on the river just beyond the entrance to lock 1.

2 Lock 24E has a guillotine-type tailgate. Read the operating instructions before use.

WALKING & CYCLING

Throughout both the Huddersfield Broad Canal and the adjoining Narrow Canal the towpath is in excellent condition making an attractive off-road trans-Pennine route for both walker and cyclist alike. To negotiate the section of canal in Huddersfield that tunnels under the floor of a factory, follow the copious blue and white signs along a succession of streets between Bridges 22 and 25.

● **Huddersfield**

W. Yorks. All services. Huddersfield is in the best tradition of Victorian industrial towns: all built to a grand scale of dark local stone, in a happy mixture of 19th-C styles. The most striking part of the town is around the railway station, built in 1847 with its powerful classical façade of Corinthian columns, considered one of the finest examples of railway architecture. The renowned Huddersfield Choral Society operates from the 19th-C town hall.

Art Gallery Princess Alexandra Walk, Huddersfield HD1 2SU (01484 221964; www.kirklees.gov.uk/ leisure/museumsGalleries/huddersfieldArtGallery). Above the library. Presents an international programme embracing all media together with changing displays from the permanent collection. *Open Mon–Fri 10.00–17.00, Sat 10.00–16.00.* Free.

Castle Hill and Victoria Tower off Lumb Lane, Almondbury, Huddersfield HD4 6TA (07968 426312; www.kirklees.gov.uk/events/ venuedetails.asp?vID=45). A striking local landmark occupied since the Stone Age and now topped by a Victorian tower. Splendid views and an exhibition tracing the hill's 4000 years of history. Charge. Bus No 341 from Huddersfield stops at the bottom of the hill. Open on occasional days throughout *the summer from Apr onwards.* Visit the website for further details.

Colne Valley Museum Cliffe Ash, Golcar, Huddersfield HD7 4PY (01484 659762; www.colnevalleymuseum.org.uk). The hand weaver's working life c.1850 depicted in a working exhibit in period settings. Also clog making by gas light and a range of changing craft exhibitions. Books, gifts and light refreshments available. *Open weekends and B Hols 14.00–17.00.* Small charge.

Regular buses – Nos 301A, 302, 303 and 304 – from Huddersfield bus station; or walk up from Holme Mill Bridge on the Narrow Canal.

Holmfirth Nr Huddersfield. An essential visit for all *Last of the Summer Wine* devotees, easily accessible by bus from Huddersfield. Exhibition gallery contains photographs and memorabilia dating from the series beginning in 1972. *Sat* craft market and galleries.

Holmfirth Tourist Information Centre 49–51 Huddersfield Road, Holmfirth HD9 3JP (01484 222444; www.kirklees.gov.uk). *Open Mon–Fri 09.00–17.00, Sat 10.00–17.00, Sun 11.00–16.00.*

Kirklees Light Railway Park Mill Way, Clayton West, near Huddersfield HD8 9XJ (01484 865727; www.kirkleeslightrailway.com). Scenic ride on a narrow-gauge railway along a disused branch line. Children's playground and miniature fairground rides. Café. *Open weekends and most days throughout the summer.* Telephone for full details of event times. Charge. Bus nos. 80 or 81 from Huddersfield.

Tolson Museum Ravensknowle Park, Wakefield Road, Huddersfield HD5 8DJ (01484 223830). Fine Italianate mansion housing natural history, archaeology and local history exhibits. Workshops, events and children's activities. *Open Mar–Oct, Tue–Fri 11.00–17.00 & Sat–Sun 12.00–17.00. Nov–Feb Tue–Fri 11.00–16.00 & Sat–Sun 12.00–16.00.* Free.

Tourist Information Centre Huddersfield Library, Princess Alexandra Walk, Huddersfield HD1 2SU (01484 223200; www.kirklees.gov.uk). *Open Mon–Wed 09.30–17.00, Thu–Fri 09.00–17.00 & Sat 09.00–16.00.*

Pubs and Restaurants

✗Canalside Café Cooper Bridge, Huddersfield Immediately to the west of Cooper Bridge, in the middle of an industrial estate, above a dyeworks. Real down-to-earth café (in spite of its first floor location) serving an impressive selection of extremely inexpensive food from breakfasts (they come in all sizes) through sandwiches, hot drinks, soups and snacks, to a variety of full-blown meals. *Open Mon–Fri 07.00–14.00, Sat 07.00–12.00.*

▥✗The Royal and Ancient Country Inn 19 Dalton Bank Road, Colne Bridge, Huddersfield HD5 0RE (01484 425461; www.royal-ancient.co.uk). East of bridge 2. A fine pub, tastefully furnished, achieving a balance between genuine olde worlde and traditional comfort. An intimate, cosy atmosphere in the separate restaurant area, together with interesting wall decorations and an intriguing array of curios to captivate the eye. An elaborate, varied and exciting range of food is available in both the bar and restaurant *daily 12.00–21.00 (Sun 20.00)* and a good selection of real ales is dispensed from a bar dominated by a dark burr-oak post, uncarved, but appearing to depict the head of a Hereford bull. Children welcome as are well-behaved dogs (outside water provided). Patio seating. Open fires *in winter*. Wi-Fi.

▥✗The Slubbers Arms 1 Halifax Old Road, Huddersfield HD1 6HW (01484 429032). ¼-mile west of Hillhouse Lane Bridge 12. With 150 years of history under its belt, this hostelry still dispenses real cider, perry and real ales, together with good value bar meals *all day, every day*. Patio drinking area and real fires. *Open 12.00.*

▥The Vulcan 32 St Peters Street, Huddersfield HD1 1RA (01484 302040). ¼-mile south west of Gas Street Bridge 14. Popular, town-centre pub open from *09.00 (until very late)* serving a wide range of real ales and excellent value *L* food *daily*. Outdoor drinking area, traditional pub games and sports TV. *Sun* live music.

▥The Sportsman 1 St John's Road, Huddersfield HD1 5AY (01484 421929; www.undertheviaduct.com). ½-mile west of Gas Street Bridge 14. A CAMRA Heritage Conservation Pub serving a wide range of real ales, real cider, perry and food *daily L and E*. Outside drinking area, open fires and Wi-Fi. Dog- and family-friendly. *Open 12.00.*

There are plenty of pubs and restaurants in Huddersfield. These are just a selection close to Aspley Basin:

▥Ship Inn Market Street, Huddersfield HD1 4SH (01484 425569). Large, one-roomed student pub with a poster-covered ceiling. Seven real ales always on tap. Live music *Thu* and quiz *Sun*.

✗▱Memsahib Eastern Eatery 37–39 Queensgate, Huddersfield HD1 2RD (01484 422002). Indian cuisine from a restaurant whose proprietor takes a real interest in serving authentic, regional dishes using fresh ingredients. Excellent value and *open E*. Children welcome. Takeaway service – within jogging distance of the basin.

▥The Aspley Table Table Aspley Basin, St Andrews Way, Huddersfield HD1 6SB (01484 544250; www.tabletable.co.uk). Real ales and food available in both bar and restaurant *all day, every day*. Children welcome. Canalside seating and moorings.

WILDLIFE

The *Freshwater Crayfish* was formerly common and widespread, but has become somewhat scarce and endangered today. Its numbers are threatened by pollution and the disturbance of favoured river and stream habitats, and by competition from the introduced North American species. It needs fast-flowing, well-oxygenated water and, during the daytime, hides under stones, in holes in the bank and in gaps in dry-stone walls. During the restoration of the canal in Huddersfield, Canal & River Trust were able to create special habitat sites for the crayfish during construction of new tunnels built under factories that had been built over the canal. The crayfish has also successfully adopted the Rochdale Canal (*see* page 172).

LANCASTER CANAL

MAXIMUM DIMENSIONS	MANAGER
Preston to Tewitfield	0303 040 4040;
Length: 72'	enquiries.northwest@canalrivertrust.org.uk
Beam: 14'	**MILEAGE**
Headroom: 8'	*PRESTON* to
Glasson Branch	Garstang: 16¼ miles
Length: 70'	Junction with Glasson Branch: 24 miles
Beam: 14'	Lancaster: 29¼ miles
Headroom: 8'	Carnforth: 37¼ miles
Ribble Link	*CANAL TERMINUS:* 41¼
Length: 62'	No locks
Beam: 10' 6"	
Headroom: 8'	Glasson Branch: 2¾ miles, 6 locks
Draft: 2'	Millennium Ribble Link: 4 miles, 9 locks

Construction on the Lancaster Canal began in 1792. The chosen route included several aqueducts, but only eight locks, at Tewitfield. By 1799 the canal between Tewitfield and Preston, including the aqueduct over the Lune, and the separate section between Clayton and Chorley, was opened. The route north was extended to Kendal in 1819, and the short, and very attractive, arm to Glasson Dock, falling through six locks, was opened in 1826, finally providing a direct link with the sea. In 1968 the canal north of Tewitfield was abandoned with the building of the M6 motorway (although eventual restoration now seems fairly certain), and the route in Preston was shortened by about a mile. What remains is remarkably rural, surprisingly quiet and worthy of exploration. The Ribble Link, opened in 2002, now provides a connection with the national network.

NAVIGATIONAL NOTES

1   You will need a Watermate key to use the locks on the Glasson Branch.
2   Those who wish to navigate the Ribble Link should visit www.canalrivertrust.org.uk/canals-and-rivers/ribble-link to download a variety of information including a Skippers Guide, Booking form and general Guidance Notes. These are also obtainable by telephoning 0303 040 4040. *Passage can be booked up some time ahead, for this popular waterway, so advanced planning is necessary. Passage is free to CRT long term licence holders. Operating times are dictated by tides in the Ribble estuary, but a journey can be made during daylight hours as directed by CRT.* The staircase and sea lock are manned, and the link operates one way each day. There is no mooring on the Link. As the River Ribble is tidal, boats should carry, *as a minimum*: anchor, chain and warp, VHF radio or mobile phone, lifejackets for all on board, fire-fighting equipment, coastal flares. Your engine must be sufficiently powerful to cope with tidal conditions. Be sure to check that your boat insurance covers tidal waters.
3   If you need help or advice while on the River Ribble, contact Preston Riversway Control on VHF channel 16 (working on channel 14), or telephone 01772 726871.
4   If you wish to visit Preston Docks, contact Preston Riversway Control on 01772 726871.
5   Navigators entering the Rufford Branch of the Leeds & Liverpool from the sea should remember that they will need a Watermate key and a windlass to open the locks.
6   *At least 24hrs* notice of a booking cancellation must be given to CRT or a fee will be charged.

CATFORTH

73

34 Whinnyfield Bridge
33 Woodplumpton Aqueduct

Stone Chimneys
Bridge 31   **SWILLBROOK**

30 Roots Bridge   Marina
Swillbrook 32   Swillbrook
Bridge   House

29 Kellet's Bridge

M55 Motorway

Preston

The canal in Preston, shortened many years ago by nearly a mile, now starts on an embankment just beyond Ashton Basin. To the south west on Riversway (beside the old Albert Edward Dock) there is a useful retail park which includes a large *supermarket*, incorporating a *chemist, café and garage*. From its terminus the canal runs through urban areas until Haslam Park appears at bridge 12, where there is a CRT *sanitary station and showers*. The Ribble Link leaves the main line just east of bridge 16 (*see* Navigational Notes on page 69) to link the Lancaster Canal with the rest of the network. A tall sculpture, *Gauging the Ripple*, overlooks the first new lock. Soon Preston is left behind and the canal reaches Salwick, where the moorings are administered by the Duchy of Lancaster. At Kellet's Bridge the navigation turns sharply east towards Catforth. At Swillbrook Bridge there is one of the few boatyards on this canal: the proprietor's house was formerly the old canal cottage.

28 New Bridge

27 Six Mile Bridge

26 Salwick Bridge
Aqueduct

Wilson's Bridge 25

Salwick Hall 24
Bridge

Ward's House
Bridge 23

18 Lea Malt Kiln Bridge

Lea Lane Bridge 22   19 Quaker's
21 Brier's Bridge   Bridge

Leyland Bridge 6

Lock 7

Ribble Link Navigation

10 Lock

Savick Bridge

9 Rotating Sealock

**To the River Ribble and
the Leeds & Liverpool Canal**

Boatyards

Ⓑ **Arlen Hire Boats** Ashton Basin, Tulkuth Brow, Preston PR2 2SD (01772 769183; www.arlen-hireboats. co.uk). 🛒🔧Ⓓ Pump out, gas, narrowboat hire, overnight and long-term mooring, solid fuel.
Ⓑ **Pendle Marine** at the Jolly Roger The Boat House, Catforth Road, Preston PR4 0HE (07864 822905; www. pendlemarine.co.uk). Ⓓ Day boat hire, long-term mooring, holiday mooring, winter storage, engine sales and repairs including outboards (Tohatsu agents), boat sales and repairs, chandlery, shower, toilet, café.

- **Preston**

Lancs. All services. A large industrial town granted a Royal Charter by Henry II in 1179, with the right to hold a Guild Merchant. An outdoor market was also established and still thrives today. The teetotal movement was founded in Preston in 1834, and Joseph Livesey's Temperance Hotel (the world's first) used to stand at the corner of Church Street and North Road. There are many churches, such as St Walburge's (south east of the terminus), whose tall spires are a distinctive feature of the town. There is a good shopping precinct and a large modern bus station. Preston was awarded city status by the Queen in April 2002, in celebration of her Golden Jubilee.

Harris Museum & Art Gallery Market Square, Preston PR1 2PP (01772 258248; www.harrismuseum.org.uk). The largest gallery space in Lancashire, containing a specialised collection of the Devis family of painters and exhibits illustrating 18th-C and 19th-C art, including ceramics and costume. *Open Mon 11.00–17.00, Tue–Sat 10.00–17.00.* Free.

Tourist Information Centre Guild Hall, Lancaster Road, Preston PR1 1HT (01772 253731; www.preston.gov.uk). *Open Mon–Sat 10.00–17.30.*

Pubs and Restaurants

The Olde Dog & Partridge 44 Friargate, Preston PR1 2AT (01772 252217). Unpretentious, city-centre pub dispensing real cider and real ales, together with excellent value *L* food *Mon–Sat.* Quiz *Thu, monthly* live music and a DJ *Sun.* Outside seating and traditional pub games. *Open 11.00 (Sun 12.00).*

The Black Horse 166 Friargate, Preston, Lancashire PR1 2EJ (01772 204855; www.blackhorse-preston.co.uk). Historic, Grade II listed hostelry (complete with a hall of mirrors seating area) serving a wide range of real ales and real cider. Homemade food is available *L Mon–Sat* in the upstairs **Graze and Grog Café**. Open fires in an original, unspoilt interior. *Open 10.30 (Sun 12.00).*

The Grey Friar 144 Friargate, Preston PR1 2EJ (01772 558542; www.jdwetherspoon.co.uk/home/pubs/the-grey-friar). Bustling, city-centre pub, in an ex-carpet store, serving real cider, a wide range of real ales and food *from 08.00 onwards.* Children welcome. Wi-Fi and large-screen TV.

The Old Vic 78 Fishergate, Preston, Lancashire PR1 2UH (01772 254690). Popular pub, close to the railway station, serving a wide range of real ales and food *daily 12.00–17.00 (Sun 13.00–16.00).* Outside seating, Wi-Fi, traditional pub games and sports TV. *Open 11.30 (Sun 12.00).*

The Hand & Dagger Treales Road, Salwick, Preston PR4 0SA (01772 690306; www.handanddagger.com). Canalside at bridge 26. Once the Clifton Arms. A welcoming country pub serving real ale and freshly prepared food *all day.* Dog-friendly; children welcome if dining. Mooring and camping. Quiz *Wed.* *Open 12.00 Tue-Sun.*

WALKING & CYCLING

The towpath is in good condition throughout. Cycling on the towpath is allowed only on a short stretch near Preston and between bridges 95 and 129. The Preston area is well-served with footpaths, including 'The Ribble Way', a 70-mile route following the river and its valley from the sea to its source (www.lancsenvironment.com/countryside/ribbleway), and the 23-mile 'Round Preston Walk' – a booklet is available at the Tourist Information Centre.

Bilsborrow

Passing the marina at Moons Bridge, the canal gently meanders along its remote route to eventually enter the village of Bilsborrow on a minor embankment: the A6 joins the canal here, as does the West Coast Mainline to Scotland, and the M6. Generally these rival transport routes keep their distance and the canal is for the most part delightfully quiet, still passing through peaceful green farmland, while the foothills of the Pennines begin to converge from the east. 'Owd Nell's' and 'Guys Thatched Hamlet' provide a single colourful intrusion. The River Brock is crossed on an aqueduct, with a good view to the west. There is a handy *garage and shop (solid fuel)* at Bridge 49, with limited temporary moorings giving direct access.

Boatyards

Ⓑ**Moons Bridge Marina** Hollowforth Lane, Woodplumpton, Preston PR4 0BD (01772 690627; www.moonsbridgemarina.co.uk). Ⓓ Gas, long-term mooring, winter storage, slipway, boat lift, boat and engine sales and repairs, chandlery, gifts, DIY facilities.

BIRD LIFE
The *Moorhen* is a widespread and familiar wetland bird: often wary, in urban areas they can become rather tame. The adult has brownish wings but otherwise mainly dark grey-black plumage. It has the distinctive yellow-tipped red bill and a frontal shield on its head, with white feathers on the sides of the undertail and a white line along the flanks. Juvenile birds have pale brown plumage. The moorhen's legs and long toes are yellowish. It swims with a jerky movement, with tail flicking. In flight the moorhen shows dangling legs.

Pubs and Restaurants

✕♀**Barton Bangla Bistro** 913 Garstang Road, Barton, Preston PR3 5AB (01995 640236; www.bartonbanglabrasseriepreston.co.uk). Family orientated Indian restaurant offering à la carte, set menu and *Sun* buffet. *Open Mon-Fri from 13.00.* Takeaway service available.

◗✕**Owd Nell's** Canalside, St Michael's Road, Bilsborrow, Preston PR3 0RS (01995 640010; www.guysthatchedhamlet.co.uk). At bridge 44. A farmhouse-style thatched pub and restaurant complex, with all sorts of attractions. There are craft shops, a thatched terrace, a timber castle and games areas with cricket pavilion. Generous bar meals, with a children's menu *all day, every day*. When in season, local game features on the menu, as well as fresh fish dishes. Real ales, with a choice of well furnished bars in which to drink them. Children welcome. Wi-Fi. B&B.

◗✕**Roebuck** Garstang Road, Bilsborrow, Preston PR3 0RE (01995 640234; www.chefandbrewer.com/pub/roebuck-bilsborrow-preston/s6624). A pub/restaurant/lodge serving real ale and meals *daily 12.00-22.00 (Sun 21.00).* Children welcome, and there is a large garden. *Open 11.00 (Sun 12.00).* B&B.

◗**The White Bull** Garstang Road, Bilsborrow, Preston PR3 0RE (01995 640324; www.thewhitebull.co.uk). Friendly Canalside at bridge 44. Friendly village local with an open fire, dispensing real ales. Children welcome and there is a garden. *Open Sun-Thu L and E; Fri-Sat all day from 12.00.*

FROM PRESTON TO KENDAL, BY WATERBUS
In an age when there is great personal freedom of movement, it is not always easy to imagine that canals, in their time, provided much the same opportunities as buses and trains today. As well as regular water bus services, special excursions were organised. Indeed as early as 1776 boats carried pleasure seekers from Beeston to the Chester Races, on what is now the Shropshire Union Canal.
Such services were scheduled on the Lancaster Canal until 1849. Initially a regular daily service operated between Kendal and Preston, the journey taking 14 hours, with refreshments being provided. In 1833, in order to compete with the stage coaches, an express service was introduced, cutting the journey time to 7 hours 15 minutes, and carrying an incredible 14,000 passengers in the first six months.
'For safety, economy and comfort no other mode of transport could be so eligible.'

BOAT TRIPS

The wide-beam boat *Jungle Queen* operates public trips from Guy's Thatched Hamlet *Sat and Sun, 12.00-14.00*. The boat can also be chartered for private cruises. Contact Lancaster Canal Cruises, Olde Duncombe House, Bilsborrow Wharf, Garstang Road, Bilsborrow, PR3 0RE (01995 602943/07748 324221; www.party-boats.co.uk) for further details. Day boat hire, narrowboat hire and B&B also available.

● **Bilsborrow**

Lancs. PO, tel, stores, fish & chips, off-licence, garage. A village which straggles along the A6. The church of St Hilda, built 1926–7, is set apart, up on a hill; there are three pubs very close to the canal. The fish and chip shop serves breakfast *until 10.30*.

Garstang

There is a flurry of canal
interest around the Calder Aqueduct
and Catterall Basin, and those who
moor here and walk up the hills to the east of
bridge 54 will also be rewarded with splendid views
over Cockerham Sands and the Fylde. The canal then temporarily
moves away from the hills and the remains of Greenhalgh Castle to cross the
River Wyre on a fine stone aqueduct, 110ft long and 34ft high, attributed to John Rennie.
There are steps down if you wish to have a better look at it. The attractive town of Garstang
is soon reached; the area around Garstang Basin is a popular mooring for pleasure boats.
The town lies to the north east as the canal passes a marina and continues to wind through
countryside that is as green and pleasant as ever, but which is now overlooked by the steep
slopes of the Pennines.

Boatyards

ⓑ **Bridge House Marina** Nateby Crossing Lane,
Nateby, Garstang PR3 0JJ (01995 603207;
www.bridgehousemarina.co.uk). Between bridges
64 and 66. 🏠🏠🔧 Gas, winter storage, slipway,
crane, chandlery, boat sales, boat and engine
repairs, day hire, toilets, solid fuel, toilets, showers,
telephone. DIY facilities. Also caravan park.

Pubs and Restaurants

The Kenlis Arms Hotel Ray Lane, Barnacre, Preston PR3 1GD (01995 603307) East of bridge 54. A handsome red-brick pub serving home-cooked food *Thu-Sun 12.00-20.00 (Sun 18.00)*. Children are welcome, and there is a family garden with a play area. *Closed L Mon-Wed.* B&B.

Th'Owd Tithebarn The Wharf, Church Street, Garstang, Preston PR3 1PA(01995 604486; www. tithebarngarstang.co.uk). Canalside at bridge 62. A uniquely old-fashioned establishment overlooking the canal basin. Real ale is served together with food *Mon-Fri L and E & Sat-Sun all day 12.00-20.00*. Children welcome and there is a garden. Traditional pub games and open fires. Quiz *Wed. Open 11.30.*

The Royal Oak Hotel Market Place, Garstang, Preston PR3 1ZA (01995 603318; www. royaloakhotelgarstang.co.uk). A coaching inn, dating from the 1670s but with parts surviving from 1480. Real ale is served and food is available *Mon-Sat L and E & all day Sun*. Children and dogs welcome. Traditional pub games and open fires. Beer gardens. B&B. *Open 11.00.*

Eagle & Child 3 High Street, Garstang, Preston PR3 1EA (01995 602139). Serves real ale. Children welcome, and there is a small garden. Disco *Fri-Sat,* karaoke *Sun.* Traditional pub games and Wi-Fi. *Open 11.00.*

The Crown 34-37 High Street, Garstang, Preston PR3 1EA (01995 602152/07887 486728; www. thwaitespubs.co.uk/the-crown-hotel-garstang). Serving real ales and food *L and E*. Children welcome and there is outside seating. Traditional pub games and sports TV. *Open 12.00.*

The Kings Arms High Street, Garstang, Preston PR3 1EA (01995 602101). A sport-orientated pub serving real ale and home-made bar meals *L and E*. Children welcome, outside seating. Traditional pub games and sports TV. Music *Fri-Sat. Open 11.00.*

Pipers Restaurant 46 High Street, Garstang, Preston PR3 1EA (01995 606665; www.pipersrestaurant. co.uk). Set in a quaint, 18th-C building, this restaurant serves modern English cuisine in the form of bistro-style *lunches* and an à la carte *dinner* menu. Open *Tue-Wed E; Thu-Sat L and E* and *Sun 12.30-19.30.*

The Wheatsheaf 1 Park Hill Road, Garstang, Preston PR3 1EL (01995 600486; www.thewheatsheafgarstang.co.uk). Once a farm house, this Grade II listed hostelry now dispenses real ale and food *Wed-Sun 12.00-20.00 (Sun 19.00)*. Sports TV, garden and traditional pub games.

● **Claughton Hall** 1/4 mile east of the canal. This hall was originally an Elizabethan mansion built next to the village church for the Croft family, but in 1932-5 the whole house, except for one wing, was dismantled and reassembled on top of the moor north of the village. It was quite a remarkable undertaking and still stands in defiant isolation.

● **Greenhalgh Castle** Just north of the canal on a grassy knoll are the modest ruins of Greenhalgh Castle. It was built in 1490 by the Earl of Derby, who placed Richard III's crown on Henry Tudor's head after the victory at Bosworth Field. In the 17th C it was destroyed by the Roundheads during the Civil War, when the Royalists made a final stand there. Ask at the adjacent farm to visit the ruins.

● **Garstang**
Lancs. PO, tel, stores, banks, chemist, fishmonger, baker, butcher, delicatessen, hardware, off-licence, fish & chips, takeaways, library, garage. A friendly place, referred to as 'Cherstanc' in the Domesday Book, lying north east of the canal, which retains the atmosphere of a small market town. In the 18th C Garstang was a popular stopping point for coaches en route from London to Edinburgh and the traditional market which still takes place every Thursday dates back to 1310, in the time of Edward II. Near the canal is the 18th-C church of St Thomas, surrounded by a tidy churchyard. Opposite the cobbled market place is an interesting town hall with diminutive bell-tower. Built 1755-64 to acknowledge the town's promotion by the king to borough status, it was rebuilt in 1939. The market cross, erected in 1754, is an elegant column topped by a ball. There was at one time a dozen ale houses in the town; a surprising number still remain!

Visit Garstang Centre 1 Cherestanc Square, Garstang PR3 1EF (01995 602125; www.visitwyre.co.uk). *Open Apr-Oct, daily 10.30-16.30; Nov-Mar, daily 11.00-15.00.*

75

Potters Brook

Continuing northwards through quiet, modest and unspoilt pasture land, the canal passes countryside which is empty of villages but full of farms and houses which are dotted about the landscape. The absence of any locks certainly makes this an ideal waterway for restful cruising, while the wildlife and the generously proportioned stone-arched bridges always supply interest along the way. From Potters Brook Bridge (81) a lane across the A6 leads to a *telephone* and hotel beside what used to be Bay Horse Station. Just north of Potters Brook is the Ellel Grange estate with its remarkable spired church, ornamental canal bridge and the Grange itself, shrouded by tall trees; unfortunately the estate is private.

● **Ellel Grange** Bay Horse, Ellel, Lancaster LA2 0HN (01524 751651; www. ellelministries.org). On the banks of the canal. A very fine Italianate villa built for William Preston, a merchant, in 1857–9. It is a large mansion with two broad towers that compete in vain with the graceful spire of the charming little church of St Mary, built in 1873 at a cost of £7000, which stands in the grounds of the house. It was also built by William Preston. Purchased in 1986 by the Ellel Ministries, it was the first of their centres to be established and it still remains the international headquarters of the work. As well as holding Healing Retreats and Training Courses, Ellel Grange accommodates the Special Ministries Unit which provides longer-term help for those in need.

Pubs and Restaurants

🍺✕**The Bay Horse Inn** Bay Horse, Ellel LA2 0HN (01524 791204; www.bayhorseinn.com). North east of bridge 81, across the A6. Real ale is served in this friendly and cosy country pub, which has an open fire *during the winter*. Restaurant and bar meals are available *Wed-Sun L and E*. Children are welcome if you are eating, and there is a garden. *Open Wed-Sun L and E.*

BIRD LIFE

The *Grey Heron* is a familiar large, long-legged wetland bird. The adult has a dagger-like, yellow bill and a black crest of feathers. The head, neck and underparts are otherwise whitish except for black streaks on the front of the neck and breast. The back and wings are blue-grey. In flight, the wings are broad and rounded with black flight feathers; the heron employs a slow, flapping wingbeat and holds its neck folded in a hunched 's' shape close to its body. The juvenile is similar to the adult but the markings are less distinct and the plumage more grubby in appearance. The heron is often seen standing motionless for hours on end on long, yellow legs, sometimes with its neck hunched up. It will occasionally actively stalk prey which comprise mainly amphibians and fish, especially eels. The call is a harsh and distinctive 'frank'. The heron nests in loose colonies mainly in trees but sometimes seen on coasts in winter.

The *Green Woodpecker*, despite its size and bright, colourful plumage, can be surprisingly difficult to see. It is usually rather wary and often prefers to hide behind tree trunks rather than show itself. Sometimes it is seen feeding on lawns or areas of short grass when the green back, greenish buff underparts and red and black facial markings can be seen. It uses its long tongue to collect ants. If disturbed the green woodpecker flies off revealing a bright yellow-green rump. The spiky tail gives support when climbing tree trunks. Its presence is often detected by a loud and distinctive yaffling call. The stout, dagger-like bill is used to excavate wood for insect larvae and to create nest holes. It favours open, deciduous woodland.

WALKING & CYCLING

The 260-mile Lancashire Cycleway (Routes 90/91) comprises two circular routes, which meet in the historic village of Whalley in the Ribble Valley. In places the Cycleway intersects with the canal, while following minor roads wherever possible. It takes you through a host of different landscapes from the rugged Bowland Hills and West Pennine Moors, to the rich pastures of the Fylde Plain and the outstanding coastal scenery at Silverdale. Part of the Cycleway at Rivington was used in the 2001 Commonwealth Games.

The northern loop explores the remote Bowland Fells, the rich Fylde Plain and the lush valleys of the Lune and Ribble,

while the southern loop takes you past mighty Pendle Hill (with its associations with witchcraft) and across the brooding West and South Pennine Moors. In between the moors there are attractive valleys with ancient weavers' villages in which to rest. Away from the hills, the Cycleway crosses the rich West Lancashire plain, with its market gardens, before returning to the Ribble Valley.

A guidebook to the Cycleway by Jon Sparks is available from Cicerone Press 2 Police Square, Milnthorpe, Cumbria LA7 7PY (01539 562069; www.cicerone. co.uk).

A host of other cycling routes in Lancashire can be viewed at www. lancashire.gov.uk/corporate/web/?siteid=3732&pageid=12416.

The Glasson Branch

Double Bridge marks the end of a rocky cutting and the junction with the Glasson Branch. Just around the corner on the main line is Galgate and a large boatyard and mooring site. The extremely attractive Glasson Branch leads off down to the west to connect the Lancaster Canal with the Lune estuary via Glasson Dock. The branch was finished in 1826, long after the main line of the canal was completed, and provided the canal with its only direct link with the sea. There are six wide locks whose bottom gates feature the same excellent type of sliding paddles seen on the Leeds & Liverpool Canal (*see* Navigational Note 2). Gates must be locked after use, and the locks left *empty*, even when going up. The arm falls through the Conder Valley, a pleasant, quiet stretch of countryside whose proximity to the sea is betrayed by the many seagulls cruising around. After the bottom lock, the canal runs in a straight line through saltings and marshland to Glasson Basin, where there is a large boatyard, mainly for seagoing yachts, and moorings.

The main line of the canal continues northwards through beautiful undulating green countryside, then passes through an unusually long wooded cutting, marked by Deep Cutting Bridge, and ends in the outskirts of Lancaster.

NAVIGATIONAL NOTES

1 Glasson Basin Lock 7 will take boats up to 87' 10" x 26' 3" with 11' 9" draught. Anyone wishing to use this lock (*for which 24hrs notice is required*) should contact the Canal & River Trust 0303 040 4040; enquiries.northwest@canalrivertrust.org.uk. The dock links to a sea lock which operates from *2hrs* before high water and is under the jurisdiction of Lancaster Ports Commission (01524 751724). You must give them at least *24hrs notice during winter months* while *summer opening* is arranged around the times of high water.

2 The locks on the Glasson Branch will take boats up to 67' 6" x 16' with 3' 10" draught. You will need a Watermate key to operate them. Gates must be locked after use, and the locks left *empty*, even when going up.

Pubs and Restaurants

◆✕**The Mill Inn** Mill Lane, Conder Green LA2 0BD (01524 752852; www.themillatcondergreen. co.uk). Near Sixth Lock. Real ale and food served *L and E* in a sympathetically restored, 17th-C grain mill. Gardens, with moorings close by. Dog-friendly; Wi-Fi. *Open 12.00.*

◆**The Dalton Arms** Ten Row, West Quay, Glasson Dock, Lancaster LA2 0BZ (01524 753007; www. daltonarms.info). Traditional family-run country pub. Real ale. Food available *Mon-Tue E; Wed-Sat L and E & Sun 12.00-20.00*. Children welcome, patio. *Open 12.00 (Mon-Tue 16.00).*

✕**Lantern O'er the Lune Café** West Quay, Glasson Dock, Lancaster LA2 0BY (01524 752323). Overlooking the basin, this friendly café does main meals along with cakes, teas and coffee.

✕**Lock Keepers Rest** Glasson Basin. Beside the Swing Bridge. This converted caravan has provided tea, coffee, cakes and burgers to visitors for many years.

◆**The Victoria Inn** Victoria Terrace, Glasson Dock, Lancaster LA2 0BT (01524 751423). A friendly welcome, real ale and inexpensive tasty food are all available at this harbourside pub. Children welcome, outside seating.

◆**The Plough** Main Road, Lancaster, Galgate LA2 0LQ (01524 751337; www.plough-galgate.co.uk). Real ale and food (*all day*) is dispensed in this 16th-C coaching inn. Garden, open fires and Wi-Fi. Sports TV and traditional pub games. Dogs welcome. *Open 12.00.*

Boatyards

Ⓑ**Galgate Marina** Main Road, Galgate, Lancaster LA2 0LG (01524 751491; www.bwml.co.uk/marinas/galgate_marina). 🏠🏠⚓ **D** Pump out, long-term mooring, slipway, toilets, showers, laundry. See Glasson Basin Marina below for boat hoist, chandlery, laundrette.

Ⓑ**Glasson Basin Marina** Glasson Dock, School Lane, Lancaster LA2 0AW (01524 751491; www.bwml.co.uk). 🏠🏠 ⚓ **D** Gas, long-term mooring, winter storage, boat hoist (50 ton), slipway, boat sales and repairs, chandlery, books and maps, showers, toilets, laundrette.

WALKING & CYCLING

The Lune Millennium Cycleway, which also forms part of the Lancashire Cycleway, follows a former railway line and connects Glasson to Lancaster and Bull Beck picnic site to the north. The route of this footpath/cycleway runs through Lancaster before heading up-stream on the River Lune towards Caton.

● **Galgate**

Lancs. PO, tel, stores, off-licence, fish & chips. An unassuming village on the A6, dominated by the main railway to Scotland. The back of the village up the hill is quiet; by the church of St John, built 1906–7, are the buildings of what is apparently the oldest surviving silk spinning mill in England, built in 1792. There is another, apparently older, built originally as a corn mill, close by. Some of the nearby cottages were built for the mill-workers.

Canalside Craft Centre Pear Tree Barn, Main Road, Galgate Lancaster LA2 0LQ (01524 752223). A craft shop next to the marina. Tea, coffee, snacks and full meals. *Open 10.00–17.00, closed Mon except B Hols.*

● **Glasson**

Lancs. PO box, tel, stores, off-licence. A fascinating tiny port built in 1787 to serve Lancaster. The huge basin is now only occupied by an assortment of pleasure boats using its excellent sheltered moorings. In the tidal dock, however, there are often coasters which discharge into lorries and there is still an active smokehouse.

Lancaster

The canal now enters Lancaster, losing its rural identity as buildings close in. There are useful *stores* just west of bridge 98. At bridge 100 the towpath returns to the west side of the canal, where it stays for the rest of the journey northwards. The canal passes through the heart of Lancaster, passing well-restored mills, including Moor Lane with its conspicuous red-brick water tower and now the home of Reebok UK, and continues north, passing an old dry dock by bridge 103, to cross an aqueduct, built in 1961, over the A683. The imposing aqueduct which carries the canal over the River Lune quickly follows, affording fine views along the Lune valley. The canal then rejoins the side of the valley, turning west, then north again to head towards the sea at Hest Bank.

● **Lancaster**

Lancs. All services. Today Lancaster's quay, once a great shipping port handling more cargo than Liverpool, is a quiet backwater, with pleasant walks. There are some fine canalside buildings.

Lancaster Castle Castle Parade, Lancaster LA1 1YJ (01524 64998; www.lancastercastle.com). On the site of Roman fortifications, this is a mainly 13th-C and 14th-C construction, except for the Norman keep, which is surmounted by a beacon tower. *Open daily 10.00–17.00.* Guided tours (Court sittings permitting) from *10.30–16.00.* Charge. Gift shop.

Cottage Museum 15 Castle Hill, Lancaster LA1 1YS (01524 388716). Opposite the castle, this is part of a 1739 house containing the artifacts of an artisan, c. 1820. Activities. *Open 13.00–16.00.* Charge.

Lancaster Priory & Parish Church Castle Hill , Lancaster LA1 1YZ (01524 65338; www.lancasterpriory. org). There has been a church on this site since AD 630. The present building is an attractive 15th-C church in late Perpendicular style, with an original Saxon western doorway. Church *open all year round 09.30–17.00.* Free. Guided tours *on request.* Refectory *open Easter–Oct, 10.00–16.00.* Interesting book stall. Nearby are the excavated remains of a Roman bath house.

Lancaster City Museum Old Town Hall, Market Square, Lancaster LA1 1HT (01524 64637; www.lancashire.gov.uk). Lancashire's past, the King's Own Regiment Museum, portraits and landscapes, changing exhibitions, events and activities. *Open Mon–Sat 10.00–17.00.* Free.

Ashton Memorial Well House Wyresdale Road, Lancaster LA1 3JJ (01524 68460; www.lancaster.gov).

Dominated by the Ashton Memorial folly, which contains an exhibition gallery. Also tropical butterfly house and over 50 acres of parkland including landscaped gardens, children's playground and an ornamental lake. Shop and café. *Open Easter–Oct, daily 10.00–17.00; winter, daily 11.00–16.00.* Charge.

Maritime Museum Old Customs House, St George's Quay, Lancaster LA1 1RB (01524 382264; www.lancaster.gov.uk). Walk towards the river from bridge 99, turning left into Damside. Lifeboats, fine models and artefacts from Glasson Dock. *Open Easter–Oct, daily 11.00–17.00; winter 12.30–16.00.* Charge. Café. The riverside path to the west connects with Glasson Dock about 5 miles away.

Visitor Information Centre The Storey, Meeting House Lane, Lancaster LA1 1TH (01524 582394; www.citycoastcountryside.co.uk/lancaster-city). *Open Mon–Sat 10.00–16.00.*

● **Lune Aqueduct**

This splendid edifice carries the navigation for some 600ft across the River Lune, which is 60ft below. Designed by John Rennie, it was built between 1794–7 by Alexander Stevens, a Scotsman who died before it was completed. The bottom of the channel is apparently 7 or 8ft deep, containing a layer of puddled clay about 3ft thick. There is said to be a plug which can be pulled to drain the structure into the River Lune below. Its total cost was £48,320 18s 6d.

● **Hest Bank**

Lancs. PO box, tel, takeaway, fish & chips. The seashore is only a couple of hundred yards from the navigation, and at low water miles of sandy beach are uncovered.

Pubs and Restaurants

◗✕**The Water Witch** Aldcliffe Lane, Lancaster LA1 1SU (01524 63828; www.thewaterwitch.co.uk). Canalside between bridges 98 and 99. Warm and friendly, with a stone floor and a good variety of freshly-cooked food available *daily 12.00–21.00 (Sun 20.00).* Real ale is served together with real cider *in summer.* Outside seating, moorings, open fires and Wi-Fi. Quiz *Thu.* Open 11.00.

◗✕**White Cross** Quarry Road, Lancaster LA1 4XT (01524 33999; www.thewhitecross.co.uk). Canalside at bridge 100. Real cider, real ales and food *daily 12.00–21.00.* Children welcome, patio and moorings. Large-screen TV, traditional pub games and Wi-Fi. *Open 11.30.*

◗**The Waggon & Horses** 27 St George's Quay, Lancaster LA1 1RD (01524 846094; www.wagonandhorseslancaster.co.uk). Worth a look in if you

are visiting the Maritime Museum, this pub serves real ale, and food *Mon–Fri L and E; all Sat-Sun.* B&B. *Open 11.00.*

◗✕**Hest Bank** 2 Hest Bank Lane, Lancaster LA2 6DN (01524 824339). Canalside at bridge 118. You can still see the window for the guiding light, which once showed the way across the sands. Now this old coaching inn, which dates from 1554, is justly popular and you can share the shelter it once offered to abbots and monks, soldiers and highwaymen, the Duke of Devonshire and Prince Frederick of Prussia. Real ale and fresh local food, and seafood *L and E, daily.* Children welcome (not in the public bar), and there is a fine canalside garden. Quiz *Wed.* Mooring.

WALKING & CYCLING

Themed walks and tours, local history walks, ghost and murder walks and treasure hunts are run in the Lancaster area by Catwalks (01524 792089;www.catwalks-lancaster.co.uk). There are guided tours of many of Lancaster's historic landmarks, plus Old Calendar Walks which leave from John O'Gaunt Gateway at Lancaster Castle at *19.00* on *New Year's Eve, Valentine's Day, St George's Day, May Day, Midsummer Eve, Michaelmas Day, Hallowe'en and St Nicholas' Day*, contact the Visitor Information Centre (01524 582394; www.citycoastcountryside.co.uk/lancaster-city for details.

BOAT TRIPS

Lancaster Canal Boats operate boat trips and a waterbus service *May-Sep* along the waterway in the Lancaster and Carnforth areas. Telephone 01524 389410 or visit www.budgietransport for a timetable and further details.

118 Hest Bank Bridge
HEST BANK
117
116 Rakes Head Bridge
Blind Lane Bridge 115
114 Belmont Bridge
113 Williamsland Bridge
Folly Bridge 112
Milestone Bridge 111A
Hammerton Hall 111 Bridge
110 Beaumont Turnpike Bridge
Beaumont Hall Bridge
109
Halton Road Bridge
108
107 Lune Aqueduct
106 Bulk Road Aqueduct
Footbridge
105 Dolphinlee Bridge
104 Ridge Lane Bridge
Dry Dock (remains)
103 Dry Dock Footbridge
102 Moor Lane Bridge
101 Nelson Street Bridge
CATHEDRAL
Friarage Bridge 100
99 Penny Street Bridge
Footbridge
Aldcliffe Road Bridge 96
Haverbreaks Bridge 95

12m 0L
Borwick
Glasson
Branch
5¼m 0L

LANCASTER

82

79

81

Carnforth

The canal now passes Hest Bank and Bolton-le-Sands, with the sea never far away to the west and the A6 beside and below. As the waterway comes into Carnforth, it often affords grand views over Morecambe Bay before sneaking quite inconspicuously through the town, mostly in a cutting, passing a *sanitary station, pump out and showers*. Carnforth railway station offers an excellent jumping off point to explore the attractions of the Lake District coast and the train journey to Carlisle, via Barrow-in-Furness, is an excitement in itself, much of the track being virtually on the beach! Indeed three suggested visits, within easy reach of the line, are listed on page 83. Carnforth is also the starting point for possibly the ultimate 'railway ring' – one that can be comfortably accomplished in a day. Travelling in an anti-clockwise direction: take the train to Hellifield, thence north up the extraordinary Settle-Carlisle line; returning via the aforementioned Cumbrian coast railway. Soon after leaving Carnforth the navigation dives under the motorway spur road and finds itself diverted along a new channel for several hundred yards before going under the main line of the M6: this diversion was presumably cheaper to build than a long, finely-angled skew motorway bridge over the navigation. Beyond the motorway lies peaceful green countryside backed, unmistakably, by the foothills of the Lake District. At Capernwray the canal crosses the River Keer on a minor aqueduct built by John Rennie in 1797; the nearby railway, which goes to Leeds, also crosses the Keer, on a very impressive viaduct.

- **Bolton-le-Sands**
  Lancs. PO, tel, stores, off-licence, butcher, chemist, takeaways, fish & chips, garage. A pleasant village of narrow streets, with a pub at each end and the shops strung out over more than a mile.

- **Carnforth**
  Lancs. PO, tel, stores, banks, chemists, takeaways, off-licence, hardware, baker, library, station. Not particularly attractive but useful for supplies, especially the superb selection of pies at Madisons in Market Street, 01524 732021, and of interest as an important railway junction. It is possible to catch trains not only north-south but east over the beautiful green hills to Skipton and Leeds, west to Barrow and right round the coast to Carlisle. Carnforth was the last town in the country to lose its regular British Rail steam locomotive service in 1968: it is now a centre for steam-hauled railtours over the national railway

BOAT TRIPS

There are regular boat trips available *May–Sep* operated by Lancaster Canal Boats. Telephone 01524 389410 or visit www.budgietransport for a timetable and further details.

Boatyards

Ⓑ**Nu-Way Acorn** Lundsfield, Carnforth LA5 9NB (01524 734457). Pump out, gas, overnight mooring, long-term mooring, winter storage, slipway, boat and engine sales and repairs, toilets, showers, DIY facilities.

system. The Tearooms, as featured in the film *Brief Encounter*, have been restored (as has the famous clock) and there is a small museum. There is a useful cycle shop – Dyno Start 1-3 Scotland Road, Carnforth LA5 9JY (01524 732089; www.dynostart.com) – *open Mon-Sat 09.00-17.00 (Sat 16.30)* – which also houses a small museum.

Leighton Moss Nature Reserve Storrs Lane, Silverdale, Carnforth LA5 0SW (01524 701601; www.rspb.org.uk/reserves/guide/l/leightonmoss). ¼-mile south of Silverdale railway station – just one stop away from Carnforth. Leighton Moss is the largest reed bed in north west England, and home to rare birds such as breeding bitterns, bearded tits and marsh harriers. Also deer and a wide range of butterflies. You can choose from a selection of trails and hides, most of which are suitable for wheelchairs, and get right to the heart of the reed bed. Or take the nature trail alongside two coastal lagoons to see a variety of wading and water birds. Reserve *open dawn to dusk;* café and Visitor Centre *open daily 09.30-17.00 (Dec-Jan 16.30).* Free entry to Visitor Centre and café. Charge for nature trails and hides – although free for those who arrive by public transport or cycle.

Ravenglass and Eskdale Railway Ravenglass, Cumbria CA18 1SW (01229 717171; www.ravenglass-railway. co.uk). 1¾-hours travel from Carnforth, adjacent to the railway station. Known locally as La'al Ratty, this narrow gauge railway runs from Ravenglass (the only coastal village in the Lake District National Park) across the estuary and through the hills, passing seven request stops. At times there are 1:40 gradients on the route to its final destination at the Dalegarth for Boot Station. The journey itself was one of Wainwright's favourites, crossing seven miles of spectacular scenery to the foot of England's highest mountains, the Scafell Range (3,209ft) at their peak. *Regular daily timetable mid Mar-Oct; limited timetable Nov-mid Mar.* Telephone of visit the website for full details. Charge.

The Lake District Coast Aquarium South Quay, Maryport CA15 8AB (01900 817760; www.coastaquarium. co.uk). 2¾-hours travel from Carnforth and worth it for the journey alone! This is the point where the coastal line heads inland for Carlisle so a good place to de-train and enjoy the fascinations of this aquarium. It houses over 55 themed tanks containing a variety of the marine life found around the Cumbrian coastline, from fish to crustaceans, as well as a purpose built tropical marine community reef tank. A must for all those fascinated by everything that goes on under the water! Friendly café and gift shop. *Open daily 10.00-17.00.* Charge.

Pubs and Restaurants

✗**Miaitalia** Bye-Pass Rd, Bolton-le-Sands, Carnforth LA5 8JA (01524 823323). The real flavour of Italy with all the excellent food freshly prepared. Proper Italian ice creams contrast with a warm, friendly welcome, especially to children, who are provided with entertainment. Real coffee and pastries. *Open Mon-Fri 09.30-21.00 (Fri 22.00); Sat 10.00-22.00 & Sun 11.00-21.00.*

🍺**The Royal Hotel** Main Road, Bolton-le-Sands, Carnforth LA5 8DQ (01524 732057; www. royalhotelbls.co.uk). A choice of real ale, plus a good range of excellent food *daily 12.00-21.00 (Sun 20.00).* Dart board, pool table and sports TV. Children welcome. Garden, quiz *Thu.* B&B. *Open 12.00.*

🍺✗**The Canal Turn** Lancaster Road, Carnforth LA5 9EA (01524 734750; www.thecanalturn.co.uk). A very attractive canalside pub in cottages once known as 'Pig & Piano Row', and which housed workers from nearby iron and gas works. Meals are served *all day from 11.30.* Dogs and children welcome. Quiz *Tue.* Patio, mooring, traditional pub games and Wi-Fi.

🍺**The Shovel Inn** North Road, Carnforth LA5 9NA (01524 733402). West of bridge 128. A friendly pub serving real ale. Children welcome, and there is a garden. Dogs welcome. Traditional pub games, Wi-Fi, open fires and sports TV. *Open 12.00.*

🍺✗**Royal Station Hotel** Market Street, Carnforth LA5 9BT (01524 733636; www. theroyalstationhotelcarnforth.co.uk). Bang in the centre of town, this handsome establishment played host to Trevor Howard, Celia Johnson and Stanley Holloway in the Noel Coward film 'Brief Encounter', which was filmed around Carnforth Station. Queen Victoria is also reputed to have stayed here. They offer real ale, plus food *Mon-Fri L and E & Sat-Sun 12.00-20.00 (Sun 19.00).* Dog- and child-friendly. Beer garden, sports TV, traditional pub games and Wi-Fi. Quiz *Thu. Open 08.00.*

🍺**The Snug** Unit 6, Carnforth Gateway Building, Carnforth LA5 9TR (01524 396861). Minimalist pub in the old station buildings serving real ales and real cider *Tue-Sat 12.00-14.00 & 17.00-21.00.* Snacks, conversation and the whoosh of passing trains greet the visitor, as does the striking floor to ceiling, glazed wooden drinks cabinet. Traditional pub games.

Borwick

Beyond Keer Aqueduct and the railway viaduct is the Capernwray Arm, a short branch to a worked-out quarry, and now offering some attractive sheltered moorings. The canal then winds around the hillside to end abruptly just beyond Borwick and right beside the M6: only the very hard of hearing will be able to enjoy a sojourn here! The abandoned Tewitfield locks begin across the road from the present terminus, and it is well worth taking the fenced path by the motorway and under the bridge to go and have a look, and to imagine how they will look when hopefully restored! It is possible to walk the 14 miles from Tewitfield to the original terminus at Kendal (and get a bus back). Boats can be left at the moorings here. There are the usual boater services here, together with *toilets and showers, a pump out and recycling facilities.*

● **Borwick**
Lancs. PO box, tel. A small, old and attractive village, spread around a green. Overlooking the canal is Borwick Hall, a large and sombre Elizabethan manor house, built around a high 15th-C tower and with extensive gardens.
Capernwray Dive Centre Jackdaw Quarry, Capernwray Road, Over Kellet, Carnforth LA6 1AD (01524 735132; www.dive-site.co.uk). ¼-mile south west of Capernwray Bridge 131. Large flooded former quarry, now operated as an inland scuba diving site.

Equipment hire and tuition. Café and accommodation. *Open Mon-Fri 10.00-17.00 & Sat-Sun 09.00-17.00.* Charge. Advanced booking recommended.
Greenlands Farm Village Tewitfield, Carnforth LA6 1JH (01524 784184; www.greenlandsfarmvillage.co.uk). A short walk north east from the terminus, along A6070. Family fun from an amalgam of soft play, an open farm, donkey rides, artisan village, picnic area, go-karting, straw barn frolicking, climbing wall – to name but a few. Café. *Open daily 10.00-17.00.* Charge.

Pubs and Restaurants

🍴✕**Longlands Hotel** Tewitfield Locks, Tewitfield, Carnforth LA6 1JH (01524 781256; www. longlandshotel.co.uk). Just north east of the canal terminus. This popular country pub serves real ale and home-made bar and restaurant meals *Mon-Sat L and E & Sun all day. Breakfast Mon-Fri from 07.30 & Sat-Sun 08.00.* Dog- and Child-friendly, outside seating. B&B and holiday cottages. Wi-Fi.

Boatyards

Ⓑ**Tewitfield Marina** Chapel Lane, Tewitfield, Carnforth LA6 1JH (01524 782092; www. tewitfieldmarina.co.uk). 🚿🛒🔧 Long- and short-term moorings, showers, toilets, laundry, holiday accommodation.

LEEDS & LIVERPOOL CANAL

MAXIMUM DIMENSIONS

Liverpool to Wigan, and Leigh Branch
Length: 72' 0"
Beam: 14' 3"
Headroom: 8' 0"

Wigan to Leeds
Length: 60' 0"
Beam: 14' 3"
Headroom: 8' 0"

Rufford Branch
Length: 62' 0"
Beam: 14' 3"
Headroom: 8' 0"

MANAGER

0303 040 4040
enquiries.northwest@canalrivertrust.org.uk

MILEAGE

LIVERPOOL. Canal terminus to Burscough,
junction with Rufford Branch: 24½ miles
Wigan, junction with Leigh Branch: 35 miles
Johnson's Hill Locks: 47¼ miles
Blackburn, Top Lock: 56 miles
Burnley: 72½ miles
Skipton: 98 miles
Bingley Five Rise: 110¾ miles
Apperley Bridge: 118 miles
LEEDS, River Lock: 127¾ miles
Locks: 91
Leigh Branch: 7¼ miles, 2 locks
Rufford Branch: 7¼ miles, 8 locks

With a length of 127¼ miles excluding branches, the Leeds & Liverpool Canal is the longest single canal in Britain built by a single company. The canal has its beginnings in the River Douglas, a little river made navigable by 1740 from Wigan to Parbold, Tarleton and the Ribble estuary. Several ambitious trans-Pennine canal schemes had been mooted; one for a canal from Liverpool to Leeds, to connect with the head of the Aire & Calder Navigation. The Leeds & Liverpool Canal was authorised in 1770, and construction began at once, with John Longbotham as engineer. The first (lock-free) section from Bingley to Skipton was opened within three years; by 1777 two long sections were open from the Aire & Calder at Leeds to Gargrave (incorporating many new staircase locks) and from Wigan to Liverpool. The L & L bought out the River Douglas navigation at an early stage to gain control of its valuable water supply. It was replaced by a proper canal branch to Rufford and Tarleton, where it joined the (tidal) River Douglas. In 1790 work began again, with Robert Whitworth as the company's engineer; but after 1792 and the outbreak of war with France, investment in canals declined steadily. The whole of the main line from Leeds to Liverpool was finished by 1816 actually *sharing* the channel of the Lancaster Canal for 10 miles from Wigan Top Lock to Johnson's Hill Bottom Lock. The Lancaster used to branch off up what became the Walton Summit Branch. In 1820 a branch was opened to join the Bridgewater Canal at Leigh. A short branch (the Springs Branch) was also made to rock quarries at Skipton and an important 3-mile-long canal from Shipley to Bradford. The cut down into the Liverpool Docks was made in 1846. The prosperity of the company after 1820 was not, at first, greatly affected by the advent of railways. The scale of the navigation (the locks were built as broad locks 62ft by 14ft, allowing big payloads to be carried along the canal) contributed to the high dividends paid to shareholders for several years. Water supply was, however, a problem and in spite of the building of copious reservoirs, the canal had to be closed for months on end during dry summers, driving carriers' custom away to the railways. Use of the navigation for freight declined throughout the last century; the hard winter of 1962/63 finished off many traders. Today this canal offers boaters, walkers and cyclists an exhilarating link between two superb cities.

Liverpool

The Liverpool Canal Link was officially opened to boaters on 20 April 2009. It runs from the bottom of the existing Stanley Locks and linking Stanley Dock to Canning Dock, via the old West Waterloo Dock; Princes Dock and an underground section near Pier Head, in front of the Royal Liver Building. Canning Dock in turn provides a link into the revitalised Albert Dock which will, for the first time in its history (it is hoped), play host to a regular influx of narrowboats.

Navigation now begins just north of Vauxhall Bridge B. It runs north from the city centre for about 6 miles, parallel and close to Liverpool Docks, before turning east to Aintree, Wigan and the Pennines. Liverpool, while at one time not an attractive place from the canal, is slowly changing and although some factories still have their backs to the waterway, considerable effort has been made to improve the access to the towpath which is alive with walkers, fishermen and cyclists. The water, however, is surprisingly clear. Eldonian Village forms an attractive backdrop to the moorings in the terminus basin. There is a *PO* beside bridge 2A together with a very comprehensive range of *shops*.

NAVIGATIONAL NOTES

1 Just north of the terminus is the Stanley Dock Branch, until recently used only by intrepid navigators as a useful link into the tidal River Mersey. Today this compact flight of locks gives access to the newly completed Liverpool Canal Link, leading across the historic Pier Head, in front of the Royal Liver Building and ultimately into Salthouse Dock. There are four locks on this branch leading down into Stanley Dock. Contact CRT North West Office (0303 040 4040); enquiries.northwest@canalrivertrust.org.uk for information or to book a passage through to Salthouse Dock in the heart of Liverpool.
2 Levels within the old docks – traversed as part of the Liverpool Link – can vary, with the partially infilled West Waterloo Dock providing as little as 2' 6" draught.
3 Navigators wishing to enter the Mersey should contact the Mersey Docks and Harbour Company (0151 949 6000) – the lock is operated *24hrs a day*.
4 Those navigating the Leeds & Liverpool Canal will need, as well as a windlass, a Canal & River Trust handcuff lock key and a Watermate key.
5 Mooring at unrecognised sites in the city centre is not recommended.
6 If you wish to navigate between Liverpool and Aintree and need assistance or details of safe mooring locations, contact CRT North West Office (0303 040 4040); enquiries.northwest@ canalrivertrust.org.uk.

● **Liverpool**
Merseyside. All services. In the first century AD it was 'lifrugpool', a settlement next to a muddy creek; now it is one of Britain's largest ports. Famous worldwide as the place where the Beatles began their march to fame, and equally well known for the exploits of Liverpool Football Club. Club. There is much to be seen in this ancient port. The Anglican Cathedral, begun in 1904 and finished in 1978, is the largest in the world; the Roman Catholic Cathedral has stained glass by John Piper and Patrick Reyntiens. On the pierhead is a memorial to the engineers lost on the *Titanic*, which sank in 1912. The superb Albert Dock development and Liverpool Tate and The Walker Art

Pubs and Restaurants

There are many to be found here.

Galleries, together with a wide range of theatres and museums, are attracting an ever increasing number of tourists. As a city it has more Georgian buildings than Bath, a UNESCO World Heritage waterfront and has convincingly re-established itself upon a reputation as a cultural and leisure centre which was recognised with the award of City of Culture 2008.

91

Litherland Road Bridge 2B
Pipe Bridge
Stanley Road
2A
2 Changeline Bridge
1 Caroline Street
Changeline Bridge

STA

STA

Oriel
Rd Sta
N

M
STA

K

Bank STA
Station

Sandhills
13
H

FERRY
SHIP
Belfast

Langton
River Entrance

FERRY
SHIP
Dublin

Kirkdale

Alexandra Dock

Langton
Dock

Brocklebank
Dock

Canada
Dock

Huskisson Dock

Sandhills
Sta

Boundary Bridge E
Leigh Bridge D
Lightbody
Street Bridge C
Vauxhall Bridge

Collingwood
Dock
Salisbury Dock
Victoria
Tower

Nelson
Dock
Stanley
Dock AA
Footbridge

4 Locks 44'0"
BB
Eldonian
Basin M

24½m 0L
Burscough

Liverpool
Canal Link

ELDONIAN
VILLAGE

Central Docks
Channel

LIVERPOOL

CC

Kingsway
Road Tunnel Toll

West
Waterloo
Dock
River Ent

DD

AQUARIUM
Floating
Stage

BOAT
TRIPS

33

Princes
Dock

Princes Dock Lock 5
Tunnel

EE

FERRIES
CATAMARAN
Douglas (Summer only)
Dublin (Summer only)
SHIP
Douglas (Winter only)

Royal Liver
Building

Canning
Dock

Mersey Ferry

Mann Island Lock 6

Queensway
Mersey Tunnel Toll

Albert Dock

Salthouse Dock

ART
GALLERY

Lime St
Station

Univ

University
Moorfields
Sta

Univ
Hall

Central
Sta

The Fact
Centre

CATHEDRAL

Chinese
Arch

Albert Dock The Colonnades, Albert Dock, Liverpool L3 4AF (0151 707 0729; www.albertdock.com). The largest grouping of Grade I listed buildings in England–opened in 1846 as warehousing for a range of precious cargo from around the world, these buildings have been transformed into an award-winning tourist destination including shops, cafés, restaurants, galleries and museums.

Beatles Story Britannia Vaults, Kings Dock Street, Liverpool L3 4AD (0151 709 1963; www.beatlesstory.com). The title says it all. *Open daily 09.00-17.00.* Charge.

Bluecoat Arts Centre Bluecoat Chambers, School Lane, Liverpool L1 3BX (0151 702 5324; www.thebluecoat.org.uk). A striking 18th-C building housing a varied selection of visual and performing arts. Also educational programmes, artists' studios, shops and a café. *Open daily 08.00-18.00 (Sun 10.00).*

Bluecoat Display Centre College Lane, Liverpool L1 3DS (0151 709 4014; www.bluecoatdisplaycentre.com). Craft and design centre in an adjacent street. *Open Mon-Sat 10.00-17.30, Sun 12.00-17.00.*

Chinese Arch Berry Street, Liverpool. The largest outside China from where it was originally shipped, the arch stands 15m high and spans Nelson Street complete with its five roofs and 200 ornate dragons.

Citysightseeing Pier Head, Canada Boulevard, Liverpool L3 1DP (0151 203 3920; www.citysightseeingliverpool.com). Hop on and hop off open-top buses where a ticket lasts for *24hrs. Operates daily throughout the year from 09.50.* Charge. Also **Maghull Coaches** (0151 933 2324/922 4284; www.cityexplorerliverpool.co.uk) operate a similar service *daily throughout the year (except over Xmas Hols).* Charge.

Croxteth Hall & Country Park Muirhead Avenue East, Liverpool L11 1EH (0151 233 3020; www.liverpoolcityhalls.co.uk/croxteth-hall). Once the ancestral home of the Molyneux family, the Earls of Sefton, the estate now offers the opportunity to visit the historic Hall, the 500- acre Country Park, the Walled Garden and the Home Farm. Only the Country Park is free. *Open Easter-Sep 10.30-17.00* and farm, café and shop *open weekends Oct-Easter.*

Empire Theatre Lime Street, Liverpool L1 1JE (0151 702 7320; www.liverpoolempire.co.uk). Year-round programme of ballet, opera, musicals and large scale-theatre in a 2300-seat auditorium.

Everyman Theatre Williamson Square Liverpool L1 1EL (0151 709 4776; www.everymanplayhouse.com). A popular theatre with a diverse programme of in-house productions and touring shows.

Fact 88 Wood Street, Liverpool L1 4DQ (0151 707 4444; www.fact.co.uk). Exciting, purpose-built arts centre, completed in 2003, housing a range of galleries, a café, restaurant and bar. *Open Sun-Fri 12.00-18.00, Sat from 11.00.* Free.

24 Hour Museum Guide Visit www.24hourmuseum.org.uk/cityheritage to plan your day out and gain a unique perspective on the heritage of English cities. Non-commercial and free to use.

Liverpool Cathedral St James Mount , Liverpool L1 7AZ (0151 709 6271; www.liverpoolcathedral.org.uk). The largest Anglican cathedral in Britain, resplendent in red sandstone, built to the design of Sir Giles Gilbert Scott and begun in 1904. The 331ft tower extends the full width of the building and is home to the heaviest ringing peal of bells in the world–all 30 tons of them. Inside there are soaring gothic arches, a massive organ and together with worship there are regular recitals and concerts. Refectory and shop. *Open daily 08.00-18.00 (attractions 10.00-17.00).* Free-donations. Charge for Tower and Embroidery Gallery.

Liverpool Heritage Walk Liverpool (www.liverpoolworldheritage.com/visitingthewhs/trails/index.asp). Provides a structured approach to explore Liverpool's unique historical and architectural features. The Heritage Walk comprises 75 gunmetal markers set in footways and pedestrian areas throughout the city centre. Themed sub-trails within the heritage walk provide an opportunity to focus on three specific areas of the city's rich architectural legacy: 1) Maritime and Commerce; 2) Arts and Heritage and 3) Learning and Religion. Contact the TIC for further details.

Martin Mere Fish Lane, Ormskirk L40 0TA (01704 895181; www.wwt.org.uk/wetland-centres/martin-mere). A major Wildlife & Wetlands Trust site approaching 600 acres that in winter hosts thousands of migratory wetland birds. There is plenty to do and see at all times of the year and it makes a worthwhile visit either from the city (Merseyrail train to Ormskirk and then a No 3 bus) or as you follow the canal east through Burscough. Café, shop and picnic area. Children's activities. *Open Apr-Oct 09.30-18.00 & Nov-Mar 09.30-16.30.* Charge.

Mendips & 20 Forthlin Road 251 Menlove Avenue, Liverpool L25 7SA (0151 427 7231; www.nationaltrust.org.uk/beatles-childhood-homes). Where Sir Paul McCartney lived with his parents and John Lennon grew up with his aunt and uncle. Both homes have been sensitively restored and can be visited on a tour commencing either in the city centre or from Speke Hall. Booking essential–no direct access to either property. Tours *Mar-Nov 10.00, 11.00 & 14.15* from Jurys Inn Hotel 31 Keel Wharf, Liverpool L3 4FN and *mid Mar-Oct 15.15* from Speke Hall (see page 91). Charge (can be booked online).

Mersey Ferries Pier Head, Georges Parade, Liverpool L3 1DP (0151 236 7676; www.merseyferries.co.uk). Long ago made redundant by road and rail tunnels under the Mersey, these fine vessels now offer a variety of River Explorer Cruises and regular trips along the Manchester Ship Canal. Telephone or visit the website for details. *Open 08.00-20.00.*

Merseyside Maritime Museum Albert Dock, Liverpool L3 4AQ (0151 478 4499; www.liverpoolmuseums.org.uk/maritime/). The chance to discover Liverpool's maritime heritage from tales of the Titanic to the transatlantic slavery trade. Shop and restaurant. *Open daily 10.00-17.00.* Free.

MerseyTravel PO Box 1976 Liverpool L69 3HN (0151 330 1234; www.merseytravel.gov.uk). Also National Rail Enquiries 08457 48 49 50 *(24hrs).* Offers a journey planner, bus train and ferry timetables and regular promotions.

Metropolitan Cathedral Mount Pleasant, Liverpool L3 5TQ (0151 709 9222; www.liverpoolmetrocathedral.org.uk). Standing on the site once occupied by the Poor Law Institute, today's striking building, with its interior lantern tower of multi-coloured glass, has had a somewhat chequered career. Of the original design by Sir Edwin Lutyens, dating from 1933, only the Crypt was built and after the war inflation had raised the estimated cost of completion to £27m. Sir Frederick Gibberd produced a design that met the new brief, namely, that the cathedral should be completed within five years, incorporate the original crypt and cost no more than £1m. Building recommenced in 1962 and the finished cathedral–known locally as 'Paddy's wigwam'–was consecrated in May 1967. Café bar and gift shop. *Open daily 07.30-18.00.* Free – donations welcome.

Mr Hardman's Photographic Studio 59 Rodney Street, Liverpool L1 9EX (0151 709 6261; www.nationaltrust.org.uk). The complete studio, housed in an elegant Georgian terrace, where one of the city's best known portrait and landscape photographers lived and worked. *Open mid Mar-Oct Wed-Sat 11.00-15.30 & B Hol Mon.* Charge for timed ticket and guided tour.

Museum of Liverpool Pier Head, Liverpool L3 1DG (0151 478 4545; www.liverpoolmuseums.org. uk/mol/). An opportunity to explore the richness of Liverpool's cultural diversity in a striking new building rearing up over the Liverpool Link. *Open daily 10.00-17.00.* Shop and café. Free.

Prince's Road Synagogue Synagogue Chambers, Prince's Avenue, Liverpool L8 1TG (0151 709 3431; www.princesroad.org). Arguably Europe's finest example of Saracenic or Moorish revival style of synagogue in a Grade II listed building. Guided talks covering its architecture and history available.

Radio City Tower St John's Beacon, 1 Houghton Street, Liverpool L1 1RL (0151 472 6800; www.radiocity.co.uk). Stunning views over the city and the Mersey estuary from the top of the 440ft Radio City Tower. Tours *daily 11.00-17.30 (Sat 10.30).* Charge. Refreshments and Wi-Fi.

Rice Lane City Farm Rawcliffe Road, Walton, Liverpool L9 1AW (0151 530 1066; www.facebook. com/RiceLaneCityFarm). 224 acres of countryside–11 of which are woodland. There is a variety of rare breeds of farm animals together with ponies, goats and poultry. *Open daily 10.00-15.30.* Free – donations welcome.

Royal Court 36 Hope Street, Liverpool L1 1HL (0870 787 1866; www.royalcourtliverpool.co.uk). An impressive, 1,500-seat Grade II listed building

presenting a major events programme including drama, opera, comedy and popular music gigs.

Royal Liverpool Philharmonic Hall Hope Street, Liverpool L1 9BP (0151 709 3789; www.liverpoolphil.com). Art Deco building opened in 1939 to replace the original which was destroyed by fire and now home to the Royal Liverpool Philharmonic Orchestra. The hall hosts around 60 orchestral concerts a year together with drama, film and other arts.

St George's Hall St George's Place, Liverpool L1 1JJ (0151 225 6909; www.stgeorgesliverpool.co. uk). A stunning reflection of the City's prosperity in the 19th C, built in the neo-classical style to house the law courts and as a music venue. One of the first buildings to greet the visitor arriving at Liverpool Lime Street Station. Heritage Centre and Tourist Information *(open daily 10.00-17.00)* and Café *open daily 08.30-16.30 (Sun 16.00).* Hall *open to visitors 10.00-16.00.* Free.

Sefton Park Palm House Sefton Park, Liverpool L17 1AP (0151 726 2415; www.palmhouse.org.uk). An octagonal, three-tiered, Grade II listed Victorian glasshouse housing Liverpool's botanical collection. Inside and outside the palm house are beds of formal bedding and statues. Regular events which may *curtail opening. Open daily Apr-Oct 10.30-17.00 (Sun 16.00) & Nov-Mar 10.30-16.00).*

Seized Albert Dock, Liverpool L3 4AQ (0151 478 4466; www.liverpoolmuseums.org.uk). The museum tells the exciting story of smugglers and duty men, from the 1700s to the present day. Shop and café. *Open daily 10.00–17.00, last admission 16.00.* Free.

Speke Hall The Walk, Liverpool L24 1XD (0844 800 4799; www.nationaltrust.org.uk). Black and white, half-timbered house dating back to 1490 complete with priest hole, fine Jacobean plasterwork, a Great Hall, Victorian kitchen and servants' hall. Restaurant and children's play area. Charge. *Open Wed-Sun, Apr-Oct & Nov-Mar weekends Nov, Dec, Feb and Mar: Estate & Gardens 10.30-17.00; Hall 12.30-17.00 and Hall tours 10.30-12.30.*

Sudley House Mossley Hill Road, Liverpool L18 8BX (0151 478 4016; www.liverpoolmuseums. org.uk/sudley/). Take the train to either Airburth or Mossley Hill stations. Victorian interior decoration and craftsmanship together with fine examples of 18th- and 19th-C art – the art collection of a Victorian merchant in its original setting. *Open daily 10.00-17.00.* Free. Café *open Apr-Oct 11.00-16.30 (Sat-Sun 10.00) & Nov-Mar 11.00-16.00 (Sat-Sun 10.00).* Wi-Fi.

Tate Liverpool Albert Dock, Liverpool L3 4BB (0151 702 7400; www.tate.org.uk/liverpool). One of the largest galleries of contemporary and modern art outside London housed in part of the splendidly converted Grade I listed warehouses surrounding Albert Dock. Shop and Café. *Open daily 10.00-17.00.* Free. Charge for touring exhibitions

The Walker Art Gallery William Brown Street, Liverpool L3 8EL (0151 478 4199; www.liverpoolmuseums.org.uk/walker). One of Europe's foremost art galleries with outstanding collections from 1300 to the present day. *Open daily 10.00-17.00.* Shop and Café. Free.

Victoria Gallery and Museum University of Liverpool, Ashton Street, Liverpool L69 3DR (0151 794 2348; www.vgm.liverpool.ac.uk). Collection of modern and classical art with works by Epstein, Audubon and Freud. *Open Tue-Sat 10.00-17.00,* café *closes 16.00 (Sat 14.00).* Free.

Western Approaches - Liverpool War Museum 1-3 Rumford Street, Liverpool L2 8SZ (0151 227 2008; www.liverpoolwarmuseum.co.uk). Re-creation of the underground centre that orchestrated the Battle of the Atlantic during World War II. Shop. *Open Mar-Oct, Mon-Thu & Sat 10.30-16.30. Last admission 15.30.* Charge.

Williamson Tunnels Heritage Centre The Old Stableyard, Smithdown Lane, Liverpool L7 3EE (0151 709 6868; www.williamsontunnels.co.uk).

A unique labyrinth of tunnels under Edge Hill created by 19th-C philanthropist Joseph Williamson– 'The Mole of Edge Hill.' The Visitor Centre offers an insight into the life and underground world of one of Liverpool's most eccentric characters. Also 45-minute guided tours through a small section of the tunnel system. *Open Tue-Sun 10.00-17.00 (Thu-Sun in winter).* Charge.

World Museum William Brown Street, Liverpool L3 8EN (0151 478 4393; www.liverpoolmuseums. org.uk/wml). Thousands of exhibits, including an exploration of the Earth and cosmos, with themes ranging from the oceans to the stars–much very hands-on and interactive. A wide ranging and ever changing programme of events for all the family. Shop and Café. *Open daily 10.00-17.00.* Free.

Tourist Information Centres Anchor Courtyard, Albert Dock L3 4AS (0151 233 2008; www. visitliverpool.com). *Open Apr-Sep 10.00-17.30 & Oct-Mar 10.00-17.00.* Also at Platform 7 Lime Street Station, Liverpool L1 1JD *open daily 09.30-17.00.*

Liverpool Link, Pier Head, Liverpool (see page 87)

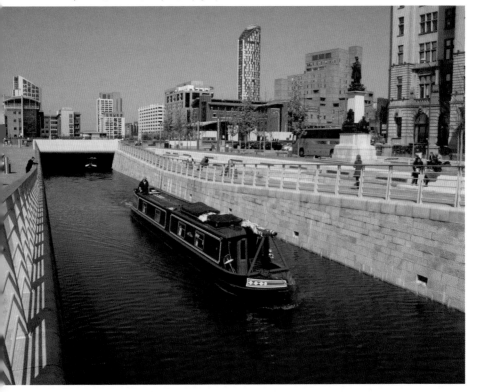

Litherland

North of Litherland the canal turns east to Aintree. Soon the first of many swing bridges is encountered; for the first few miles these bridges have to be locked to combat vandalism. All navigators should ensure that they have both a Watermate and a Handcuff key before reaching these bridges.

● **Bootle**
Merseyside. All services. Now a busy suburb of Liverpool, this settlement was described in early Victorian times as 'containing, with the township of Linacre, 808 inhabitants. The village comprises several good houses and is very much resorted to during summer for the benefit of sea-bathing.'

Maghull

Aintree marks the limit of Liverpool's outskirts and here is of course the Aintree Race Course. At the east end of the racecourse is another swing bridge; this carries a main road and traffic lights are installed, but boat crews operate the bridge themselves. The canal turns north again and emerges into open countryside, although Maghull soon interrupts this with a series of swing bridges. On the offside, between bridges 13 and 14, there is a *PO, a bank and a variety of restaurants and takeaways.*

● **Melling**
Merseyside. Tel. The village stands on an isolated hillock at a safe distance from the big city. The church is a landmark in the area; it was built in the 15th C with rock from an adjacent quarry.

● **Maghull**
Merseyside. All services. A small town astride the canal, convenient for supplies.

St Andrew's Church Damfield Lane, Maghull, Liverpool L31 6DD. Just north of bridge 12A. Though separated from the rest of the town by a dual carriageway, it is well worth a visit. It was built in the late 19th C, but its style is in imitation of that of the 13th C to accord with the tiny 700-year-old chapel, known as Old St Andrew's, which sits in its grounds. To the west of 11B Drapers Bridge, close to the railway station, there is a pub and a useful parade of shops including a late closing store.

Pubs and Restaurants

◖╳**The Bootle Arms** Rock Lane, Melling, Liverpool L31 1EN (0151 526 2886; www. bootlearmspub.co.uk). Family-friendly pub serving real ale and food *daily 12.00-22.00 (Sun 21.00).* Beer garden and children's play area. *Open 11.30.*

◖**The Hare & Hounds** 53 Liverpool Road North, Maghull, Liverpool L31 2HP (0151 526 1447; www. emberinns.co.uk/the-hare-and-hounds-maghull). Near bridge 14. Real ales and traditional bar meals are available *daily 12.00-22.00 (Sun 21.00)* in this open-plan, roadside pub. Patio seating area, children welcome and Wi-Fi. *Open 11.30.*

◖**The Frank Hornby** 38 Eastway, Maghull L31 6BR (0151 520 4010; www.jdwetherspoon.co.uk/

home/pubs/the-frank-hornby). ¼-mile east of Bridge 14A. Named after the famous inventor of Meccano and the Hornby model trains (and not totally devoid of examples of his work!) this suburban pub serves a good selection of real ales and food *all day from 08.00.* Family-friendly, patio drinking area and Wi-Fi.

◖**The Coach & Horses** 164–166 Liverpool Road North, Maghull, Liverpool L31 2HP (0151 520 0425). On A567 east of the canal between bridges 15 and 16. Snacks and bar meals are available *L and E daily* together with real ales. Children outside only. Garden and children's play area.

NAVIGATIONAL NOTES

1 Those heading towards Liverpool, who wish to continue beyond Hancock's Swing Bridge 9, should contact Canal & River Trust (0303 040 4040; enquiries. northwest@canalrivertrust.org. uk) for assisted passage into Eldonian Village, giving *at least 48hrs* notice. You can also seek advice on where and where not to moor.

2 However, an application form must be submitted for passage along the Liverpool Canal Link into Liverpool Docks. Together with booking and travel details, it can be downloaded at www. canalrivertrust.org.uk/canals-and-rivers/liverpool-canal-link) and at *least 48hrs* notice is also required. Numbers are limited so it is advisable to book early during potentially busy periods of the year.

95

16 Bell's Swing Bridge

Wks

Bell's Lane

Upper Gore Farm

re Houses

11¾m 0L
Burscough
Terminus
12¾m 0L
Schs

15 Methodist Swing Bridge

14A

14 Shaw's Swing Bridge

13 Red Lion Bridge

MAGHULL

12A Northway Bridge

Maghull Hall

12 Swing Bridge

Drapers Bridge 11B

11A

M58 Bridge

Weavers Lane

Bradshaw's Farm

MELLING

11 Melling Stone Bridge

MELLING

M 58

Wood Hall Farm

7

M 57

Brewery Lane

Brooklea

New House Farm

Waddicar

10 Holmes Swing Bridge

Perimeter Road

91

Carr Cottage

Brooklands Farm

7 Copy Bridge

7A Dunning's Bridge

STA

Old

7D Old Roan Bridge

7C

Aintree Hall Farm

Ledson's Bridge 9C

M57 Bridge

Bull Bridge

AINTREE

8 Blue Anchor Bridge

Weir

Aqueduct

P

AINTREE VILLAGE CP

Retail & Business Park

AINTREE RACE COURSE

Golf Driving Range

9 Hancock's Swing Bridge

FB

AINTREE RACE COURSE

Co Const & CP Bdy

Boro Const & Met Dist Bdy

CH

Haskayne

The canal now enters continuous open countryside, which soon establishes itself as extremely flat and intensively cultivated lowlands: indeed it is more akin to Cambridgeshire or Lincolnshire than to the rest of Lancashire. However, it is pleasant enough and the canal forms one of its more important features – a view which is borne out by the large number of people usually to be seen walking and boating upon it, as well as the hundreds of anglers enjoying their sport in this well-stocked length of canal. As if in compensation for the unexciting landscape, the traveller is offered a truly astonishing number (and variety) of pubs on or near the canal, all the way from Lydiate to Wigan. The digging of the canal is reputed to have commenced in the low cutting between bridges 24 and 25, and this clearly provided an excellent source of stone for local bridges.

● **Haskayne**
Lancs. PO box, tel. There are just two pretty houses here: the old post office and a thatched cottage opposite. The remainder of the village sprawls away from the navigation but there is no sign of a church.

FERTILE RELIEF

This was once an area of low lying marshland, much of it below sea level and, consequently, thinly populated. The original course of the River Douglas ran close by, joining the sea near Southport. At some point its course was blocked – possibly by giant sand dunes thrown up by a great storm – and it found a new, northern mouth in the Ribble estuary, leaving behind the area known today as Martin Mere. This once extended to 15 square miles but in 1787 Thomas Eccleston of Scarisbrick Hall, with the help of John Gilbert, set about draining it for agricultural use (it was Gilbert who, as agent to the Duke of Bridgewater, enlisted James Brindley's help in constructing Britain's first major canal). Once drained the mere required vast quantities of manure to raise its fertility for crop production. 'Night soil' was shipped in along the canal from the large conurbations of Liverpool and Wigan and off-loaded at a series of small wharfs, some still visible today. Part of the mere remains undrained, a haven for migrating geese.

Pubs and Restaurants

The Scotch Piper Southport Road, Lydiate, Liverpool L31 4HD (0151 526 0503). 500yds west of canal, access from bridge 19, left at A567 junction. An attractive old world, thatched pub dispensing real ales and good conversation in generous measure. No large (or small) screen TV, fruit machines or juke boxes. Dogs are most welcome but strictly no children. Garden.

The King's Arms Delf Lane, Haskayne, Ormskirk L39 7JJ (07903 408749). Just north of Haskayne Bridge 21A. Friendly pub serving a rotating range of real ales. Open fires, traditional pub games and quiz *Thu. Open 13.00.*

The Ship 6 Rosemary Lane, Haskayne, Ormskirk L39 7JP (01704 840077; www.jwlees. co.uk/locations/the-ship-inn). Canalside at Ship Bridge 22. A well-known canal pub with a garden and waterside terrace serving real ale. Excellent fresh food served in a homely, dark-beamed bar tastefully decorated with horse brasses available – including seafood, steaks and pasta – *daily 12.00-21.00 (Sun 20.00)*. Children welcome. Reputed to be the first pub on the canal, which was started in the adjacent cutting. *Regular* live music, traditional pub games garden and play area. Dog-friendly and open fires. *Open 12.00.*

The Saracen's Head 100 Summerwood Lane, Halsall, Ormskirk L39 8RH (01704 840204; www. thesaracensheadhalsall.co.uk). Canalside, at Halsall Warehouse Bridge 25. Real ales together with a wide range of food served *Mon-Sat L and E, Sun all day until 19.45.* Afternoon tea is available *14.45-16.45.* Children welcome *until 20.00*; garden with children's play area.

Halsall

Lancs. PO, tel, chemist, garage. ½ mile west of canal. There is a handsome tall 14th–15th-C church here (St Cuthbert's), with a fine spire. The choir vestry, erected in 1592, was formerly a grammar school. There is an interesting pair of pulpits/lecterns. One of them is generously illuminated by a solitary overhead window; the other, more sheltered, gives the occupant the unfortunate air of being behind bars… The chemist and PO *(open Mon & Thu 14.00-17.00)* are both to be found in the rather unlikely location of the sports pavilion, to the north east of the village.

Boatyards

Ⓑ **Fettlers Wharf Marina** Southport Road, Ormskirk L40 8HQ (01704 841924; www.fettlerswharfmarina.co.uk/html/scarisbrick_marina.html). 🚿🛁🔧D Gas, pump out, solid fuel, long- and short-term mooring, boat repairs, boat sales, showers, toilets, laundry, Wi-Fi. Tearoom *open daily from 09.00.*

Ⓑ **Red Lion Caravan Centre** Scarisbrick Bridge, Southport Road, Ormskirk L40 8HQ (01704 840032; www.rlcaravans.co.uk). 🔧D E Gas, solid fuel, narrowboat hire, large selection of spares and parts for caravans, many of which are 'boat compatible'.

Burscough

On now past a massive caravan site on one side and attractive woods containing the private Scarisbrick Hall on the other; then out again into the open flatlands. An attractively produced information board, at the north end of bridge 27A, offers a fascinating insight into the history of the parish and the past habitation of the hall. The Southport–Manchester line converges from the north west; it runs near the canal all the way into Wigan, and has some wonderfully remote stations. A flurry of swing bridges brings the canal into Burscough; just beyond is the junction with the Rufford Branch.

● **Burscough**

Lancs. PO, tel, stores, chemist, bank, hardware, tool hire, fish & chips, takeaways, off-licence, library, garage, stations. Formerly a canal village and a staging post on the one-time Wigan–Liverpool 'packet boat' run, this place attaches more significance nowadays to the benefits of road and rail transport. It still boasts two stations (one is on the Preston–Liverpool line) and suffers from heavy through traffic. A very convenient place for taking on provisions. Recent developments around the old wharf have added a range of amenities and generally brought an area of redundant buildings back to life – an initiative that should be applauded. They include craft and food emporiums, an arts centre and a music school. There is a useful cycle shop just north of Bridge 32A – Jack Parker Cycles 62–64 Liverpool Road North, Burscough L40 4BY (01704 892442; www.jackparkercyclesburscough. co.uk) *open Mon-Sat 09.00-17.30.*

Boatyards

Ⓑ**Scarsbrick Marina** Southport Road, Scarsbrick L40 9RH (01704 841924; www.fettlerswharfmarina. co.uk/html/scarsbrick_marina.html). 🛉🛒🛢D Pump out, gas, long- and short-term mooring, toilets, showers, laundry, slipway, solid fuel, bottom blacking, Wi-Fi. Tearoom open *daily 09.00.*
Ⓑ**Lathom Marina** The Workshop, Crabtree Lane, Burscough, Ormskirk L40 0RW (01704 894782). Winter storage, slipway, chandlery, boat and engine sales and repairs, salvage, canopy manufacture and repairs.

Ⓑ**The Burscough Boat Trading Ltd** Unit 5, Osprey Place, Guys Industrial Estate North, Burscough L40 8TG (01704 891675/897762; www. burscoughboats.com). Boat building and fitting out, self-drive boat hire and a variety of cruises from Bridge 32A.

NAVIGATIONAL NOTES

You will need a Watermate key, and a windlass, to open bridge 32.

Pubs and Restaurants

✗♀**The Blue Elephant** Southport Road, Scarisbrick L40 8HQ (01704 841222). Near Scarisbrick Bridge 27A. Formerly the Red Lion, now turned into a good, reasonably priced Indian restaurant.

🍺✗**Heatons Bridge Inn** Heatons Bridge Road, Scarisbrick L40 8JG (01704 840549). Friendly unspoilt canalside pub, at bridge 28. Real ales together with inexpensive, traditional pub food served *L and E*. Children welcome (not in bar area); dogs welcome outside restaurant space. Garden and Moorings. Open fires. Traditional pub games and Wi-Fi. *Closed Mon & Tue.*

🍺✗**The Martin Inn** Martin Lane, Burscough L40 0RT (01704 892095). 200yds north of bridge 29. Restaurant and inn attracting a wide-ranging clientele and serving real ale and an à la carte menu *L and E*. Children and dogs welcome. Patio seating.

🍺✗**The Farmers Arms** 36 New Lane, Burscough L40 8JA (01704 896021; www. farmersarmsburscough.co.uk). Canalside, by bridge 31. A bright, friendly pub of great character with an open fire, serving real ale. Full à la carte menu together with a wide and interesting range of bar food *L and E daily*, served in nicely furnished surroundings. Child- and dog-friendly. Open fires, large-screen TV, traditional pub games and Wi-Fi. Moorings and quiz *Wed*.

🍺**The Slipway** 48 Crab Tree Lane, Burscough L40 0RN (01704 897767). Attractive canalside setting (beside bridge 32) for this pub serving real ales and food *daily 12.00-20.00*. Family-friendly, a large garden, traditional pub games and Wi-Fi. *Open 11.00.*

✗**The Ponderosa Café** 3 Mart Lane Burscough L40 0SD (07968 688156). Unpretentious and inexpensive café serving breakfasts, snacks, tea, coffee and sandwiches. *Open Mon-Fri 07.00-13.00 & Sat 08.00-12.00.*

✗**Infusions Café** 4 Orrell Lane, Burscough L40 0SQ (01704 893356; www.infusionscoffeeburscough. co.uk). Family-run coffee shop serving a tasty range of paninis, jacket potatoes, sandwiches, wraps, cakes, coffees, teas, smoothies and milk shakes. *Open Mon-Fri 08.30-16.30; Sat 09.00-16.00 & Sun 10.00-14.00.*

✗♀**The Blue Mallard** Unit 14 Burscough Wharf, Liverpool Road North, Burscough (01704 893954; www.thebluemallard.co.uk). Spacious, light, airy restaurant offering relaxed, canalside dining *Mon-Sat L and E (not Mon E) & Sun 12.00-20.00*. Reasonably priced, appetising food – a mix of regional and traditional dishes – served by friendly staff. Visit website for details of special evenings.

✗♀**The Sinners Club** Burscough Wharf, Liverpool Road North, Burscough L40 5RZ (01704 891756; www.thesinnersclub.co.uk). Highly regarded, family-run establishment serving an American (ribs, fries and burgers – to name but a few dishes) menu from *12.00 'til late*. Friendly staff, cool blues and mellow rock. Food *available until 21.30*.

🍺**The Bridge** 73 Liverpool Road North, Burscough L40 0SA (01704 894172). Traditional village pub serving real ale and food *L and E*. Children welcome and outside drinking area. Takeaway service.

🍺✗**The Hop Vine** Liverpool Road North, Burscough L40 4BY (01704 893799; www. thehopvine.co.uk). Between Bridge 32A and the railway station. Popular brew-pub serving its own real ales and guests, together with appetising food *Mon-Sat L and E and all day Sun*. Children welcome, outside seating area and open fires. *Open 10.30.*

Parbold and Rufford

The Rufford Branch leaves the Leeds & Liverpool main line just east of Burscough, through an imposing arched bridge dated 1816. A canal settlement, now a conservation area, surrounds the top lock and the roomy dry dock here (also *showers* and the usual *facilities*). The locks come thick and fast to begin with, as the canal falls through the fertile and gently sloping farmland towards the distant Ribble estuary and a connection with the Lancaster Canal. The country is generally quiet, flat and unspectacular. At times the busy A59 intrudes noisily. There is a useful *farm shop* (01704 892599) on this road just west of Bridge 5A. East of the junction with the Rufford Branch, the canal meanders through the flat countryside to the village of Parbold with its ancient sail-less windmill. Here the canal crosses the River Douglas and then joins the Douglas Valley, a pretty, narrow wooded valley which the canal shares with the railway. Appley Lock is reached: there are two locks alongside, now semi-derelict and therefore only the lock on the main line is in operation. The shallower locks were once used as a navigable sidepond for boats passing in opposite directions. **As with all subsequent locks, the gates should be closed and the paddles lowered and padlocked after use to combat vandalism and wastage of water.**

NAVIGATIONAL NOTES

You will need a Watermate key to open bridges 33 and 36 and a windlass and Watermate key to operate Lock 1 and Bridge 1 on the Rufford Branch.

● **Parbold**

Lancs. PO, tel, stores, chemist, bank, hardware, delicatessen, takeaways, fish & chips, greengrocer, off-licence, library, garage, station. Parbold is prettiest near the canal bridge, where the brick tower of the old windmill is complemented by an equally attractive pub. Unfortunately the rest of the village is being engulfed by acres of new housing. Local landmarks are the tall spires of Parbold's two churches, and Ashurst's Beacon high on a hill to the south. The latter was built in 1798 by Sir William Ashurst in anticipation of an invasion by the French. The beacon was intended as a local warning sign.

● **Douglas Navigation**

The little River Douglas, or Asland, was made navigable in the first half of the 17th C, well before the great spate of canal construction. It provided the Wigan coalfield with a useful outlet to the tidal River Ribble, from which the cargoes could be shipped over to Preston or along the coast. When the Leeds & Liverpool Canal was built, the old river navigation became superfluous. The new company constructed their own branch to the Ribble estuary (the Rufford Branch). Between Parbold and Gathurst it is possible to find many traces of the old navigation, including several locks.

Pubs and Restaurants

🍺**The Ship Inn** 4 Wheat Lane, Lathom L40 4BX (01704 893117; www.shipatlathom.co.uk). Near second lock down, on Rufford Branch. An old canal pub formerly known as the 'Blood Tub' – black puddings were once made here, and a bucket of pig's blood could be exchanged for a pint of beer. Busy, welcoming, comfortable with real ales and excellent food served *daily 12.00-21.00 (Sun 20.00)*. Family-friendly, garden, open fires and Wi-Fi.
🍺**The Ring O'Bells** Ring O'Bells Lane, Lathom L40 5TE (01704 893157; www.ainscoughs. co.uk/The-Ring-O-Bells/welcome-to-the-ringo-bells.html). Canalside at bridge 34. Tastefully modernised country pub serving an interesting variety of bar meals *daily Mon-Fri L and E and all day Sat-Sun* along with real ales. Canalside seating, real fires, dog- and family-friendly and traditional pub games. *Open 11.00 Mon-Fri and 10.00 Sat-Sun.*
✗**Yours is the Earth** 2 Mill Lane, Parbold WN8 7NW (01257 462999; www.yoursistheearth. co.uk). Canalside, bridge 37. Traditional chintzy tearoom serving coffee, lunch and tea. Tasty ice creams. All food home-made including soups and cakes. *Open Mon-Sat 10.00-17.00 (Sat 10.30) & Sun 10.30-16.30.*
🍺**The Windmill Hotel** 3 Mill Lane, Parbold WN8 7NW (01257 462935; www.thewindmillatparbold. co.uk). Beside bridge 37. Old village local dispensing real ale, and an imaginative selection of traditional, home-cooked food *Mon-Sat L and E & Sun all day*. Children welcome *until 20.00*. A huge collection of brassware decorates the pub, and there is outside seating. *Open 12.00.*
🍺**The Railway** 1 Station Road, Parbold WN8 7NU (01257 462917; www.therailwayparbold.co.uk). Friendly, welcoming pub, serving real ales together with pies, muffins and coffees. Quiz *Tue*. Outside seating, dog-, boater- and rambler-friendly. *Open Mon-Thu 16.00 & Fri-Sun all day.*
🍺✗**The Stocks Tavern** 16 Alder Lane, Parbold WN8 7NN (01257 462874; www.thestockstavern. co.uk). South of bridge 37. Fine traditional country pub, dating from 1810 and serving Spanish and English menu serving food *Mon-Fri L and E & Sat-Sun all day (Sun breakfast from 10.00)*. Sports TV, open fires, beer garden and family-friendly.
🍺✗**The Wayfarer** 1-3 Alder Lane, Parbold WN8 7NL (01257 464600; www.wayfarerparbold.co.uk). South of bridge 37. Dating back to before 1668 this cosy pub-cum-restaurant serves real ale and food *Mon-Thu L and E & Fri-Sun all day*. Open fires and a garden. *Open 12.00.*
🍺**The Boathouse** Mill Lane Appley Bridge WN6 9DA (01257 252057; www. appleybridgeboathouse.com). East of Bridge 42. Newly refurbished pub offering a range real ales and excellent food *Mon-Sat L and E & Sun 11.00-19.00*. Large garden and moorings. Family- and dog-friendly. Wi-Fi. *Open 11.00.*
🍺**The Wheatsheaf** 287 Miles Lane, Appley Bridge WN6 9DQ (01257 252299). Village pub serving real ales, real cider and bar snacks. Quiz *Tue*. Family-friendly, garden, traditional pub games and Wi-Fi. *Open Mon-Fri 15.00 (Fri 14.00) & Sat-Sun 12.00.*

PARBOLD

A5209

Sch

Parbold Hill
Parbold Beacon

38 Alder Lane Bridge

Towing Path

Wood Lane

Delf House Wood

Chapel House 39 Bridge · FB

Gillibrand House

FB

40 Gillibrand Bridge

Leeds & Liverpool Canal

41 Hand Lane Bridge

ngton's Farm

Blackbird's Farm

Prior's Wood Farm

Fish Farm

91 Appley Locks 12' 0"

APPLEY BRIDGE

East Quarry

Prior's Wood Hall

Deep Lock

Appley Bridge Station

STA

102

Tarleton

A line of trees and the spire of Rufford church are followed by the beautiful Rufford Old Hall, on the west bank. Then the waterway leads back out into open, flat and fairly featureless countryside, with the River Douglas never far away but initially out of sight. Beside Spark Bridge 8A there are *facilities including a pump out, showers and a toilet.* At Sollom there used to be a lock, but now it is no more. This is where the canal turns into the old course of the River Douglas, and it twists and turns as though to prove it. The 'new' course of the Douglas (which was once navigable from the sea right up to Wigan) comes alongside the canal at the busy road bridge near Bank Hall, a house hidden by trees. From here it is only a short distance to the final swing bridge and Tarleton Lock, where the canal connects with the tidal River Douglas – which in turn flows into the River Ribble near Preston forming the newly opened Ribble Link with the Lancaster Canal.

NAVIGATIONAL NOTES

1   Navigators entering the Rufford Branch canal from the sea should remember that they will need a padlock key – as well as a windlass – to open the locks up the branch. Both available from James Mayor's boatyard.

2   Those who wish to navigate the Ribble Link should visit www.canalrivertrust.org.uk/canals-and-rivers/ribble-link to download a variety of information including a Skippers Guide, Booking form and general Guidance Notes. These are also obtainable by telephoning 0303 040 4040. *Passage can be booked up some time ahead, for this popular waterway, so advanced planning is necessary. Passage is free to CRT long term licence holders. Operating times are dictated by tides in the Ribble estuary, but a journey can be made Easter–Oct during daylight hours, Nov–Easter on request.* The staircase and sea lock are manned, and the link will operate one way each day. There is no mooring on the Link. As the River Ribble is tidal, boats should carry, *as a minimum*: anchor, chain and warp, VHF radio or mobile phone, lifejackets for all on board, fire fighting equipment, coastal flares. Your engine must be sufficiently powerful to cope with tidal conditions, and be sure to check that your boat insurance covers tidal waters.

3   If you need help or advice while on the River Ribble, call Preston Riversway Control on VHF channel 16 (working on channel 14), or telephone 01772 726871.

4   If you wish to visit Preston Docks, contact Preston Riversway Control on 01772 726871.

5   *At least 24hrs* notice of a booking cancellation must be given to CRT or a **fee** will be charged.

● **Rufford**
Lancs. PO box, tel, chemist, stores, garage, station. The church is a small Italianate Victorian building containing many monuments to the Heskeths who owned Rufford Hall for several centuries; obviously a prolific family, judging by one large sculpture depicting a brood of 11 children, dated c.1458. The family now resides in Northamptonshire. *Gas and coal* are available in the garage where there is a very small *stores*.
Rufford Old Hall NT 200 Liverpool Road, Rufford L40 1SG (01704 821254; www.nationaltrust.org. uk). On the west bank of the canal. A medieval timber-framed mansion with Jacobean extensions given to the National Trust in 1936. The interior is magnificently decorated and furnished in period style, especially the great hall with its hammerbeam roof and 15th-C intricately carved

movable screen – one of the few still intact in England. The Hall also houses a folk museum and an exhibition. Gardens and tearoom. *House open daily mid Mar–Oct 11.00– 17.00 (except Thu and Fri). Gardens as per house.* Charge.
Note: although the Hall is beside the waterway, it is not possible to enter the grounds directly from the canal. Navigators should therefore tie up near bridge 8, walk up to the village and turn left at the main road. The entrance is a few hundred yards along the wall on the left.

● **Tarleton**
Lancs. PO, tel, stores, bank, butcher, baker, chemist, delicatessen, hardware, takeaways, off-licence, fish & chips, library, garage. A large village luckily avoided by the A59 road. There are some useful shops, and a good takeaway pizzeria opposite the Cock & Bottle.

Pubs and Restaurants

🍺✕ **The Rufford Arms** 380 Liverpool Road, Rufford L40 1SQ (01704 822040; www.ruffordarms.com). Immediately west of bridge 8A. Restaurant with a bar open to diners serving reasonably priced food. Children welcome. *Open L and E and all day Sat and Sun.* Private hotel accommodation – bookings via the website. Wi-Fi.

🍺 **The Hesketh Arms** 81 Liverpool Road, Rufford L40 1SB (01704 821009). In the centre of the village, majoring on beers from local microbreweries, this spacious hostelry serves real ale and food *throughout the day.* Beer garden, family-friendly and quiz *Tue. Open 12.00.*

🍺✕ **The Cock & Bottle** 70 Church Road, Tarleton PR4 6UP (01772 812518; www.thwaitespubs.co.uk/ the-cock-and-bottle-tarleton). West of bridge 12. Village-centre pub dispensing real ale. Bar snacks and meals served *daily L and E.* Garden, sports TV and *regular* live entertainment. *Open 12.00.*

✕♀ **Whittles Farm Restaurant** 94 Church Road, Tarleton PR4 6UP (01772 817435; www. whittlesfarm.com). Light bites, à la carte and table d'hôte menus, together with *Sun* specials are all within the repertoire of this welcoming restaurant, set in an upmarket shopping complex. Booking recommended. Limited *Mon* menu. *Open daily 10.00-16.30 (Sun 11.00).*

🍺 **The Village Inn** Mark Square, Tarleton PR4 6TU 01772 815959; www.villageinntarleton.co.uk). Known for its excellent food – *available Mon-Sat L and E & Sun 12.00-19.00* – served in generous portions, this modern, open-plan pub (also known as the Lord Lilford) serves real ales.

Boatyards

Ⓑ **Fettlers Wharf Marina** 20 Station Road, Rufford L40 1TB (01704 821197; www.fettlerswharfmarina.co.uk). 🛏️🛢️🧺 **D** Pump out, gas, long- and short-term mooring, toilets, showers, laundry, slipway, solid fuel, bottom blacking, Wi-Fi.

Ⓑ **St Mary's Marina** Diamond Jubilee Road, Rufford L40 1TD (01704 823697; www.stmarysmarina.co.uk). 🛏️🛢️🧺 **D** Pump out, slipway, hard standing, repairs and servicing, long- and short-term mooring, boat sales, boat painting, toilets and showers, laundrette, library service and visiting PO *Tue 10.00-15.00.* Also ✕ **The Boathouse Brasserie** open *Tue-Sun 09.30-17.00.*

Ⓑ **James Mayor** The Boatyard, Tarleton PR4 6HD (01772 812250; www. tarletonboatyard.com). 🧺 **D E** Overnight mooring, long-term mooring, winter storage, slipway up to 65 feet, 3-ton crane, boat transportation, boat and engine sales, engine repairs, showers, toilets.

Wigan and the Douglas Valley

The canal now goes through Appley Bridge and runs up the rural Douglas Valley. Passing three consecutive swing bridges, one soon reaches Dean Locks. East of the locks the valley widens out. Ell Meadow and Pagefield Locks lead the canal up towards the centre of Wigan. The Leigh Branch leaves the main line of the Leeds & Liverpool Canal in Wigan, just to the east of lock 52 and descending through two locks enters the lock-free level, that extends all the way along the Bridgewater Canal to Preston Brook and Runcorn, over 40 miles away. The famous Wigan Pier, a coal staithe, is by bridge 51 and has been rebuilt.

Wigan is an attractive town running up and down a gentle incline and offering a surprisingly large range of shops within a short walk of the waterway. There are several shopping arcades, both old and new, and all the well-known retail outlets are represented. Many of the older buildings employ a deep red, terracotta brick and the municipal buildings, particularly the town hall, speak of a past industrial prosperity. The two railway stations (one on the West Coast Mainline) and conveniently placed within 50 yards of one another, offer easy access to all parts of the country. It is advisable to use the secure moorings outside the CRT offices, below Henhurst Bridge, if stopping overnight in the town.

Pubs and Restaurants

✕♀**The Baby Elephant** 162 Gathurst Lane, Gathurst, Shevington WN6 8HZ (01257 251155; www. babarelephant.co.uk/shevington.html). Formerly the Navigation Inn, now a restaurant serving contemporary Indian cuisine and a tapas bar. *Open daily from 17.30 (Sun 13.00).*

🍺**The Crooke Hall Inn** Crooke, Standish Lower Ground, Wigan WN6 8LR (01942 204451; www. allgatesbrewery.com/our_pubs/crooke_hall). Near bridge 47. Cosy village pub, with friendly atmosphere, in the pretty Douglas Valley serving a selection of real ales. Traditional, homemade meals *Mon-Wed L and E & Thu-Sun all day.* Canalside garden and play area. Traditional pub games, real fires and sports TV. *Thu* folk and acoustic night. Tea, coffee and hot chocolate. *Open 12.00.*

🍺**The Moon Under Water** 5-7a Market Place, Wigan WN1 1PE (01942 323437; www.jdwetherspoon.co.uk/home/ pubs/the-moon-under-water-wigan). Real ale dispensed in a busy, town centre, ex-building society premises. Food available *daily from 08.00.* Children welcome, large-screen TV and Wi-Fi.

🍺**The Orwell** 4 Wallgate, Wigan WN3 4EU (01942 242456; www.rogandbucket.com/wigan_website). Large converted cotton warehouse on Wigan Pier serving real ales and food *Thu-Sun 12.00-19.00.* Canalside seating *in summer.*

🍺**The Anvil** Dorning Street, Wigan WN1 1ND (01942 239444; www.allgatesbrewery.com/our_pubs/ the_anvil). 100yds west of Wallgate railway station. Popular town-centre hostelry serving an excellent range of real ales together with real cider. Also draught and bottled continental beers. Sports TV and outside seating area – no children. *Open 11.00.*

● **Appley Bridge**
Lancs. PO, tel, stores, station. Canalside hamlet with a useful *café* in the Old Station House WN6 9AE (01257 255140).

● **Wigan**
Gt Manchester. All services. A large, heavily industrialised town whose skyline is now a mixture of industrial chimneys and towering concrete blocks of offices and flats. There is a covered market hall in the traditional mould, and an Olympic-size swimming pool.
All Saints Church 192 Atherton Road, Hindley, Wigan WN2 3XA (www.wiganparishchurch.org). A very large and impressive parish church surrounded by beautiful rose gardens. There are several fine stained-glass windows, including a charming William Morris example depicting St Christopher.
Museum of Wigan Life Library Street, Wigan WN1 1NU (01942 828128; www.wlct.org/wigan/museums-archives/mowl). Lively displays depicting everything from sport to World Wars. *Open Mon-Tue & Thu-Fri 10.00-17.00 and Sat 11.00-15.00. Free.*

Trencherfield Mill Heritage Way, Wigan WN3 4EF (01942 828128/777566; www.wlct.org/wigan/museums-archives/trencherfield). Although converted to apartments, the engine shed – home to probably the largest working steam-powered mill in Europe, installed in 1907 when the mill was constructed – has been retained. The engine is in beautifully restored condition; its operators are very knowledgeable and there is an audio-visual presentation linked to some clever lighting that shows off the engine to its best. There is also a range of working cotton spinning machinery which is used to demonstrate the processes that were carried out at this mill. This is a marvellous opportunity to get to grips with what made this area such a hub of the industrial revolution: a revolution whose successful was, to a large extent, dependant upon the presence of the Leeds and Liverpool Canal. *Open Sun 11.00* for tours and the engine is in steam *alternate Sun* – visit website for details. Charge.
Tourist Information Wigan Library, College Avenue, Wigan WN1 1NN (01942 827619; www.wlct.org). Helpful library staff will try to assist with any enquiries.

NAVIGATIONAL NOTES

1 You will need a Watermate key to open Bridge 43; however Bridges 43-45 are usually left open.
2 The locks (nos 85-1) between Wigan and Leeds are 60ft long and cannot accommodate a full-length narrowboat.
3 You will require a Canal & River Trust handcuff key.
4 CRT have a dry dock for hire in Wigan. Contact CRT North West Office (0303 040 4040); enquiries. northwest@canalrivertrust.org.uk

2 Moss Bridge

Plank Lane

The Leigh Branch passes through a landscape once spoiled by mining but now painstakingly restored as parkland – a wildlife haven. For most of the way, the canal is on an embankment, well above the level of the surrounding landscape; this is a relatively new situation and is due to severe

mining subsidence in the area. The canal has had to be built up – appropriately with pit waste – while the land on either side has sunk considerably. It continues eastwards past the Dover Lock Inn, once the site of two locks moved to Wigan as a result of the local subsidence, towards Plank Lane swing bridge (actually a lift bridge and site of another defunct lock) which is mechanically operated (*see* page 105). Past the bridge, in Leigh, the canal suddenly becomes the Bridgewater Canal (without the customary stop lock), giving access to Manchester and the Trent & Mersey via Preston Brook (*see* page 44). This navigation is owned by the Manchester Ship Canal Company: boats licensed by Canal & River Trust may use the Bridgewater without further charge for up to seven consecutive days (but not Pomona Lock into the River Irwell). There is a useful *supermarket* on the offside, immediately before the A572 Leigh Bridge 11.

● **Leigh**
Gt Manchester. All services. Once the archetypal mill town, most of the tall buildings and chimneys have now been demolished. In the market place you can see the fine Edwardian baroque town hall, built 1904-7, facing the battlemented church of St Mary. This church was originally built in 1516 but was extensively rebuilt in the late 19th C and is the burial place of Thomas Tyldesley, killed at the battle of Wigan Lane.

Pennington Flash Country Park off St Helen's Road, Leigh WN7 3PA (01942 605253; www.wlct. org). 1100-acre park centred on the flash or lake. Walks, birdwatching, sailing, fishing, golf, picnic areas and information centre. *Open daily 08.30-dusk.*
Three Sisters Recreation Area Three Sisters Road, Bryn, Ashton-in-Makerfield WN4 8DD (01942 720453; www.wlct.org). Site of the Wigan Alps: three colliery spoil tips now landscaped to provide

Pubs and Restaurants

The Dover Lock Inn Warrington Road, Abram WN2 5XX (01942 866300; www.thedoverlockinn.co.uk). Canalside at Dover Bridge on the Leigh Branch. Real ales are served together with bar meals and snacks *L and E*. Children welcome. Large garden and moorings.

The Red Brick Inn Twist Lane, Leigh WN7 4DP. A warm, comfortable boater-friendly pub offering real ales. Food available *Tue–Sun L and E until 20.00*. Children welcome away from the bar. Outside seating. Disco *Fri*, karaoke *Sat*. B&B.

The Waterside Inn Twist Lane, Leigh WN7 4DB (01942 605005; www.gkpubs.co.uk/pubs-in-leigh/waterside-inn-pub). This pub is contained within very handsome grade II listed canalside buildings, one a two-storey stone warehouse dated 1821, the other a brick warehouse dated 1894. A distinctive wooden tower adjoins. Real ale is

served, and food is available *daily 11.00-21.00*. Open fires, a garden, moorings and family-friendly. *Weekend discos 'til late*.

The White Lion 6A Leigh Road, Leigh WN7 1QL (07814 575883; www.allgatesbrewery.com/our_pubs/the-white-lion-leigh). ¼ mile north of Leigh Bridge 11. Situated opposite Leigh's historic parish church, this friendly All Gates Brewery pub serves a range of their own (and guest) real ales, real cider and bar snacks. Quiz and food *Thu*. Traditional pub games. *Open Sun-Thu 12.00 & Fri-Sat 11.00*.

The Thomas Burke 20A Leigh Road, Leigh WN7 1QR (01942 685640; www.jdwetherspoon.co.uk/home/pubs/the-thomas-burke). Named in honour of a famous local tenor – the 'Lancashire Caruso' – this striking pub serves a large range of real ales and food *all day from breakfast onwards*. Large screen TV and Wi-Fi. Children welcome and outside drinking area. *Open from 08.00*.

an international karting circuit (01942 270230), racing circuit, boating lake, picnic area and visitor centre. Telephone for details or visit their website.

Turnpike Gallery Civic Square, Leigh WN7 1EB (01942 404469; www.wlct.org). Home to major touring arts exhibitions. *Open Tue-Fri 10.00-17.00 & Sat 10.30-15.30*.

NAVIGATIONAL NOTES

Plank Lane Swing Bridge 8 is now boater operated and requires a Watermate Key. It is available for use at all times outside the periods *Mon-Fri 08.00-09.30 & 16.00-18.00*. Any difficulties contact CRT (0303 040 4040; enquiries.northwest@canalrivertrust.org.uk).

Wigan Locks

Leaving the junction with the Leigh Branch, the main line reaches the Wigan flight of 21 locks. The Kirkless Hall at the top lock offers an embellished certificate to all boaters who complete the ascent, and the nearby boater *facilities* provide both *toilets and showers*. Here is a T-junction as the canal meets what used to be the southern end of the Lancaster Canal. Turning left, the traveller is soon aware of the great height climbed as the navigation winds along a hill.

New Springs

Gt Manchester. A suburb of Wigan. Once an industrial hub with collieries and ironworks lining the canal as it struggled up the 21 locks to the summit. The acres of partially landscaped waste ground today belie the past activity of Rose Bridge Colliery (near bridge 54) and Ince Hall Coal and Cannel Company higher up (cannel is a dull coal that burns with a smoky, luminous flame). Hardest of all to imagine is the massive operation of Wigan Coal and Iron Co. who, at the turn of the century, employed 10,000 people at their works beside the top nine locks of the flight. Then one of the largest ironworks in the country, it mined 2 million tons of coal to produce 125,000 tons of iron annually. The skyline here was dominated by 10 blast furnaces, 675 coking ovens and a 339ft high chimney. It must have been an impressive sight on the night skyline, viewed from the streets of Wigan.

Haigh Hall Copperas Lane, Haigh, Wigan WN2 1PE (01942 832895; www.wlct.org). On east bank of the canal. The pre-Tudor mansion was rebuilt by its owner, the 23rd Earl of Crawford, between 1830 and 1849. The reconstruction was designed and directed by the Earl, and all the stone, timber and iron used on the job came from the estate. The Hall is now owned by Wigan Corporation, who allow the citizens to use it for private wedding receptions, etc. There is little to see in the house and it is not normally open to the public. The park and grounds around the hall are *open daily all year, except 25–26 Dec and 1 Jan* and contain much that caters for the family: there are children's amusements, gardens and woodlands, a nature trail and selection of waymarked walks, miniature railway, a model village, crazy golf course, shop and cafeteria. Entry to the park is free but there is a charge for the amusements which are *open May–Sep.* Audio trail for the blind and partially sighted using a braille map and tape player.

Stables Centre Haigh Country Park, Copperas Lane, Haigh, Wigan WN2 1PE (01942 832895). Daily art and craft workshops for groups and individuals. Hands-on creativity painting, batik, stencilling, clay, canal art for adults and children. *Available Apr–Nov 09.00–16.30. Weekends by arrangement.* Charge.

Pubs and Restaurants

🍺**The Kirkless Hall Inn** New Springs, Wigan WN2 1JW. Canalside near Wigan Top Lock. Distinctive black and white building housing spacious and comfortable bars. A wide range of excellent food is offered *L and E daily.* Dogs welcome together with children until *20.30. Regular* live music, garden, real fires and sports TV. Traditional pub games. *Open 12.00.*

🍺**The Colliers Arms** 192 Wigan Road, Wigan WN2 1DU (01942 831171). North of Springs Bridge 59A. Real ale dispensed in a charming 17th-C listed hostelry overlooking the canal. Children welcome *until 21.00.* Patio seating. Quiz *Sun.* Open *13.30 (Wed-Thu 19.30).*

🍺**The Crown Hotel** 106 Wigan Road, Aspull, Wigan WN2 1DP (0800 068 6678; www. thecrownatworthington.co.uk). South of Springs Bridge 59A. Roadside pub serving real ales and food *daily 12.00-21.30 (Sun 20.30). Regular* live music, open fires and beer garden. Quiz *Thu.* B&B.

NAVIGATIONAL NOTES

1 The locks between Wigan and Leeds (nos 85–1) are 6oft long and, therefore, cannot accommodate a full-length narrowboat.

2 The Wigan Flight is not quite the daunting prospect it once was. It is *open throughout the year (Nov-Mar 08.30-16.30).* CRT volunteers are sometimes available to assist boaters *daily 08.30--16.30).* It is possible to stop on the flight, between locks 77 and 78 where, to the east of bridge 54, there are *stores, takeaways and a PO.*

3 You will require a Canal & River Trust handcuff key.

Adlington

The canal continues to run as a 9-mile lock-free pound – known as the Lancaster Pool – along the side of the valley from which the industries surrounding Wigan can be viewed in the distance. It enjoys a pleasant and quiet isolation in this lightly wooded area. Already the navigation is well over 300ft above the sea, and the bleak hills up to the east give a hint of the Pennines that are soon to be crossed. The conspicuous tower east of Adlington stands on a hill that is over 1500ft high. Wandering northwards, beyond the village, the waterway remains hemmed in for much of the way by woodland and is undisturbed by the railway and main roads that for a while follow it closely. Soon the greenery gives way to views of Chorley's rows of rooftops across the valley. The canal crosses this valley, but shuns the town. There is a *slipway* just to the north of Cowling Bridge 75A, on the towpath side.

Pubs and Restaurants

The Bridge 11 Park Road, Adlington PR7 4HZ (01257 480507). Beside Bridge 69. Welcoming, family- and dog-friendly establishment serving real ale. Moorings, a garden and *regular* live music. Sports TV, traditional pub games and Wi-Fi. *Open Mon-Thu 14.00 & Fri-Sun 12.00.* There is a *greengrocer* further west, along Park Road.

The White Bear 5A Market Street, Adlington PR7 4HE (01257 482357). East of Bridge 69. An old roadside pub serving real ales and inexpensive bar food available *Tue-Sat L and E & Sun all day.* Dogs and children welcome, garden and play area. Open fires, sports TV, traditional pub games and Wi-Fi. B&B. *Open 12.00.*

✕ **The Marina Café** Park Road, Adlington PR7 4HZ (01257 266311; www.brothersofcharity.org.uk/What-We-Do/Social-Enterprises/The-Marina-Caf%C3%A9.aspx). East of bridge 69, beside the marina. Friendly establishment managed by the Brothers of Charity, serving hearty meals, snacks and daily specials. *Open Mon-Fri 09.00-16.00.*

The (Bottom) Spinners Arms 23 Church Street, Adlington PR7 4EX (01257 483331). One of two pubs in the village with the same name, this hostelry serves the 'Bottom Enders' of Lower Adlington – close to the canal – dispensing real ale and tasty bar meals *daily L and E.* No intrusive pub games, an open log fire, sports TV and Wi-Fi. Dog- and child-friendly. *Open 12.00.*

The (Top) Spinners Arms 105 Railway Road, Adlington PR6 9QZ (01257 481 234). Despite its quirky bar (with a sloping floor) this pub still manages to serve a full pint of real ale! Child- and dog-friendly, outdoor patio seating (on the level), sports TV and traditional pub games. Wi-Fi. *Open 16.30 (Sat-Sun 12.00).*

The Elephant & Castle 1 Bolton Road, Adlington PR6 9NH (01257 475826). Pleasant, open-plan pub serving real ales and hosting *regular* live music. Children welcome, garden and real fires. Sports TV, traditional pub games and Wi-Fi. *Open 15.00 (Sat-Sun 12.00).*

✕ **The White Horse** 32 Chorley Road, Heath Charnock PR6 9JS (01257 481766). East of bridge 71, top of Rawlinson Lane. Smart, welcoming pub serving real ale. Family-and dog-friendly, garden, sports TV and traditional pub games. *Regular* live music. *Open 16.00 (Sat-Sun 12.00).*

Boatyards

ⓑ **White Bear Marina** Park Road, Adlington PR7 4HZ (01257 481054; www.bwml.co.uk). 🚿🚽🔧D Pump out, slipway, gas, overnight mooring, long-term mooring, winter storage, laundrette, showers, toilets, solid fuel, waterway guides, café (next door). Office *open Tue-Sat until 14.30.*

ⓑ **Ellerbeck Narrowboats** Rawlinson Lane, Heath, Charnock PR7 4DE (01257 480825; www.boatstohire.co.uk). D Pump out, gas & coal, daily and evening narrowboat hire, long-term moorings, toilets, boaters bathroom and laundrette, chandlery.

ⓑ **P B Mechanical Services** Rawlinson Lane, Heath Charnock PR7 4DE (01257 474422; www.pbmechanical.co.uk). New, second hand and vintage engine sales, engine servicing, repairs and overhauls, electrical and plumbing work, chandlery.

- **Adlington**
  Gt Manchester. PO, tel, stores,
  chemist, baker, off-licence,
  takeaway, fish & chips, garage,
  station. A small industrialised
  town very useful for pubs and
  supplies – the local licensed store
  east of bridge 69 is *open late most*
  evenings and there is a park nearby.

- **Chorley**
  Lancs. All services. On the west bank
  of the canal, a busy town based on
  the manufacture of textiles and spare
  parts for commercial and public service
  vehicles. (Leyland, where the vehicles
  are built, is just a few miles away to
  the north west.) Chorley has avoided too
  much industrial grimness by maintaining
  its market town traditions and by extensive
  new housing development. Today there
  are two major markets: the Flat-Iron
  Market, dating from 1498, *held on Tue* and
  the Covered Market *held on Tue, Thu, Fri*
  and Sat. A collectors' market is also *held*
  on Mon. Sir Henry Tate, the founder of
  the Tate Gallery in London, was born in
  Chorley in 1819 and began his career here
  as a grocer's assistant.

  St Laurence's Church Church Brow,
  Chorley (01257 231360; stlaurencechorley.
  googlepages.com). Surrounded by trees in
  the centre of the town, parts of the church
  date back to the 14th C. The bones that are
  enshrined in a recess in the chancel are
  believed to have belonged to St Laurence
  and to have been brought back from
  Normandy.

  Astley Hall Museum and Art Gallery
  Astley Park, Chorley PR7 1NP (01257
  515151). At the north west end of the town
  just over a mile from Botany Bridge (78A).
  Set in 105 acres of wooded parkland beside
  an ornamental lake, the appearance of this
  Elizabethan mansion is very striking, for in
  the 17th C the existing timber framing was
  replaced by a new façade that is lacking
  in symmetry. The interior – more home
  than museum piece – is very fine,
  with splendid restoration ceilings,
  furnishings, tapestries and pottery.
  Open Apr–Oct, Sat and Sun, 12.00–
  17.00. Free.

  Tourist Information Contact
  Chorley Council on 01257
  515151; www.chorley.gov.uk.

Withnell Fold

The canal sidesteps Chorley to the east, passing instead some large and resplendent outlying textile mills. There is a *slipway* just to the north of the M61 bridge, on the off-side. Now the boater enters a most delightful stretch of waterway. The junction with the old Walton Summit Branch features a canal cottage and the bottom lock in the Johnson's Hill flight. A short but energetic spell of windlass-wielding is required here, for the seven locks are very close together. It is rewarding work, for the steep countryside yields good views, and the locks are tidily maintained and painted. Near the middle lock is an old toll house and a *telephone*, while at the top lock there is a pub, a boatyard and, together with the usual facilities, *showers, toilets and a self-operated pump out*. The canal now changes course to north east and flows along a beautifully secluded and often wooded valley at a height of over 350ft above sea level. Even the old paper mills at Withnell Fold, which once brought a glimpse of industry, have been converted into small, discreet, industrial units. There is an excellent nature reserve developed in the old filter beds and sludge lagoons opposite which, derelict for many years, gradually infilled with silt and reedswamp to provide natural plant and animal habitats.

Pubs and Restaurants

Malt 'n' Hops 50-52 Friday Street, Chorley PR6 0AH (01257 260967). Near the railway station. Guest real ales that change on a daily basis are dispensed in the congenial surroundings of this displaced antique dealer! Also real cider. Dog- and child-friendly, garden, real fires, sports TV and Wi-Fi. *Open Mon-Thu 16.30; Fri 14.00; Sat 12.30 & Sun 13.00.*

Malt House Farm Moss Lane, Whittle-Le-Woods, Chorley PR6 8AB (01257 232889; www.chefandbrewer.com). A listed farm house converted to an upmarket pub and restaurant. Open fires and exposed beams. Real ales are available together with an extensive range of home-cooked food served *daily 12.00-22.00 (Sun 21.00)*. Children welcome, dogs outside only. Large canalside garden, mooring and Wi-Fi. B&B.

The Red Lion 196 Blackburn Road, Wheelton, Chorley PR6 8EU (01254 831981). A changing selection of real ales served in a popular village pub which is open *from 12.30 (Wed-Thu 11.30)*. Dog- and family-friendly. Garden, open fires, sports TV and traditional pub games. Quiz *Wed* and curry night *Thu.*

The Red Cat 114 Blackburn Road, Whittle-Le-Woods, Chorley PR6 8LL (01257 263966; www.theredcat.co.uk). Fine English dining *Thu-Sat L and E and all day Sun from* 12.00. Booking advisable, patio.

The Top Lock Copthurst Lane, Heapey, Chorley PR6 8LS (01257 263376). Real ales served in a canalside hostelry at the top of the Johnson's Hill flight of seven locks. Well placed to slake the toiling boaters' thirst, this pub serves reasonably-priced, traditional pub food *daily 12.00-21.00*. Also real cider. Children welcome, quiz *Mon*, live music *Thu* and there is a garden. Mooring. *Open 11.00.*

The Dressers Arms 9 Briers Brow, Wheelton, Chorley PR6 8HD (01254 830041; www.dressersarms. co.uk). ¾ mile east of Bridge 82. This superb pub was totally destroyed by fire on 24th April 2014. However, it is expected to reopen by the end of the year so visit the website or telephone for details.

Wan's Cantonese Restaurant Briers Brow, Wheelton, Chorley PR6 8HD (01254 830171). Originally above the Dressers Arms (see above) so telephone for details.

The Golden Lion 398 Blackburn Road, Higher Wheelton, Chorley PR6 8HP (01254 833681; www.thwaitespubs.co.uk/the-golden-lion-hotel-chorley). A pleasant walk up the footpath south of bridge 86. Real ales in a small, welcoming main road pub. Food available *daily L and E*. Dog- and child-friendly. Garden, sports TV, open fires and traditional pub games. Wi-Fi. *Open 12.00.*

Boatyards

Ⓑ **Botany Bay Boatyard** 7 Botany Bay, Chorley PR6 9AE (07967 380464/07770 576288; www.botanybayboatyard.co.uk).Next to Bridge 78A. 🅱 Boat sales and repairs, engine sales and repairs, boat fitting out, hard standing and winter storage, bottom blacking, DIY facilities, painting and sign writing, short-term moorings, boat transport, cranage.

Ⓑ **Wheelton Boatyard** Kenyon Lane, Heapey, Chorley PR6 8EX (01254 831475/07984 617385/07767 037127; www.wheeltonboatyard.co.uk). Gas, solid fuel, chandlery, DIY facilities, Crane (30 ton), hard standing, boat sales and repairs, engine sales and repairs, hull blacking, painting and sign writing, boat fitting out (www.fortonboatfitters.co.uk).

Wheelton
Lancs. PO, tel, stores, off-licence, laundrette, garage. The village is best accessed by walking east from bridge 82.

Walton Summit Branch
The short branch used to be part of the Lancaster Canal, originally projected to run south from Preston to the Bridgewater Canal. The Lancaster Canal Company, after arranging with the Leeds & Liverpool Company to share a common course between Johnson's Hill Locks and Wigan Top Lock, was daunted by the prospect of constructing an expensive aqueduct over the River Ribble in Preston. A 'temporary' tramroad was built to connect the two lengths of canal between Preston and Walton Summit. The tramway, which opened in 1803, featured a short tunnel and a light trestle bridge over the Ribble. The tramroad was never replaced by a canal; indeed the whole line was closed by 1880. However in 2002, more than 200 years after the truncated Lancaster Canal was completed, the navigation has finally been connected into the rest of the waterways system with the opening of the Ribble Link, using the tidal rivers Douglas and Ribble. Most of the canal branch has been severed by the building of a motorway, although plenty of it still remains in an unnavigable state.

Botany Bay Village Botany Bay, Chorley PR6 9AF (01257 261220; www.botanybay.co.uk). Canalside near bridge 78A. Themed shopping centre in a converted mill together with restaurants and children's play area.

Withnell Fold
Lancs. A remarkable, small estate village, built to house workers at the canalside paper mills which are now demolished. Grouped around three sides of a spacious square, the terraced cottages present an intimately united front which is almost unnerving to the casual visitor – especially as on the fourth side of the square is an old set of wooden stocks.

Blackburn

Passing under the new M65 extension the canal curls round a steep and thickly wooded valley, crossing it on a high embankment before entering the outskirts of Blackburn. Close to bridge 95 the delightfully named suburb of Cherry Tree provides an excellent range of *shops and takeaways*. It seems to take a long time to get through this large town, as there is a flight of six locks here, raising the canal's level to a height of over 400ft above sea level, affording excellent views. Careful thought should be given to choosing a mooring site in Blackburn, especially if staying more than a few hours. There are *showers and toilets* beside Bridge 100 and a good towpath exists throughout the city.

Pubs and Restaurants

The Boatyard Inn Bolton Road, Riley Green PR5 0SP (01254 209841; www.boatyardinn.co.uk). Beside Bridge 91A. Serving real ale and food available *Mon-Fri L and E, Sat-Sun 12.00-21.00 (Sun 20.00)*. Children welcome, dogs in the Coffee Shop *(open daily 09.00)* only. Canalside terrace and mooring for customers. WiFi. Chalet B&B.

The Royal Oak Blackburn Old Road, Riley Green PR5 0SL (01254 201445; www.royaloak-rileygreen. co.uk). North of bridge 91A. An oak-beamed pub dating from 1620 which serves real ale. Meals and snacks *Mon-Fri L and E & Sat-Sun 12.00-21.00*. Dog- and child-friendly. Garden, open fires and Wi-Fi. *Open 11.30.*

The Station Hotel 391 Preston Old Rd, Blackburn BB2 5LW (01254 201643). Beside Cherry Tree railway station, Bridge 95. An excellent place to sample the full range of local brewer, Thwaites, range of real ales. Outdoor drinking area, large-screen TV and traditional pub games. *Open Mon-Thu 15.00 & Fri-Sun 11.00.*

The Navigation Inn 2 Canal Street, Mill Hill, Blackburn BB2 4DL (01254 53230; www.thwaitespubs. co.uk/navigation-inn-blackburn). Canalside at Bridge 96A. Real ales are available *from 10.00 (Sat-Sun 11.00)* from this waterside pub. Dogs welcome. Sports TV and *regular* live music.

Blakeys Café Bar King George's Hall, Northgate, Blackburn BB2 1AA (01254 503238; www.kinggeorgeshall.com/food-drink). Café serving breakfast, light lunches, snacks, coffee and the like *08.30-16.00. Last food orders 15.00. Open on show nights* for pre-performance suppers.

NAVIGATIONAL NOTES

1   Gates giving access to the towpath in Blackburn are locked at night and those providing access to a secure mooring in the town can be opened with a CRT Handcuff Key. For suitable moorings consult the lock keeper.

2   There is the usual range of services, together with *showers and toilets*, immediately above bridge 99.

3   Locks 57–52 require a Handcuff Key.

● Blackburn

Lancs. All services. Few of the Pennine towns which sprang up with the Industrial Revolution can be described as beautiful. In an attempt to rectify this, Blackburn has taken drastic steps in recent years to construct a new town centre. Nevertheless the most impressive features of the town are still the old cotton mills.

Blackburn Cathedral Cathedral Close, Blackburn BB1 5AA (01254 503090; www.blackburncathedral. com). Dating from 1820–6, the parish church was raised to cathedral status in 1926. Extensive renovations have been made inside. Very striking 13ft sculpture of 'Christ the Worker' in aluminium and black iron by John Hayward. Large churchyard.

King George's Hall Northgate, Blackburn BB2 1AA (01254 582579; www.kinggeorgeshall.com). Entertainment complex promoting a wide-ranging programme of music and theatre. Charge.

Museum & Art Gallery Museum Street, Blackburn BB1 7AJ (01254 667130; www.blackburn.gov.uk). Exhibits include natural history, pottery, early manuscripts and a large collection of English, Greek and Roman coins. In the art gallery are over 1200 beautiful Japanese prints, as well as English watercolours of the 18th C–20th C. Also incorporated is the Lewis Textile Museum: a series of period rooms demonstrating the development of the textile industry from the 18th C by means of full-size working models, including Hargreaves' Spinning Jenny. *Open Wed-Sat 12.00-16.45; closed B Hols.* Free.

Waves Water Fun Centre Nab Lane, Blackburn BB2 1LN (01254 268800; www.blackburn. gov.uk). The town's own tropical paradise. Cafeteria. Full disabled access. Technical tours by arrangement. Charge.

Witton Country Park Preston Old Road, Blackburn BB2 2TP (01254 55423; www.blackburn.gov.uk). Nearly 500 acres of magnificent parkland, including the beautiful landmark, Billinge Hill. Tree and nature trails; wayfaring course; picnic sites and children's play area. *Open Mon-Fri 06.30-21.00 & Sat-Sun 09.00-16.00. Reduced opening hours in winter.*

Tourist Information Centre Blackburn Library, Townhall Street, Blackburn BB2 1AG (01254 688040; www.visitblackburn.co.uk).Tourist and travel information, gift shop selling souvenirs, locally produced preserves, books and maps. *Open Mon-Sat 09.00-17.00 (Sat 16.00). Closed B Hols.*

Hoghton Tower Hoghton, Nr Blackburn PR5 0SH (01254 852986; www.hoghtontower.co.uk). Past the Royal Oak at bridge 91A. So enjoyable was a joint of beef devoured during a visit, that James I knighted the remains 'Sir Loin'. More recently this 16th-C fortified hilltop mansion is visited for its dungeons, doll's houses, picturesque gardens, as well as for the magnificent banqueting hall. *Open Jan-Apr 3rd Sun of month 11.00-17.00 (last tour 16.00); May-Sep, Sun-Thu 11.00-17.00 (last tour 16.00); Oct, Tue-Thu & Sun – tours at 13.30 and 14.30.* Charge.

Leeds & Liverpool Canal   Blackburn

Rishton

Of particular interest to those on the canal are the fine canopied wharves of the Depot at Eanam Wharf, now converted for business use and also incorporating a pub. The canal leaves Blackburn and embarks upon a course of twists and turns that emphasise the hilliness of the countryside. The scenery varies all the time between heavy industrial development (and its effects) and – just around a corner – green fields, farms and distant views of wild moorlands. The Calder Valley motorway (M65) follows the line of the canal to Burnley. Of interest is the fine wharf building with a large central arch at Simpson's Bridge, now in a serious state of dereliction. Beyond Church, the first of four swing bridges appears (nos. 113, 114 and 115 require a handcuff key and a windlass): they are the only ones between Wigan and Gargrave.

● **Rishton**
Lancs. PO, tel, stores, chemist, butcher, baker, takeaways, DIY shop, fish & chips, off-licence, library, garage, station. A small grey town that grew up around the cotton mills in the 19th C by courtesy of the Petre family of the Dunkenhalgh Estate, who used to be lords of the manor and are still local landowners. For more about the industrial archaeology of the Rishton area visit www.rishton.net.

● **Church**
Lancs. PO box, tel, fish & chips, garage, station. An industrial community which was originally based on calico printing, established on the canal bank by the family of the famous statesman Sir Robert Peel. The row of terraced houses is characteristic of so many of the towns in this industrial area. The parish church of St James is right on the banks of the canal; only the tower and font remain from the original 15th-C building. There are two delightful windows designed by Edward Burne Jones. To arrange a visit telephone 01254 725450. The canal is close by and there are excellent moorings at this, the central point of the Leeds and Liverpool Canal, which is depicted by a sculpture. **Dunkenhalgh Hall** Clayton-le-Moors. Standing in 16 acres of gardens and woodland, it is a beautiful Elizabethan mansion, extensively altered in the 19th C. Its name is said to be derived from a Scottish raider named Duncan, who chose to settle there. The hall is now used as a hotel.

Boatyards

Ⓑ**Altham Marine** Canal Wharf, Moorfield Close, Moorfield Industrial Estate, Altham BB5 5TX (01254 383900; www.althammarine.co.uk). Marine engineering, on-site and mobile services. Also mooring, cranage, storage, boat sales and chandlery.

Pubs and Restaurants

The Rishton Arms Station Road, Rishton BB1 4HF (01254 886396; www.thwaitespubs.co.uk/rishton-arms-rishton). Worth the walk for the friendly welcome in this comfortable local beside the railway station. A traditional pub with two rooms serving a range of ales (including a mild) from local brewer Thwaites. Dogs welcome, outside seating. Sports TV, *regular* live music and traditional pub games. *Open Mon-Thu 17.00; Fri 14.00 & Sat-Sun 12.00.*

The Walmsley Arms 51 High Street, Rishton BB1 4LD (01254 602004; www.thwaitespubs.co.uk/walmsley-arms-rishton). Welcoming pub serving real ale and food *L and E.* Child- and dog-friendly. Beer garden, Wi-Fi and *regular* live entertainment. *Open 12.00.*

✕♀**The Auberge Restaurant** 106 High Street, Rishton BB1 4LQ (01254 882343; www.aubergerestaurant.org). Housed in the old Nat West building, this restaurant offers both a table d'hôte and an à la carte menu *Tue-Sat E from 18.00 and Sun 12.00-19.00,* featuring traditional English cuisine with Continental influences. Coffee lounge.

Hapton

The navigation continues to wind eastwards along the side of what turns out to be the Calder Valley with the M65 motorway to the south. High ground rises on each side of the valley, and in the distance the summit of Pendle Hill (1831ft high) can be clearly seen when it is not obscured by cloud. This is an attractive length of canal, unspoilt by industry and greatly enhanced by the ever-changing views from the side of the hill along which the canal is cut, although the motorway is uncomfortably close throughout. Soon the distant mass of dwellings is recognisable as the suburbs of Burnley and the canal ducks through Gannow Tunnel (559yds long) to swing sharply over the M65. At Rose Grove there are *moorings* together with *a pump out, showers and toilets* with full disabled access

Pubs and Restaurants

●The Railway Inn 17 Manchester Road, Hapton, Burnley BB12 7LF (01282 773719). Traditional local's drinking pub. Pool, darts, sports TV and Wi-Fi.

●✕ The Hapton Inn Accrington Road, Hapton BB11 5QL (01282 771152). ¾ mile south of Hapton Bridge 121, past the station. Popular eatery serving real ale and food *Mon-Fri L and E and all day Sat, Sun & B Hols.* Outside seating and children welcome. *Open Mon-Thu L and E & Fri-Sun 11.30 (Sun 12.00).*

●Gannow Wharf 168-170 Gannow Lane, Burnley BB12 6QH (07855 315498). Canalside at bridge 127A. 6 constantly rotating real ales are served in this friendly, canalside pub. Children welcome until 18.00. *Occasional weekend* live music. Traditional pub games and sports TV. Secure moorings. *Open Mon-Fri 17.30 (Fri 17.00) & Sat-Sun 15.00.*

●The Dugdale Arms Dugdale Road, Burnley BB12 6DW (01282 423909/07766 101003; www.dugdalearms. co.uk). Approach from western end of Gannow Tunnel. Thwaites beers served in a large, modern suburban pub. Children allowed and good disabled access. Sports TV, beer garden and traditional pub games. Live entertainment *Sat,* Karaoke *Fri* and Quiz *Sun. Open Mon-Thu 15.00 & Fri-Sun 12.00.*

Shipley (see *page 132*)

Boatyards

Ⓑ**Knott's Bridge Moorings** 13 Water Street, Hapton BB12 7LJ
(01282 774868; 07790 534517). 🏠⚓E Pump out, overnight mooring,
long-term mooring (24/7 security), DIY facilities, engine repairs.

WALKING & CYCLING

To rejoin the canal beyond Gannow Tunnel leave the towpath and follow the subway under the
motorway. Bear round to the right under the A67 and take the path leading uphill to the right of the
Derby Hotel. Cross the road and go up the steps and then follow the straight path leading steadily
downhill to the eastern tunnel portal. The town of Accrington lies a little to the south of the waterway
but is the centre for the Hyndburn District which covers Rishton, Church and Clayton-le-Moors.
There is a beautifully produced range of walking and cycling guides to this area which can be obtained
(for the most part free) from Accrington Information Centre at the Town Hall (01254 380293; www.
hyndburn.gov.uk). *Open Mon-Fri 09.00-16.00.*

● **Hapton**
*Lancs. PO box, tel, stores, takeaway, laundrette,
station.* A small and unmistakably northern village,
with regular streets of
terraced houses.

Burnley

This is an industrial stretch where the canal was once a main artery for the town and its industries. The area around bridge 130, known as the Weavers' Triangle, has been recognised to be of great interest – fine warehouses, tall chimneys and loading bays flank the canal here. At Burnley Wharf there is a museum in the old toll house and wharf master's house. The huge Burnley Embankment carries the navigation across part of the town – called 'the straight mile' it is 3/4 mile long, but no less dramatic for that; 60ft high, it incorporates an aqueduct over a main road. The whole area of the embankment has been tidied up and the towpath opened up offering excellent access to a wealth of pedestrianised shopping, together with good *moorings*. The town is within easy reach and the attractive Thompson Park (good play area and boating lake) can be found north of the aqueduct after bridge 130H. Now the canal negotiates a landscape which alternates between open country, towns and semi-towns, with the massive distant bulk of Pendle Hill in the background. Cobbled streets of terraced houses run down to the canal and old wharves, some disused and overgrown, are under renovation for offices and housing. There is excellent *mooring* immediately south of bridge 140 on the offside, together with an attractive children's playground opposite.

● **Burnley**
Lancs. All services. A large industrial northern town, which has worked hard to improve its appearance. It was once the world centre for cotton weaving. The excellent shopping centre is only 10 minutes' walk from Finsley Gate Bridge, and if you feel like a swim, a sauna or a solarium, the Thompson Centre (01282 664444) is even closer.
Burnley Mechanics Theatre Manchester Road, Burnley BB11 1BH (01282 664400; www.burnleymechanics.co.uk). Built in 1854 and converted into a theatre in 1979, this Grade II* listed building now houses a thriving arts centre and real ale bar. *Regular* performances and events – visit the website or telephone for details.
Pendle Village Mill Hollin Bank, Brierfield BB9 5NG (01282 442424; www.pendlevillage.co.uk). Just south of Bridge 139. A mill shop selling fabrics, clothes, crafts and gifts. Tearoom – see **Pubs and Restaurants** page 121. *Open Mon-Sat 10.00-17.30 (B Hols 17.00) & Sun 10.30-16.30.*
Queen Street Mill Textile Museum Harle Syke, Burnley BB10 2HX (01282 412555; www.lancashire. gov.uk). North east of Burnley Embankment, along Eastern Avenue and Briercliffe Road from the football ground. This is Britain's only working 19th-C weaving mill: 300 looms powered by the 500hp steam engine 'Peace'. Virtually unchanged until it closed in 1982, the mill has now found a new lease of life, with some of the former employees back again to work the looms. *Mill shop and café. Open May-Sep, Tue-Sat 12.00-17.00; Oct & Apr, Tue-Fri 12.00-17.00; Nov & Mar Tue-Thu 12.00-16.00 and B Hol weekends Apr-Sep.* Charge.

Reel Cinema Hollywood Park, Manchester Road, Burnley BB11 2EJ (01282 416329; www.reelcinemas.co.uk/cinema-info-burnley.html). Multi-screen cinema not far from the canal.
Towneley Hall Museum Towneley Park, Burnley BB11 3RQ (01282 424213; www.burnley.gov.uk). On the southern outskirts of Burnley, 1¼ miles south east of the CRT yard. Set in extensive parkland with two golf courses (one 9-hole and the other 18-hole) and play area, the grandiose, battlemented house dating from the 14th C was the home of the Towneley family until 1902. It is now an art gallery and museum with rooms lavishly furnished in period style. *Open Sat-Thu 12.00-17.00.* Charge.
Weavers' Triangle Manchester Road, near town centre. The area between bridges 129B and 130B is one of the best-preserved 19th-C industrial districts in the country – there are weaving sheds with 'north light' roofs, engine houses, spinning mills and well-preserved terraces of 19th-C houses. An explanatory leaflet and town trail guide are available from: the Tourist Information Centre or the **Visitor Centre**, Burnley Wharf, 85 Manchester Road, Burnley BB11 1JZ (01282 452403; www.weaverstriangle. co.uk). *Open Easter-Sep, Sat-Tue 14.00-16.00 & Oct, Sat-Sun 14.00-16.00.* Free – donations welcome.

● **Brierfield**
Lancs. PO, tel, stores, chemist, bank, hardware, off-licence, takeaways, fish & chips, butcher, greengrocer, library, garage, station. A small industrial town merging into Burnley at one end and into Nelson at the other. The parish church of St Luke in Colne Road is a Victorian building with an unusually designed clock tower culminating in a steep pyramid roof.

Pubs and Restaurants

▮◨╳ **The Inn on the Wharf** Manchester Road, Burnley BB11 1JG (01282 459951; www.theinnonthewharf.co.uk). Beside bridge 130B. A weaver's warehouse featuring the original beams, stonework and flagstone floors now dispensing real ale. Varied menu *L and E Mon-Fri and all day Sat, Sun and B Hols*. A family pub. Canalside seating, mooring. Quiz *Mon* and Karaoke *Fri*. Takeaway service. *Open 11.00.*
▮◨ **The Mechanics Theatre** Mechanics Institute, Manchester Road, Burnley BB11 1JA (01282 664400; www.burnleymechanics.co.uk). Town centre bar, part of the local arts centre, *open Mon-Fri 12.00-16.00 & Sat 10.00-12.45.* Children and guide dogs welcome.

The Bridge Bier Huis 2 Bank Parade, Burnley BB11 1UH (01282 411304; www.thebridgebierhuis. co.uk). ¼ mile north west of Aqueduct 130G. Real ales and more than 40 foreign, bottled beers (7 on tap) are served from this town centre pub with its open-plan bar and small snug. Food is available *Wed-Sun 12.00-19.00 (Sun 17.00)* and there is a quiz *Wed*. Open fires, traditional pub games and outside drinking area. *Open Wed-Sun 12.00 (and Tue 17.00 if Burnley FC are playing at home!)*

Talbot Hotel 65 Church Street, Burnley BB11 2RS (01282 412074; www.talbotburnley.co.uk). ¼ mile south west of Godley Bridge 130H. A wide selection of real ales is available in one of the town's oldest buildings, together with live music *Fri-Sat E and Sun afternoon*. Sports TV, open fires, traditional pub games and a secure beer garden. *Open Mon-Thu 17.00, Fri 16.00 & Sat-Sun 12.00.* B&B.

The Brun Lea 31-39 Manchester Road, Burnley BB11 1HG (01282 463700; www.jdwetherspoon.co.uk/home/pubs/ the-brun-lea). ¼ mile north east of Manchester Road Bridge 130B. Busy, town centre pub serving a good range of real ales (and real cider) and food *07.00-22.00*. *Weekend* live music. Children welcome, large-screen TVs and Wi-Fi.

✕ **The Queen Victoria** Queen Victoria Road, Burnley BB10 3EF (0871 527 8174; www.premierinn.com/ en/hotel/BURQUE/burnley). North of bridge 130H. Pub and Premier Inn serving real ale. Food *available all day*. Indoor and outdoor children's play areas. Canalside seating. Moorings. B&B.

✕ **Pendle Village Mill Tearooms** Hollin Bank, Brierfield BB9 5NG (01282 442424; www.pendlevillage.co.uk). Just south of Bridge 139. Part of the Mill retail complex, this tearoom serves breakfast, full meals, 'lite bites', a children's menu, sandwiches and snacks, tea and coffee. *Open Mon-Sat 10.00-17.30 (B Hols 17.00) & Sun 10.30-16.30.*

Boatyards

ⓑ **Bank Hall Dock** Thompson Park, Colne Road, Burnley BB10 1LA (01282 788686/07702 795735/07702 795737; www.bankhalldrydock.co.uk). Fully serviced, covered dry dock, DIY, bottom blacking, boat maintenance and repairs.

ⓑ✕ **Reedley Marina** (01282 420333; www.reedleymarina.co.uk). 🚿🚽♨️DE Gas, pump out, solid fuel, visitor moorings, short- and long-term moorings, toilets, showers, laundry. Also the Kingfisher Café Bar (01282 450531). Office *open 10.00-16.00*.

ⓑ **Hapton Valley Boats** Reedley Marina, Barden Ln, Reedley, Lancashire BB12 0DX (01282 771371/07554 994701; www.canal-cruises.co.uk). Narrowboat hire, dayboat hire.

Foulridge

The navigation winds as it follows the hillside; but this ceases at Nelson, where it crosses the valley on a minor aqueduct and begins to climb the pretty Barrowford Locks, having finally seen off the motorway. Immediately to the north of Bridge 141C, on the offside, there is a *canal users recycling point*, complete with its own *mooring*. This is a refreshing stretch, in which the canal leaves the succession of industrial towns. It rises through the seven Barrowford Locks, passing Barrowford Reservoir (in which the summit level's surplus water is stored), and at the beautifully kept top lock reaches the summit level of the whole canal. Soon various feeder streams can be seen, continuously pouring vital water supplies into the navigation. Meanwhile, distant mountainous country frames beautiful old stone farms nearer at hand. Before long everything is blotted out by Foulridge Tunnel; at the other end there is an old wharf (*café, toilets and showers*) where it is possible to moor to visit the village.

WALKING & CYCLING
To rejoin the canal beyond Foulridge Tunnel follow the waymarked route along minor roads and footpaths, skirting one of the navigation's extensive water supply reservoirs. Further afield, there is a selection of walks leaflets featuring a variety of treks (from 5 to 45 miles) around Pendle Moors whilst 'Bowland by Bike' is a selection of 10 on- and off-road rides around the area. Available from TICs. National Cycle Route 68 uses this section of the towpath.

- **Nelson**
  Lancs. All services. Nelson is a conglomerate of a number of small villages that combined in the 19th C to form one industrial town. The centre has been redeveloped with a large covered shopping precinct. One of Nelson's more valuable assets is the easy access to the beautiful Moors and Forest of Pendle, behind which looms Pendle Hill.

- **Barrowford**
  Lancs. PO, tel, stores, chemist, butcher, off-licence, greengrocer, takeaways, fish & chips. There are still some attractive terraces of stone cottages in this village, which lie a short walk to the west of the locks. The Toll House, the last intact survivor from the old Marsden (Nelson) to Long Preston turnpike road, together with the 17th-C Park Hill (the birthplace of Roger Bannister, the first 'four minute miler') now houses:
  Pendle Heritage Centre Colne Road, Barrowford, Nelson BB9 6JQ (01282 677150; www.htnw.co.uk). *Open daily 10.00–17.00 (Dec-Feb 10.00–16.00 except Xmas).* Exhibition on Pendle Witches; 18th-C walled garden and woodland walk; cruck barn with animals; parlour shop and tearoom-cum-restaurant. Also Pendle Arts Gallery. *Charge.* John Wesley preached from the packhorse bridge in the 1770s; there is a fine park by the river containing traces of a mill dating from 1311.
  Tourist Information Centre – details as per Pendle Heritage Centre.

- **Foulridge**
  Lancs. PO box, tel, takeaway. Attractive around the green, where alleys festooned with washing lines give the place a homely air. In the surrounding countryside are scattered the reservoirs that feed the summit level of the canal. There is a reception centre housing a small museum in the old warehouse on the wharf.

- **Foulridge Tunnel**
  1640yds long, with no towpath, this tunnel is, not surprisingly, barred to unapproved boats. The hole in the hill sprang to fame in 1912 when a cow fell into the canal near the tunnel mouth and for some reason decided to struggle through to the other end of the tunnel. The gallant but weary swimmer was revived with alcohol at the Foulridge end. The tunnel roof drips liberally.

NAVIGATIONAL NOTES

Entrance to Foulridge Tunnel is restricted and controlled by lights. Please obey signs giving instructions.

BOAT TRIPS

M.V. Marton Emperor operates canal trips *May-Oct Sun 14.30* from Foulridge Wharf, just north of the tunnel. Also trips through the tunnel to Barrowford run on *selected Sun May-Sep 11.00* – see website. Private charters available throughout year in centrally heated boat. For further details telephone 01282 844033 or visit www.boattrips.info.co.uk.

Pubs and Restaurants

The White Bear Inn Gisburn Road, Barrowford, Nelson BB9 6EP (01282 440931; www.thewhitebearinn.co.uk). Attractive village local serving real ales and food *all day.* Children welcome. Outside seating. Quiz nights. Barrowford can be accessed via a footpath near the top of Barrowford Locks. *Open 11.00.*

Ristorante Zio Gisburn Road, Barrowford BB9 6DT (01282 601999; www.baccirestaurants. co.uk/italian_restaurant/restaurants/Zio). Friendly restaurant serving classic Italian regional dishes together with traditional Lancashire cuisine. Children welcome. *Open daily L and E.*

Bombay Lounge 117B Gisburn Road, Barrowford BB9 6EW (01282 616006). Well-respected Indian restaurant, with attentive staff, that also offers a free delivery on £10+ orders within a 5-mile radius. *Open 17.00 (Sun 14.00).*

Turners 117A Gisburn Road, Barrowford BB9 6EW (01282 619606; www.turnerwines. co.uk). Hard to pin down – this emporium is both delicatessen (majoring on cheeses) and wine merchant, whilst simultaneously performing the rôle of bistro, wine bar, tearoom and coffee shop to considerable acclaim. *Open Mon-Tue 09.00-17.00; Tue-Sat 09.00-23.00 & Sun 11.00-19.00.*

The New Inn Skipton Old Road, Foulridge, Colne BB8 7PD (01282 870913; www. thwaitespubs.co.uk/the-new-inn-foulridge). A popular village pub serving good food and real ales. Traditional home-cooking with *weekly* specials available *L and E Wed-Sun.* Children welcome *until 21.30;* dogs in snug area only. Outside seating. *Open 12.00.*

Barnoldswick

Meanwhile the navigation continues northward through this very fine countryside to Salterforth, crossing over the little 'County Brook' between bridges 149 and 150. This is one of the more remote sections of the whole canal and probably the most beautiful. There is also much canal interest, for just south of bridge 153 was the junction, now disappeared, of the Rain Hall Rock Branch, essentially a linear quarry where the limestone was loaded directly from the rock face onto the boats. Walk up the road from the bridge (east) and turn right at the top where it will come into view, straddled by a tall three-arched viaduct. A mile further along one rounds a corner and is confronted by Greenberfield Top Lock (*showers, toilet, camping and an attractive picnic area with refreshments*), which introduces the beginning of the long descent towards Leeds – the feeder from the distant Winterburn Reservoir enters the canal at the top lock. The three locks here were built in 1820 to replace the original flight (the old dry bed of the earlier route can be seen on the towpath side) and are set in beautiful uplands – for the next few miles the canal winds through scenery that is composed of countless individual hillocks, some topped by clumps of trees. Beyond are distant mountains.

Boatyards

Ⓑ**Lower Park Marina** Kelbrook Road, Barnoldswick BB18 5TB (01282 815883; www.lowerparkmarina.com). 🛠️🅳 Pump out, gas, overnight mooring, long-term mooring, day boat hire, boat sales, winter storage, cranage, DIY facilities, wet dock, solid fuel, boat repairs, chandlery, gifts, books and maps, hot drinks and fresh milk.

● **Salterforth**
Lancs. PO box, tel. A small village of narrow streets and terraced houses in an upland setting. Children will enjoy the playground north of bridge 151.

● **Barnoldswick**
Lancs. PO, tel, stores, banks, chemist, butcher, baker, hardware, takeaways, off-licence, fish & chips, garage. Set back from the canal, the mainstay of this town's existence is the Rolls Royce factory, where experimental work is done on aero engines. The centre of the town is compact and dominated by the modern Holy Trinity Church completed in 1960.
Bancroft Mill Engine Trust Gillians Lane, Barnoldswick BB8 5QU (01943 602118; www.bancroftmill.org.uk). A 600 hp steam engine and its two boilers, once powering the looms of Bancroft Mill, saved for preservation. *Regular* steaming and weaving demonstrations. Cafeteria and shop. *Open every Sat 11.00-15.30* for static viewing. Free. Visit website for details of steaming days when the engine runs *13.00-16.30* with guided tours at *12.00 & 14.00.* Charge.
Tourist Information Centre Post Office Buildings, Fernlea Avenue, Barnoldswick BB18 5DL (www.pendle.gov.uk/tourism). *Open Mon, Wed, Thu-Fri 09.00-16.00 (closed 13.00-13.30).*
Pennine Way The Pennine Way is a walking route covering 268 miles of Pennine highland from Edale in the south to Kirk Yetholm in the north. Because of the nature of the route much of the Way is rough, hard walking, but it gives a superb view from the mountains. At East Marton the Pennine Way shares the canal towpath for a short distance – you will notice that the stones here abound with fossils.

Pubs and Restaurants

🍺✕**The Anchor Inn** Salterforth Lane, Salterforth, Barnoldswick BB18 5TT (01282 813186). Canalside, at bridge 151. An historic village canalside pub serving real ales, where a second building was built on top of the first – hence where you now drink was once the bedrooms. Real ale and wide range of good, traditional pub food served *L and E and all day Sat, Sun.* Built beside the old packhorse road, the downstairs room (and now the cellar) hosts a spectacular display of stalactites. Garden. Good moorings, children's menu and outdoor play area. Traditional pub games, open fires and sports TV. Dogs welcome. *Open 12.00.*
🍺✕**The Fountain Inn** 14 Church Street, Barnoldswick BB18 5UT (01282813412; www.fountaininnbarnoldswick.com). Town-centre pub, majoring on real ale, together with real cider and appetising food *daily.* Family-friendly, open fires, and a beer garden. *Regular* live music *Thu.* B&B. *Open 12.00.*

West Marton

124
Swillber Hill
Langber Hill
Pennine Way

Marton Hall
Bale New Plantation
Bell Flat Hill
Langber
FB
Stock Bridge Hill
Stock Bridge Laithe
Town Hill
Ransa Hill
Threlsay Hill
South Field
South Field 159 Bridge
Risebrigg Hill
Turney Cliff Hill
Hayfield Hill
Castleber Hill
Dodge Carr Laithe
Old Cote
Copy Hill
Risebrigg Plantation
Shed Laithe
Risebrigg Hill
Thornton-in-Craven
Church Hill
A 6263
Greenberfield Changeline Bridge 158
Pendle
Nutter Cote Farm
Hotel
Locks 44-42 Greenberfield 3 Locks 29' 1"
42 Bottom Lock
Church Road
Thornton Hall Farm
43
Gilbeber Hill Earthwork
Reservoir
Greenberfield Bridge 156
Gilly CH
157 Greenberfield Lock Bridge
GREENBER FIELD
44 Top Lock
FB
Cemy
Skipton
Ghyll Lane
Banks Bridge
11m 15L Skipton
Wigan 52m 41L
Ghyll Fields
Loughber Hill
154A Coate's Bridge
Coates
RAINHALL
QUARRY (DIS)
Little Cut
Rain Hall Rock Branch
Hall
153 Long Ing Bridge
SWIMMING POOL
Pendle Way
MARINA
152 Cockshott Bridge
BARNOLDSWICK
High Close Hill
Bawmier
North Holme
Lescliff Hurse Hill Letcliff
Higher Park
151A Park Bridge
SALTERFORTH
Dye House Farm
151 Salterforth Bridge
Spen Farm
Sough Bridge
SALTERFORTH CP
Green Hill
Bashfield Farm
KELBROOK
Park Cl Aqueduct
LEEDS AND LIVERPOOL CANAL
Booth House Farm
Dry Hill Laithe
Heather Leigh
150 Hatters Bridge
120

WALKING & CYCLING
At bridge 158 walkers can pick up the Pendle Way, details of which are available from local TICs.

Gargrave

Around East Marton, after skirting the isolated church, the surroundings change briefly: the navigation enters a cutting, passes under a double-arched main road bridge and enters a sheltered fold housing a farm, *a pub* and some *moorings*. A steep wooded cutting leads the canal back into the rugged moorlands. There is a useful *shop* and *restaurant* at Wilkinsons Farm, together with *B&B* and *camping*, by bridge 162, which can also be reached via a lane to the side of the Cross Keys. This is another outstanding stretch, in which the navigation continues to snake extravagantly around the splendid green and humpy hills that fill the landscape. The six Bank Newton Locks lower the canal into Upper Airedale, yielding excellent views across the valley to the hills and moors beyond. The River Aire flows in from the north, accompanied by the railway line to Skipton and Leeds from Morecambe, Settle and distant Carlisle. The canal crosses the river by a substantial stone aqueduct. Meanwhile, yet more locks take the canal round Gargrave; the beauty of the area may be judged by the fact that the Yorkshire Dales National Park borders the navigation along here.

● **Gargrave**
N. Yorks. PO, tel, stores, chemist, garage, station. A very attractive and much-visited village. Holding an enviable position near the head of Airedale between the canal and the river, this place is the ideal centre for boat crews to explore the surrounding countryside. The River Aire cuts Gargrave in two, and the bridge over it forms the centre of the village. There is a charming station, and some pretty stone cottages along the green. The church is mostly Victorian, except for the tower, which was built in 1521. There is a coal and firewood merchant beside bridge 171 and the village store *stays open until late.*

Yorkshire Dales National Park Some of England's finest walking country is contained in this area of fine views, deep valleys, open moorland and rugged hills. Designated as a National Park in 1954 the Dales, covering 680 sq miles, are hardly scarred by habitation.

Pubs and Restaurants

✕🍷**Abbot's Harbour Restaurant** Sawley House, East Marton, Skipton BD23 3LP (01282 843207). Charming canalside restaurant set in a 12th-C building constructed by Cistercian monks who worked the land and provided shelter to travellers between abbeys. Traditional English home-cooked food available *daily 10.00-17.00*. Children, walkers, cyclists and boaters most welcome. Outside seating.

🚤✕**The Cross Keys Inn** East Marton, Skipton BD23 3LP (01282 844326; www.thecrosskeys.uk.com). Traditional 16th-C inn, overlooking the canal. A range of real ales is available together with a modern English menu served *Mon-Sat L and E & Sun 12.00-19.00*. Children and dogs welcome. Outside seating. Quiz *Mon*. Moorings. *Open 12.00.* Telephone nearby.

🚤✕**The Anchor Inn** Hellifield Road, Gargrave, Skipton BD23 3NB (01756 749666; www.premierinn.com/en/hotel/SKIANC/skipton-north-gargrave). By Anchor Lock. Usual Brewers Fayre pub serving food *daily 11.30-21.45 (Sun 12.00)*. Breakfast available *from 06.30 (Sat-Sun 07.00)*. Large garden with children's play area. B&B. Wi-Fi.

✕**The Dalesman** 45 High Street, Gargrave, Skipton BD23 3LX (01756 749250). 500 yards from Higherlands Lock and bridge 170. A one-room replica of a boater's cabin. Home made meals and 200 varieties of old-fashioned sweets. Dogs and children welcome. *Open Tue-Sun 09.00-16.30.*

🚤**The Mason's Arms** Marton Road, Gargrave, Skipton BD23 3NL (01756 749304; www.masonsarmsgargrave.co.uk). An attractive old local pub with a bowling green at the rear dispensing real ales and food *daily 12.00-20.30*. Also real cider. Child- and dog-friendly, garden, real fires and sports TV. Wi-Fi. B&B. Takeaway service available. *Open 12.00.*

🚤✕**The Old Swan** 20 High Street, Gargrave, Skipton BD23 3RB (01756 749232). Imposing village centre pub and restaurant serving real ales and traditional home-cooked food *daily 12.00-20.30. Winter* log fires. Children and dogs welcome; children's play area. Garden and pub games. Sports TV and Wi-Fi. B&B. *Open 12.00.*

WALKING & CYCLING

The Pennine Cycleway, which is National Cycle Route 68 and runs from Berwick-upon-Tweed to Derby, joins the waterway west of Gargrave and runs west along the towpath as far as Burnley, before heading south to meet the Rochdale Canal at Hebden Bridge.

NAVIGATIONAL NOTES

Locks 41–30 require a Handcuff Key.

Skipton

The canal now turns south east and proceeds down Airedale, a valley which contains it from here right through to Leeds. Upper Airedale is a flat, wide valley defined by tall steep hills. The countryside is open, unploughed and very inviting to walkers, especially with the moorlands stretching away over the top of the hills. In this robust landscape the navigation hugs the hillsides just above the valley floor, enjoying a lock-free pound that is 17 miles long – although the navigator's relief at the absence of locks may be tempered by the abundance of swing bridges. Entering Skipton, which is usually bristling with pleasure boats, the navigator will see the Springs Branch, a little arm packed with moored craft, that leads off past the town centre and soon finds itself in what is virtually a ravine, overlooked by the castle more than 100ft above. (Navigation is limited – see Navigational Note, see page 128.) At the junction is a boatyard: next door is a restored canal warehouse. On leaving Skipton the canal continues along the hillside down the valley of the River Aire, with the main road just beside and below the navigation. Excellent views are offered up and down this splendid valley and the surrounding countryside. The village of Bradley has an attractive waterfront and the pub is well worth the 1/4 mile uphill walk (take the first turning on the right over the lift bridge). Visitor moorings are *on the towpath side only.*

Pubs and Restaurants

There is a wide choice of pubs in Skipton. This is just a selection within reach of the canal:

Herriots Hotel Broughton Road, Skipton BD23 1RT (01756 792781; www.herriotsforleisure.co.uk). Canalside, near bridge 176. Home-made food to suit all tastes is on offer *L and E* in this bar and à la carte restaurant. Children welcome. Conservatory with open fire. Outside courtyard. B&B.

The Yorkshire Rose 10 Coach Street, Skipton BD23 1LH (01756 793884;www. yorkshireroseskipton.com). By the junction with the Springs Branch. Real ale is served in this town-centre pub, together with food *10.30-20.00 (Sun 18.00).* Breakfast and *afternoon* tea available. Children and dogs welcome. Garden, sports TV and Wi-Fi. Quiz *Thu.*

The Royal Shepherd Canal Street, Skipton BD23 1LB (01756 797507) Friendly, welcoming family-run pub (overlooking the Springs Branch) offering home-cooked food *L and E* and a selection of real ales and real cider. Dogs welcome. Garden, open fires, traditional pub games and Wi-Fi. *Open 12.00 (11.00 in summer).*

Bistro des Amis Jerry Croft, Skipton BD23 1ED (01756 797919; www.lebistrodesamis.co.uk). Everyone (including children) is made welcome in this French bistro with a modern twist, whether visiting for a special meal, a pint of real ale or just a coffee. The relaxed, homely atmosphere is highly inductive to enjoying the quality food, fine wines and the sounds of the recorded chansons, jazz or blues. Food available *Mon-Sat L and E and all day Sun. Open 10.00 (Sun 11.00).*

Bean Loved 17 Otley Street, Skipton BD23 1DY (01756 791534; www.beanloved.co.uk). Coffee bar offering wide range of coffees, homemade bread, soup and sandwiches, sit-in and takeaway. *Open Mon-Sat 07.30-17.00 (Sat 08.00) & Sun 09.00-17.00.*

The Cock & Bottle 30 Swadford Street, Skipton BD23 1RD (01756 794734; www.cockandbottle. co.uk). Exposed stone walls and beamed ceilings make this 18th-C coaching inn a congenial pub in which to enjoy a good selection of real ales. *Open from 09.00 (Sun 10.00),* serving breakfast *09.30-12.00 (Sat-Sun 10.00) and L 11.00-16.00 (Sun 12.00).* Children and dogs welcome. Quiz *Wed* and *regular* live music. Open fires, garden, traditional pub games and Wi-Fi.

The Narrow Boat 38 Victoria Street, Skipton BD23 1JE (01756 797922; www.markettowntaverns. co.uk). A lively real ale drinkers pub that pays homage to the traditional brewery and to the canal. Furnished with old pews, this hostelry dispenses at least six ever-changing cask ales and a variety of Belgian and German bottled beers, together with real cider. Food available *Mon-Fri L and E; Sat-Sun & B Hols all day (Sun until 18.00).* Outside seating; folk *Mon* and quiz *Wed.* Dogs welcome and Wi-Fi. *Open 12.00.*

The Bay Horse Kieghley Road, Snaygill, Bradley, Nr Skipton BD20 9HB (01756 797711; www. vintageinn.co.uk/thebayhorseskipton). Close to the canal, this pub serves real ale and food *all day.* Children welcome, canalside garden and mooring. *Open 12.00.*

The Slaters Arms Crag Lane, Bradley BD20 9DE (01535 632179; www.theslatersarms.co.uk). Near bridge 182A. 18th-C quality local complete with a warm welcome,inglenook fireplace and log fires in *winter.* Well kept real ales together with an appetizing range of homemade food is available *Mon-Sat L and E and Sun all day.* Children welcome *until 21.00;* dogs at any time in the tap room if food is not being served. Large garden overlooking the canal and Aire Valley. *Open 11.00.*

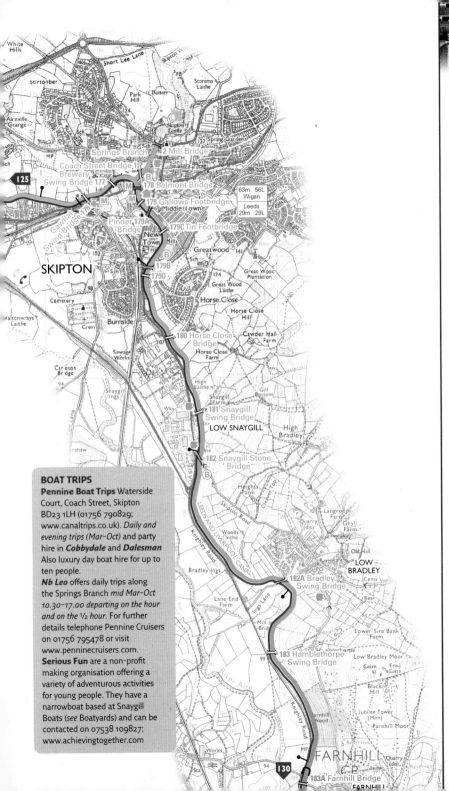

125

63m 56L
Wigan

Leeds
29m 29L

Springs Branch
2 Mill Bridge
Coach Street Bridge
Brewery
Swing Bridge 177
178 Belmont Bridge
179 Gallows Footbridge
Middletown
Pinder 179A
Bridge
179C Tin Footbridge
New
Town
SKIPTON
179B
179D
Greatwood
Great Wood
Plantation
Great Wood
Laithe
Horse Close
Burnside
180 Horse Close
Bridge
Horse Close
Farm
Cawder Hall
Farm
Snaygill
Ings
181 Snaygill
Swing Bridge
LOW SNAYGILL
High
Bradley
182 Snaygill Stone
Bridge

LEEDS AND LIVERPOOL CANAL

Keighley Road

Skipton Road

LOW
BRADLEY
182A Bradley
Swing Bridge
183 Hamblethorpe
Swing Bridge
Low Bradley Moor
Jubilee Tower
(Mon)
Farnhill Moor

River Aire
Keighley Road

FARNHILL
C.P.
130
183A Farnhill Bridge

BOAT TRIPS

Pennine Boat Trips Waterside
Court, Coach Street, Skipton
BD23 1LH (01756 790829;
www.canaltrips.co.uk). *Daily and
evening trips (Mar–Oct)* and party
hire in *Cobbydale* and *Dalesman*
Also luxury day boat hire for up to
ten people.

Nb Leo offers daily trips along
the Springs Branch *mid Mar–Oct
10.30–17.00 departing on the hour
and on the ¹/₂ hour*. For further
details telephone Pennine Cruisers
on 01756 795478 or visit
www.penninecruisers.com.
Serious Fun are a non-profit
making organisation offering a
variety of adventurous activities
for young people. They have a
narrowboat based at Snaygill
Boats (*see* Boatyards) and can be
contacted on 07538 109827;
www.achievingtogether.com

127

Springs Branch at Skipton

NAVIGATIONAL NOTES

1 Bridges 173–176, 181, 183–185 and 188–191 require a handcuff key. Bridges 177, 182A and 187 require a Watermate Key. *See* Navigational Notes on pages 136 and 139 for keys required for structures closer to Leeds.
2 Turning in the Springs Branch is restricted and craft over 35ft should be confident that they can reverse out avoiding moored craft. Craft less than 35ft may still have to reverse to find a turning area.

Boatyards

Ⓑ**Pennine Cruisers** The Boat Shop, 19 Coach Street, Skipton BD23 1LH (01756 795478; www.penninecruisers.com). At junction with Springs Branch. ⚓ D E Pump out, gas, narrowboat hire, day-hire craft, overnight mooring, long-term mooring, winter storage, dry dock, boat building, boat sales, chandlery, books, maps and gifts, engine repairs, covered wet dock, solid fuel.

Ⓑ**Snaygill Boats** Skipton Road, Bradley, Nr Skipton BD20 9HA (01756 795150; www.snaygillboats. co.uk). At bridge 182. 🛁🚿 D E Pump out, gas, narrowboat hire, overnight mooring, long-term mooring, chandlery, dry docks for narrow and wide beam boats, books, maps and gifts, engine repairs, toilet, shower.

● **Skipton**
*N. Yorks. All services (including cinema) and
excellent shops.* Skipton is probably the most
handsome town along the whole Leeds &
Liverpool Canal. It is an excellent place for visiting
from the canal, for one can moor snugly and
safely about one minute's walk away from the
centre. It still maintains its importance as a
market town, which is referred to in its name:
Saxon 'Scip-tun' means sheep-town. The wide
High Street is very attractive, lined with mostly
Georgian houses, and headed at the northern end
by the splendid castle and the well-kept graveyard
of the parish church. There is an interesting water
mill beside the Springs Branch.
Church of the Holy Trinity High Street,
Skipton BD23 1NJ (www.holytrinityskipton.org.
uk) Standing opposite the castle, it is a long
battlemented church, encircled by large lawns
and flourishing gardens. It is in Perpendicular
style dating from the 14th C, though it was
greatly renovated after suffering serious damage
during the Civil War. It has a fine oak roof and a
beautifully carved Jacobean font cover.
Craven Museum Town Hall, High Street, Skipton
BD23 3RA (01756 706407; www.cravenmuseum.
org). Outstanding local geology and archaeology
collection together with a colourful insight into
life in the Craven Dales. *Open Mon & Wed-Sat
10.00-16.00.* Free.
Cycle Hire Dave Ferguson Cycles 3 Albion Yard,
Rope Walk, Otley Street, Skipton BD23 1ED
(01756 795367; www.davefergusoncycles.com).
Spares, repairs, sales and bike hire. *Open Mon-Sat
09.30-17.30.*

● **Springs Branch**
A short (770yds) but very unusual branch that
leaves the Leeds & Liverpool Canal, passes the
centre of Skipton and soon finds itself in what is
virtually a ravine, overlooked by the castle that
towers 100ft above. The branch is navigable by
small craft, and makes an interesting diversion
by boat or foot. (The towpath continues past
the arm, into Skipton Woods.) It was built by the
Earl of Thanet, the owner of Skipton Castle, to
carry limestone away from his nearby quarry.
It was extended by 240yds in 1797 from the

water-mill bridge through the deep rock cutting,
and 120ft-chutes were constructed at the new
terminus to drop the rock into the boats from
the horse tramway that was laid from the quarry
to the castle. The quarry still flourishes, but the
canal and tramway have not been used since
1946. Trains and lorries have replaced them.
Now a picturesque backwater the Springs Branch
acted for many years as a feeder to the Leeds
& Liverpool Canal, taking water from Eller Beck,
which runs beside it.
Skipton Castle Skipton BD23 1AW (01756
792442; www.skiptoncastle.co.uk). A magnificent
Norman castle, with 17th C additions, that
dominates Skipton High Street. After a three-
year siege during the Civil War, Cromwell's
men allowed the restoration of the castle, but
ensured that the building could never again be
used as a stronghold. The six massive round
towers have survived from the 14th C and other
notable features are the 50ft-long banqueting
hall, a kitchen with roasting and baking hearths,
a dungeon and the 'Shell Room', the walls of
which are decorated with sea shells. Picnic area,
licensed tearooms and shop. *Open daily 10.00–
18.00 (16.00 Oct–Feb). Closed Sun until 12.00.*
Charge.
Tourist Information Centre Coach Street,
Skipton BD23 1LQ (01756 792809;
www.skiptononline.co.uk). *Open Mon–Sat 10.00–
17.00 and Sun 11.00–15.00.*
Skipton Woods Fine woods leading up the
little narrow valley from the Springs Branch. For
access, just keep on walking up the towpath of
the branch.
Embsay and Bolton Abbey Steam Railway
Bolton Abbey Station, Skipton BD23 6AF (01756
710614; www.embsayboltonabbeyrailway.org.uk).
Talking timetable (01756 795189). 1 mile north
of Skipton off the A59/65 bypass. Bus service
from Skipton. A 4-mile round-trip either steam
or diesel-hauled. Bookshop, café and picnic site
(at all stations). Disabled access at Bolton Abbey
Station. *Services throughout year.* Visit website or
telephone the talking timetable (01756 795189)
for details of upcoming events.

THE SETTLE-CARLISLE RAILWAY

O.S. Nock, the well-known railway writer, described this line (accessible from Skipton station) as 'the
only mountain railway in the world built for express trains'. Completed in 1876, at a cost of almost £3.5
million; 72 miles long – including 20 large viaducts, 14 tunnels and no sharp curves and, in common
with so many canal projects, some 50% over budget, it very nearly fell to the neo-Beeching axe. It
was both one of the most awesome feats of Victorian railway engineering and one of the most fiercely
contested closure battles. It is, therefore, fortunate that in the light of today's burgeoning rail freight,
common sense finally prevailed, saving the line for a rapidly growing commercial traffic – and our
wonder and enjoyment. A regular service connecting the isolated communities along the line (swelled
by tourist traffic in the summer months) together with ever-increasing pressure on the West Coast Main
Line, will undoubtedly ensure the future of this route.

Silsden

There is a fine wooded stretch north of Kildwick; then one curves sharply round the outcrop on which crouches Farnhill Hall, a mellow stone building. The intriguing village of Kildwick has some well-restored canalside buildings now used as private residences. There are good moorings here prior to quieter country: the main road and the railway cut the valley corner while the canal takes the longer route round to Silsden. Overlooking Airedale, the green hills are very steep and beautifully wooded in places. The distant rows of chimneys, factories and terraced houses across the valley comprise Keighley; most of its industrial and suburban tentacles are quickly passed by the canal, although the constant succession of little swing bridges regularly impedes a boat's progress.

This type of swing bridge is prone to intermittent stiffness due to the elements, and all require a handcuff key. There are a *PO* and *stores* south of bridge 197, and an attractive *mooring* by woods, to the east of bridge 195.

Pubs and Restaurants

The White Lion Priestbank Road, Kildwick BD20 9BH (01535 632265; www.thewhitelionkildwick.co.uk). 17th-C coaching Inn, close to the canal, serving real ales and *food Mon-Sat L and E & Sun 12.00-16.00.* Garden with views over the Aire Valley; dog- and child-friendly. Traditional pub games and Wi-Fi. *Open 12.00.*

The Robin Hood 19 Kirkgate, Silsden BD20 0AJ (01535 643397). Decorated with pictures of old Silsden, this pub serves real ales and food *daily 12.00-20.00.* Outside drinking area, open fires, pool and Wi-Fi. Dogs welcome. Disco *Sat. Open 11.00.*

The Red Lion Hotel 47 Kirkgate, Silsden BD20 0AQ (01535). Two-roomed, locals' pub serving real ales and food *Mon-Fri L and E & Sat-Sun L.* A real fire, traditional pub games and sports TV. *Open 11.00.*

The Punch Bowl Inn Bridge Road, Silsden BD20 9ND (01535 652360). Comfortable, two-roomed pub, to the west of the canal, serving real ales and food *L. Wed* live music. Beer garden, sports TV and pool. *Open 11.30.*

The King's Arms Bolton Road, Silsden BD20 0JY (01535 653216). Friendly, welcoming pub serving real ales and food *Tue-Sat 12.00-18.00 & Sun L.* Real cider or perry. Music *Tue and Thu,* quiz *wed.* Dogs and well-behaved children welcome. Beer garden, open fires and Wi-Fi. *Open 12.00.*

The Boltmaker's Arms 117 East Parade, Keighley BD21 5HX (01535 661936; www.boltmakers.com). Intimate, one-roomed pub – the de facto Timothy Taylor tap – dispensing real ales, real cider and at least 50 single malt whiskies. Dogs welcome, Children *until 20.00.* Open fires, beer garden, traditional pub games, sports TV and Wi-Fi. Live music *Tue* and quiz *Tue* (accompanied by free pie and peas). *Open 11.00.*

The Globe Inn 2 Parkwood Street, Keighley BD21 4QR (01535 610802; www.timothytaylor.co.uk/globe-inn-keighley). Well worth the walk and an excuse to view the K&WV Railway close up. This genuine, friendly local offers excellent real ale free from the distractions of any machines. Dogs welcome. Traditional pub games. *Open Mon-Fri 16.00 & Sat-Sun 12.00.*

There are plenty of other pubs in Keighley.

Boatyards

Ⓑ**Silsden Boats** Canal Wharf, Elliot Street, Silsden, nr Keighley BD20 0DE (01535 653675; www.silsdenboats.co.uk). 🚽🛢️ D Pump out, gas, narrowboat and wide-beam boat hire, slipway, books, maps and gifts, toilets.

● **Kildwick**

W. Yorks. Tel. An interesting and unusual village spilling down the hillside. The streets are extremely steep; one of them goes under the canal through a narrow skewed aqueduct. There is a *part-time PO* in the Institute on Main Street, Farnhill on the opposite side of the canal.

● **Silsden**

W. Yorks. PO, tel, stores, chemist, bank, off-licence, butcher, takeaway, garage, station nearby. A well-contained, stone-built industrial town spreading uphill from the canal. In addition to its proximity to the Yorkshire Dales National Park, it offers plenty of shops near the canal. The canalside warehouses are attractive; there is also an old corn mill dated 1677.

● **Keighley**

W. Yorks. All services. Compared with some other industrial centres in the area, Keighley is a clean and pleasant town. It boasts a large new shopping centre, much modern housing and some handsome older stone terraces. The oldest part is around the parish church of St Andrew, a large Perpendicular building whose main attraction is its shady churchyard.

Cliffe Castle Spring Gardens Lane, Keighley BD20 6LH (01535 618231; www.bradfordmuseums.org/ venues/CliffeCastle). Once the home of the Butterfield family, it has been completely restored and now houses the museum and art gallery. Local exhibits illustrate the archaeology, natural history and industrial history of the area. There are reconstructed craft workshops and a textile room. Picturesque grounds where band concerts are held. *Open Tue-Fri 10.00-16.00 & Sat-Sun 11.00-16.00. Also B Hol Mon. Free.*

Keighley & Worth Valley Railway Bradford Road, Keithley BD21 5JA (01535 645214; www.kwvr.co.uk). Privately preserved by volunteers of the Keighley & Worth Valley Railway Preservation Society, the line runs for 5 miles from the British Rail station at Keighley up to Haworth, the home of the Brontë family, and Oxenhope. British Railways closed the line in 1961, but the Society eventually succeeded in reopening it in 1968 with a regular service of steam trains. In the mornings, the service is operated by diesel railbuses, but in the afternoons magnificent steam engines puff their way along the track. In the goods yard at Haworth the Society has a splendid collection of steam engines and carriages, mostly ancient. The line was made famous by the film *The Railway Children. Open every weekend, most school holidays and throughout the summer.*

Tourist Information Centre 2/4 West Lane, Howarth BD22 8EF (01535 642329; www.haworth-village.org. uk/visitors/visiting-bronte-country/visitor-information.asp). *Open Apr-Sep 10.00-17.00 & Oct-Mar 10.00-16.00 (Wed 10.30).*

197 Stockbridge Swing Bridge
197A Granby Swing Bridge

RIDDLESDEN

EAST RIDDLESTON HALL

West Morton

Dane Hole

East Morton

Green End

Skipton		Leeds	
10¾m	0L	18¼m	29L

198 Swine Lane Bridge

198A Morton Swing Bridge

Micklethwaite

199 Micklethwaite Swing Bridge

A.B.C. Swing Footbridge (Fixed open)

STA

Five Rise Locks Swing Bridge 200
Locks 29-25
Bingley Five Rise
Locks 60' 0"

Locks 24-22
Bingley Three Rise
Locks 29' 11"

201 Three Rise Locks Swing Bridge

202 Park Bridge

BINGLEY

Dubb Bridge 203

Maud Bridge 204

Bingley and Shipley

The impressive Bingley Five-Rise staircase locks (*see* page 135) mark the end of the long level pound from Gargrave, and from here to Leeds there are no more views of a sweeping, uncluttered river valley. Just a few hundred yards south of the five locks are the three-rise staircase locks, which bring one steeply down into Bingley. The canal was moved sideways, over a distance of 400yds, in 1994 to allow the construction of a new road. Offside visitor moorings have been provided adjacent to the Damart mill. The waterway bisects this town, but one can see little of the place from the water. Leaving Bingley, trees lead to Dowley Gap and the two staircase locks. At the foot of the locks the towpath changes sides and the navigation crosses the River Aire via a massive stone aqueduct. Woods escort the canal along to the single Hirst Lock; from here one moves past the big mills at Saltaire and right through Shipley. There is a useful *fresh fruit and vegetable shop beside Bridge 197A*.

Pubs and Restaurants

🍺**the Marquis of Granby** 1 Hospital Road, Riddlesden BD20 5EP (01535 607164). At swing bridge 197A. Real ales are served at this long-established canalside pub. Children welcome *until 20.00*. Beer garden and moorings outside. *PO and stores* south of bridge 197.

🍺**The Brown Cow** Ireland Bridge, Bingley BD16 2QX (01274 564345; www.thebrowncowbingley. co.uk). ¼ mile west of bridge 202. An excellent selection of real ales and good quality home-cooked food at pub prices served *L and E Mon–Sat and Sun L*. Children and dogs welcome. Garden and ghost. Live music *weekends*. Real fires and Wi-Fi. *Open Mon–Thu L and E and Fri–Sun all day.*

🍺**The Ferrands Arms** 4 Queen Street, Bingley BD16 2JS (01274 563949; www.ferrandsarms.co.uk). 250yds south of bridge 202. Lively pub with a late night licence (*until 02.00 Fri–Sat*) dispensing real ales. Children welcome *until 20.00*. Pool and Wi-Fi. Sports TV and Karaoke Thu. *Open Mon–Fri 16.00 & Sat–Sun 12.00.*

✕**Five Rise Locks – Café & Store** 2 Beck Lane, Bingley BD16 4DS (01274 569664; www. fiveriselockscafe.co.uk). An inexpensive selection of hot and cold, freshly made sandwiches, paninis, jacket potatoes, full English breakfasts, homemade cakes, tea, coffee and a children's menu. Dogs, babies and children welcome. *Open Apr–Oct, Tue–Fri 10.00–17.00 (& Jul–Aug Mon) & Sat–Sun 09.30–17.30; Nov–Mar, Tue–Sun 10.00–16.00.*

🍺**The Fishermen's Inn** Wagon Lane, Bingley BD16 1TS (01274 511886; www. fishermansbingley.co.uk). Canalside, above Dowley Gap locks. A comfortable pub serving real ales and home-made food *daily 12.00–21.00*. Dog- and child-friendly. Patio with fine views, open fires and Wi-Fi. *Open 12.00.*

🍺✕**The Boathouse Inn** Victoria Road, Saltaire BD18 3LA (01274 585690; www.theboathouseinn. co.uk). Between river and canal at bridge 207A. Flying in the face of a century and a quarter of local tradition this is the first licensed premises in Saltaire, and it dispenses real ale. Food *all day*. Children welcome. Riverside terrace and beer garden. Try also: 🍺**The Victoria** 192 Saltaire Road, Saltaire BD18 3JF (01274 593725) and 🍺**Fanny's Ale & Cider House** 63 Saltaire Road, Saltaire BD18 3JN (01274 591419).

🍺**The Ring o' Bells** 3 Bradford Road, Shipley BD18 3PR (01274 584386). ½ mile south west of Victoria Street Bridge 207B. A traditional and homely pub, serving real ale and food *Mon–Thu L and E & Fri–Sun 12.00–16.00*. Sports TV, dog-friendly, a garden, Traditional pub games and Wi-Fi. *Occasional* live music. *Open 11.00.*

✕**The Waterside Restaurant & Bar** Wharf Street, Shipley BD17 7DW (01274 594444; www. waterside-restaurant.co.uk). Well-thought off, small and intimate candle-lit restaurant serving a modern British menu. Canalside seating *in summer. Open Tue–Fri & Sun L and Tue–Sat E.*

🍺**The Sir Norman Rae** Victoria House, Market Square, Shipley BD18 3QB (01274 535290; www. jdwetherspoon.co.uk/home/pubs/the-sir-norman-rae). Named after a local benefactor, mill owner and politician, this popular pub serves a wide range of real ale, real cider and food *08.00–22.00*. Children welcome, large-screen TV and Wi-Fi.

Bingley Five-Rise Locks

● **Baildon**
W. Yorks. All services. 1½ miles north of Shipley.
A very old industrial town huddled on a hilltop on
the edge of Baildon Moor. Stretching from Baildon
to Bingley is the Glen, a wooded valley that curves
below the heights of the moor. A splendid scenic
tramway carrying two tramcars connects the coach
road to the higher parts of Baildon Moor – *in summer
a frequent service operates, but in winter it is arranged
only to suit the needs of residents at the upper level.*

Shipley
W. Yorks. All services. A dark stone town built on a
generous scale and based on textile and engineering
industries. There are powerful- looking mills to
be seen, as well as the town hall and a suitably
battlemented Salvation Army citadel. Shipley is
lucky enough to be on the edge of Baildon Moor and
Shipley Glen. The 3-mile-long Bradford Canal used to
join the Leeds & Liverpool in Shipley, by bridge 208,

but this has all been filled in for years. There is a pub
and restaurant beside bridge 207C together with a
useful canalside supermarket between bridges 207D
and 208. There are public moorings at Ashley Lane
– near bridge 207B – with town centre shopping a
relaxed 5 minutes' walk away.

● **Saltaire**
*W. Yorks. PO, tel, stores, chemist, off-licence,
takeaways, fish & chips, butcher, garage, station.* An
estate village that owes its existence to the Utopian
dream of Sir Titus Salt, a wealthy Victorian mill
owner. He was so appalled by the working and living
conditions of his workers in Bradford that he decided
to build the ideal industrial settlement. This he did in
1850 on the banks of the canal and the River Aire –
hence the name Saltaire. He provided every amenity
including high standard housing, but no pub – for
he was a great opponent of strong drink. The village
has changed little since those days (save the recent

addition of a pub!); everything is carefully laid out and the terraced houses are attractive in an orderly sort of way. There is an Italianate church near the canal, and a large park beside the river. Admirers of David Hockney's work should visit the art gallery.

Salts Mill Saltaire BD18 3LB (01274 531163; www.saltsmill.org.uk). The 1853 Gallery showing David Hockney's work, further galleries and a local history exhibition; an inexpensive diner and a café, and three floors of shops. *Open Mon–Fri 10.00–17.30, and Sat,Sun 10.00–18.00 except Xmas.*

Tourist Information Centre Salt's Mill 2 Victoria Road, Saltaire BD18 3LA (01274 437942). *Open Apr–Sep, daily 10.00–17.00 & Oct–Mar daily 10.00–16.00.*

● **Bingley**
W. Yorks. All services. An industrial town now known nationally as a centre for thermal underwear. Standing at the south east end of the town, amidst several old cottages, is the large parish church of Holy Trinity, with its massive spire conspicuous from the canal.

Bingley Five-Rise Locks A very famous and impressive feature of the canal system built in 1774 in 'staircase' formation. They are all joined together rather than being separated by pounds of 'neutral' water. The top gates of the lowest lock are the bottom gates of the lock above, and so on. This means it is not possible to empty a lock unless the one below is itself empty. The rapid elevation thus resulting is quite daunting. The CRT Sanitary Station is housed in a handsome old stable, where towing horses were once rested.

East Riddlesden Hall Bradford Road, Keightly BD20 5EL (01535 607075; www.nationaltrust. org.uk/east-riddlesden-hall). Just south of swing bridge 197A. A 17th-C stone manor house complete with tithe barn. Fine collection of Yorkshire oak furniture, textiles, pewter, paintings and armour. The house is set in mature grounds with beech trees, ducks and a pond and the Starkie Wing provides a striking backdrop to a garden planted with lavender, flowers and a fragrant herb border. Also an orchard garden with wild flowers, bulbs, perennials and, of course, apple Blossom. Open times vary so telephone or visit the website for details. Shop, picnic area and tearoom (*open as per house except 12.00 on Sat*). Events. Charge.

NAVIGATIONAL NOTES

1 Bridges 188–196 require a Handcuff key, although Bridges 189–91 are usually left open. Bridges 197, 197A, 198A and 199 need a Watermate key. Bridge 209 needs a Watermate key and a windlass.

2 Locks 29–14 and 12–4 require a Handcuff key. Locks 13 and 2 require a Handcuff key and are security locked outside opening hours – *see* note 3. Lock 1 requires a Watermate key.

3 Opening times for Bingley Five-Rise, Bingley Three-Rise and Field Locks: *mid Mar–Oct first passage commencing 08.00 & last passage commencing 17.00 (Oct 16.00)*. They may be used only under the supervision of the lock keeper. To confirm times contact CRT 0303 040 4040; enquiries.northwest@canalrivertrust.org.uk.

4 See also Navigational Note on page 139.

Boatyards

Ⓑ**Hainsworth Boatyard** Fairfax Road, Bingley BD16 4DR (01274 565925; www. boattransporter.co.uk). 200yds above the five-rise. 🛠 Pump out, gas, overnight and long-term mooring, winter storage, slipway, chandlery, solid fuel, boat sales and repairs, engine repairs, toilets. International boat transporters. *24hr emergency call-out.*

Ⓑ**Gallows Bridge Moorings** Apperley Bridge, Bradford BD10 0UR (01274 616961; www. apperleybridgemarina.co.uk). In Shipley – just east of Gallows Footbridge 207D. Short- and long-term moorings.

Apperley Bridge

This section sees the end of the wide open moorlands that frame the scenery further upstream: from now on, industry and housing begin to feature more as one approaches the outskirts of Leeds. The navigation, however, is thankfully sequestered from these intrusions into the landscape. Leaving Shipley, the adjacent railway cuts through a 500ft-high hill in two mile-long tunnels. The canal goes all the way round this delightfully wooded hill, tenaciously following the Aire Valley. Halfway round the long curve are Field Locks. Beyond the main railway bridge is a Canal & River Trust maintenance yard at the head of Dobson Locks and housed in a former canal warehouse. There are also *showers, toilets and a pump out* here. Temporarily traversing a built-up area, the navigation emerges yet again onto a wooded hillside overlooking the still rural and charming valley that contains the River Aire.

NAVIGATIONAL NOTES

Bridge 214 needs a Watermate key. Bridges 215–219 require a Handcuff key. Bridge 215 is usually padlocked open to the canal.

● **Rodley**
W. Yorks. PO box, tel, takeaway, off-licence. Rodley has long been associated with the woollen industry with fulling mills and scribbling mills powered by the swift-flowing waters of the River Aire. It is still a useful village with two pubs, several shops and good visitor moorings.

Pubs and Restaurants

■The **Woolpack** Main Street, Esholt, Shipley BD17
7QZ (01274 809495; www.thewoolpackesholt.co.uk).
As featured in the TV series *Emmerdale*. From bridge
211 follow the footpath north west to the main
road, turn right, then take the turning to the right
signposted Esholt. Real ale together with food *daily
12.00-20.00 (Sun 18.00)* served in this well-known
pub. Children's room and garden. Quiz *Thu*.

■The **Dog & Gun** 1001 Harrogate Road, Apperley
Bridge BD10 0LT (01274 611388). Just south of
Bridge214A. Friendly local serving real ale and food
Wed-Fri E & Sat Sun 12.00-20.30. Beer garden, open
fires, sports TV and Wi-Fi. *Open Mon-Thu 16.00 &
Fri-Sun 12.00*.

■✕The **Stansfield** Apperley Lane, Apperley
Bridge BD10 0NP (0113 250
2659; www.gctaverns.
co.uk).

A beautifully beamed pub, dating from 1543, serving
real ales and food *daily 12.00-22.00*. It welcomes
children, walkers, cyclists and dog owners. Open fires
and a garden. Quiz *Sun. Open 11.00*.

■The **Railway Inn** Calverley Bridge, Rodley LS13
1NR (0113 257 6603). Beside bridge 216A. Traditional
canalside pub serving real ale and food *L and E*.
Children welcome, and dogs welcome outside.
Moorings and outside seating. *Open 11.00*.

■The **Rodley Barge** 184 Town Street, Rodley LS13
1HP (0113 257 4606; www.therodley-barge.co.uk).
Unpretentious canalside pub by bridge 217 serving
real ale and food *daily L*. All canal and towpath users
are welcome – children *until 20.00*. Canalside garden,
open fires, Wi-Fi and moorings. Quiz *Mon, Wed & Sun*.
Open 12.00.

■✕The **Owl Hotel** I Rodley Lane, Rodley LS13 1LB
(0113 255 7355). An attractive old pub serving real
ales and food *daily 12.00-21.00*. Beer garden and dogs
welcome. *Open 12.00*.

✕**Café Fraîche** 33 Rodley Lane, Leeds LS13 1LB
(0113 236 3520; www.cafefraiche.co.uk).
Open daily 08.30-16.00 (Sun 14.30), this
friendly, family-run café serves an
appetising selection of light meals,
sandwiches, wraps, paninis, salads
and specials together with an
all day breakfast. Tea and
coffee. Canal users most
welcome.

Boatyards

ⓑ**Apperley Bridge Marina**
Apperley Bridge, Bradford
BD10 0UR (01274 616961; www.
apperleybridgemarina.co.uk) 🚿🏠🔧 D Pump
out, gas, short- and long-term mooring with
24hr CCTV coverage, solid fuel, chandlery, toilets,
showers.

ⓑ**Swiftcraft** The Boathouse, Parkin Lane, Apperley
Bridge, Bradford BD10 0NF (01274 611786/07850
249449/07789 076314; www.swiftcraftboats.co.uk).
Gas, overnight mooring, long-term mooring, DIY
facilities, boat fitting out and repairs, boat sales, boat
condition surveys, BSS surveys, Gas Safe registered.

ⓑ**Rodley Boat Centre** Canal Wharf, Canal Road,
Rodley, Leeds LS13 1LP (0113 257 6132; www.
rodleyboatcentre.com). By Bridge 217. 🚿🏠🔧D E

Pump out, overnight
mooring, long-term
mooring, winter storage,
slipway, chandlery, books and
maps, marine engineers (inboard
and outboard), generators and electrics.
24hr emergency call out.

Leeds

This is a section full of contrasts; and it probably represents the most pleasant way of entering the city of Leeds. Although the area becomes more and more built up as one travels eastward, the canal remains unaffected by it, maintaining its privileged position on the wooded south side of the narrowing Aire Valley. Leaving the ruined Kirkstall Abbey on the other side of the river, the navigation passes the old Mackeson brewery, now imaginatively converted to student accommodation, and borders for a while the steeply sloping edges of an extensive park. The site of the old Kirkstall Power Station is reached, with its own private canal 'lay-by': until the mid 1960s, scores of barges used to come up to fuel this establishment every week; now both dock and power station have disappeared. Beyond, by bridge 225, is the Leeds Industrial Museum. The route of the Aire & Calder to Castleford and Wakefield is continued on page 16.

Pubs and Restaurants

The Abbey Inn 99 Pollard Lane, Newlay, Leeds LS13 1EQ (0113 258 1248). A small, friendly country pub – once used by the nearby Abbey as a morgue – but now serving real ales and excellent food *Mon-Sat 12.00-20.00 (Fri-Sat 20.30) & Sun L.* Also real cider. Children welcome, outside seating, open fires, traditional pub games and Wi-Fi. *Open 12.00.*

West End House 26 Abbey Road, Leeds LS5 3HS (0113 278 6332; www.westendleeds.co.uk). Traditional, old, stone-built hostelry close to Kirkstall Abbey, serving real ale, real cider and appetising food *Mon-Fri L and E; Sat 11.30-19.30 & Sun 12.00-8.00.* Outdoor drinking area. *Open 11.30 (Sun 12.00).*

- **Leeds**
  W. Yorks. All services. See also page 18.
  Leeds Industrial Museum Armley Mills, Canal Street, Leeds LS12 2QF (0113 263 7861; www.leeds.gov.uk/museumsandgalleries/Pages/armleymills.aspx). There have been corn and fulling mills on this site since at least 1559, with the present building dating from 1805. When built it was the most advanced in the country and it now houses a superb range of real-life exhibits demonstrating the local textile, heavy engineering, tanning and printing trades. There are working cranes, locomotives and waterwheels, and a cinema of the 1920s. *Jack* the locomotive runs on 'steaming up' days. Shop and picnic area. Disabled access. The little stone bridge over the canal here dates from around 1770. *Open Tue-Sun 10.00-17.00; Sat 13.00-17.00 & B Hols 10.00-17.00.* Charge.
  Kirkstall Abbey Kirkstall LS5 3EH (0113 230 5492; www.leeds.gov.uk/kirkstallAbbey/). The large elegant ruins of a Cistercian abbey founded in the 12th C. The remaining walls narrowly escaped demolition in the late 19th C, but are now carefully preserved, surrounded by a small, attractive park. *Open daily during daylight hours.* Free
  Abbey House Museum Abbey Walk, Kirkstall LS5 3EH (0113 230 5492; www.leeds.gov.uk/museumsandgalleries/Pages/Abbey-House-

Museum.aspx). This splendid folk museum illustrates the life and work of the people of Yorkshire during the last 300 years. As well as exhibiting toys, costumes and pottery, it houses three streets of fully furnished 19th-C shops, cottages and workshops. *Open Tue-Fri & Sun 10.00-17.00; Sat 12.00-17.00 and B Hols 10.00-17.00.* Charge.
Tourist Information Centre Leeds Railway Station, New Station Street, Leeds LS1 4DT (0113 242 5242; www.leeds. gov.uk). *Open Tue-Sat 09.00-17.30, Sun 10.00-16.00 & Mon 10.00-17.30.*

NAVIGATIONAL NOTES

In the interests of safety and water conservation Newlay, Forge and Kirkstall Locks cannot be operated outside the hours *08.15–18.00 mid-Mar-Oct* when CRT staff will be in attendance to provide assistance as required. However, please note that when travelling east the latest departure time from Newlay Top lock is *15.00* in order to arrive in Leeds Canal Basin by *18.00*. The latest departure time from Leeds, when travelling west, in order to clear Newlay Top Lock by *18.00*, is *15.00*. To confirm times and the availability of assistance contact CRT on 0303 040 4040. Uninterrupted passage between Granary Wharf and Newlay is advised.

Boatyards

ⓑ**Fallwood Marina**
Pollard Lane, Leeds LS13 1ER (0113 258 1074; www.fallwood-marina.co.uk). By bridge 221. 🚿🏠♿ Winter storage, crane, gas, paraffin, slipway, boat and engine repairs, showers, toilets. No dogs.
ⓑ**Aire Valley Marina** Redcote Lane, Kirkstall, Leeds LS4 2AL (01575 560275; www.narrowboats.org/canal-service/15/aire+valley+marina). 🏠♿E Gas, overnight mooring, long-term mooring, winter storage, slipway, DIY facilities, toilets, showers, launderette.

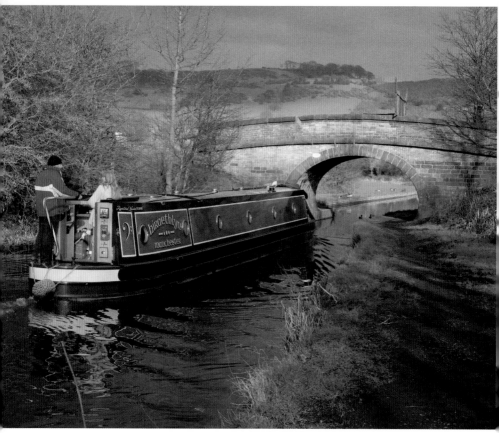

Boating at Macclesfield (see page 148)

KEEPING THINGS ON THE LEVEL

The Macclesfield Canal adheres to a mainly level course, with all the locks (aside from the stop lock at Hall Green) in a single group at Bosley. Had the visionary scheme proposed by J. F Pownall, in his work *The Projected Grand Contour Canal to Connect with Estuaries and Canals in England* (1942), come to fruition, the Macclesfield would have formed a part of his grand plan:

'Through the heart of England there runs a *natural canal line*, as I shall term it. This is a line so naturally favourable for canal construction that a canal can follow it easily for miles at a time whilst remaining throughout at the same level. The old canal surveyors saw this line. . . A canal following this contour would therefore proceed right through the country solely on one level. . . it (also) proceeds in direct reaches for long-distances at a time. . . The natural canal line creates the remarkable possibility, never before known, of having a canal go through the length of the country and serve the great industrial areas without any variation from one level.

(There) are very great advantages. The Grand Contour Canal (would be) uniformly level at 310ft above sea level to serve London, Bristol, Southampton, Birmingham, Manchester, Leeds and Newcastle. All the existing canals would be branches from it. The waterway would be large enough to accommodate coastal vessels of a fair size. The Grand Contour Canal would become the primary water distributor of the country. Along the canal there will be formed a special layer in the bed. . . in this layer pipelines for the transport of commercial liquids and gases would be embedded.

Precisely because it expresses a natural feature, the Contour Canal will lie unobtrusively on the land and will have a characteristic scenery of its own.' *Precisely*.

MACCLESFIELD CANAL

MAXIMUM DIMENSIONS

Length: 70' 0"
Beam: 7' 0"
Headroom: 7' 0"

MANAGER

0303 040 4040;
enquiries.manchesterpennine@canalrivertrust.org.uk

MILEAGE

HARDINGS WOOD JUNCTION
(Trent & Mersey Canal) *to:*
Congleton Wharf: 5¾ miles
Bosley Top Lock: 11½ miles
Macclesfield: 17 miles
Bollington: 20 miles

MARPLE JUNCTION
(Peak Forest Canal): 27¾ miles

Locks: 13

With the completion of the Trent & Mersey Canal in 1777, demand was created for an alternative canal link between the Midlands and Manchester, and a direct line through the manufacturing town of Macclesfield was an obvious choice. But it was not until 1825 that Thomas Telford was asked by promoters of the canal to survey a line linking the Peak Forest Canal and the Trent & Mersey Canal. The 28-mile line he suggested was the canal that was built, from Marple to just north of Kidsgrove, although Telford did not supervise the construction, leaving to go and build the Birmingham & Liverpool Junction Canal (now the Shropshire Union). William Crosley was the canal's engineer.

The canal, which runs along the side of a tall ridge of hills west of the Pennines, does, however, bear the distinctive hallmarks of Telford's engineering. Like the Shropshire Union, the Macclesfield is a 'cut and fill' canal, following as straight a course as possible, and featuring a many great cuttings and embankments. Apart from the stop lock at Hall Green, where a 1ft rise was insisted upon as a water preservation measure by the Trent & Mersey Canal Company – to whose Hall Green Branch the Macclesfield Canal connected at the stop lock, all the locks are grouped into one flight of 12 at Bosley. The canal is fed from nearby reservoirs, at Bosley and Sutton.

In spite of intense competition from neighbouring railways and the Trent & Mersey Canal, the Macclesfield carried a good trade for many years. Much of this was coal, along with cotton from the big mills established along its northern reaches. Following its purchase in 1846 by the Great Central Railway Company, the canal began a slow, but steady, decline. The Macclesfield Canal today is an extremely interesting cruising waterway, and forms part of the popular 100-mile Cheshire Ring canal circuit. Look out for the original, and very large, stone milestones showing distances from Hall Green stop lock (the original end of the canal) and Marple. These were removed during World War II in fear of helping invading forces. They have been lovingly restored to their former glory by the Macclesfield Canal Society.

Hardings Wood

The junction of the Macclesfield Canal with the Trent & Mersey Canal is exciting and unusual. The Macclesfield leaves the Trent & Mersey on the south side at Hardings Wood Junction, then crosses it on Poole Aqueduct after the T & M has fallen through two locks. The Macclesfield Canal then crosses Red Bull Aqueduct to begin its journey to Marple. It is thus a busy area, with canalside pubs, Canal & River Trust moorings and plenty of boats contributing to an interesting canal scene. Leaving Hardings Wood, the Macclesfield Canal passes through a stop lock in the cutting at Hall Green, to enter glorious open countryside at Kent Green. To the east, Mow Cop crowns the ridge of tall hills that stretches parallel to the navigation for miles to come. You can take a good walk to the top, on footpaths to the east from bridge 85. Beyond this point, the canal loses itself in splendid countryside for several miles as it approaches Congleton.

Boatyards

Ⓑ**David Smithsons Solid Fuel and Caravan Centre** Liverpool Road, Kidsgrove ST7 1EA (01782 787887). Near bridge 132. D Calor gas, solid fuel, caravan fittings which can be used as chandlery. Also bicycles and bicycle spares for sale.

Ⓑ**Red Bull Services** Red Bull Basin, Congleton Road South, Church Lawton, Stoke-on-Trent ST7 3AJ (01782 779033). Haul out, engine repairs, hull blacking, boat repairs and welding.

Ⓑ**Heritage Narrowboats** Heritage Marina, Station Road, Scholar Green ST7 3JZ (01782 785700; www.heritagenarrowboats.co.uk). RSWDE Gas, pump out, narrowboat hire, day boat hire, long- and short-term mooring, solid fuel, boat sales, boat painting and sign writing, boat repairs and servicing, wet dock, chandlery, toilets, Wi-Fi, holiday bungalow to let. *Open daily 08.30-17.00.*

continued in Book 4

- **Little Moreton Hall**
Newcastle Road, Congleton, Cheshire
CW12 4SD (01260 272018; www.nationaltrust.
org.uk/little-moreton-hall). Just 3/4 mile west
of the canal by footpath from bridge 86 (beware
nettles and brambles!). This fabulous moated
house is arguably the finest example of black
and white timbered architecture in the UK, and
is well worth the walk from the canal. It was built
between 1559 and 1580 with carved gables and
ornate windows, and has scarcely changed since.
It contains a fine collection of oak furniture and
pewter. Restaurant. *Open mid Feb-Oct, Wed-Sun
& B Hols 11.00-17.00; also Jul-Aug, Mon-Tue
11.00-17.00; Nov-Dec, Sat-Sun 11.00-16.00.*
Charge.

- **Mow Cop**
(www.mowcop.info). NT. Walk east from bridge
85. A hill nearly 1100ft above sea level, which
gives a magnificent view across the Cheshire
Plain, beyond Stoke and into Wales, which looks
particularly good at night. On top of the hill is
Mow Cop Castle, an imitation ruin built in 1754
by Randle Wilbraham, a local squire. It was on
this spot that Hugh Bourne, a wheelwright,
climbed to the summit to create the Primitive
Methodists in 1807. Their first meeting lasted
14 hours, and was an endeavour to create a
simpler form of religion. The memorial church
was erected in 1862 on the site of this meeting.
A hundred years later 70,000 disciples climbed
to the top to worship on what had become, for
them, a Holy Mountain. Bourne died at the age
of 80, having seen over 5000 Methodist chapels
founded. Coal from collieries to the east of Mow
Cop was carried down to the canal by a tramway
known as 'The Brake'.

- **Scholar Green**
Cheshire. PO, tel, stores, off-licence, takeaway.
Bisected by the busy A34, the village is best
known for the 18th-C Rode Hall, a Grade II* listed
building that hosts a Farmers Market *on 1st Sat of
the month*. The shop is *open late* and lies west of
Bridge 90.

NAVIGATIONAL NOTES

The Macclesfield Canal is generally quite shallow, and mooring is usually only possible at
recognised sites.

WALKING & CYCLING

The towpath is in good condition throughout the length of this canal. Ambitious walkers will want
to walk to the top of Mow Cop, which is best accessed from bridge 85. From the top you can follow a
section of The Gritstone Trail north towards the Old Man of Mow, a 65ft-tall gritstone pillar left as the
rock around it was quarried away. Just before a radio mast turn downhill as waymarked to pass through
Roe Park Woods, then bear right to reach the lane leading to Ackers railway crossing and the canal. The
Staffordshire Way leaves Mow Cop to head towards Kinver, on the Staffordshire & Worcestershire Canal.

Pubs and Restaurants

The Blue Bell 25 Hardingswood, Kidsgrove
ST7 1EG (01782 774052; www.bluebellkidsgrove.
co.uk). Canalside, at Hardings Wood Junction.
Friendly, quiet, one-bar local, winnner of many
CAMRA awards. Real ale, plus a range of specialist
bottled beers, including many from Belgium,
plus real cider and perry. No juke box, pool table
or gaming machines. Note the trapdoor in the
lounge ceiling. Well-behaved children welcome
until 21.00. Dogs welcome. Snacks are available
*at weekends. Open Tue-Fri 19.30-23.00; Sat
13.00-16.00, 19.30-23.00; Sun 12.00-22.30 (all
day during summer). Closed Mon.*

The Red Bull Hotel Congleton Road South,
Church Lawton ST7 3AJ (01782 782600; www.
redbullchurchlawton.robinsonsbrewery.com).
By lock 43. Popular pub close to Hardings Wood
Junction, serving real ale and bar meals, including
fish dishes *L and E*, along with good wine.
Children welcome. Canalside seating area. Real
fires and moorings. Wi-Fi. *Open all day.*

The Bleeding Wolf Hotel 121 Congleton
Road North, Scholar Green, Stoke-on-Trent ST7
3BQ (01782 782272; www.thebleedingwolf.
co.uk). Near bridge 94. A large and lively thatched
country pub with a conservatory, offering real ale
and food (including a carvery *Sun 12.00-15.00)
Mon-Fri L and E & Sat-Sun all day*). Family-
friendly, garden, open fires and Wi-Fi. *Open 11.00
(Sun 12.00).*

The Travellers Rest 175 Congleton Road
North, Scholar Green, Stoke-on-Trent ST7 3HA
(01782 782359; www.thetravs.com). Traditional
country pub serving real ale, together with food
daily L & Tue-Sat E. Children welcome and there
is outside seating. *Open Mon-Thu L and E & Fri-
Sun all day from 12.00.*

The Rising Sun 112 Station Road, Scholar
Green, Stoke-on-Trent ST7 3JT (01782 776235;
www.brilliantpubs.co.uk/risingsuncheshire).
Beside Bridge 87. A friendly and welcoming pub
offering real ale, and excellent home-cooked
food *Mon-Fri L and E & Sat-Sun all day*. Children
welcome, open fires and a patio. *Open Mon-Thu L
and E & Fri-Sun from 12.00 (Fri 09.30).*

Congleton

The canal continues north east, crossing Watery Lane Aqueduct. To the east the ever-present range of hills is a reminder that the Pennine Chain lies just beyond. Passing a golf course, the embanked wharf which overlooks Congleton soon appears, with an aqueduct over the road that runs down into the town. The handsome warehouse at the wharf has now been converted into apartments. There is a useful *parade of shops (including a PO, stores, chemist, off-licence, takeaway, greengrocer, fish & chips)* just to the south east of Bridge 75. Beautifully elegant 'roving' bridges, 76 and 77, follow. These are known locally as 'snake bridges' and, in the days of horse-drawn boats, changed the towpath from one side to the other without having to un-hitch the horse. Past Congleton railway station, the canal is carried on a high embankment – a common feature of the Macclesfield – across a narrow valley, affording a good view westward of the tall and elegant railway viaduct crossing the same valley. Meanwhile the looming fell known as the Cloud, over 1000ft high and topped with remains of ancient earthworks, is given a wide berth as the navigation continues on its lonely lock-free course through this very fine landscape. There is a good walk to the top of the Cloud along footpaths east of bridge 71. The canal then continues its lonely course, turning east to cross the River Dane on an embankment – not very impressive from the boat, but superb when viewed from the river – and arrives at the foot of Bosley Locks, in a really delightful setting which is semi-wooded and semi-pastoral. There are good, quiet moorings here.

● **Astbury**
Cheshire. PO box, tel, stores, delicatessen, butcher, baker, greengrocer. About 1 mile north west of bridges 79 and 80. A pretty village set just off the A34. St Mary's Church is amazing: its light interior and wide aisles are complemented by generous battlements along the roof and a tower standing quite separate from the body of the church. The *shops* are to be found at Glebe Farm.
Glebe Farm Astbury Congleton CW12 4RQ (01260 273916; www.glebefarmastbury.co.uk). An interactive day out for children and an opportunity for some retail therapy for adults! An example of total farm diversification offering animal petting, tractor rides, indoor and outdoor play areas, craft shops, a coffee shop and a farm shop, delicatessen, butcher, baker and a visiting fish monger *Thu 10.45-16.45.* Coffee shop *open Mon-Sat 08.30-16.30 (Sat 17.00) & Sun and B Hols 09.30-16.00.* Farm & Shop *open Mon-Sat 08.30-18.00 & Sun and B Hols 09.30-16.00.* Free entry.

● **Congleton**
Cheshire. All services. A compact and busy market town.
Tourist Information Centre Town Hall, High Street, Congleton CW12 1BN (01260 271095; www.visitcheshire.com/visitor-info/visitor-information-centres). *Open Apr-Sep, Mon-Fri 09.00-17.00 & Sat 10.00-16.00; Oct-Mar Mon-Fri 01.00-17.00 & Sat 10.00-14.00.*
● **Bosley Locks**
Effectively the only locks on all the 27 miles of the Macclesfield Canal, these handsome constructions are deep, raising the canal level by fully 118ft to well over 500ft above sea level. Each lock has a pair of mitred top gates instead of the more usual single one, and are a good example of Telford's practice of grouping locks together in flights; here there are 12 within just one mile.

Pubs and Restaurants

▶✕**The Egerton Arms** Astbury CW12 4RQ (01260 273946; www.egertonarms.co.uk). A handsome and justly popular village pub built c.1560 opposite the 11th-C church, serving real ale. Home-cooked food is available in both the bar and restaurant *L and E, daily.* Children, with well-behaved parents, are welcome *until 21.00,* and there is a large garden and play area. Wi-Fi and camping. B&B. *Open 11.30.*
▶**The Queen's Head** Park Lane, Congleton CW12 3DE (01260 272546; www.queensheadpub.org.uk). Just north of Bridge 75, this welcoming pub serves real ales and food *Mon-Sat L and E & Sun 12.00-16.00.* Open fires, garden and children's play area. Sports TV, dogs welcome, traditional pub games and a boules pitch. Quiz *Mon* and Wi-Fi. B&B. *Open 12.00.*
▶**The Beartown Tap** 18 Willow Street, Congleton CW12 1RL (07858 728856; www.beartownbrewery.co.uk). Main outlet for the Beartown Brewery, just across the road, this warm friendly pub serves a selection of their real ales, together with real cider. Dogs welcome. Patio drinking area, real fires, sports TV and Wi-Fi. *Open Mon-Thu 16.00 & Fri-Sun 12.00.*

▶**The Young Pretender** 30-34 Lawton Street, Congleton CW12 1RS (01260 273277; www.youngpretenderbeerparlour.co.uk). Thriving town pub, established in a renovated toy shop, serving a range of local real ales and world beers. Bar food is available *L.* Live music *Thu,* quiz *Sun.* Dog- and family-friendly (children *until 20.00*). Wi-Fi. *Open 12.00.*
▶**Railway Inn** Biddulph Road; Congleton CW12 3JS (01260 272527; www.therailwayinncongleton.co.uk). Near Congleton station, by bridge 75. A large family pub offering food *L and E daily.* Seats overlooking a bowling green. Quiz *Thu,* pool, wide-screen TV, free Wi-Fi..
▶✕**The Robin Hood** Buxton Road, Buglawton, Congleton CW12 3PE (01260 295241; www.therobinhoodcongleton.co.uk). South west of bridge 61. A choice of real ale is served in this suburban pub dating from 1787. It was once the Buglawton Court Room and, although noted for its ghost sightings, still dispenses real ale together with food *L and E.* Children welcome and there is a garden.

145

Oakgrove

The Macclesfield Canal completes the climb of Bosley Locks and resumes its lonely journey through open, attractive countryside. The facilities block beside Bridge 54 includes a *shower, toilets and a laundry*. Approaching Oakgrove the foothills and mountains of the Pennines, some over 1200ft high, spill right down to the canal. The swing bridge at Oakgrove was once a notorious obstacle on the canal, often requiring two very strong individuals to prise it open. Thankfully those days have long passed. The navigation now follows the contour of the land as it begins to swing around the hills, passing the large flat expanse of Danes Moss and approaching Macclesfield, now clearly visible to the north. If you choose to moor by Gurnett Aqueduct to visit the pubs nearby, take a look at the plaque on a cottage wall 25yds to the east. It commemorates the training here of James Brindley, the canal builder and civil engineer, between 1733–40 – he was apprenticed to Abraham Bennett. Just beyond the aqueduct, bridge 43 is a superb example of a typical 'snake bridge'.

- **Sutton Lane Ends**
Cheshire. PO, tel, stores, farm shop. This village was the home of Charles Tunnicliffe, 1901–79, the bird artist.
- **Oakgrove** A delightful spot with a pub and a superb backcloth of tall, green hills which are ideal for energetic walks. The lane west of the bridge leads to Gawsworth. Sutton Reservoir is just north.
- **Gawsworth**
Cheshire. PO box, tel, stores, off-licence, delicatessen. 2 miles west of Oakgrove. A refreshingly unspoilt village with several small lakes and a lovely 13th-C church, approached by a long avenue of elm trees. Facing the church is the old rectory, a half-timbered house built by Rector Baguley in 1470.
Gawsworth Hall Church Lane, Gawsworth, Macclesfield SK11 9RN (01260 223456; www.gawsworthhall.com). Close to the church, this is a beautiful black and white manor house,

parts of which date from Norman times. It was once the home of Mary Fitton, possibly the Dark Lady of Shakespeare's sonnets. The park encloses a medieval jousting ground, and there is a *summer season* of open-air theatre. The house is *open May-Sep, Sun 14.00-17.00 & daily Jul-Aug 14.00-17.00*. Charge. Fine tea room, selling excellent cake and *regular* events are held at the Hall.

Maggoty's Wood In this pleasant wood just outside the village is the grave of the eccentric fiddler and playwright, Maggoty Johnson. After being totally rejected by London critics he returned to Gawsworth where he died in 1773, having ordered that he should be buried far from the vulgar gentry who did not appreciate his genius.

- **Sutton Reservoir**
Close to the canal north of bridge 49, this reservoir holds up to 94 million gallons of water. The public are welcome to ramble and picnic here.

Pubs and Restaurants

Sutton Hall Bullocks Lane, Macclesfield SK11 0HE (01260 253211; www.brunningandprice.co.uk/suttonhall). South of Bridge 44. A 16th-C manor house, family home of the Earls of Lucan (and subsequently a convent) now dispensing real ales and excellent food *daily 12.00-22.00 (Sun 21.30)*. Well-behaved children and leashed dogs welcome. Open fires, a multitude of alchoved rooms and Wi-Fi. *Booking advisable – especially at weekends. Open 11.30 (Sun 12.00).*

The Church House Inn Church Lane, Sutton Lane Ends SK110DS (01260 252436). Well worth the ½ mile walk from Gurnett Aqueduct to enjoy this friendly and comfortable village local serving real ale, and good food *L and E, and all day Sat-Sun*. Children welcome away from the bar, and there is a patio with children's playthings. Dogs welcome. Open fires, traditional pub games, Wi-Fi and camping nearby. *Open 12.00.*

The Lamb Inn 13 Hollin Lane, Sutton, Macclesfield SK11 0HL (01260 252000). South of Gurnett Aqueduct. Named after Lady Caroline Lamb, Lord Byron's consort, this friendly village local dispenses real ale and homemade food as *per opening times*. Family-friendly, open fires and a garden. *Open Tue 18.00; Wed-Thu L and E & Fri-Sun all day from 12.00.*

Ye Old Kings Head 30 Bradley Smithy, Byrons Lane, Gurnett SK11 0HD (01625 423890; www.yeoldkingshead.co.uk). Below the aqueduct. A coaching house and smithy dating from 1695, which was visited by Bonnie Prince Charlie. This comfortable beamy pub serves real ales, and meals *Tue E; Wed-Fri L and E & Sat-Sun 12.00-21.00 (Sun 20.00)*. Regular live music, garden, open fires and Wi-Fi. Child- and dog-friendly. Camping nearby. *Open Mon-Tue 17.00 & Wed-Sun 12.00.*

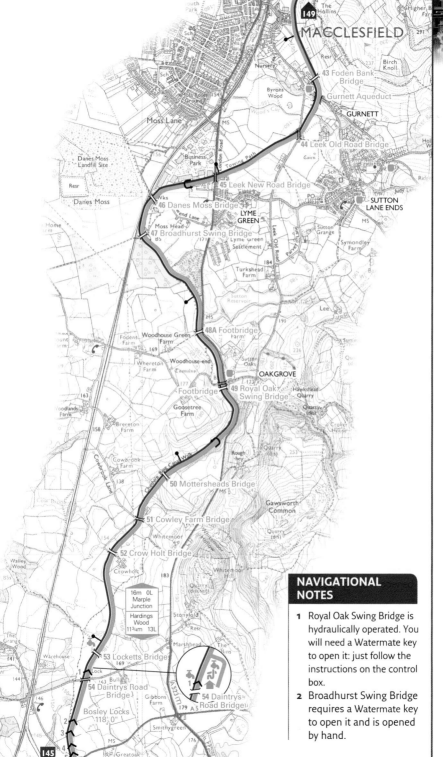

149

43 Foden Bank Bridge

Gurnett Aqueduct

GURNETT

44 Leek Old Road Bridge

SUTTON LANE ENDS

45 Leek New Road Bridge

46 Danes Moss Bridge

LYME GREEN

47 Broadhurst Swing Bridge

48A Footbridge

OAKGROVE

Footbridge

49 Royal Oak Swing Bridge

50 Mottersheads Bridge

51 Cowley Farm Bridge

52 Crow Holt Bridge

16m 0L
Marple Junction

Hardings Wood
11¾m 13L

53 Locketts Bridge

54 Daintrys Road Bridge

54 Daintrys Road Bridge

Bosley Locks 118'0"

145

55 Peckerpool Wood Bridge

NAVIGATIONAL NOTES

1 Royal Oak Swing Bridge is hydraulically operated. You will need a Watermate key to open it: just follow the instructions on the control box.

2 Broadhurst Swing Bridge requires a Watermate key to open it and is opened by hand.

147

Macclesfield

Leaving green and hilly countryside, the navigation enters the outskirts of Macclesfield, where some new housing incorporates a canal crane. A very wide stretch of water is overlooked by a vast and beautifully restored flour mill converted into up-market apartments, marking the site of the original Macclesfield Canal Company. This, the Hovis Mill, was built in the 1820s, and was the birthplace of the famous flour. The word Hovis is derived from the Latin 'hominisunvis' meaning 'power to the man'. Note the archway entrance off the canal, now blocked. The town itself is down the hill; the best place to moor is south of bridge 37, which is also handy for shops (stores, off-licence, takeaway, greengrocer – all to the east of the bridge). The tree-lined canal continues northwards to Bollington, passing through glorious open countryside with views of the hills all around, to the Adelphi Mill, once a silk mill and now converted into offices. A 60ft-high embankment and two aqueducts then carry the navigation across the valley towards the huge Clarence Mill, a textile mill now converted into thriving small manufacturing units. High on a hilltop to the south east of the town (directly east of Greens Bridge) is the White Nancy monument, recently renovated. This was erected by the Gaskell family in the 19th C at the northern end of the Kerridge Ridge, to commemorate the Battle of Waterloo, and was used by his family as a summerhouse.

Pubs and Restaurants

The Dolphin Inn 76 Windmill Street, Macclesfield SK11 7HS (01625 616179; www.thedolphin. robinsonsbrewery.com). West of Bridge 40. A traditional, community local serving real ales. Child- and dog-friendly. Sports TV, beer garden, real fires, traditional pub games and Wi-Fi. *Open Mon-Fri L and E and Sat-Sun all day from 12.00.*

The Macc Bar 1 Mill Green, Macclesfield SK11 7PE (01625 423704; www.maccbar.co.uk). West of Bridge 41, beyond the park. This popular hostelry, dispensing a wide range of real ales, real cider, continental and American beers, bottled and craft ales, is a beer lovers paradise. Food is available *daily until 20.30.* Child- and dog-friendly. Open fires, beer garden, traditional pub games and live acoustic music *Tue. Open Mon-Thu 16.00 & Fri-Sun 12.00.*

The Navigation 161 Black Road, Macclesfield SK11 7LF (01625 422777). South west of bridge 38. A Victorian local built for the original canal navvies. Real ale, a beer garden, sports TV and traditional pub games. Children and dogs welcome. *Open Mon-Thu 16.00 & Fri-Sun 12.00.*

The Puss in Boots 198 Buxton Road, Macclesfield SK10 1NF (01625 263378; www.thepussinboots.co.uk). Beside Bridge 37. Canalside pub, with moorings, serving real ale and food *Mon-Fri E and Sat-Sun 12.00-20.00. Sun* carvery. Children welcome, open fires, sports TV, Karaoke *Fri* and quiz *Wed. Open Mon-Fri 16.00 & Sat-Sun 12.00.*

The Wharf 107 Brook Street, Macclesfield SK11 7AW (01625 261879; www.thewharfmacc.co.uk). Just west of the boatyard. Popular pub serving a wide range of real ales, real cider and bottled beers from around the world. *Regular* live music. Dog- and child-friendly, garden and open fires. Sports TV, traditional pub games and Wi-Fi. *Open Mon-Fri 16.00 & Sat-Sun 12.00.*

The Treacle Tap 43 Sunderland Street, Macclesfield SK11 6JL (01625 615938; www.thetreacletap.co.uk). South west of railway station. A relaxed atmosphere pervades this former saddlery shop, which now dispenses real ale, bar meals and snacks *daily*, together with tea and coffee. Dogs and children welcome, *regular* live music and a quiz *Sun.* WI-Fi and newspapers. There is a fascinating range of events, far too varied to list. *Open 12.00.*

The Waters Green Tavern 96 Waters Green, Macclesfield SK11 6LH (01625 422653). Just west of railway station. Run by the same landlord for more than 30 years (now with the assistance of his son) this welcoming pub serves a wide selection of rotating guest ales, together with real cider. Dogs welcome, open fires, garden and traditional pub games *(when quiet). Open daily L and E.*

The Three Crowns 38 Rainow Road, Hurdsfield, Macclesfield SK10 2PF (01625 348237; www. threecrowns.robinsonsbrewery.com). East of bridge 34. A tiny Victorian stone terraced pub with a garden. Real ale is dispensed *Mon-Fri from 17.00 & Sat-Sun 12.00.* Sports TV, patio seating, traditional pub games, Wi-Fi and newspapers. Children and dogs welcome.

The Dog & Partridge 97 Palmerston Street, Bollington SK10 5JX (01625 575979; www. dogpartridgebollington.robinsonsbrewery.com). West of Bollington Aqueduct and bridge 27. A sociable village pub with an open fire. Real ale. There is a bridewell (prison), built in 1831, at the rear. Sandwiches available *L.* Dog- and family-friendly, garden, traditional pub games, sports TV and Wi-Fi. *Regular* live music. *Open 12.00.*

The Vale Inn Adlington Road, Bollington, Macclesfield SK10 5JT (01625 575147; www.valeinn. co.uk). Community focused pub, with its own microbrewery, dispensing real ales and real cider. Appetising, homemade food is available *Mon-Thu L and E & Sat-Sun all day.* Open fires, garden, children welcome. *Open Mon-Thu L and E & Fri-Sun all day from 12.00.*

WALKING & CYCLING

The White Nancy Monument can be reached by walking south from Kerridge Bridge (27) and following the path. It was a folly constructed in 1817 by John Gaskell – whose ancestral home was the nearby Ingersley Hall – to commemorate the victory at the Battle of Waterloo. It was probably named after one of his daughters, although another theory has it that it bears the name of the lead horse that hauled all the building materials to the top of the ridge. Once at the top you will find it an excellent spot for a picnic, and you can walk along the Saddle of Kerridge, enjoying extensive views. For a refreshing pint and a meal there is a handy pub **The Bulls Head** 2 Oakhouse, Kerridge SK10 5BD (01625 575522; www.thebullsheadsk10.co.uk) nearby.

The Middlewood Way follows the line of the former Macclesfield, Bollington and Marple Railway and is a well surfaced, 10-mile route suitable for walkers, cyclists, pushchairs and wheelchairs. In conjunction with the canal towpath it can be used to form a circular walk with starting/finishing points at Bollington, Poynton and Marple. A PDF detailing the trail is downloadable from the website (01625 383700; www.cheshireeast. gov.uk/leisure,_culture_and_tourism/ ranger_service/countryside_sites/ middlewood_way.aspx). See also **Walking & Cycling** page 151.

BOAT TRIPS

White Nancy Cruising operate 12-seater restaurant boats from Bollington Wharf, Grimshaw Lane, Bollington SK10 5JB. Book well in advance on 01625 573100; www.white-nancy.co.uk. Also self-drive day hire boats available.

153

26 Sugar Lane Bridge

Clarence Mill

26A

Bollington Aqueduct

27 Kerridge Bridge

Grimshaw Lane Aqueduct

BOLLINGTON

Adelphi Mill

28 Greens Bridge

Kerridge

29 Clarke Lane Bridge

30 Woods Bridge

HIGHER HURD

33 Higherfold Bridge

34 Chapel-en-le-Frith Bridge

35 Barrack Road Bridge

Smyths Bridge 36

Buxton Road Wharf

37 Buxton Road Bridge

Hovis Mill

38 Black Road Bridge

39 Hollands Bridge

40 Leadbeaters Bridge

41 Verdons Bridge

MACCLESFIELD

147

11m	0L	Marple Junction
Hardings Wood	16¾m	13L

Ⓑ**Macclesfield Canal Centre** Swettenham Wharf, Brook Street, Macclesfield SK11 7AW (01625 420042; www.freedomboats.co.uk). 🛒 D Pump out, gas, day-hire craft, overnight mooring, long-term mooring, winter storage, slipway, boat and engine sales and repairs, toilets, books and maps, solid fuel, well-stocked chandlery, ice creams, overnight parking.

Ⓑ**Peak Forest Cruisers** The Wharf, Buxton Road, Macclesfield SK11 1LZ (01625 424172). Long-term mooring. *Nearby* 🛒 either side of bridge 37.

Ⓑ**Bollington Wharf** Grimshaw Lane, Bollington SK10 5JB (01625 575811; www.bollington-wharf. com). 🛒🛒🛒 D Pump out, gas, overnight and long-term mooring, winter storage, boat building, boat sales, boat fitting out, coal and kindling, paraffin, engineering workshop (parts manufactured).

Ⓑ**Kerridge Dry Dock** The Barn, Oaklands Farm, Kerridge SK10 5AP (01625 574287). Between bridges 28 and 29. Long-term mooring, winter storage, dry dock, boat and engine repairs, bottom blacking, marine engineering. Call out *(during daylight hours)*.

● **Macclesfield**
Cheshire. All services. Earliest records of a settlement are to be found in the Domesday Book, when the area was detailed as part of the land of Earl Edwin of Mercia. The town grew rapidly until it became the most important town in east Cheshire, being recognised as a borough in 1220. At that time it was the administrative centre for the Macclesfield Forest, and was granted its charter in 1261. Following set-backs resulting from the Battle of Flodden Field in 1513, the town was granted a new charter in 1595, and this was replaced by yet another, granted by Charles II, in 1684. Now the town is an interesting combination of modern industry and old market town, with cobbled streets and a picturesque medieval Market Place, encircled by busy modern roads. There are several fine classical buildings, making the most of the local stone, and detailed in the fine Town Trail leaflet available at the Tourist Information Centre. In the 18th C the town was one of the leading silk producing centres, but now there are only two small manufacturers left. One interesting feature of the town is the Unitarian Chapel in King Edward Street, approached through a narrow passage and guarded by a lovely wrought-iron gate: it is dated 1689 and is 'for William and Mary's subjects dissenting from the Church of England'.
St Michael's Church Market Place, Macclesfield SK10 1HW (01625 421984; www.stmichaels-macclesfield.com). Very little remains of the original structure founded in 1278 by Queen Eleanor and then known as All Hallows, although the Savage Chapel, the oldest stone building in the town, survives. The church still contains many fine monuments.
Silk Museum & Paradise Mill Park Lane, Macclesfield SK11 6TJ (01625 612045; www.silkmacclesfield.org.uk/museums/paradise-mill). Built 1820-60, this handloom silk-weaving mill finally closed down in 1981. Here you can see Jacquard handlooms in action, authentic room settings and an exhibition of a whole wealth of

material connected with one of Macclesfield's major industries. *Open Mon-Sat 10.00-16.00.* Guided Mill tours *11.45, 13.00 & 14.15.* Charge.
Silk Museum Heritage Centre Galleries Roe Street, Macclesfield SK11 6UT (01625 613210; www.silkmacclesfield.org.uk/silk-museum). The first museum in the country devoted entirely to the study of the silk industry: audio-visuals, costume, textiles, room settings and even parachutes. Visit also the Heritage Centre in the old 1813 Sunday School building. *Open Mon-Sat 10.00-16.00.* Charge.
West Park Museum Prestbury Road, Macclesfield SK10 3BJ (01625 613210; www.silkmacclesfield.org.uk/museums/west-park-museum). Opened in 1898, and situated in a park containing the largest bowling green in Europe, the collections include fine and decorative art, local history and Egyptian antiquities, plus a section devoted to Charles Tunnicliffe (1901-79), the famous bird artist. *Open Tue-Sat 13.30-16.30.* Free.
Macclesfield Leisure Centre Priory Lane, Macclesfield SK10 4AF (01625 383981; www.everybody.org.uk/centres/mlc). Three swimming pools, six squash courts and a host of other facilities. *Open 09.00 until late (Wed & Fri 07.30).*
Tourist Information Centre Town Hall, Market Place, Macclesfield SK10 1DX (01625 378123; www.visitcheshire.com/visitor-info/visitor-information-centres). *Open Apr-Sep, Mon-Fri 09.00-17.00 & Sat 10.00-16.00; Oct-Mar, Mon-Fri 10.00-16.00 & Sat 10.00-15.00.*

● **Bollington**
Cheshire. PO, tel, stores, chemist, butcher, takeaway, garage. There is a good view of this stone-built town from the huge canal embankment which cuts across it. From here it is only 1 mile to the boundary of the Peak District National Park. The white tower on the ridge south of the town is called White Nancy (see **Walking & Cycling** page 150).
Bollington Leisure Centre Heath Road, Bollington SK10 5EX (01625 574774; www.bollingtonleisure.co.uk). Squash courts, a swimming pool and other facilities. *Open Mon-Fri 06.45 & Sat-Sun 07.45 until late.*

WALKING & CYCLING

There are many stimulating walks available throughout Cheshire, several in the Macclesfield area that are within reach of this waterway. You will find details at www.bootsandpaws.co.uk/acheshire.html). The Middlewood Way (see also www.macclesfield.gov.uk) is a level 10-mile footpath and cycleway (part of Route 55 of the National Cycle Network) along the course of the old Macclesfield, Bollington and Marple Railway. It runs between Macclesfield and Marple. For much of its length it closely follows the Macclesfield Canal and there are several options for circular walks. The railway was opened for passenger traffic in 1869, just 38 years after the Macclesfield Canal was completed, and for goods on 1 March 1870. Cotton, silk, coal and passengers were carried, but the railway always struggled to make a profit. It was finally closed in January 1970 and converted for recreational use in 1985. Dr David Bellamy performed the opening ceremony and then, having proclaimed it 'tewiffic', removed his socks and shoes and waded into a nearby pond.

BIRD LIFE

The *Great Tit* is a common woodland and garden species, appreciably larger than the blue tit alongside which it is often seen at bird feeders. The great tit has bold black and white markings on its head and a black bib forming a line running down its chest, broader in the male than the female. The underparts are otherwise yellow and upperparts mainly greenish. Juveniles have sombre plumage with no white on the head. Their song is extremely variable but a striking 'teecha teecha teecha' is rendered by most males. In summer the birds feed mainly on insects.

A snake bridge at Congleton (see page 144)

Higher Poynton

This isolated stretch is typical of the Macclesfield Canal and in its beautifully quiet, rural isolation it represents much of the charm that most canals possess. Winding northwards along the summit level at over 500ft above the sea, the navigation generally follows the contours of this upland country, but crosses several valleys on embankments with fine aqueducts. There is a pleasant *picnic area* south of Hag Footbridge 16, good *moorings* by the Miners Arms, bridge 18, and between bridges 20 and 19, and a fine shady, wooded section between bridges 22 and 21. There are few centres of population near the canal, just the odd pub here or there, and the countryside is quite unspoilt. Around Higher Poynton the canal becomes wider, the result of ancient subsidence from a coal mine, which necessitated the continual raising of the canal banks and bridges to hold the water in the sinking canal. Be sure to adhere to the main channel here. An old branch near bridge 15 used to lead to the mine; now it is used by a boatyard.

● **Higher Poynton**
Cheshire. PO box, tel. Considered by some to be the most pleasant moorings on the canal, where the wide water supports large families of ducks, geese and swans. There is a recreation field adjacent, and a handy *pub.* Poynton itself, with its wide selection of facilities, is 1½ miles west of Brownhills Bridge 15.
Anson Engine Museum Anson Road, Poynton SK12 1TD (01625 874426; www.enginemuseum. org). A working display of early internal-combustion engines, with emphasis on those made in the Manchester area. Tearoom and shop. *Open Easter-Oct, Fri-Sun 10.00-17.00 & B Hols.* Wi-Fi. Charge.
Lyme Park Disley, Stockport SK12 2NR (01663 762023; www.nationaltrust.org.uk/lyme-park). Two miles east of Higher Poynton. Pedestrian entrance at West Parkgate, ¼ mile south east of bridge 17 or footpath from bridge 15. In the centre of a

1400-acre park containing deer is this magnificent Italianate palace which was transformed from a Tudor house by the Venetian architect Leoni. Some of the original Elizabethan interiors can still be seen. There are Mortlake tapestries, a large collection of English clocks, Grinling Gibbons wood carvings, countless works of art, and four Chippendale chairs claimed to be covered with material from a cloak worn by King Charles I at his execution. The Victorian garden has a sunken parterre, an Edwardian rose garden, a reflection lake, a ravine garden, a Wyatt conservatory and an 18th-C hunting tower. The house featured in a BBC adaptation of *Pride and Prejudice* as 'Pemberley'. Children's playground. Restaurant, café, tearoom and shop. The garden, park, shop and café are open *daily throughout the year* while the house and restaurant *opening times vary.* Check the website for details. Charge.

Pubs and Restaurants

◗✕**The Windmill Inn** Holehouse Lane, Whiteley Green SK10 5SJ (01625 574222; www.thewindmill. info). 250yds west of bridge 25. Dating from the 15th C, when it was recorded as a farm house, it became a pub in 1674. Real ale is served, along with food available *Mon-Fri L and E & Sat-Sun 1 2.00-21.30 (Sun 20.00).* Child- and dog-friendly, open fires and a garden. Newspapers and Wi-Fi. *Open 12.00.*
◗**The Miners Arms** Wood Lane North, Four Lane Ends, Adlington SK10 4PF (01625 872731). Near bridge 18. A big, bustling, lively and thriving country pub which is pleasantly family orientated, having extensive gardens and amusements for children.

Real ale is served, along with a good choice of food and a children's menu *daily 12.00-21.00 (Sun 20.30).*
✕▯**Lyme Breeze Restaurant** Wood Lane East, Adlington SK10 4PH (01625 871120; www. lymebreeze.co.uk). You will receive a warm, friendly and relaxed welcome here for restaurant meals. Conveniently located near to Lyme View Marina. *Open Wed-Sun L & Fri-Sat E.*
◗**The Boar's Head** 2 Shrigley Road North, Higher Poynton SK12 1TE (01625 876676). Down the hill from bridge 15. An imposing, ivy-clad, red-brick pub serving real ale and food *L.* Garden with children's play area, traditional pub games and sports TV. Open *Mon-Fri L and E & Sat-Sun all day from 12.00.*

WALKING & CYCLING
The Gritstone Trail passes through Lyme Park and continues up onto the moors, passing White Nancy (*see* page 148). The Middlewood Way (*see* page 151) continues to the west of the canal. Jacksons' Brickworks (01625 383700; www.cheshireeast.gov.uk/leisure,_culture_and_tourism/ranger_service/countryside_sites/ jacksons_brickworks_lnr.aspx) in Higher Poynton, reclaimed by nature after its industrial interlude, is now a valuable wildlife resource. The 22-acre site is managed as a mosaic of different habitats including Wetland, Grassland, Semi-natural Woodland and scrub. It is especially important for the great crested newt. It is accessible from Bullocks Bridge 13.

Boatyards

Ⓑ**Lyme View Marina** Adlington Basin, Adlington SK10 4PH (01625 858176; www.lymeviewmarina.co.uk). ⬛🔧D Pump out, gas, long-term mooring, slipway, solid fuel.

Ⓑ **Braidbar Boats** Lyme Road, Higher Poynton, Stockport SK12 1TH (01625 873471; www. braidbarboats. co.uk). Near bridge 15. Narrowboat hire, boat building, boat sales and repairs, engine repairs, boat painting and signwriting, covered wet dock.

Ⓑ**Bailey's Trading Post** Lyme Road, Higher Poynton, Stockport SK12 1TH (01625 872277; www. baileystradingpost.co.uk). Near bridge 15. ⬛🔧D Pump out, gas, day-boat hire, chandlery, books and

maps, gifts, café, solid fuel.

Ⓑ**Classic Maritime Diesels** Anson Engine Museum, Poynton, SK12 1TD (07712 052635; classicdiesel@hotmail. com). Specialists in diesels. Major overhauls and rebuilds, parts made.

POYNTON
1 mile

BOAT TRIPS

Mary Sunley A 12-berth craft, suitable for those with special needs, available for charter from Lord Vernon's Wharf Lyme Road, Higher Poynton SK12 1TH (01477 537458; www.macclesfieldcanal.org.uk/ msunley.htm). Telephone *Mon-Fri 09.00-17.00* for details.

153

Marple Junction

Another massive embankment and a tall aqueduct, this time over a railway, are crossed on the way into High Lane. The canal proceeds northwards in a cutting through High Lane, passing the junction with the short High Lane Arm – well protected and now used as a club mooring site – and a children's play park. There are *moorings* between the arm and bridge 11, with *shops* close by. Beyond the town is a restored mill; then open country intervenes, offering views westward of Stockport and the southern outskirts of Manchester. There is a useful *little shop* down the hill from bridge 6. At Bridge 3 there are *fish & chips and a laundrette*. Goyt Mill appears, thankfully restored and now housing workshops, heralding the start of Marple, a busy boating centre much enjoyed by the citizens of Manchester. The area of the junction with the Peak Forest Canal is delightful: an old turnover bridge, mellow wharf buildings and the nearby flight of Marple Locks are framed by the distant mountainous country across the Goyt Valley. The canal here is 500ft above sea level.

Boatyards

Ⓑ**Canal & River Trust Marple Yard** Marple Junction, on the Macclesfield Canal (0303 040 4040; enquiries.manchesterpennine@canalrivertrust.org.uk). 🛉🛈⚓ Overnight mooring.

● **High Lane**
Gt Manchester. PO, tel, stores, chemist, off-licence, takeaway, fish & chips, delicatessen, library, station. More of a spread than a village, but there are good moorings and it is useful for supplies. High Lane is effectively at the south east corner of the Manchester conurbation, and is quite indistinguishable from its neighbours. The very long Disley Railway Tunnel passes deep underneath.

● **Marple**
Gt Manchester. All services. A typical residential town, serving as a dormitory base for Stockport and Manchester. Elements of the old village can still be seen, buried amongst the suburbia, but much the most attractive part is by the canal. The rugged Ludworth Moor is not far away, where 'Robin Hood's Picking Rods' still stand, the supposed remains of a Celtic Druid's temple.

● **Marple Locks**
The 16 locks at Marple were not built until 1804,

four years after the rest of the Peak Forest canal was opened. The 1-mile gap thus left was bridged by a tramway, while the Canal Company sought the cash to pay for the construction of a flight of locks. This was obviously a most unsatisfactory state of affairs, since limestone from Doveholes had to be shifted from wagon to boat at Buxworth Basin, from boat to wagon at Marple Junction, and back into boat again at the bottom of the tramway. Not surprisingly, a container system was developed – using iron boxes with a 2-ton payload – to ease the triple transhipment. However, this was no long-term solution, and when the necessary £27,000 was forthcoming the company authorised construction of the flight of locks. Today they stand comparison with any flight on the network. Note especially Samuel Oldknow's superb warehouse by lock 9, opposite the lock keeper's house, now tastefully converted to offices.

Pubs and Restaurants

🍺**The Bull's Head** 28 Buxton Road, High Lane SK6 8BH (01663 766195). Immediately east of Bridge 11. Recently refurbished, this pub serves real ale and food *L and E*. Children welcome, sports TV and a garden. *Open 12.00.*

🍺**The Horseshoe Inn** 1 Buxton Road, High Lane SK6 8AA (01663 762487; www.horseshoehighlane. robinsonsbrewery.com). Traditional village local serving real ale and food *Wed-Thu L & Fri-Sun 12.00-18.00.* Children welcome, garden and traditional pub games. *Open Mon-Tue 14.00 & Wed-Sun 12.00.*

🍺**The Royal Oak** Buxton Road, High Lane SK6 8AY (01663 766827). Friendly establishment serving real ale and food *Mon-Fri L and E & Sat-Sun*

12.00-18.00. Dog- and child-friendly. Garden, open fires and traditional pub games. *Open 12.00.*

🍺✕**The Ring O'Bells** 130 Church Lane, Marple SK6 7AY (0161 427 2300; www.ringobellsmarple. co.uk). By Bridge 2. An award-winning, comfortable and friendly traditional pub serving real ale and freshly prepared bar and à la carte meals *daily L and E.* Dogs and children welcome. Open fires and canalside garden. B&B. *Open 12.00.*

Try also: 🍺✕**The Red Lion** 112 Buxton Road, High Lane SK6 8ED (01663 765227; www.redlionhighlane. co.uk) and 🍺✕**The Dog & Partridge** 88 Buxton Road, High Lane SK6 8HJ (01663 762413; www. crowncarveries.co.uk/thedogandpartridgestockport). See also **Pubs and Restaurants** on page 173.

WALKING & CYCLING

There are excellent walks in the Marple area, where stunning scenery combines with the often unexpected remains of early industry. The late Gordon Mills has written an excellent series of six inexpensive guides for the local community council which take you on some of the finest walks this area has to offer: Marple Dale; The Roman Bridge & Lakes; Marple Locks & Brabyns Park; Chadkirk; From Way to Cut and Donkey Wood. No walk is longer than 4 miles, and each is fully described, with maps and old photographs. You can obtain them from Marple Library or local bookshops, and find details at www. marple-uk.com/walkso.htm. Mr Mills was quite happy for you to download the walks, in exchange for a donation to the British Heart Foundation.

MANCHESTER BOLTON & BURY CANAL

MAXIMUM DIMENSIONS
Length: 68' 0"
Beam: 14' 2"
Headroom: 6'
Draught: 3' 6"

MANAGER
Canal & River Trust (0303 040 4040;
enquiries.manchesterpennine@canalrivertrust.
org.uk).

**MANCHESTER BOLTON &
BURY CANAL SOCIETY**
Meadowbank, Ringley Road, Radcliffe,
Manchester M26 1FW
manchesterboltonandburycs@waterways.org.uk
www.mbbcs.org.uk

MILEAGE
SALFORD junction with the River Irwell to:
Park House Bridge 22: 2½ miles
Clifton Aqueduct: 4¾ miles
Giants Seat: 6¼ miles
Nob End: 8 miles

BOLTON: 11 miles
NOB END junction with the Bolton Branch to:
Radcliffe: 2½ miles
Elton reservoir: 3¾ miles
BURY canal terminus: 5 miles

Note: With the exception of approximately two
miles through Salford, and a slightly lesser distance
approaching Bolton, it is possible to follow most
of the original line of the canal, although not all
of it is in water. However, the Manchester Bolton
& Bury Canal Society has produced an excellent
towpath guide, packed with fascinating historical
detail, available through their website above. This
forms an essential companion to this guide.
**Most bridges (and all the locks) shown on
the mapping date from the time before the
canal was abandoned.** However, many have
since vanished. Missing bridge numbers, within the
sequence, will usually relate to structures spanning
culverts, arms or sluices and have been omitted for
clarity. A second bridge number shown in brackets
denotes a spurious number recently applied to the
bridge by the then, British Waterways.

The initiative for the construction of this navigation stemmed, in 1790, from a group of Bolton
men who commissioned Matthew Fletcher (of Wet Earth Colliery and a man with close links to
the Mersey & Irwell Navigation) to make an initial survey and prepare an estimate. His finding
were largely supported by a second survey, carried out a year later by Hugh Henshall – builder
of the Trent & Mersey and Chesterfield Canals – and an Act was passed for its construction in
the autumn of 1791.

The first engineer was Charles Roberts, who was succeeded by John Nightingale (Matthew
Fletcher's nephew) in 1793, for failing to discharge his duties with proper discretion and
'oeconomy.'

The canal was to be for narrowboats and by the time meetings took place with the Leeds &
Liverpool Company, with a view to a possible junction with their broad-beam waterway at Red
Moss (4½-miles west of Bolton) a five-mile section – between Oldfield Road, Salford and
Rhodes Lock – had already been built. Consequently plans were amended and the offending
stretch re-modelled.

The first tolls were taken in 1795 and the length to Rhodes Lock was opened mid-1796. The
Bury Arm remained navigable for narrowboats only until a year later and the final connection
with the Irwell was ultimately completed in December 1808. The total cost was put at £115,500
and included the impressive Prestolee Locks: two staircases, of three locks each.

The navigation was subsequently worked by both wide-beam craft and 68ft narrowboats which
predominated, each one carrying nine boxes containing between 35cwt and 2 tons of coal: an
early and efficient form of containerisation.

In 1809 the proprietors of the MB&B Canal heard of the Leeds & Liverpool's intention to build a
branch from Wigan to Worsley (connecting with the Bridgewater Canal) thereby scotching any
likelihood of a Red Moss extension.

Traffic, although steady, was modest with coal from the Clifton area up to Bolton and Bury and down to Manchester being the staple. In 1835 this amounted to 120,000 tons and was accompanied by building and road stone, flagstones and limestone, groceries and various sundries.

Passenger-carrying flyboats were popular, initially between Bolton and Manchester and, from 1810, from Bolton to Bury. Passengers taking the former service changed at Prestolee Locks, transferring via a covered walkway to save the wait while six locks were worked.

In the 1830's the canal company morphed into a railway and canal company with a view to constructing a Manchester to Bolton line 'upon or near the Line of the ... Canal.' In the event the line was built – but quite separately from the navigation.

Over its lifetime the waterway remained a coal-carrying canal, although it suffered from subsidence, especially along lengths bordering the River Irwell and during the 1880's many miles of retaining walls were constructed, along with re-puddling of the bed.

In 1905 the annual tonnage included bricks, salt, manure, pulp and cotton while, in 1941, a seven-mile section was initially abandoned by Act of Parliament, with the final stretch – between Ladyshore Colliery and Bury – remaining operational until 1951. The final Act of Abandonment came exactly a decade later.

Prestolee Aqueduct carrying the canal over the River Irwell

Salford

From Oldfield Road, the canal – its original course somewhat displaced by the arrival of the Manchester & Bolton Railway – ducks under the line and more or less shadows the trackbed (immediately to the east), until it finally becomes fully visible again, immediately beyond the Lafarge Tarmac works. Here it is reassuringly complete, in water and boldly delineated by the robust masonry of the towpath coping stones. In summer months the water is populated by a riot of colourful plants, while this surprisingly tranquil environment (for an area so close to the city centre) is disturbed only by the regular passing of trains. Most of the original bridges are intact and evidence of past industry is not difficult to detect. At Clifton the River Irwell appears on the right, emphasising just how perilously close the two water courses run – both here and at many other points along this navigation's length.

● **Salford**
Gt Manchester. All services. Although now merged with Manchester, Salford was granted its charter in 1230, 71 years before that of its now larger neighbour. It has a fine new University, dating from 1967 and a Roman Catholic cathedral consecrated in 1848. It is, however, most widely known as being the subject of many paintings by the artist L S Lowry (1887-1976). What is less widely known is that he gained his inspiration by walking the streets of Salford for many years as a rent collector, only painting in the evenings and at weekends – a fact to which he would never willingly admit. His work is exhibited at The Lowry, Salford Quays (see below).
Clifton Country Park Clifton Hose Road, Swinton M27 6NG (0161 793 4219; www.visitsalford.info/wetearthcolliery.htm). Amongst other things, the Park features the industrial remains of Wet Earth Colliery. Established around 1740, the colliery was one of the first deep mines to be sunk in the Irwell Valley and is important on at least three counts: the first application of steam winding in the area, its very long working life (1740-1928), and because of its association with James Brindley and his ingenious hydraulic pumping scheme – in continuous use from 1756 to 1924. Visit the website to download PDFs giving further, fascinating insight.

The Lowry Pier 8 Salford Quays, Salford M50 3AZ (0870 066 6849; www.thelowry.com). Rising up from the regenerated docklands, this glass and metallic building (opened in 2000) houses two main theatres and studio space for performing arts, presenting a full range of drama, opera, ballet, dance, musicals, children's shows, popular music, jazz, folk and comedy, together with gallery space. It also shows the work of L S Lowry alongside contemporary exhibitions. Restaurant, café, bars and shops. Gallery *open daily 11.00-17.00 (Sat 10.00)*. Free.
Ordsall Hall 322 Ordsall Lane, Salford M5 3AN (0161 872 0251; www.salfordcommunityleisure.co.uk/culture/ordsall-hall). The Hall is a Grade I listed Tudor manor house, was first recorded in 1177. Since then, it has been home to medieval gentry, Tudor nobility, Catholics loyal to the crown, butchers, farmers, an Earl, an artist, priests, scout troops, mill workers, cows and several ghosts! Today it is an engaging heritage site, surrounded by landscaped grounds. Café and shop. *Open Sun-Thu 10.00-16.00 (Sun 13.00)*. Charge.
Salford Art Gallery and Museum Peel Park, The Crescent, Salford M5 4WU (0161 778 0800; www.salford.gov/salfordmuseum). In the centre of Salford University campus. Stroll down a Victorian street, admire the Landau carriages and discover a Victorian heritage. Test your strength or listen to the Victorian

WALKING & CYCLING
This is a rewarding navigation for the walker, while the experienced cyclist will also find it possible to follow the waterway throughout, using a suitable machine. The most realistic starting point is Salford Crescent Station, although the canal can be followed from its junction with the River Irwell, the first quarter of a mile having been restored. However, this stretch is scheduled for development and it may, therefore, be necessary to start from Ordsall Lane or from Oldfield Road, where it intersects the Salford Crescent to Salford Central railway line.
From Oldfield Road turn left down Upper Wharf Street, right up Back Hulme Street and left along Hulme Street to intersect The Crescent dual carriageway, turning left.
After 300yds turn left into Old Fire Station Square, exiting right along Christchurch Avenue into University Road West, which becomes University Road beside Salford Crescent Station.
Follow this until approximately 100yds after it turns sharply to the right, taking the path on your left through the trees. Take the next path on your left, through a passageway between the houses to join Strawberry Hill. Turn left and then 1st right down Lissadel Street. Cross Fredrick Street and continue to the junction with Broughton Road, turning right. Take the 1st left along Langley Road South and follow this for approximately 1 mile to the Lafarge Tarmac plant on the left. Turn left up Park House Bridge Road to join the line of the canal, (now in water), which can be followed to Clifton Aqueduct. *(continued on page 161)*

Top 20. Experience the sight and sounds of Victorian Salford with original shop fronts and fascinating interiors. Victorian gallery with paintings, pottery and fine art. Temporary exhibition programme, from hands-on activities to modern art. Coffee shop. *Open all year, Mon-Fri 10.00-16.45; Sat & Sun 13.00-17.00.* Free.

Working Class Movement Library 51 The Crescent, Salford M5 4WX (0161 736 3601; www.wcml.org.uk). The Working Class Movement Library records over 200 years of organising and campaigning by ordinary men and women. The collection provides a rich insight into working people's daily lives as well as their thoughts, hopes, fears and the roles they played in the significant events of their time. Bookshop and gallery. *Open Tue-Fri 10.00-17.00 & 3rd Sat in month 10.00-16.00. Closed B Hols.* Free.

Travel Information Traveline 0871 200 22 33 Train Tracker 0871 200 4950 or Text 8 49 50. Charge.

Tourist Information Salford no longer has its own, staffed Information Centre, so see page 38 for details of the Manchester Centre or visit www.visitsalford.info.

For Manchester attractions see page 182.

NAVIGATIONAL NOTES

1 See page 39 for details of the Manchester Ship Canal transit and using the Pomona Lock connection between the River Irwell and the Bridgewater Canal in Manchester.
2 Contact Canal & River Trust (0303 040 4040; enquiries. manchesterpennine@canalrivertrust.org.uk) for details on accessing the first ¼ mile of the navigation from the River Irwell.

Pubs and Restaurants

■**The Mark Addy** Stanley Street, Salford M3 5EJ (0161 834 7271). Named after a local hero and publican, famous for saving people from drowning in the adjacent River Irwell, this hostelry still serves real ale. *Regular* live music, an outside drinking area and Wi-Fi. *Open 11.30.*

■**The New Oxford** 11 Bexley Square, Salford M3 6DB (0161 832 7082; www.thenewoxford.com). Friendly, welcoming pub serving a superb selection of real ales, continental draught lagers, real cider and over 100 bottled continental beers. Appetising, freshly cooked bar meals are available *Mon-Sat 12.00-16.00 (Sat 15.00)*. Outside seating, sports TV and Wi-Fi. Quiz *Tue.* Open *12.00.*

■**The Kings Arms** 11 Bloom Street, Salford M3 6AN (0161 839 8726; www. kingsarmssalford.com). An eclectic mix of beer, food, film, music and the performing arts, this Grade II listed pub serves real ale and homemade food *daily – Sun* roasts *14.00-20.00.* Downstairs lies the pub part, whilst upstairs is devoted to the community-led Studio Salford. Beer garden. Knitting club *Mon. Open 12.00.*

■**The Eagle Inn** 18 Collier Street, Salford M3 7DW (0161 819 5002) Traditional, back street local, known to its regulars as the Lamp Oil, serving real ale and real cider in its unadulterated, Grade II listed, 1903 interior. The attached cottage has been converted into a live music venue. Patio, traditional pub games and Wi-Fi. *Open 12.30.*

For **Pubs and Restaurants** in Manchester *see* page 181.

Manchester Bolton & Bury Canal Salford

Ringley

By any standards the Clifton Aqueduct is an impressive structure and serves as a foretaste of the engineering glories that this waterway has yet to disclose. The motorway represents the first real obstacle to restoration but the broad track under its Irwell flyover suggests at least one immediate solution. To the north three electricity pylons are planted squarely in the navigation's bed which, together with Rhodes Lock, is firmly fenced off making it a somewhat forbidding proposition. However, the tantalising views of the river, some 40-feet below, glimpsed through the boughs of the ensuing sylvan glade, are more than compensation.

● **Clifton Junction**
Gt Manchester PO box, tel, station (limited service). As its name suggests, this was the point where the now defunct Manchester, Bury & Rossendale Railway met the Manchester & Bolton Railway. The former crossed the River Irwell on the Clifton Viaduct, just downstream of the aqueduct and known locally as the Thirteen Arches. Battery and pottery manufacture are also to be found in the district, although there is little to mark its centre.
Fletcher's Canal This early navigation ran north, for approximately one mile, along the west bank of the River Irwell, from its intersection with the Manchester Bolton & Bury Canal beside the Clifton Aqueduct, serving Wet Earth Quarry (*see* Clifton Country Park on page 160). Little evidence of its existence remains today.

● **Stoneclough**
Gt Manchester. PO, tel, stores, station (Kearsley). Once home to a power station, a cotton mill and a paper mill, Stoneclough is effectively a suburban area of Kearsley and embraces Prestolee and Ringley. St Saviour's Church, with its detached tower, sits in a field between the Horseshoe pub and the Irwell, overlooking Ringley Old Bridge. The original church was erected in 1625, rebuilt in 1820 and totally replaced in 1854 with the current edifice, which contains the Rococo chancel rails, communion table and some stained glass from the original. The tower dates from the 17th-C structure.

Milestone 8 3/4 at Ladyshore (page 164)

● **Farnworth**
Gt Manchester. PO, tel, stores, chemist, baker, butcher, greengrocer, hardware, banks, off-licence, takeaways, fish & chips, station. The town lies on the northern limits of the Duke of Bridgewater's Worsley Navigable Levels: the 46-mile interconnected, underground arrangement of canals linking a series of coal mines with the Bridgewater Canal at Worsley Delph. Commenced in 1757, this system employed a complex series of inclined planes and narrow, wooden craft known as 'starvationers'. Iron foundries and cotton and paper mills were also established in the area.
Farnworth Little Theatre Cross Street, Farnworth, Bolton BL4 7AJ (0845 643 0808; www. farnworthlittletheatre. weebly.com). Long standing, amateur theatrical company who put on approximately five productions per year to great acclaim. Telephone or visit the website for further details.
Farnworth Market King Street, Farnworth BL4 9DL (01204 336840; www.bolton.gov.uk/website/Pages/ FarnworthMarket.aspx). A well-established, traditional street market selling everything from fruit and vegetables to meat clothing and toys. *Open Mon & Fri-Sat 09.00-17.00.* Flea market *Sat 07.00-14.00.*

● **Moses Gate**
Gt Manchester. PO box, tel, stores, chemist, hardware, takeaways, fish & chips, off-licence, garage, station. A corruption of the words Moss – a boggy place – and the old English 'gata' meaning a road. The Industrial Revolution brought chemical works, paper mills and a bleach works, all since demolished.
Moses Gate Country Park Hall Lane, Farnworth BL4 3DN (01204 334343). A 750-acre site situated at Moses Gate in the Croal and Irwell Valleys, part of which is also known as Crompton Lodges. *Open dawn to dusk.*

WALKING & CYCLING

Clifton to Ringley: Cross the river on the Clifton Aqueduct and head north towards the M6o, taking the path that runs between the lagoons and the Irwell – negotiating the motorway through the Irwell flyover – picking up the towpath and line of the navigation (now protected by a chain link fence) just beyond the electricity pylon.

Follow the towpath, running between the river and canal bed, to its intersection with Red Rock Lane, at Giant's Seat. Beyond the garden centre, and just before the sewerage works, take the path leading uphill to the right to regain the towpath and follow the line of the waterway running above the works boundary fence to its junction with Ringley Road – crossing Fold Road beside the Horseshoe pub. (continued on *page 164*).

Pubs and Restaurants

◗╳**The Horseshoe** 395 Fold Road, Ringley, Stonelough M26 1FT (01204 571714; www. thehorseshoeinnringley.com). Beside Bridge 41, and opposite the old Packhorse Bridge crossing the River Irwell, this popular pub serves real ale and food *daily 12.00-21.00*. Dog- and child-friendly, garden, open fires and Wi-Fi. Booking advisable *Thu-Sun L. Open 12.00.*

╳♀**La Roma Restaurant and Bar** Kearsley Hall Road, Stonelough M26 1GT (01204 707932; www. laromarestaurant.co.uk). Situated in the old Lord Nelson pub, overlooking the Irwell, this restaurant serves all the Italian classic dishes and is *open Mon-Sat L and E and Sun 12.00-21.00*. Children welcome.

◗**The Grapes** 47 Market Street, Stonelough M26 1HR (07809 484271). Friendly local, in the village centre, serving real ale and food *daily L and E*. Dog- and family-friendly, real fires and outside seating. Sports TV, traditional pub games and Wi-Fi. *Open 12.00.*

◗**The Market Street Tavern** 131 Market Street, Stonelough M26 1HF (01204 572985). Compact local serving a rotating range of real ale. Dogs and children welcome; *regular* live music. Outside seating, traditional pub games and Wi-Fi. *Open Mon-Fri 14.00 & Sat-Sun 12.00.*

◗**The Britannia Inn** 34 King Street, Farnworth BL4 7AF (01204 416331). Friendly local serving real ale and food *L*. Outside drinking area, sports TV, traditional pub games and Wi-Fi. *Open 11.00.*

◗**The Wellington Inn** 56 Market Street, Farnworth BL4 7NY (01204 862180). Bearing a name that is often abbreviated locally to an item of waterproof footwear, this community pub dispenses well-kept real ale and good conversation, together with food *L. Regular* live music, sports TV, traditional pub games and Wi-Fi. *Open 11.30.*

◗**The Railway Hotel** Egerton Street, Moses Gate BL4 7JZ (01204 571858; www.joseph-holt.com/ pubs/view/railway-hotel). Imposing, two-roomed pub serving real ale and food *L. Regular* live music, bingo *Tue* and Karaoke *Fri-Sat*. Traditional pub games, sports TV and Wi-Fi. *Open 13.00.*

161

Bolton

Across Hall Lane, Moses Gate, there was originally a substantial aqueduct, followed by a second a few hundred yards along Fogg Lane, and their absence represent the next two restoration challenges. However, they pale into insignificance beside the missing Damside Aqueduct which, until 1965, spanned the River Tonge, only to fall to an act of unprovoked barbarity. The final mile or so of the Bolton Arm, which terminated at Church Wharf (just beyond the railway viaduct carrying the Bolton – Blackburn line) is, for the most part, obliterated by the A666 dual carriageway.

● **Bolton**

Gt Manchester. All services. From the time that Flemish weavers first settled in the area during 14th C, Bolton has been a focus for textile production which, with the invention of Arkwright's Spinning Jenny and Carding Machine, together with Crompton's Spinning Mule, saw the town rise to become one of the world's largest centres of cotton spinning during the 1920's. By 1930 there were 216 cotton mills and 29 dyeing and bleaching works, yet just 50 years later production had virtually come to a standstill. At the turn of the 20th C, Bolton was heralded as the third largest engineering centre in Lancashire (after Manchester and Oldham) producing everything from railway locomotives to wrought iron, yet today there is, again, but scant evidence of this industry. However, gracious buildings and wide-open leafy squares still testify to the town's past glories and the swathes of generous, pedestrianized streets make walking through the centre a positive delight. The 700 listed buildings and 26 conservation areas remain as a lasting witness to the prosperity brought about through previous endeavour.

Aquarium Le Mans Crescent, Bolton BL1 1SE (01204 332853; www.boltonmuseums.org.uk/aquarium). An extensive collection, containing a wide range of fresh water fish from all over the world. *Open Mon-Sat 09.00-17.00 (Wed 09.30) & Sun 10.00-16.00. Free.*

Hall i' th' Wood Green Way, off Crompton Way, Bolton BL1 8UA (01204 332377/332853; www.boltonmuseums.org.uk/historic-halls). Originally a late medieval yeoman farmer's house, later inhabited by Samuel Crompton and finally purchased by Lord Leverhulme in 1899, who restored the building and donated it to Bolton Corporation in 1902. *Open Tue 10.00-15.00 & Sat 12.00-16.00. Free.*

Market Ashburner Street, Bolton BL1 1TJ (01204 336825; www.bolton.gov.uk/website/Pages/BoltonMarket.aspx). This award-winning market has a growing reputation as the premier food market in the North West. *Open Tue & Thu-Sat 09.00-17.00.*

Museum and Art Gallery Le Mans Crescent, Bolton BL1 1SE (01204 332211; www.boltonmuseums.org.uk/museum). Fine and decorative art; botany; local history and Egyptology. Family-friendly events and exhibitions all the year round. *Open as per Aquarium. Free.*

Smithills Hall Smithills Dean Road, Bolton BL1 7NP (01204 332377/332853; www.boltonmuseums.org.uk/historic-halls). Grade I listed building, containing fine examples of architecture through the ages, from medieval and Tudor right through to Victorian times. The hall is set in formal gardens overlooking the west Pennine moors. *Open Wed-Fri 10.00-15.00 & Sun 12.00-16.00. Charge.*

Tourist Information Centre Central Library, Le Mans Crescent, Bolton BL1 1SE (01204 334321; www.visitbolton.com). *Open Mon-Tue and Thu 08.00-19.30; Wed and Fri 08.00-17.30 & Sat 09.00-17.00.*

WALKING & CYCLING

Moses Gate to Bolton: At the light controlled, equestrian crossing over A6053 (Hall Lane) head north into the woods, along Fogg Lane (in reality just a path!) until, after approximately 1/3rd mile, two paths appear, heading uphill on the right. Take the second one that runs at approximately 45° to Fogg Lane to re-join the line of the towpath, distinguished (as in so many places along this waterway) by the row of substantial coping stones.

Beyond Smithy Bridge 57 a tarmac path leads to the start of the demolished Damside Aqueduct, which can be negotiated by taking the path into Crossen Street and turning right beside No 5, descending the steps onto Radcliffe Road and again turning right. Follow the road over the River Tonge and turn immediately left into Chapel Place, along a track (beside the Lever Bridge pub) signposted Restricted Byway. At the brick wall take the path up to the right where evidence of the canal again becomes visible amongst the trees.

By the time A666 St Peter's Way strikes in from the left, there is little left to do save more or less follow its course along grassy, meandering pathways, first walking under the redundant Burden Railway Viaduct. After approximately ¼ mile, having passed behind a housing estate, the path joins Hilden Street, which can be followed to its junction with A579, Bradford Street. Turn left and, having crossed the road, take the path right, through trees, again paralleling St Peter's Way to its intersection with the railway viaduct, picking up the underpass and a path leading up Church Bank, into the town. Sadly, the last mile or so of waterway now lies beneath the pounding wheels and tarmac of the busy A666.

Iconic steam crane at Ladyshore used as the MB&BCS logo

Pubs and Restaurants

The Levers Arms 3 Top O'th Lane, Darcy Lever, Bolton BL3 1SS (01204 392486). 200yds north west of 59 Bentley Bridge. Friendly, welcoming community pub serving real ale and real cider. Dogs welcome. Garden, sports TV and traditional pub games. *Open Mon-Fri 15.00 & Sat-Sun 12.00.*

The Volunteer 276 Radcliffe Road, Bolton BL3 1RS (01204 524271). On the Crossen Street towpath diversion. Lively, community local serving real ale. Garden, traditional pub games and sports TV. *Open 12.00.*

The Farmers Arms 357 Radcliffe Road, Bolton BL3 1RU (01204 524106; www.farmersarmsbolton.co.uk). Beside Smithy Bridge 57. Comfortable, rambling hostelry, serving real ale and food *Wed-Fri L and E & Sat-Sun all day (Sun until 18.30). Occasional* live music. Family-friendly, garden and traditional pub games. Quiz *Wed. Open Wed-Sun 12.00 – (Sun until 21.00).*

The Lever Bridge Inn 206/210 Radcliffe Road, Bolton BL2 1PF (01204 393866). Crouching beneath the disused Bolton to Bury Railway Viaduct, this pub hosts *regular* live music and offers sports TV, traditional pub games and outside seating.

The Spinning Mule Nelson Square, Bolton BL1 1JT (01204 533339; www.jdwetherspoon.co.uk/home/pubs/the-spinning-mule). Named after the invention which revolutionised the cotton industry (giving Bolton world-wide fame) this pub now serves real ale, real cider and food *daily 08.00-22.00.* Children welcome. Sports TV and Wi-Fi. *Open 08.00.*

The Dog & Partridge 22-26 Manor Street, Bolton BL1 1TU (07708 377229). Majoring on local microbreweries, this pub serves a wide range of real ales and ciders, *opening at 17.00 (Sat 16.00). Weekend* live music, garden and traditional pub games.

The Barristers Bar 2-4 Churchgate, Bolton BL1 1HJ (01204 365174). Part of the Swan Hotel – a listed building dating from 1845 – this attractively panelled pub serves an excellent selection of real ales and food *L.* Live background music *most evenings.* Heated courtyard seating. *Open 12.00.*

Nob End

The two Ringley Locks lie hidden in the trees where the towpath is regained, across the main Kearsley Road and soon the navigation is again in water, perched above Prestolee, flanked by thin sandstone 'fencing' slabs. In parts the towpath is cobbled. Rounding a corner Nob End comes into view, heralded by the imposing Wellfield House and, upon crossing the striking Prestolee Aqueduct, the navigation arrives at the basin below the two sets of staircase locks. The aqueduct, locks, basins, bridges and waterway junction form a spectacular engineering ensemble, fully deserving to qualify in the forefront of any list of waterway wonders of the world, topped off with the contemporary twist of Liam Curtin's delightful Meccano bridge. The first ¾-mile of the Bolton Arm is in water and has in the past hosted several trailboat rallies, while the start of the Bury Arm is spacious and soon arrives at the site of a spectacular breach – dating from 1936 – and never repaired. Most of the length to Bury is in water, it being the last section in use and it hugs the contour, never far from the course of the Irwell, burbling along far below, often separated by only a thin screen of trees. Beyond Radcliffe, Elton Reservoir comes into view as trams rattle close by before the final evidence of the waterway vanishes in a short, shallow cutting.

WALKING & CYCLING

North of A667 Kearley Road the towpath can be regained at the site of the two Ringley Locks and followed through to the basin below Prestolee Locks. Here a track on the left leads downhill to Wilson's Bridge (over the River Croal) and a 10-minute walk to Farnworth Railway Station. Uphill, the track leads to the junction of the Bolton and Bury Arms – the former being in water with a good towpath through to Moses Gate Country Park (see Walking & Cycling *page 163*).

The Bury Arm can be followed without difficulty through to the outskirts of the town, where it intersects the roadway into an industrial estate. Bear right and pass under Daisyfield Railway Viaduct and along Wellington Street to its junction with Bolton Road. This is close to the terminus of the navigation. To access the town (and public transport) turn right, cross the river and follow signs through the underpass to avoid the busy main road. National Cycle Route 6 uses the towpath between Radcliffe and Bank Top Bridge 80.

See also the Irwell Sculpture Trail (*page 166*) for another possible series of walks, which could be planned in conjunction with towpath exploration, to make up a circular perambulation.

● **Little Lever**
*Gt Manchester. PO,
tel, stores, chemist, bank,
hardware, off-licence, takeaways,
fish & chips, library, garage.* Close to
the three branches of the Manchester
Bolton & Bury Canal, the village was
home to a variety of industry that relied
to great extent on the navigation to
bring in raw materials and export coal
and the finished products. In 1880 there
were 10 working coal mines listed in the
area, together with cotton and paper mills,
bleach and terracotta manufacture. There
was also a rope works. Boats were built and
repaired at the Canal Company's workshop
at Nob End.

● **Radcliffe**
*Gt Manchester. PO, tel, stores, chemists,
banks, butcher, off-licence, takeaways, fish &
chips, tram stop.* Evidence of the town as a
habitation goes back to the Mesolithic period
– approximately 6,000 BC – while more recent
activity is documented in the form of a medieval
hall and nearby Roman road. Water power, from
the River Irwell, was available long before the
invention of the steam engine so cotton spinning
and weaver, on an industrial scale, came early to the
settlement. This was followed by extensive coal mining,
paper-making, a chemical industry and brick production.
Little sign of all this past activity is apparent today.

● **Bury**
Gt Manchester. All services (but trams not trains). A Roman Urn,
containing small bronze coins dating from between AD 253-282,
was found immediately north of the present day town centre,
which has always been closely identified with the cotton industry,
together with its greatest son, Sir Robert Peel. Calico printing and light
engineering also figured as pillars of the area's industrial prowess, only
to decline in the second half of 20th C. Today, in common with many of the
prime textile producing areas of Lancashire, Bury seeks a new identity in retail, the
service industries and as a dormitory town for the nearby city of Manchester.

Bury Art Museum Moss Street, Bury BL9 0DR (0161 253 5878; www.bury.gov.uk/index.aspx?articleid=2537).
Housed in a distinctive Edwardian building, that is a work of art in itself, this welcoming and friendly
establishment is the perfect place to enjoy art and find out more about the rich history of Bury and the
surrounding area. Also a showcase for international and local art. Shop and coffee shop. *Open Tue-Sat 10.00-
17.00 (Sat 16.30).* Free.

Bury Castle Castle Armoury, Castle Street, Bury BL9 0LB. An early medieval, moated and fortified manor house,
dating from 1469. A leaflet detailing the history behind Bury Castle is available from the Tourist Information
Centre and all local libraries. *Open at any reasonable time.* Free.

Bury Market 1 Murray Road, Bury BL9 0BJ (0161 253 6520; www.burymarket.com). Dating from 1444, the present day market robustly promotes itself as both 'World Famous' and 'Really Large' which, with its impressive market hall and extensive spread of covered stalls, is rarely in dispute. Black pudding features prominently in any catalogue of Bury's native provender. Market Hall *open Mon-Sat 09.00-17.00*; Fish and Meat Hall *open Mon-Sat (not Tue afternoon) 09.00-17.00*; Open Market *Wed & Fri-Sat.*

East Lancashire Railway Bolton Street Station, Bury BL9 0EY (0161 764 7790; www.east-lancs-rly. co.uk). An award-winning restored railway offering a mainly steam-hauled service along the picturesque Irwell Valley. Shop and refreshments. Trains operate at *weekends and B Hols throughout the year and Apr-Sep, Wed-Fri.* Charge.

Fusilier Museum Moss Street, Bury BL9 0DF (0161 763 8950; www.fusiliermuseum.com). Home to the collection of the Lancashire Fusiliers and the Royal Regiment of Fusiliers – together they record more than 300 years of history and heritage. Shop and café (with Wi-Fi). *Open Mon-Sat 10.00-17.00 (Sat 16.00).* Charge.

Irwell Sculpture Trail (0161 253 5891; www.irwellsculpturetrail.co.uk). Winding its way from Bacup to Salford Quays and featuring over 70 artworks by locally, nationally and internationally renowned artists, this 33-mile trail links a series of clusters of thought provoking sculptures. It passes through Bury (with a cluster in the town, together with a second one in Burrs Country Park, just to the north), Radcliffe (one cluster in the town with a second in Outwood Country Park to the south), Clifton Country Park (where the M60 intersects the canal) and thence south into Salford linking into clusters at Chapel Street and Ordsall. Visit the website for further information and to download a detailed map.

Ladyshore Bolton Countryside Service (01204 334343). Immediately south of Ladyshore Bridge 68. A picturesque site, sandwiched between the canal and the River Irwell, rich in wildlife.

Tourist Information Centre The Fusilier Museum, Moss Street, Bury BL9 0DF (0161 253 5111; www.bury. gov.uk/index.aspx?articleid=2070). *Open Mon-Sat 10.00-17.00 (Sat 16.00).*

Pubs and Restaurants

▶✕The Jolly Carter 168 Church Street, Little Lever BL3 1BW (01204 411966). Popular local serving real ale and appetising food *Tue-Sun 12.00-20.00 (Sun 19.00)*. Family-friendly and *regular* live entertainment. Beer garden, sports TV, traditional pub games and Wi-Fi. Quiz *Sun*. B&B. *Open 12.00.*

▶The New Inn 56 Church Street, Little Lever BL3 1BE (01204 794611; www.newinnatlittlelever.co.uk). A sports orientated pub with 3D TV, serving real ale. *Regular* live music, newspapers, outside drinking area and traditional pub games. *Open 12.00 (Sat 11.00).*

▶Henighans 71 Lever Street, Little Lever BL3 1BA (01204 862664; www.henighans.com/little-lever). A warm, welcoming friendly atmosphere blends with well-kept real ales and food *available Fri-Mon 12.00-19.00*. Family-friendly. Newspapers, Wi-Fi and *regular* live music and quizzes. Large-screen TV, beer garden and traditional pub games. *Open 12.00.*

▶The Queen Anne 26 High Street, Little Lever BL3 1NB (01204 572640). Imposing, traditional local serving real ales. Dog- and family-friendly. Newspapers, sports TV, beer garden and traditional pub games. *Open Mon-Thu 16.00; Fri 14.00 & Sat-Sun 12.00.*

▶The Stopes Tavern 185 Stopes Road, Little Lever BL3 1NW (0161 723 4337). Friendly community local serving real ale and food *L and E*. Beer garden, newspapers and traditional pub games. *Open Mon-Wed 19.00; Thu 17.00 & Fri-Sun 12.00.*

▶The Bridge Tavern 8 Blackburn Street, Radcliffe M26 1WW (0161 425 1252). Friendly community pub dispensing real ale and food *L and E*. Child- and dog-friendly. Enclosed beer garden and *regular* live music. Wi-Fi, newspapers, traditional pub games and sports TV. Karaoke *Fri*. *Open 11.00 (Sun 12.00).*

▶✕The Lock Keeper 4 Mill Bank, Pilkington Way, Radcliffe M26 1AJ (0161 723 3502; www.all-inns.co.uk/pub/the-lock-keeper). Family-orientated establishment, in reality some 2½ miles from the nearest locks at Nob End, serving real ale and food *daily 12.00-22.00 (Sun 21.00)*. Indoor children's play area. Dogs welcome, sports TV, beer garden and Wi-Fi. *Open 11.30 (Sun 12.00).*

▶✕The Lamb Inn 533 Tottington Road, Woolfold, Bury BL8 1UB (0161 764 2714). Friendly, welcoming hostelry – with a landlord who is passionate about his beer – serving a range of real ales and food *Sat 13.00-17.00 & Sun 13.00-19.00*. Dogs and children welcome. Open fires, garden, sports TV, traditional pub games and Wi-Fi. Quiz *Thu (fortnightly)* and *Sat (fortnightly)* live entertainment. *Open Mon-Fri 16.30 & Sat-Sun 13.00.*

▶The Black Bull 8 Lowercroft Road, Bury BL8 2EY (0161 761 5961; www.theblackbullbury.co.uk). Award winning and welcoming hostelry serving real ale, real cider and appetising food *Mon-Sat L and E (not Sat L) & Sun 12.00-19.00*. Children and dogs welcome. Newspapers and Wi-Fi. Sports TV, open fires and a garden. Booking advisable. *Open 12.00.*

✕♟The Jewel in the Crown 102 Bolton Street, Bury BL9 0LP (0161 764 2211; www.jewelinthecrownbury. co.uk).

Try also **▶The Unicorn** 351 Bolton Road, Radcliffe M26 3QQ (0161 723 3307); **▶The Royal Oak** 28 Water Street, Radcliffe M26 4TW (0161 723 3581); **▶Wyldes** 4 Bolton Street, Bury BL9 0LQ (0161 797 2000; www.joseph-holt.com/pubs/view/wyldes); **▶The Robert Peel** 10 Market Place, Bury BL9 0LD (0161 764 7287; www.jdwetherspoon.co.uk/home/pubs/the-robert-peel); **▶The Old White Lion** 6 Bolton Street, Bury BL9 0LQ (0161 764 2641; www.guesthouse-bury.co.uk).

PEAK FOREST AND ASHTON CANALS

MAXIMUM DIMENSIONS
Length: 70'
Beam: 7'
Headroom: 6'

MANAGER
0303 040 4040;
enquiries.manchesterpennine@
canalrivertrust.org.uk

MILEAGE
PEAK FOREST CANAL
WHALEY BRIDGE to:
Marple Junction: 6½ miles
Dukinfield Junction: 14½ miles
Locks: 16

ASHTON CANAL
DUCKINFIELD JUNCTION to:
Ducie Street Junction: 6½ miles
Locks: 18

THE PEAK FOREST CANAL

This canal runs from Whaley Bridge and Buxworth through Marple to the Ashton Canal at
Dukinfield Junction. Authorised by Act of Parliament in 1794, it was aimed at providing an outlet
for the great limestone deposits at Doveholes, south east of Whaley Bridge. However, since
Doveholes is over 1000ft above sea level, the canal was terminated at Buxworth (Bugsworth as
it was then known), and the line was continued up to the quarries by a 6½-mile tramway.
The canal was completed by 1800 except for the flight of locks at Marple, which were not built
until 1804. A second, temporary, tramway bridged this gap in the meantime. Bugsworth soon
became a busy interchange point where the wagons bringing the stone down from Doveholes
tipped their load either into canal boats or into lime-kilns. This traffic, and the boats bringing
coal *up* the canal for firing the kilns, accounted for the greatest proportion of the canal
company's revenue.
The Peak Forest was also boosted by the opening of the Macclesfield Canal to Marple top lock
in 1831, making it part of a new through route from Manchester to the Potteries. The Cromford
& High Peak Railway was opened in 1831, joining up Whaley Bridge with the Cromford Canal
on the far side of the Peak District.
By the early 1840s the Peak Forest Canal was suffering from competition from the Trent &
Mersey Canal Company and two new railways. It was leased in perpetuity to the Sheffield,
Ashton-under-Lyne & Manchester Railway, later the Great Central. In 1922 the Bugsworth
traffic finished, while (through) traffic on the 'lower' Peak Forest Canal had disappeared by
World War II. Along with the Ashton, full navigation was restored in 1974 and now the splendid
Buxworth line is also open.

THE ASHTON CANAL

Authorised in 1792 and opened shortly afterwards, the Ashton was a strong rival of the
Rochdale Canal – with which it connects in Manchester. The two canals were constructed
simultaneously, partly to tap the big coal-producing area around Oldham. The Ashton also
opened a new trade route from Manchester to the textile mills of Ashton, while the Rochdale
served as a broad canal link over the Pennines between the Mersey and the rivers of Yorkshire.
In 1831 completion of the narrow Macclesfield Canal made the Ashton part of a through route
from Manchester to the Potteries.
The 1830s saw the peak of the Ashton Canal's prosperity. The canal company sold out to the
forerunner of the Great Central Railway Company in 1846, who continued to maintain and
operate the canal. Traffic declined in the present century and by 1962 it was unnavigable. A
determined effort by the Peak Forest Canal Society, the IWA, local councils and the BWB (as
was) resulted in its reopening in 1974.

Upper Peak Forest

The former Whaley Bridge Branch, now the
main line of the Peak Forest Canal, terminates
in a small basin at the north end of the town.
There is a building here of great interest to industrial
archaeologists: it covers a dock and was built in 1832 at
this, the junction of the Peak Forest Canal and the Cromford
& High Peak Railway. Here transshipment between canal boat and
railway wagon could take place under cover. The former railway's Whaley
Bridge inclined plane (now a footpath) rises to the south of this historic building. South
of bridge 34 the canal splits: the original main line turns east across the Goyt on an aqueduct to
Buxworth (its name changed from the supposedly less desirable Bugsworth) with its fascinating
basin complex overlooked by a fine *pub*. There is a handy *supermarket* which can be accessed from
bridge 37A. The Peak Forest Canal leads off to the north west; and it rapidly becomes apparent that
this is a navigation set in a robust, handsome landscape. Clinging desperately to a wooded hill-side
overlooking the steep, wide Goyt Valley, it winds its precarious way to New Mills. The trains that
traverse the opposite side of the valley look like tiny models on the distant hills. The A6 road and
the railway are always close to the navigation, but they detract not at all from its isolation. There
are charming stations at New Mills, Furness Vale and Whaley Bridge: from these one may take a
magnificent railway trip past two canal-feeding reservoirs and over the hills to the summit, 1200ft
above sea level, then down to the old Roman town of Buxton, now unfortunately the end of the
line. The canal continues north west along the hill-side towards New Mills. It is an enchanting
stretch, passing plenty of woods, pastures and grazing horses. As you approach New Mills you will
notice the smell of sweets in the air – Matlows, the makers of 'Swizzels', have their factory here.
Near Disley, another railway pops out of the long Disley Tunnel, way below the canal; while yet
another line appears above and beside the canal, from High Lane. Thus around New Mills the valley
contains three very picturesque railways. One of the pleasant features of this terrain is the easy
co-existence of woods, fields and a canal on the one hand, and a certain amount of industry on the
other. There are good moorings at bridge 24, where a public footpath gives easy access to Strines.

BOAT TRIPS

Judith Mary II Canal Street, Whaley Bridge SK23 7LS (01663 732408/07540 895615; www.judithmary.co.uk).
A long-established and fully equipped 70ft, 42-seater narrowboat available for private charter *all year*. Also
occasional public trips – telephone for details.
Phoenix is a day boat available for hire from Whaley Bridge Basin. Contact Trafalgar Marine Services Victoria
Works, Woodside Street, New Mills SK22 3HF (07934 750787/07790 748860; www.trafalgarmarineservices.
co.uk/dayboathire/phoenix for further details.

NAVIGATIONAL NOTES

1 You will need an anti-vandal key for the locks and swing-bridges on the Ashton Canal. Bridge 1 on the Peak Forest also requires an anti-vandal key.
2 A Watermate key is required to operate bridge 25 and 30.
3 Bridges 22 and 24 are windlass operated.

WALKING & CYCLING

The towpath is in good condition throughout. Peter Roger's Guide gives details of some walks and bicycle rides from Whaley Bridge – details at users. breathemail.net/peter.rogers/whaley.htm. Details of local walks exploring Bugsworth (as was) Basin and the parish paths can be obtained from: PFCC, 41 Tatton Street, Knutsford, Cheshire, WA16 6AE or at users.iclway.co.uk/don.baines/maps& guides.htm. The Millennium Walkway (01663 743434/746904; www.visitpeakdistrict.com/New-Mills-Millenium-Walkway/details/?dms=3&feature=4&venue=6080107) which starts by the Heritage Centre in New Mills (*see* page 170) gives access to previously inaccessible parts of the gorge near New Mills. You can also obtain a series of leaflets from the centre giving full details of The Torrs Industrial Trail, The Bridges Trail, The Sett Valley Trail and The Waterside Way. The Goyt Way, which has an interpretation board at the canal terminus, and the Mid-Shires Way (from Buckinghamshire!) both pass through here.

Boatyards

Ⓑ**Furness Vale Marina** The Moorings, Station Road, Furness Vale SK23 7QA (01663 747475; www.aquaquero.co.uk/companies/72/furness-vale-marina). 🛢🛒 D Pump out, long term mooring, winter storage, boat sales, chandlery, dry dock.
Ⓑ**TW Marine** Station Road, Furness Vale SK23 7QA (01663 745757; www.twmarine.co.uk). Marine engineers, chandlery.
Ⓑ **New Mills Marina** Hibbert Street, New Mills SK22 3SS (01663 741310; www.canalmarinas.com/newmills_marina.html). Beside Bridge 28. D Gas, pump out, solid fuel, short- and long-term mooring, toilets, showers, laundrette, *24hr* CCTV. Public telephone nearby.

A SILK PURSE FROM A SOW'S EAR

The Ashton Canal is now a part of the Cheshire Ring, a superb 100-mile cruising circuit which can be comfortably completed in a week. Those with extra energy, or a day or two more, can add in a diversion along the Peak Forest Canal, and their efforts will reap just reward. The ability to cruise these waterways is due to those who campaigned between 1959 and 1974 to clear and restore canals that had become both an eyesore and a danger. Extensive lobbying resulted in the formation of the Peak Forest Canal Society, and with the staging of the 1966 IWA National Rally at Marple, restoration gained momentum. 'Operation Ashton', held over a weekend in September 1968, saw 600 waterway enthusiasts clear more than 2000 tons of rubbish from the canal. Local people were amazed, and began to realise that what had long been regarded as an eyesore and a danger could now become a valuable local amenity. *The corner had been turned*. Following a rally on the Rochdale Canal at Easter 1971, local authorities and the British Waterways Board (as it then was) decided to proceed with full restoration of the Ashton and Peak Forest Canals. We owe a great debt to all those involved.

● Whaley Bridge

Derbs. PO, tel, stores, chemist, baker, takeaways, fish & chips, delicatessen, bank, off-licence, library, garage, station. Built on a steep hill at the end of the canal, with good views across the Goyt valley, this is now a quiet and pleasant place, a new bypass having removed much of the traffic. The beautiful nearby hills are, however, more noteworthy than the town. There is also a useful cycle shop: The Bike Factory Vernon House, Beech Road, Whaley Bridge SK23 7BP (01663 735020; www.ukbikefactory.com). *Open Mon-Sat 09.00-17.30 (Thu-Fri 19.00).* Gas is available from the builders' merchants beside the Basin (01663 732168; www.sdrinkwaterandson.co.uk).

Cromford & High Peak Railway In the early 1820s a physical connection was planned between the Peak Forest Canal at Whaley Bridge and the Cromford Canal, way over to the south east on the other side of the Peak District, using a junction canal. However a waterway would have been impracticable through such mountainous terrain, and so a railway was constructed. Known as the Cromford & High Peak Railway, it was opened throughout in 1831, and was 33 miles long. With a summit level over 1200ft above sea level, this extraordinary standard-gauge goods line was interesting chiefly for its numerous slopes and inclined planes, up which the wagons were hauled by either stationary or tenacious locomotive steam engines (the steepest gradient on the line was 1 in 7). The C & HPR closed in 1967; now much of the route has been turned into a public footpath and bridleway. Around Whaley Bridge one may still see the remains of the short inclined plane (now a footpath) which brought the goods down the hill, then through the town to the wharf at the terminus of the Peak Forest Canal.

Toddbrook Reservoir Just south of Whaley Bridge. A very pleasant area for picnicking and walking. Private sailing club; fishing rights on this CRT reservoir are exercised by an angling club (day tickets available).

● Buxworth

Derbs. PO box, tel. The main feature in Buxworth is the fascinating old terminal basin system. This used to be a tremendously busy complex, and is of great interest to industrial archaeologists. The canal line to Bugsworth (as it was then known) was built to bring the canal as near as possible to the great limestone quarries at Doveholes, a plate tramway being constructed in 1799 via Chapel Milton to complete the connection. Known as the Peak Forest Tramway, this little line, 6½ miles long, brought the stone down the hills to Bugsworth, where it was transshipped into waiting canal boats. Throughout the history of the line, the wagons on the tramway were drawn exclusively by horse-power – except for a 500yd inclined plane in Chapel-en-le-Frith, where the trucks were attached to a continuous rope so that the descending trucks pulled empty ones up the 1 in 7½ slope. The tramway was closed by 1926, and the sidings and basins at Buxworth became disused and overgrown, but are now fully restored and open to navigation. They should not be missed!

● Furness Vale

Derbs. PO box, tel, fish & chips. A main road (A6) village, useful for supplies.

● New Mills

Derbs. PO, tel, stores, chemist, banks, hardware, butcher, takeaway, fish & chips, garage, stations. A mostly stone-built town on the Cheshire/Derbyshire border; its industries include textile printing, engineering and engraving. A boatyard occupies old canal buildings to the east of bridge 28. There is also a useful cycle shop: Sett Valley Cycles 9 Union Road, New Mills (01663 742629; www.settvalleycycles.co.uk). *Open Mon-Sat 09.00-18.00 (Sat 17.00).*

New Mills Heritage Centre Rock Mill Lane, New Mills, High Peak SK22 3BN (01663 746904; www.newmillstowncouncil.org.uk/heritage.php). North of Thornsett Road Bridge (28). Located by the path leading down into the Torrs Gorge, next to the bus station. A splendid centre where you can see a display illustrating the history of the town, with a superb model. There is also a mock mine tunnel. Local books and walk details can be purchased in the shop, and there is also a café. The Millennium Walkway starts here. *Open Tue-Fri 10.30-16.00; Sat-Sun & B Hols 10.30-16.30 (winter 16.00).*

● Disley

Cheshire. PO, tel, stores, chemist, bank, greengrocer, butcher, baker, delicatessen, takeaways, garage, station. On the south bank of the canal. The centre of the village is quite pretty, spoilt slightly by the A6 traffic. The village is up the hill, south west of bridge 26. The attractive church stands among trees above the little village square. It was greatly renovated in the last century, but the ancient tower with the griffin leering down at passers-by dates from the 16th C. Vehicular and pedestrian access to Lyme Park (*see page 154*) is from the A6 near Disley, 1½ miles south west of Bridge 26. There is also a useful cycle shop: Freeride Cycles 18-20 Market Street, Disley SK12 2AA (01663 764444; www.freeridecycles.com). *Open Tue-Sat 10.00-17.30 (Tue 19.00).*

Pubs and Restaurants

The Railway 33-35 Market Street, Whaley Bridge SK23 7AA (01663 732245). Real ale in a fine straightforward pub. Children welcome. Outside seating and sports TV. *Open 17.00.*

The Shepherds Arms 7 Old Road, Whaley Bridge SK23 7HR (01663 732384). Once a farmhouse, this unspoilt gem of a pub serves real ales from its 17th-C stone-flagged taproom. Beer garden, open fires and traditional pub games. *Open Mon-Fri 15.00; Sat 12.00 & Sun 14.00.*

The Goyt Inn 8 Bridge Street, Whaley Bridge SK23 7LR (01663 732840). An attractive pub with an open fire and a garden, close to the canal basin and shops. Real ale is served. Children are welcome, and there is a garden. *Open Mon-Fri 18.00 & Sat-Sun 12.00.*

✕**Pear Tree Café** Whaley Bridge 10 Canal Street, Whaley Bridge SK23 7LS (01663 7719811). Describing itself as a Mediterranean café/restaurant, this welcoming establishment serves breakfast, light lunches, tea, coffee and homemade cakes. *Open Tue-Fri 09.00-16.00 (Wed 15.00); Sat 09.30-16.00 & Sun 10.00-15.00.*

✕**The Navigation** Buxworth, High Peak SK23 7NE (01663 732072; www.navigationinn.co.uk). By the canal terminus, this is a superbly situated pub overlooking the old basins, beautifully decorated with some fine canal memorabilia, and with real fires *in winter*. It was built around 1794, and was once run by Pat Phoenix, *Coronation Street's* Elsie Tanner. A choice of real ale, along with restaurant and bar meals available *L and E, daily*. Garden with a playground. Children welcome *until 21.00*. Pool table and darts. *Occasional* live bands. B & B. *Open 11.00.*

The Crossings Station Road, Furness Vale SK23 7QS (01663 743642). By the level crossing, up the hill from bridge 31. A friendly pub serving real ale. Children welcome, garden. *Open Mon-Fri 17.30 & Sat-Sun 11.00.*

✕♀**Imperial Palace** 142 Buxton Road, Furness Vale SK23 7PH (01663 745777). Cantonese restaurant *open Tue-Sun 17.30-late.* Delivery service.

Soldier Dick 150-152 Buxton Road, Furness Vale SK23 7PH (01663 611010; www.soldierdick. co.uk). Welcoming, friendly pub serving real ales and good value food *L and E*. Children welcome, open fires and a garden. B&B. *Open 12.00.*

The Beehive Albion Road, New Mills SK22 3EY (01663 749222). Just along the lane opposite New Mills Wharf, by bridge 28. A welcoming stone-built pub. Real ales, *regular* live music and a comfortable upstairs lounge. Dogs welcome, sports TV, a beer garden and Wi-Fi. *Open daily 17.00-23.00.*

The White Lion 135 Buxton Road, Disley SK12 2HA (01663 762800; www.thewhiteliondisley. co.uk). South of Bridge 26. Village pub featuring a doggy dining room complete with blankets (and a meal for the price of a donation to a dogs trust). A wide selection of real ales are served, together with food (majoring on pies) *Tue-Sun 12.00-21.00 (Sun 16.00)*. Children welcome, garden, newspapers and open fires. *Open Mon 18.00 & Tue-Sun 12.00.*

✕**The Romper** Ridge End, Marple SK6 7ET (0161 427 1354; www.theromper.co.uk). ¼ mile south west of Rawton Walls Bridge 21. In an attractive setting, above the canal, this pub serves real ale and food *daily 12.00-20.30*. Family-friendly and a garden with extensive views. *Open 12.00*. Also accessible from the Macclesfield Canal by following the footpath leading off the lane east of Clough Bridge 6.

The Sportsman 105 Strines Road, Strines SK6 7GE (0161 427 2888; www.the-sportsman-pub.co.uk). Perched on the side of the Goyt Valley, this pub has superb views across wooded countryside and serves real ales, together with food *Mon-Sat L and E & Sun 12.00-20.00*. Dog- and family-friendly. Garden, open fires and traditional pub games. Folk *1st Wed of month*. Camping. *Open Mon-Fri L and E & Sat-Sun 12.00.*

Beswick Locks (see page 176)

Marple Aqueduct

The canal, accompanied by the River Goyt beyond the road to the east, reaches Marple Junction, where the Macclesfield Canal leaves to the south west by the attractive buildings of Marple Yard. The 16 Marple Locks then carry the Peak Forest Canal down 214ft towards Manchester. The locks themselves, which are spaced out over 1 mile, have an unrivalled setting in an excellent combination of built-up area, parkland, tall trees and steep hillside; the River Goyt is now hidden down in the wooded valley to the east. Look out for the interesting Possett Bridge, where there is a small tunnel for the towpath (and horse) and an even smaller one for the boatman, leading down to the lock. At the foot of the locks, where the River Goyt is crossed, there is the superb spectacle of a major canal

WALKING & CYCLING

There are excellent walks in the Marple area, where stunning scenery combines with the often unexpected remains of early industry. The late Gordon Mills has a written an excellent series of six inexpensive guides for the local community council which take you on some of the finest walks this area has to offer: Marple Dale; The Roman Bridge & Lakes; Marple Locks & Brabyns Park; Chadkirk; From Way to Cut and Donkey Wood. No walk is longer than 4 miles, and each is fully described, with maps and old photographs. You can obtain them from Marple Library or local bookshops, and find details at www. marple-uk.com/walkso.htm. Mr Mills was quite happy for you to download the walks, in exchange for a donation to the British Heart Foundation.

aqueduct with an even bigger railway viaduct alongside. West of here a narrow stretch was once Rose Hill Tunnel, long since opened out. The canal then traverses a wooded hillside before diving into Hyde Bank Tunnel, 308yds long. The towpath is diverted over the hill, passing a farm. On the other side, a couple of minor aqueducts lead the canal northwards, away from the Goyt Valley and past Romiley, Bredbury and Woodley, where there is a narrow 176yd-long tunnel, this time with the towpath continuing through it. There is a swimming pool close to the canal at bridge 14.

NAVIGATIONAL NOTES

1 There is no mooring on the Marple flight since water levels in the pounds can fall dramatically when the locks are in use.
2 Hyde Bank Tunnel, although appearing wide, does not have sufficient clearance for two boats to pass. Make sure it is clear before you enter.

● **Marple**
Gt Manchester. All services. Once a famous hat-making centre, the town is most interesting by the canal. The town centre can be accessed from bridge 18.

● **Marple Locks**
The 16 locks at Marple were not built until 1804, four years after the rest of the navigation was opened. The 1-mile gap thus left was bridged by a tramway, while the Canal Company sought the cash to pay for the construction of a flight of locks. This was obviously a most unsatisfactory state of affairs, since the limestone from Doveholes had to be shifted from wagon to boat at Bugsworth Basin, from boat to wagon at Marple Junction, and back into boat again at the bottom of the tramway. Not surprisingly, a container system was developed – using iron boxes with a 2-ton payload – to ease the triple transshipment. However, this was no long-term solution, and when the necessary

£27,000 was forthcoming the company authorised construction of the flight of locks. Today they stand comparison with any flight on the network. Note especially Samuel Oldknow's superb warehouse, by lock 9, now tastefully converted to offices.

● **Marple Aqueduct**
Deservedly scheduled as an ancient monument, this three-arched aqueduct over the River Goyt is a very fine structure, in an exquisite setting almost 100ft above the river. Designed by Benjamin Outram, its construction utilises circular pierced shoulders above each arch to reduce the weight of the rubble filling whilst providing a decorative feature. Contrast and interest are further added by the use of two different colours of gritstone in the parapets and ledges.

● **Romiley**
Gt Manchester. All services. A useful place for supplies.

Pubs and Restaurants

◆✕**The Navigation** at Lock 13 9 Stockport Road, Marple SK6 6BD (0161 427 3817; www.navigationmarple.robinsonsbrewery.com). Useful for 'lock wheelers' (remember, there is no mooring on the flight!) A large comfortable pub serving real ale. Food is available *daily 12.00-19.00.* Children and dogs welcome. Beer garden, sports TV and *regular* live music. *Open 12.00.*

✕♟**Murillo's** 48 Stockport Road, Marple SK6 6AB (0161 427 1200; www.murillos.com). Spanish restaurant and tapas bar. *Open Tue-Sun 09.00-23.00* for food and drinks.

◆**The Hatters Arms** 81 Church Lane, Marple SK6 7AW (0161 427 1529; www.hattersarmsmarple.robinsonsbrewery.com). Set in a terrace, this intimate little pub – with panelled walls and leaded lights – serves real ale and food *Sun-Thu L and Fri-Sat 12.00-21.00.* Dog- and family-friendly. Quiz *Thu* and traditional pub games. *Open 12.00.*

◆**The Railway** 223 Stockport Road, Stockport, Marple SK6 6EN (0161 427 2146; www.railwayrosehillmarple.robinsonsbrewery.com). West of Possett Bridge 18. Friendly pub, beside

Rose Hill railway station, serving real ale and food *daily 12.00-14.00 (Sun 15.00).* Children welcome. Garden, sports TV and Wi-Fi. *Open 12.00.*

◆**The Spread Eagle** Hatherlow, Romiley SK6 3DR (0161 494 5723; www.almond-pubs.co.uk/spread-eagle). A sympathetically renovated pub, dating from the 1770s, serving real ale and food *Mon-Fri L and E & Sat-Sun 12.00-21.00 (Sun 20.30).* Carvery. Children welcome *until 21.00.* Outside seating and real fires. *Open 11.30.*

◆**The Duke of York Hotel** Stockport Road, Romiley SK6 3AN (0161 406 9988). East of bridge 14. A choice of real ale in an unspoilt 18th-C pub. Food is available *daily L and E.* Garden, open fires and Wi-Fi. Quiz *Wed. Open 12.00.*

◆✕**Platform 1** 6 Stockport Road, Romiley SK6 4BN (0161 406 8686). Formerly the Railway, this pub and wine bar serves a wide range of real ales and food *daily 12.00-20.00* (accessed via separate entrance – Platform 2). Outside seating and Wi-Fi. *Open 12.00.*

See also **Pubs and Restaurants** and **Boatyards** entries on page 156.

Hyde

The canal continues northward through a landscape which becomes less rural, but increasingly interesting. Bridge 6 is a pretty roving bridge, grown wider over the years. To the north, beyond the M62 motorway, the industrial tentacles of Hyde – Greater Manchester – ensnare the canal traveller, but the approach to Dukinfield Junction and Portland Basin is still very pleasant. The towpath is tidy, with plenty of grass, trees and seats. A lift bridge, a canal arm, an aqueduct over the River Tame and a stone roving bridge provide plenty of canal interest as you approach the junction, where the Ashton canal heads south-west into Manchester, and the Huddersfield Narrow canal starts its journey east across the Pennines (see page 65) to Huddersfield. Portland Basin was constructed to allow boats to make the sharp turn here, and was nicknamed the 'weavers rest', since so many weavers had reputedly drowned themselves here during hard times, such as the famine of 1860 and the depression of the 1930s. The warehouse which faces you across the junction, built in 1834, has been well restored. The Ashton Canal takes you into Manchester proper: this is still a fine, solid industrial section of waterway, still with a few steaming factories, tall chimneys and a good clear towpath. If you pass Dukinfield Junction in mid-July, you may see the colourful Tameside Canals Festival, which has been running successfully for many years now.

Ashton-under-Lyne
Gt Manchester. All services. Walk north west from Portland Basin and you will find the church of St Michael, which was begun by Sir John de Assheton in the early 15th C and completed by his great grandson before 1516. The church is large, with a tall west tower rebuilt by Crowther in 1886–8. Particularly notable is the stained glass, depicting the Life of St Helena and dating from the 15th–16th C. A market was granted to the town in 1284, but by 1801 the population still numbered only 4800. It then expanded rapidly, due to the growth of cotton weaving in the area, and by 1851 totalled over 30,000.

Portland Basin Social & Industrial History Museum 1 Portland Place, Ashton-under-Lyne OL7 0QA (0161 343 2878; www.tameside.gov.uk; www. tameside.gov.uk/museumsgalleries/portland). This museum is housed in a superb reconstruction of a canal warehouse dating from 1834, at the junction of

the Ashton, Peak Forest and Huddersfield canals. It tells the rich story of Tameside's social, political and industrial history, drawing upon many different facets of local life. The museum features a 1920s street, working models, computer interactives, sound and film. The original waterwheel is restored to working order on the wharfside. Displays include topics such as textiles, hatting, printing, canals, coalmining, Chartism, education and politics. *Open Tue-Sun & B Hols 10.00-16.00 (Jul-Sep 17.00).* Café and shop. Free

Astley Cheetham Art Gallery Trinity Street, Stalybridge SK15 2BN (0161 338 6767; www.tameside. gov.uk/museumsgalleries/astleycheetham). Above Stalybridge Library, this gallery was built as a gift to the town in 1901. Exhibition programme of sculpture, textiles, painting and drawings, featuring work by prominent local artists and community groups. *Opening times vary so visit the website for details.* Free.

Stalybridge See page 58.

WALKING & CYCLING
Pasture and fine woodland are a feature of Haughton Dale Nature Reserve, to the west of the canal near Hyde. Paths follow the River Tame here. Details from: Park Bridge Heritage Centre, The Stable, Park Bridge, Ashton-under-Lyne OL6 6D (0161 330 9613; www.tameside.gov.uk/parkbridge). Café and Information Centre *open Thu-Sun 10.00-15.00.* Free.

Boatyards

ⓑ**Portland Basin Marina** Lower Alma Street, Dukinfield SK16 4SQ (0161 330 3133; www.portlandbasinmarina.co.uk) 🛢 D Pump out, gas, overnight and long-term mooring, winter storage, crane, 100-year-old dry dock, day boat hire, narrowboat hire, boat building and fitting out, engine repairs, chandlery, toilets, showers, books and maps, gifts, solid fuel, DIY facilities. Laundrette and supermarket close-by. *Emergency call out.*

ASHTON-UNDER-LYNE

STALYBRIDGE

59

HYDE

Pubs and Restaurants

The Ash Tree 9-11 Wellington Road, Ashton-under-Lyne OL6 6DA (0161 339 9670; www.jdwetherspoon.co.uk/home/pubs/the-ash-tree). With a name that directly reflects the town's original identity, this pub serves good value real ales, real cider and food *daily from 08.00*. Children welcome. TV screens, outside seating and Wi-fi.

The Engine Room 46 Wellington Road, Ashton-under-Lyne OL6 6DQ (0161 330 1757). Large town-centre pub, established in the old fire station, serving real ale and food *daily 09.00-21.00*. Children welcome and large-screen TV.

The Forester's Call 147 Old Street, Ashton-under-Lyne OL6 7SA (0161 330 1814; www.foresterscall.com). Town-centre local, serving real ales, with an award-winning garden and car park! Sports TV, traditional pub games, newspapers and Wi-fi. *Open 10.00*.

The Feathers Inn 62 High Street, Stalybridge SK15 1SE (0161 338 6403). A corner local serving real ale. Children are welcome *until 18.30*. Various artistes and music *weekends*. There is a useful fish and chip shop next door.

Station Buffet Platform One, Stalybridge Station, Rassbottom Street, Stalybridge SK15 1RF (0161 303 0007). A very fine refurbishment of the Victorian buffet, incorporating the stationmaster's house and ladies' waiting room. Having won many awards, it now serves real ale from a variety of breweries, along with real cider and bottled Belgian beers. Excellent food is served all day, and children are welcome. *Opens 09.30 for coffee and afternoon teas Wed 12.00-16.00. Quiz Mon*, folk night *Sat*. A short walk north of the canal.

The Wharf Tavern 77 Caroline Street, Stalybridge SK15 1PD (0161 338 2662). Traditional town pub serving a varying selection of guest real ales. Drinkers may bring in food from the *fish & chip shop* next door. Garden, sports TV and *regular* live music. *Open Mon-Thu L and E & Fri-Sun 12.00*.

BOAT TRIPS
Huddersfield Canal Society
Stillwaters is a 46-seater which operates from Portland Basin all year round for party bookings. Public trips run *most Sun and B Hols*. Telephone 07804 701249/07515 878549 for further details.

See also **Pubs and Restaurants** on page 59.

175

Droylsden

From start to finish, the Ashton Canal passes through a densely built-up area in which the canal is conspicuous as a welcome relief from the townscape which flanks it. Its clear water, excellent towpath, functional but dignified old bridges and the peace that generally surrounds it make it a haven for local school children, anglers, walkers and idlers, indeed for anyone who enjoys an environment that is quite separate from and unrelated to ordinary daily life. The rare pleasure, afforded only by an English canal, of stepping out of a city suburb into the peaceful and unpretentious atmosphere of the 18th C is once again, with continued restoration work, becoming available to all. At Fairfield Junction the top lock of the 18 which climb from Ducie Street Junction is encountered. It is a picturesque canal scene here with traditional buildings, including a shed dated 1833 standing over a canal arm, giving the area a quiet dignity. Descending the locks, you may wish to look out for the remains of several old canal arms: one of the more important was the 5-mile Stockport Branch, leaving from Clayton Junction, just below lock 11. The canal then falls through the remaining locks into Manchester. The surroundings are brightened by the well-cared-for Beswick flight of four locks, standing next to the new Stadium, where you can see the wonderful 'B of the Bang' sculpture, an explosion of spikes designed by Thomas Heathwick, to mark the success of the Commonwealth Games held here in 2002. Large-scale redevelopment has been completed at Paradise Wharf and Piccadilly Village, making this final stretch unusually gentrified, with smart flats, basins and a crane. The Rochdale Canal, joined here, stretches from Ducie Street Junction for 33 miles over the Pennines to join the Calder & Hebble Navigation, and is once again open to through navigation (*see page 180*) after many years of campaigning. The bottom mile or so of the Rochdale Canal remained navigable, from the junction with the Ashton Canal at Ducie Street down to Castlefield and its meeting with the Bridgewater Canal, and provided a vital link between the Bridgewater and Ashton Canals in the 100-mile Cheshire Ring cruising route.

NAVIGATIONAL NOTES

1 You will need a handcuff lock key for the locks on this and the Peak Forest Canal.

2 CRT advise you to cruise the Ashton lower Rochdale Canals early in the morning, and avoid school holidays if possible. Moor only at recognised sites in this area, and do not offer anyone you do not know a ride on your boat. Keep the front doors locked.

3 Bridge 21 is very low.

4 Passage through locks 1–18 should be commenced *before 10.00.*

THE CHESHIRE RING – THEN AND NOW

This route has remained one of the most popular cruising circuits for many years now – a one-week trip encompassing parts of the Trent & Mersey, the Bridgewater, the Ashton, the Peak Forest and Macclesfield canals, passing through a wide and exciting variety of canalscape. Part of the journey includes a passage through central Manchester, a pleasant experience these days, but it was not always so . . .

The problem used to be timing your passage through the city so that the 'Rochdale Nine' locks were open, and your subsequent overnight mooring was a safe one! Local children preyed upon you as you tackled the Ancoats, Beswick and Clayton flights, leaping across the locks from one side to the other, begging lifts, and 'picking up' *anything* you might have left lying around . . .

The lock machinery was stiff, water supply uncertain, and the things which fouled your propeller defied description . . .

It is, thankfully, VERY different now, and the city passage is very attractive, interesting and enjoyable. Just take the usual precautions.

Pubs and Restaurants

The Kings Head 169 Market Street, Droylsden M43 7AY (01298 277193). Decorated with military memorabilia, this busy pub attracts a mixed clientele and serves real ale, together with food *L and E*. Traditional pub games, outdoor drinking area and sports TV. Dogs welcome. *Weekend* discos and karaoke. *Open 11.00 (Sun 12.00).*

The Pearl Restaurant Bar and Lounge 119 Manchester Road, Audenshaw M34 5PY (0161 301 5680; www.thepearlrestaurant.co.uk).

South of Bridge 19. Brightly decorated, upmarket Asian restaurant, *open Mon-Fri 17.00 & Sat-Sun 12.00.* Outdoor terrace and DJ *weekends.*

The Jolly Angler 47 Ducie Street, Manchester M1 2JW (0161 236 5307). Near the junction. A small, plain and friendly pub. Real ale. Café nearby. Regular Irish and folk music sessions. Children welcome. Mooring nearby but **don't** leave your boat here overnight. *Open Mon-Fri 17.30; Sat 12.00 & Sun L and E.*

See also **Pubs and Restaurants** on page 181.

Boatyards

Droylesden Marina Lock Keepers Cottage, Droylesden (0161 330 3133). Secure pontoons for overnight and long-term moorings.

There is also a new marina being developed in **Piccadilly Basin**, Manchester.

New Islington Marina Ducie Street Junction *see page 185.*

Fairfield

Gt Manchester. PO box, tel, stores, off-licence, fish & chips, takeaway, garage. Immediately south of Fairfield Junction is a group of neat and tidy buildings around a fine chapel. This is an original Moravian settlement, established in 1785 by Benjamin Latrobe and consisting of tidy rows of cottages built in brick, intended to house the members of a self-contained community.

Velodrome Stuart Street, Manchester M11 4DQ (0161 223 2244; www.manchestervelodrome.com). Part of Sport City. Access from the bridge, west of bridge 9, and in view from bridge 8, when climbing the locks. This is the National Cycling Centre, where the track is widely regarded as one of the finest and fastest in the world. There is a full programme of exciting cycle races staged in this magnificent stadium, which recently hosted the track events of the Commonwealth Games 2002. *See also* Walking & Cycling.

City of Manchester Stadium Rowsley Street, Manchester M11 3FF (0161 438 7650; www.mcfc. co.uk). Part of Sport City. A wonderful 48,000 capacity stadium used for the 2002 Commonwealth Games. The foundation stone was laid by Tony Blair on the 17th of December 1999, and the stadium was built at a cost of £90 million.

Manchester

All services. One of Britain's finest Victorian cities, a monument to 19th-C commerce and the textile boom, its size increasing remorselessly with the building of the canals, and later railways. Unfortunately virtually no early buildings survived the city's rapid growth, although there is an incredible wealth of Victorian architecture still to be seen, in spite of redevelopment. The town hall and surrounding streets are a particularly rich area. St Peter's Square, by the town hall, was the site of the 'Peterloo Massacre' in 1819, when a meeting demanding political reform was brutally dispersed by troops carrying drawn sabres. Eleven people were killed and many more were injured. The Free Trade Hall, once the home of the Hallé Orchestra, is a little further along the road. Built in 1856, it was badly damaged in World War II, but was subsequently re-built to its original Palladian design. There is theatre, ballet and cinema, art galleries, and a wealth of interesting buildings, Victorian shopping arcades, many pubs with a choice of good beer and a variety of restaurants just a short walk from the canal. Sporting facilities are excellent, partly as a consequence of Manchester being the venue for the 2002 Commonwealth Games. The new developments at Salford Quays, on the Manchester Ship Canal, are quite breathtaking.

Manchester Visitor Information Centre Piccadilly Plaza, Portland Street, Manchester M1 4BT (0871 222 8223; www.visitmanchester.com). *Open 10.00–17.30 (Sun and B Hols 16.30).*

WALKING & CYCLING
Keen cyclists might like to visit the magnificent Velodrome (*see* above) for a 'Taster Session' where, for a very modest fee, you can hire a track bike and a helmet and ride the steeply banked circuit for an hour. Telephone 0161 223 2244 for details and times.

Bugsworth Basin (see page 169)

ROCHDALE CANAL

MAXIMUM DIMENSIONS

Length: 72' 0"
Beam: 14' 2" (Locks 40, 41 & 47: 13' 6")
Headroom: 7' 6" (7' 1" under the M62 culvert)
Draught: 2' 6" (recommended by CRT as some
sections of the western end of the canal are only
dredged to 3' 3")

MILEAGE

MANCHESTER to:
Failsworth: 5 miles
Castleton: 11½ miles
Littleborough: 16½ miles
Todmorden: 22 miles
Hebden Bridge: 26½ miles
SOWERBY BRIDGE: 32 miles

MANAGER

0303 040 4040;
enquiries.manchesterpennine@
canalrivertrust.org.uk

The Rochdale Canal is one of three Pennine canal crossings. It was authorised by an Act of Parliament in 1794 and completed exactly ten years later. With wide locks it was able to handle barges, Humber keels and even small coasters, the latter sometimes trading between the Continent and Irish ports, using the River Mersey and the Irwell Navigation at the eastern end. However, the Achilles' heel of the waterway lay in its requirement for a copious supply of water at the summit pound, together with the sheer physical effort required to operate the three locks per mile that are averaged over the canal's relatively short length.

The boom years for the canal were in the 1820s and 1830s before the inevitable railway competition began to make an impression. Passenger carrying packet boats (Manchester to Rochdale: 13 miles and 41 locks in 7 hours) and fast, light-goods-carrying fly boats (20 tons transported from Manchester to Todmorden in 12 hours) were both successful enterprises in the early 1800s.

In 1887 the canal's fortunes appeared to take an upturn when the canal company bought its own boats. Traffic included cotton, grain, coal, wool, cement, salt and timber, and whilst end to end carriage steadily declined, shorter journeys continued to thrive. At the outbreak of World War I the canal company was still ordering new craft (powered by 25hp inverted compound steam engines) which were capable, loaded, of pulling a further two laden dumb barges. However, in 1921, as competition from the roads took its toll, the fleet ceased operation and traffic became spasmodic. The last loaded boat to trade over the canal's entire length was *nb Alice*, in April 1937, carrying 20 tons of wire from Manchester to Sowerby Bridge. The navigation was officially closed by an Act in 1952, except for the stretch connecting the Bridgewater and Ashton canals in Manchester. Restoration was commenced nearly 30 years ago and the canal society had not only succeeded in protecting nearly all its original line, but also re-opened 16 miles of the eastern end. It has also, in conjunction with the local authority-based Canal Trust, inspired the construction of Tuel Lane Lock and Tunnel.

Subsequently Canal & River Trust and its partners have completed restoration at a cost of £23 million, rebuilding locks, bridges and tunnels and completing many new structures. This investment has only been possible because of projected benefits to the local community over a number of years, totalling in the region of £200 million.

Central Manchester

Departing from Dale Street Basin, the canal begins its unremitting climb into the Pennines flanked by a series of not unattractive, although somewhat unusual, stone-filled gabions. Attractively painted cast iron bridges, reflecting the livery of past railway companies, regularly span the navigation as it heaves its way up past a series of abandoned, but still impressive, cotton mills. Moving steadily onwards and upwards the waterway is accompanied by a mix of urban housing, parkland and industry; the redeveloped Victoria Mill at Miles Platting is a most impressive example. Passing Newton Heath with its canalside *market* and handy *shops*, the canal soon reaches Failsworth where there is a collection of fine mill buildings, many now in their second or third incarnations. The section of the waterway west of the A62 bridge had been built over and part of a supermarket had to be demolished during restoration; the remaining portion together with a *PO, banks and a chemist* still lies to the north beside the new footbridge. Beyond Failsworth, and several more solid mill buildings, development starts to step back from the navigation as it enters a pleasantly tree-lined section. Between here and Littleborough, the line of the canal has been designated an SSSI in recognition of its importance as a site for certain rare aquatic plants, particularly floating water plantain (*Luronium natans*). The staked-out rectangles along sections of the waterway are 'in-channel reserves' designed to protect the plant's tendrils of floating oval leaves and delicate three-petalled white flowers. The white-clawed crayfish has also adopted the canal, living in the well-oxygenated water of the lock by-washes where they remain hidden from the prying eyes of their natural predators such as herons and mink.

NAVIGATIONAL NOTES

1 See Navigational Notes 1 & 2 on page 177.
2 Volunteers are often available to assist boaters up the Flight to Failsworth and are an invaluable source of local knowledge and information. Contact Canal & River Trust (0303 040 4040; enquiries.manchesterpennine@canalrivertrust.org.uk) for further information.

Pubs and Restaurants

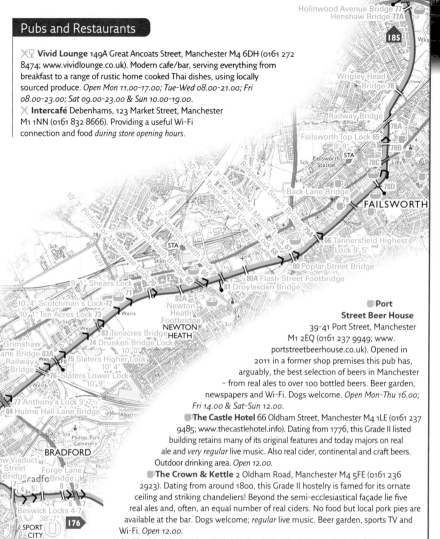

X♀ **Vivid Lounge** 149A Great Ancoats Street, Manchester M4 6DH (0161 272 8474; www.vividlounge.co.uk). Modern cafe/bar, serving everything from breakfast to a range of rustic home cooked Thai dishes, using locally sourced produce. *Open Mon 11.00-17.00; Tue-Wed 08.00-21.00; Fri 08.00-23.00; Sat 09.00-23.00 & Sun 10.00-19.00.*

X **Intercafé** Debenhams, 123 Market Street, Manchester M1 1NN (0161 832 8666). Providing a useful Wi-Fi connection and food *during store opening hours.*

Port Street Beer House 39-41 Port Street, Manchester M1 2EQ (0161 237 9949; www. portstreetbeerhouse.co.uk). Opened in 2011 in a former shop premises this pub has, arguably, the best selection of beers in Manchester – from real ales to over 100 bottled beers. Beer garden, newspapers and Wi-Fi. Dogs welcome. *Open Mon-Thu 16.00; Fri 14.00 & Sat-Sun 12.00.*

The Castle Hotel 66 Oldham Street, Manchester M4 1LE (0161 237 9485; www.thecastlehotel.info). Dating from 1776, this Grade II listed building retains many of its original features and today majors on real ale and *very regular* live music. Also real cider, continental and craft beers. Outdoor drinking area. *Open 12.00.*

The Crown & Kettle 2 Oldham Road, Manchester M4 5FE (0161 236 2923). Dating from around 1800, this Grade II hostelry is famed for its ornate ceiling and striking chandeliers! Beyond the semi-ecclesiastical façade lie five real ales and, often, an equal number of real ciders. No food but local pork pies are available at the bar. Dogs welcome; *regular* live music. Beer garden, sports TV and Wi-Fi. *Open 12.00.*

X **The Marble Arch** 73 Rochdale Road, Manchester M4 4HY (0161 832 5914; www. marblebeers.com/marble-arch). A Grade II listed building with a sumptuous interior, featuring a barrel vaulted ceiling (to rival the Crown & Kettle above) with a decorative frieze, serving real ales from their own brewery. Equally highly-regarded food is available *daily 12.00-20.45 (Sun 19.45).* Also real cider. Child- and dog-friendly. Open fires and a beer garden. *Open 12.00.*

Bar Fringe 8 Swan Street, Manchester M4 5JN (0161 835 3815). A motorbike sits atop the entrance to this somewhat quirky, Belgian-style, urban pub, serving real ales and an excellent range of continental bottled and draught beers. Also real cider. *L* food and a beer garden. *Open 12.00.*

X **The Angel** 6 Angel Street, Manchester M4 4BQ (0161 833 4786; www.theangelmanchester.com). A dining pub, free from intrusive television, which showcases the work of local artists. The 10 handpumps ensure a mini beer festival on a weekly basis, with the beers changing with unprecedented frequency! Real cider and an excellent range of food available *daily L and E (not Sun E).* Traditional pub games, open fires and an outdoor drinking area. *Open 12.00.*

X **The Millgate** Ashton Road West, Failsworth, Manchester M35 0ES (0161 688 4910; www.themillgatepub. co.uk). Carvery pub serving real ale and food *daily 12.00-20.00.* Outside seating, traditional pub games and Wi-Fi. *Open 12.00.*

The Church Inn 477 Oldham Road, Failsworth M35 0AA (0161 683 4076; www.churchinnfailsworth. robinsonsbrewery.com). Refurbished pub, east of Bridge 78B, serving real ale. Garden and children's play area. Sports TV and *regular* live entertainment. *Open 12.00.*

● **Manchester.**
All services. One of Britain's finest Victorian cities, a monument to 19th-C commerce and the textile boom, its size increasing remorselessly with the building of the canals, and later the railways. Unfortunately virtually no early buildings survived the city's rapid growth, although there is an incredible wealth of Victorian architecture surviving, in spite of redevelopment. The town hall and surrounding streets are a particularly rich area (north of Oxford Street Bridge). St Peter's Square, by the town hall, was the site of the 'Peterloo Massacre' in 1819, when a meeting demanding political reform was brutally dispersed by troops carrying drawn sabres. Eleven people were killed and many more were injured. The Free Trade Hall, once the home of the Hallé Orchestra, is a little further along the road. Built in 1856, it was badly damaged in World War II, but was subsequently re-built to its original Palladian design. There is theatre, ballet and cinema, art galleries, and a wealth of interesting buildings, Victorian shopping arcades, many pubs with a choice of good beer and a variety of restaurants just a short walk from the canal. Sporting facilities are excellent, partly as a consequence of Manchester being the venue for the 2002 Commonwealth Games. The new developments at Salford Quays, on the Manchester Ship Canal, are quite breathtaking.
Bridgewater Hall Lower Mosley Street, Manchester M2 3WS (0161 907 9000; www.bridgewater-hall.co.uk). A visually striking hall – built beside the Rochdale Canal coal wharves and its junction with the Manchester & Salford Junction Canal (its name was almost as long as the waterway itself) – and home to the Hallé Orchestra, BBC Philharmonic, Manchester Camerata and an impressive pipe organ. The auditorium seats over 2000 for classical concerts, celebrity recitals, jazz and rhythm and blues music. Conducted tours of the auditorium and backstage can be pre-booked. Telephone for programme details.
East Lancashire Railway Bolton Street Station, Bury BL9 oEY (0161 764 7790; www.east-lancs-rly. co.uk). An award-winning restored railway offering a mainly steam-hauled service along the picturesque Irwell Valley. Shop and refreshments. Trains operate *at weekends and B Hols throughout the year and Apr-Sep, Wed-Fri. Charge.*
24 Hour Museum Guide Visit www.24hourmuseum.org.uk/cityheritage to plan your day out and gain a unique perspective on the heritage of English cities. Non-commercial and free to use.

Library Theatre has combined with Cornerhouse Theatre and they are due to move to a new, purpose-built performance space during 2015, to be known as Home First Street, Manchester M15 4FN (0161 200 1500/228 7621; www.homemcr. org). Telephone or visit their website for the current situation and programme details.
Manchester Airport-Aviation Viewing Park Sunbank Lane, Altrincham WA15 8XQ (0161 489 3932; www.manchesterairport.co.uk). The chance to get a close-up of Concorde G-BOAC together with a selection of other aircraft and unrivalled views of the operational runways at Manchester Airport. Shop, snack bar, picnic and children's play areas. *Open 08.30-dusk. Charge.*
Manchester Art Gallery Mosley Street, Manchester M2 3JL (0161 235 8888; www.manchestergalleries.org.uk). Outstanding collection of 19th-C Pre-Raphaelite paintings; works from 18th-C masters (Gainsborough, Reynolds and Stubbs); contemporary art and sculpture; fine examples of Dutch and Italian painting and an internationally renowned collection of decorative art (ceramics, metalwork, furniture and textiles). Also the Clore Interactive Gallery for 5-12 year olds and their families. Shop and Gallery Restaurant. *Open daily 10.00-17.00 (Thu 21.00).* Free.
Manchester Cathedral Victoria Street, Manchester M3 1SX (0161 833 2220; www.manchestercathedral.org). Founded as a Chantry College in 1421, it became the cathedral for the newly formed diocese in 1847. 16th-C misericords render a humorous depiction of medieval life; carving in the choir stalls and canopies is exquisite as is the choir screen and the six bays that make up the nave, which are the widest of any church in England.
Manchester City Football Club Sportcity, Manchester M11 3FF (0161 444 1894; www.mcfc. co.uk). Much the same as Manchester United really except the *opening times are Mon-Sat 09.00-17.00; Sun & B Hols 10.00-17.00. Charge.*
Manchester Jewish Museum 190 Cheetham Hill Road, Manchester M8 8LW (0161 834 9879; www.manchesterjewishmuseum.com). Beautifully restored, Grade II listed building opened in 1874 and now a museum but retaining the basic layout of a synagogue. Striking architecture, stained glass and the former Ladies Gallery containing the Permanent Exhibition which tells the 200-year old story of Manchester Jewry. Heritage Trails take place *monthly Mar-Oct.* Shop. *Open Sun-Fri (10.00-16.00 (Fri 13.00). Charge.*

Manchester Museum University of Manchester, Oxford Road, Manchester M13 9PL (0161 275 2634; www.museum.manchester. ac.uk). This university museum helps to uncover the mysteries of Ancient Egypt, discover the world of neotropical frogs, tease out the intricacies of the human body and encourage you to marvel at the dinosaurs and other prehistoric beasts. Stunning displays and interactive exhibits. Shop and café. Open *daily 10.00–17.00*. Free.

Manchester United Football Club Sir Matt Busby Way, Old Trafford, Manchester M16 oRA (0870 442 1994; www.manutd.com). Museum charting the history of the club from 1878 to the present day, hall of fame and the trophy room. The tour visits the player's dressing rooms, takes in Sir Alex's dugout and lets you run down the players tunnel to the imaginary roar of the crowd. Shop and café. *Open 09.30–17.00*. Charge

Markets Piccadilly Gardens, Manchester (0161 234 7357; www.manchester.gov.uk/markets). Flower Market *Thu–Sat 10.00– 18.00;* French Market *once a month (usually 3rd week) Thu–Sat 10.00–18.00;* Farmers' Market *once a month (usually 2nd week) Fri–Sat 08.30–17.00*. Fashion Market, Tib Street *Sat 10.00–17.00.*

Museum of Science and Industry Liverpool Road, off Deansgate, Manchester M3 4FP (0161 832 2244; www.msim.org.uk). Located on the site of the world's first passenger railway station, this exciting hands-on museum has 14 galleries covering everything from steam to space, transport to textiles, and includes a working steam train, a reconstructed Victorian sewer (complete with smells!) and an interactive science centre. *Open daily 10.00–17.00*. Free. Coffee shop.

Palace Theatre and Opera House Oxford Street, Manchester M1 6FT (0871 977 3801). Two of the most prestigious theatres in the Northwest, hosting the best in musicals, drama, opera and comedy.

Royal Exchange Theatre St Ann's Square, Manchester M2 7DH (0161 833 9833; www.royalexchangetheatre.co.uk). Theatre-in-the-round set in the recently restored Royal Exchange Centre. Telephone for programme details.

Smithills Hall Smithills Dean Road, Bolton BL1 7NP (01204 332377; www.boltonmuseums.org. uk). Some of the finest examples of Medieval, Tudor and Victorian Architecture in the region exhibited in a Grade I listed building. Shop and refreshments. Guided tours. *Open Wed-Fri 10.00–15.00 & Sun 12.00–16.00*. Charge.

Travel Metroshuttle is a free city centre bus-contact Traveline for details of this and all public transport information on 0871 200 2233 *open 07.00–20.00 (08.00 weekends)*. For Metrolink Trams contact 0161 205 2000; www.metrolink. co.uk and for train travel 08457 48 49 50.

Whitworth Art Gallery University of Manchester, Oxford Road, Manchester M15 6ER (0161 275 7450; www.whitworth.manchester. ac.uk). Home to internationally renowned collections of British watercolours, textiles and wallpapers. Also an impressive range of paintings, drawings, sculptures and prints. Exhibitions and events throughout the year. Gallery Bistro (0161 275 7497) serving drinks, home-made cakes and light lunches *Mon–Sat 10.00–16.30 and Sun 14.00–16.30*. Specialist art bookshop (0161 275 7498). Gallery *open Mon-Sat 10.00–17.00 & Sun 12.00–16.00*. Free.

Manchester Visitor Information Centre Piccadilly Plaza, Portland Street, Manchester M1 4BT (0871 222 8223; www.visitmanchester. com). *Open daily Mon–Sat 10.00–17.30, Sun and B Hol Mon 11.00–16.00*.

● **Rochdale Canal Corridor Regeneration** The £24m restoration of the waterway, part of which runs through Oldham and Rochdale, is seen as a core programme of restoration acting as a catalyst for areas and communities within the canal corridor. A study commissioned by British Waterways and the two local authorities came up with proposals which include a range of accessible canalside developments where people can live and work, a series of visitor attractions, a waterside network of safe green spaces and walking routes together with good maintenance and management marketed by a cross-section of public and private groups. The Rochdale Canal Strategy will also help to create a further 15,000 jobs, the construction or re-use of 627,000 sq yds of office, leisure and shopping floorspace as well as reclamation and recovery of 1484 acres of land. A comprehensive brief has been developed to maximise the potential the navigation has to offer the local community in terms of economic regeneration, leisure, transport, tourism and movement. Hopefully this holistic approach will ultimately succeed in eliminating many of the social problems that beset the area and, in their turn, detract from the boater's enjoyment of this historic section of newly restored waterway.

● **Ancoats Mills** (www.heritageworks.co.uk) Not far out of Ducie Street Basin the canal passes, on the off side, a collection of fine old cotton spinning mills. These are of national importance and include some of the earliest mills built in Manchester. Murray's Mills were constructed between 1798 and 1804 and Old Mill – built 1798 – is the city's oldest surviving mill and is of a non-fireproof design. Of slightly later construction is Sedgewick Mill (1818-20), while Paragon and Royal Mills were the last of a whole series of buildings on this site, being completed in 1912. They ceased production around 1960.

Newton Heath
Gt Manchester. PO, tel, stores, chemist, butcher, baker, bank, hardware, takeaways, fish & chips, library, station. A satellite to Failsworth, once engaged in cotton spinning and weaving and now a useful place to stop outside the city.

Failsworth
Gt Manchester. PO, tel, stores, chemist, hardware, fish & chips, takeaways, banks, library, garage, station. Virtually the most southerly outpost of the cotton industry in Rochdale and close to the crescent-shaped Lancashire coalfield, exploited around Ashton-under-Lyne. *Gas* is available 100yds east of 78C (0161 681 1563; www.embassygas.co.uk).

Pubs and Restaurants

Boat and Horses Broadway, Chadderton, Oldham OL9 8AU (0161 681 2363; www.boatandhorsespub.co.uk). Originally dating from 1804, this pub had to be completely rebuilt in 1999 following serious foundation disturbance due to the construction of the M60. Today it serves real ales and food *daily 12.00-20.45*. There is a carvery *L and E Mon-Thu and all day Fri-Sun*. Breakfast is available *daily 09.00-11.30*. Family-friendly, garden and play area. Conservatory, sports TV and Wi-Fi. *Open 09.00*.

The Minders Arms 51 Joshua Lane, Middleton M24 2AY (0161 643 4964). Just west of Firwood Footbridge 75. A friendly local, but a stone's throw from the brewery gates, serving real ale. Dog- and family-friendly. Garden, traditional pub games, newspapers and Wi-Fi. *Open 12.00*.

Rose of Lancaster 7 Haigh Lane, Chadderton, Oldham OL1 2TQ (0161 624 3031; www.roseoflancaster.co.uk). East of Oldham Road Bridges 72 & 73. Overlooking the canal, the River Irk and open countryside, this popular pub serves real ale and food *daily 12.00-21.15 (Sun 20.45)*. Conservatory restaurant and covered patio. Open fires, sports TV,

traditional pub games and Wi-Fi. *Open 11.30 (Sun 12.00)*.

The Ship Inn 693 Rochdale Road, Slattocks M24 2RN (0161 643 5871; www.slattocks.com/the-ship-inn). Sitting beside 2nd Laneside Lock 55, this pub - dating from 1837 - serves real ale and offers canalside seating and moorings nearby.

Hopwood Arms 753 Rochdale Road, Middleton M24 2RA (01706 359807; www.hopwoodpub.co.uk). Village pub at Slattocks Top Lock serving real ale and food *L and E*. Children welcome. Outside seating. Large garden and childrens play area. Sports TV, pool and Wi-Fi.

Tandle Hill Tavern 14 Thornham Lane, Slattocks M24 2SD (01706 345297). I mile east of Slattocks Top Lock, up the severely potholed Thornham Lane. It is well worth the walk to this unusually remote hostelry, to enjoy a pint (or two) of the house ale, Bumpy Lane. Frequented by farmers, locals and walkers, this pub caters for dogs and offers *limited Sun* food and toasties at *most other times*. Real fires and a beer garden with real views. *Open Tue-Sun 17.00*.

Newton Heath Lock

Slattocks

This stretch is a mix of industry and housing, with the navigation sometimes part buried in a leafy cutting. There is only one lock in the 3-mile length. Beyond Mills Hill there is an abrupt and welcome change as, on crossing the infant River Irk, the waterway bends around to confront a stone bridge and lock in a delightfully rural setting. As it gains height the navigation has partially looped back on itself and at Higher Boarshaw the locks are interspersed with two striking examples of the Manchester & Leeds Railway's bridges. Above the second bridge, as the waterway rounds a slight bend, the Pennines first come into full view and although still distant, herald the challenge yet to come – for which the compact flight of the six Slattocks Locks provides a telling overture!

● **Slattocks**
Gt Manchester. PO box, tel, stores, garage. A long, narrow village. It is reputed to derive its name from a Northern-style amalgamation of the two words 'South Locks'. There is a small stores in the garage which is open 24hrs.

Boatyards

Ⓑ**New Islington Marina** New Urban Splash Limited, Timber Wharf , 16-22 Worsley Street, Castlefield, Manchester M15 4LD (0161 839 2999; www.urbansplash.co.uk/residential/new-islington). 🚽♿🧺 Short- and long-term moorings, toilets, showers, laundry.

See also Boatyard entries for the Bridgewater Canal pages 30 and 33.

Rochdale

Above the locks there are fine open views as the waterway bends first towards the railway then swings back to duck under the motorway, in what was a road crossing over a farm lane. No provision was made for the canal, then derelict, when the M62 was constructed and to build one retrospectively, when the navigation was restored, would have been prohibitively expensive. The ingenious solution devised was to commandeer an existing culvert, divert the line of the waterway through it, relocate lock 53 south of the motorway to correct the levels, and provide an alternative approach to the farm. Above Castleton, the canal heads into Rochdale but skirts the town itself which used to be served by an arm below Moss Locks, now derelict. The main line maintains a discrete distance and retains its Pennine vistas, stretching out ahead in a wide arc. Passing through a shallow cutting in open moorland, the navigation arrives at the charming cluster of buildings at Clegg Hall: early 19th-C weavers' cottages, an old mill from the same era and the gaunt and newly renovated hall peeping out from behind the trees. Beyond, the waterway negotiates a series of new bridges – replacing previous infilling – and passing Little Clegg, a chemical works and Smithy Bridge station, arrives in Littleborough accompanied by the railway.

NAVIGATIONAL NOTES

1 The M62 culvert is only 14' 7'' wide with a maximum draught of 3' 3'' and an air draught of 7' 1''. All craft should proceed with extreme caution. Wide boats wishing to use this culvert must give *24 hrs notice* (0303 040 4040; enquiries.northwest@canalrivertrust.org.uk) as a floating towpath has been installed.
2 The new section under the A627(M) is made up of new narrow channel, a passing place and a 121yd tunnel. As there are short sightlines throughout, boaters should proceed with caution. The channel and tunnel are only 16' 6'' wide so wide boats must give way in the passing place between the two.
3 The new channel west of Well i'th Lane Bridge (approximately ½ mile east of the A627(M) Tunnel) is 20' wide but there is a tight curve at the eastern end. Care should be taken, especially by wide boats.

Pubs and Restaurants

There are plenty of pubs at Castleton, and an excellent selection of pubs and restaurants in Rochdale, so it is worth walking up into the town.

🍺**The Blue Pits Inn** 842 Manchester Inn, Castleton OL11 2SP (01706 632151). Real ale, pub games and open fires *in winter*. Fun quiz Mon.

🍺**The Crown & Shuttle** 170 Rochdale Road, Firgrove OL16 3BU (01706 648259). South east of Wallhead Bridge. A small upstairs military museum, three comfortable rooms downstairs and real ale makes this friendly and traditional local well worth the walk. Outside seating, open fires *in winter* and pub games *all the year round*. *Open all day.*

Try also 🍺**The Gallows** Kiln Lane, Milnrow OL16 3JW (01706 642898); 🍺**The Ladybarn** 58 Harbour Lane, Milnrow OL16 4HF (01706 355412; www.theladybarn. co.uk) and 🍺**The Bobbin** 3 Dale Street, Milnrow OL16 3LH (01706 357200).

● **Castleton**
Gt Manchester. PO, tel, stores, chemist, baker, butcher, fish & chips, off-licence, takeaway, laundrette, station. A cotton-spinning town and once home to Tweedales & Smalley, a textile machinery manufacturer that specialised in the production of ring spinning machines. The works was subsequently used by Woolworths as a distribution centre. The Arrow Mill, standing beside the canal with its somewhat truncated chimney, is a fine example of a cotton mill built in 1908.

● **Rochdale**
Gt Manchester. All services. Home of the Co-operative Movement and birthplace of Gracie Fields, this is also another cotton-spinning town par excellance, although by the 18th C Rochdale was the flannel capital of Britain – a centre for the production of coarse and plain weave flannel. Lord Byron became Lord of the Manor of Rochdale in 1808 and, while residing at Hopwood Hall, Middleton, wrote a large part of *Childe Harolde*.
Touchstones Rochdale The Esplanade, Rochdale OL16 1AQ (01706 924492; www.link4life.org/centres/touchstones-rochdale). Four art galleries, museum, heritage gallery, tourist information centre and café. *Open Tue-Sat 10.00-17.00.* Free.
Rochdale Pioneers Museum 31 Toad Lane, Rochdale OL12 0NU (01706 524920; www.rochdalepioneersmuseum.coop). The Rochdale Society of Equitable Pioneers held their first meeting here on 15 August 1844 and 31 Toad Lane went on to become the world's first viable Co-operative shop. *Open Tue-Sat 10.00-17.00.* Free.
St Chad's Parish Church Sparrow Hill, Rochdale OL16 1QT (01706 645014). There has been a church overlooking the town, perched on this site, for over 1,000 years and parts of the present tower date back to Saxon times, although there have been several different buildings over the centuries. There is a striking Burne-Jones stained-glass window in the tower and further glass by William Morris. The town stocks, dating from 1688, are within the church curtilage.
● **Milnrow**
Gt Manchester. PO, tel, stores, chemist, butcher, baker, hardware, off-licence, takeaways, fish & chips, garage, station. Very much a centre for stone quarrying, open-cast and shaft mining, lying on the south east end of the crescent-shaped Lancashire coalfield. At Tunshill Farm there is a bank of old coking kilns and the remains of a fulling mill, with evidence of a paved pack-horse track and numerous local paths. Also six beehive coking ovens nearby. A mile east of Firgrove Bridge 58.
Ellenroad Engine House Steam Museum Elizabethan Way, Newhey, Rochdale OL16 4LG (07789 802632; www.ellenroad.org.uk). Home to one of the world's largest working steam mill engine and the Whitelees beam engine. Café and picnic area. The engine house is *open Tue & Sun 11.00-15.00 and Sat before steaming 12.00-15.00.* Free – donations welcome. The engine is in steam *1st Sun in each month (except Jan) 11.00-16.00.* Charge. Reglar bus service from Rochdale terminus and Newhey railway station is nearby.

187

Summit

Leaving Littleborough, the canal climbs steadily upwards past the strung-out Courtaulds factory, leaving the industrial chimneys of Rochdale far behind. The transition between sheltered valley bottom, with its compact, functional towns, and the open moorland that the waterway now heads towards, is fairly abrupt. Above West Summit Lock two contrasting, though striking features planted on the landscape are the Steanor Bottom Toll House (at the intersection of two roads to the west) and the 763yd span of the high-voltage line totally straddling the valley here. The typical moorland of the area is an acid peat overlying gritstone, poor draining and therefore agriculturally unproductive. At Longlees Lock the remote summit pound finishes. This was once the site of both a chemical and a brick works. Now reverted to coarse grasses, rushes and mosses, this section of the waterway is a haven to birdlife that can include meadow pipit, snipe, sandpiper, wheatear, dunlin, curlew and redshank. The descent into Todmorden is as scenically exhilarating as it is physically exhausting and the extended views, both in front and behind, steadily give way to the valley's intimacy.

● **Smithy Bridge**
Lancs. PO box, tel, stores, chemist, off-licence, takeaway, fish & chips, library, station.
● **Littleborough**
Lancs. All services. Laundrette. A bustling little town, busy with visitors in summer though, strangely, without a market. Opposite the solid stone parish church is the excellent Coach House Heritage Centre – a local initiative to provide tourist information established in a grade II listed building. Just round the corner, in Victoria Street, are a good butcher and baker.
Coach House Heritage Centre Lodge Street, Littleborough OL15 9AE (01706 378481; www.rochdaleonline.co.uk/sites/littleborough-coach-house). Community hub; café; exhibitions and gifts. Open daily 11.00-16.00 (Sun 13.00).
● **Summit**
Lancs. PO, tel, stores. Once a bustling woollen weaving community, the village has played an important part in three very different forms of transport. It sits beside the summit level of the canal, a place of sustenance to the thirsty boater and source of the much-needed water supply for locks descending east and west. The railway burrows underneath in a tunnel 2869yds long – the longest rail tunnel in the world when built in 1839. Some 23 million bricks were used in its construction. In 1984 a petroleum-carrying goods train caught fire and burnt uncontrollably in the tunnel for several weeks, smoke and flames belching

from the ventilation shafts. It took £4 million and six months to re-open the tunnel to traffic.
Steanor Bottom Toll House Just to the north of the village and built in 1824 at the junction of the old and new routes to Littleborough.

● **Walsden**
W. Yorks. PO, tel, stores, takeaways, fish & chips, off-licence, library, station. Meaning 'Valley of the Welsh' this textile village, just outside Todmorden, offers the boater all the important forms of sustenance.

NAVIGATIONAL NOTES

From Mar–Oct The Summit Locks are locked *in the evening* and unlocked *in the morning.* This is necessary to maintain control of water supplies.

Pubs and Restaurants

The Smithy Bridge 43 Smithy Bridge Road, Smithy Bridge OL15 oDY (01706 559747). Just east of Smithy Bridge 54.

Tophams Tavern 18 Smithybridge Road, Smithy Bridge OL15 8QF (01706 379922). Just West of Smithy Bridge 54.

Coach House Coffee Shop Lodge Street, Littleborough OL15 9AE (01706 378481). Inexpensive home-made snacks and cakes, teas and coffees served in this friendly annexe to the Heritage Centre. *Open Mon-Sat 09.00-16.30 & Sun 10.00-16.00.* Full *Sun L* and *occasional* Greek *nights.*

The Red Lion Hotel 6 Halifax Road, Littleborough OL15 oHB (01706 378195). Once a farmhouse, this very traditional old pub has been licensed since the 18th C to dispense a wide selection of regular and guest real ales. Also an excellent range of Belgian bottled beers and foreign ales – both bottled and on draught, and real cider. Pub games, open fires *in winter* and no machines. *Open Mon-Thu 14.00 & Fri-Sun 12.30 (Sun 13.00).*

The Waterside Bar and Restaurant 1 Inghams Lane, Littleborough OL15 oAY (01706 376250; www.thewatersideexperience.co.uk). Modern bar-restaurant with an exciting menu offering Mediterranean options as well as modern British food. Meals served *Wed-Sat L and E and Sun 12.00-19.30.* Children welcome; beautiful garden with decking overlooking the canal. Exciting *regular* theme nights. *Closed Mon-Tue.*

The Summit Inn 140 Summit OL15 9QX (01706 838694; www.thwaitespubs.co.uk/the-summit-littleborough-rochdale). Real ale is served in thus country pub high up in the Pennines. Children and dogs welcome. Garden and *regular* live music. *Open Mon-Fri 14.00 & Sat-Sun 12.00.*

The Cotton Weavers Café

The Border Rose Inn 772 Rochdale Road, Walsden OL14 7UA (01706 812142). Busy, upmarket pub and restaurant serving a wide range of home-made food *L and E Mon-Thu and all day Fri-Sun.* Also real ale. Children welcome. Beer garden and guinea pigs.

The Cross Keys Inn Rochdale Road, Walsden OL14 6SX (01706 815185). A homely, welcoming establishment serving a wide range of real ale together with traditional, home-cooked food *Mon-Tue from 16.00, Wed-Sun all day.* Children welcome; dogs welcome when food is not being served. Canalside patio and moorings. Traditional pub games. *Open 12.00.*

Grandma Pollard's Fish & Chips and Homemade Pies Rochdale Road, Walsden OL14 6SA (01706 815769). Something of an institution in the area, this is a chippy and pie provider of great character. *Open Mon-Tue until 15.30 & Wed-Fri until 20.00.* Tony claims that 'his little legs need a rest' as his excuse for *staying closed over the weekend!*

Todmorden

Now the descent begins in earnest with 17 locks in less than 3 miles and a spectacular railway crossing for good measure. A sweeping bend leads the waterway into the town with an immense brick retaining wall of massive proportions running all the way around the outside. The 'Great Wall of Tod' supports the railway embankment at this point and estimates of the total number of bricks used put the figure at more than 4 million. Beyond the compact town of Todmorden the countryside initially opens out revealing the disused Cross Stone Church, perched high on hills to the north of the navigation. Its badly blackened stonework is a reminder of the concentration of local industry, both past and present. Lobb Mill has finally been re-built (and turned into luxury apartments) while opposite Callis Lock there is a useful, boater-friendly *coal merchant* selling just about everything that is combustible. The waterway is now tucked tightly under a steep hillside covered by ancient deciduous woodland as the canal hugs the narrow valley bottom, interspersed, on the towpath side, with textile mills and dyeworks. The navigation approaches Hebden Bridge descending Stubbing (meaning a cleared area of woodland), Upper and Lower locks and passing gaily painted cottages, washing stretched like bunting across cobbled alleyways.

As so often happens with an aqueduct, the canal user is unaware of its beauty, grandeur or construction. So it is with Black Pit Aqueduct whose four substantial arches squat almost toad-like, close to the bed of the newly-merged rivers Hebble and Calder.

Littleborough	10m	17L
Patmos	5½m	30L
	Sowerby Bridge	

Shawplains Lock 8' 11"
Lobb Mill Canoe Bridge 26
Centre 15
Shaw Wood Bridge 25
Lobb Mill Lock 27 10' 6"
Shaw Wood
Woodhouse Bridge
17 Old Royd Lock 9' 3"
28 Kilnhurst Bridge
Kilnhurst
Baltimore Bridge 29
Millwood
Shop Lock 8' 9"
Todmorden or Library Lock 19 10' 7"
Golden Lion Bridge 30
30A
18 Salford
HISTORIC TRAIL
Dobroyd Castle
Wadsworth Mill Lock 20 10' 2"
Shade Lock 21 9' 9" (dis)
Shade
TODMORDEN
Gauxholme Lowest Lock 22 10' 8"
Gauxholme Middle Lock 23 3"
Gauxholme 30B
No Man's
Gauxholme 24
Gauxholme Arch
Knowl Wood
31
Gauxholme Highest Lock 31A 10' 3"
32 Copperas House Bridge
TODMORDEN CP
Smithyholm Lock 25 10' 5"
Pinnel Lock 26 9' 11"
Pasture Side Farm
Alma Bridge 33
10' 3" Hollings Lock 27
34 Hollings Bridge
WALSDEN 273
35 Birks Hall Bridge
28 Travis Mill Lock 9' 2"
Nip Square Lock 29
188
North Hollingworth Farm
Walsden Moor
Winterbutlee Lock 30
Cat Stones

Cross Stone
Lobb Mill Bridge

NAVIGATIONAL NOTES

1 Copperas House Bridge 32 is the lowest on the navigation and spans a short pound on which the water level can vary significantly, making the bridge very low at times. Proceed with caution.

2 Immediately below Lobb Mill Lock 17 there is a canoe centre. Approaching boaters are requested to sound their horn.

Boatyards

Ⓑ**Mobile Boat Repairers** Sandworth Street, Todmorden OL14 6NP (01706 815103/07957 869641). Mobile welding, repairs to engines, gearboxes and generators, agents for RCR. *24hr emergency call out.*

Ⓑ**Pickwell and Arnold** Unit 10, Nanholme Mill, Shaw Wood Road, Todmorden OL14 6DA (01706 812411; www.pickwellandarnold.co.uk). Below Shaw Plains Lock 15. Engine sales and repairs, boat building and repairs. *Emergency call out.*

Ⓑ**Able Fuels** Lower Underbank, Halifax Road, Charlestown HX7 6PH (01422 842284; www.ablefuels.co.uk). Opposite Callis Mill. Coal, seasoned logs, coke, sticks, charcoal, firelighters, stoves and spare parts. *Open Mon–Fri 10.00–17.30 and Sat 09.00–16.00.*

Ⓑ**Bronte Boat Hire** New Road, Hebden Bridge HX7 8AD (01706 815103; www.bronteboathire.co.uk). 🛒🚿🛁 D E Gas, pump out, narrowboat hire, day boat hire, slipway, dry dock. *24hr emergency call out.*

CHARLESTOWN RAILWAY DISASTER

In 1912 there was a serious derailment on the Charlestown curve when the 14.25 Manchester to Leeds express left the track, having effectively shattered the alignment of the rails at this point. The accident, involving a 2-4-2 radial tank engine, occurred on the stretch of line just before the railway crosses the canal on Whiteley Arches. The inspector, Colonel Druit, found at the subsequent enquiry that while the 45mph line speed at this point was suitable for normal express running, it was too high for tank engines of this type. Indeed, he went on to question the suitability of tank engines per se – with their high centre of gravity and inherent instability – for sustained high-speed traction. The derailed locomotive, together with all its carriages, toppled down the embankment, coming to rest strewn across the grounds of the old Woodman Inn.

Todmorden
W. Yorks. All services. Laundrette. 19th C manufacturing success led to the concentration of wealth in the pockets of a few individuals whose ostentation was often manifested locally in civic and domestic architecture. Todmorden is fortunate, indeed, to have benefited greatly from the philanthropy of the Fielden family, whose legacy of good taste in buildings represents a feast in stone. Their choice of architect, in John Gibson of London, proved most successful. His work both echoes the solid vernacular building from a previous era, while introducing a further wealth of styles, which in turn complement the fine stone railway viaduct that dominates the town's centre. Simple classical building sits side by side with the richly ornate, a striking example of the latter being the elaborately pedimented town hall. Originally built astride the county boundary (moved in a later reorganisation) between Lancashire and Yorkshire, this Italian Renaissance style building is fronted by six sturdy pillars, surmounted by statuary depicting, on the one half, the agriculture and engineering of Yorkshire, while on the other various facets of cotton spinning in Lancashire. In contrast the Unitarian Church, erected by Joshua and Samuel Fielden, again to a design by Gibson, is pure Victorian Gothic revival and a fitting memorial to their father, John Fielden MP. His concern for his fellow man extended to Westminster and industrial reform, being largely responsible for the Ten Hours Act of 1847 which limited the maximum working day to ten hours for any person under 18 and any woman over 18.

Craft Centre Lever Street, Todmorden OL14 5QF (01706 818170). Small family-run centre: stalls, workshops and a tearoom.
Free Library Rochdale Road, Todmorden OL14 7LB. Typifies the many individual buildings in the town displaying the skills of the stone mason in conjunction with the philanthropy of local benefactors. The library was a gift from the local Co-operative Society in 1897 and its asymmetry is pleasing in a simple way. It gives a second name to Todmorden Lock beside it, namely Library Lock.
Hippodrome Theatre 83 Halifax Road, Todmorden OL14 5BB (01706 814875). A striking building of its period.
St Mary's Church Rochdale Road, Todmorden OL14 7BS. Built on land given to the town c. 1476 it still retains its 15th-C tower. Subsequently much altered, the present Gothic Revival chancel bears little relationship to the original, although it contains a pleasing carved oak screen and attractive stained-glass windows.
Stoodley Pike The original monument was erected in 1815 to commemorate the end of the Napoleonic Wars. However, weakened by lightning, it collapsed 40 years later and was replaced by the present 120ft high structure. Visible from the canal, as you approach the town, it makes the object of a bracing walk, rewarded by stunning views across Calderdale.
Tourist Information Centre 15 Burnley Road, Todmorden OL14 7BU (01706 818181; todmorden@ytbtic.co.uk). *Open Mon–Sat 10.00–16.00.*

ON YOUR TOD

It is said that the only man-made feature distinguishable on the Earth, when viewed from the moon, is the Great Wall of China. Clearly this must be due to its length rather than its – relatively speaking – minuscule width. For a guard detachment, patrolling some of its more remote lengths, it must have been a singularly lonely and, in some cases, solitary occupation. The 'Great Wall of Tod' – the name given to the canalside railway retaining wall before Library Lock – is unlikely to hold quite such long-standing historical significance. Nor will it become a talking point amongst future lunar cosmonauts. Owing its existence to the less than prosaic function of keeping 'railway out of t'cut' it still remains, nonetheless, one of the wonders of a more local world. Building with brick (well in excess of 4 million in this instance) in the Calder Valley, rather than the local gritstone, was largely down to the advent of the railway: a phenomenon repeated throughout many other areas of the country.

BIRD LIFE

The *Nuthatch* is recognised by its rounded, short-tailed appearance and its habit of descending tree trunks head-downwards, a trait unique in Britain to this species. The nuthatch has blue-grey upperparts, a black eyestripe, white cheeks and orange-buff underparts. The chisel-like bill is used to prise insects from tree bark and to hammer open acorns wedged in bark crevices. This woodland species has a falcon-like call. It nests in tree holes, often plastering the entrance with mud to reduce its diameter.

Pubs and Restaurants

The Mason's Arms 1 Bacup Road, Gauxholme OL14 7PN (01706 812180). Close to Bridge 31 and almost lost under the railway viaduct. Once the local mortuary, this welcoming pub now serves an excellent selection of real ales and good, traditional pub food *daily L and E*. Family-friendly, open fires and a garden. *Open Mon-Thu 15.00 & Fri-Sun 12.00.*

Bramsche Bar and Restaurant 31A Rochdale Road, Todmorden OL14 7LA (01706 817633; www.bramsche.co.uk). Describing itself as 'a contemporary bar and kitchen', this establishment serves appetising food *Wed-Fri L and E; Sat 12.00-20.00 & Sun 12.00-17.00*. Real ales are available – at least one from a local microbrewery. *Open 12.00.*

The Polished Knob 31 Burnley Road, Todmorden OL14 7BU (01706 810480; www. thepolishedknob.co.uk). Originally the Black Swan, and sporting a fine façade, this pub now serves real ales and food *Wed-Sun 12.00-16.00*. Live music *Fri-Sat*. Outside seating, sports TV, open fires and Wi-Fi. Dogs and children welcome. B&B. *Open 11.00.*

The Rope and Anchor 132 Halifax Road, Todmorden OL4 5QR (01706 816054). With an interior somewhat reminiscent of a ship's galley, this hostelry in fact dispenses real ale and there is *regular* live entertainment. Traditional pub games, large-screen TV and dogs are welcome. *Open 12.30.*

The White Hart Station Approach, Todmorden OL14 8JR (01706 811760; www.jdwetherspoon. co.uk/home/pubs/the-white-hart-todmorden). Imposing mock-Tudor building replacing the 1728 original that once housed the local court. Today it dispenses real ale and food *daily 08.00-22.00*. Outside seating, children welcome and Wi-Fi.

Stubbing Wharf King Street, Hebden Bridge HX7 6LU (01422 844107; www.stubbingwharf. com). A good range of real ales (and real cider) are dispensed in this canalside, family pub, together with excellent food *daily 12.00-21.00 (Sun 20.30)*. Canalside seating, mooring, open fires and quiz *Thu*. *Open 12.00.*

The Fox and Goose 9 Heptonstall Road, Hebden Bridge HX7 6AZ (01422 842649...; www.foxandgoose.org). A community-owned, real ale pub that is serious about its beer and cider. Alongside its real ales, many from local microbreweries, is an excellent range of bottled continental lagers and ciders. Dogs welcome, hillside beer garden, open fires, traditional pub games and Wi-Fi. *Regular* live music. Quiz *Mon*. *Open 12.00.*

Greens Vegetarian Café New Oxford House, 24 Albert Street, Hebden Bridge HX7 8AH (01422 843587; www.greensvegetariancafe. wordpress.com). Friendly establishment serving appetising vegetarian meals, homemade cake, tea and coffee. *Open Wed-Sun 11.00-15.00; B Hols & Fri-Sat from 18.30.*

Jolly Roger

Leaving Hebden Bridge (there is a useful *coal merchant* close to Bridge 16 – 01422 842526), the canal continues its

steady descent through open countryside, passing Walkley's Canalside Mill and heading for Mytholmroyd. There is a slightly incongruous but very striking ape sculpture beside Broadbottom Lock 7. Beyond is the hamlet of Brearley (*pub, telephone box, children's playground and public toilets*) perched on a hill to the north, while the River Calder, still little more than a grubby grey beck, flows to the south. All around the waterway offers views of a tranquil rural scene: one of tiny stone-walled fields reaching up steep hillsides to the nearby horizon. Dotted here and there with crouching stone homesteads, it is a chequer-board landscape of rich pasture grazed, for the most part, by sheep and horses. All too soon the navigation burrows into more shady surroundings and, despite sharing the often narrow defile of the infant Calder Valley with road, rail and river, it manages to preserve a seclusion and an intimacy, hemmed in as it is by woodlands and spanned by solid stone bridges. The Rochdale Canal terminates at Sowerby Bridge where for many years the waterway had lain forlorn, a ribbon of water languishing in a supermarket car park, its contact with the Calder & Hebble Navigation a tantalising 50yds away, severed by infilling beneath a road junction. Today it is again accessible by craft travelling the inland waterways system and offers an unrivalled ascent into the undisturbed uplands of the Pennine chain.

● **Hebden Bridge**
W.Yorks. All services. Developed as a settlement in late medieval times, providing both a meeting point of packhorse routes and a river crossing. However, it was not until the late 19th C, with the advent of steam power, the building of canal and railway, together with the mechanisation and centralisation of the textile industry, that the town attained its present size and layout. Displaying a variety and delicacy of stonework – towers, turrets and pediments at every turn – houses and mills peel off from the market square to straggle haphazardly up steep hillsides. The first bridge to cross the River

Hebden was wooden, dating from 1477 and replaced by the present stone packhorse bridge some 30 years later. This solid structure contrasts with the delicate ironwork of the cast iron Victorian road bridge, sited upstream beside the ornate council offices, which incorporate the original fire station. Double-decker housing and a diversity of religious non-conformism are also characteristic of this strikingly compact mill-town.
Hebden Bridge Alternative Technology Centre Hebble End Mill, Hebden Bridge HX7 6HJ (01422 842121; www.alternativetechnology. uk). Information line 08453 304930. Working from

a strong base within the local community, this charitable organisation – in making sustainability sustainable and simply irresistible – aims to provide inspiration, practical innovation, information and advice. By setting a stimulating and exciting example, it seeks to enable people to improve all aspects of their lives and environment. Permaculture garden, plastic pipe recycling, 'renewables' and shop. *Open daily Mon–Fri 10.00– 17.00; Sat 12.00–17.00 and Sun 12.00–16.00. Extended opening on B Hol weekends.*
Hardcastle Crags NT, Hollin Hall Office, Hebden Bridge HX7 7AP (01422 844518; www.nationaltrust.org.uk). Large tract of Trust-managed countryside, 1½ miles north of Hebden Bridge, easily accessible by bus. Rich in natural history and famous as the seat of the hairy wood ant. Regular events and guided walks – telephone for details. *Open all year. Free.*

Visitor and Canal Centre Butlers Wharf, New Road, Hebdon Bridge HX7 8AF (01422843831; www.calderdale.gov.uk/advice/tourism/ touristinformation/hebdenbridge.html). *Open daily 10.00–17.00.*
Metro (0113 245 7676; www.wymetro.com). Contact for all local travel information or a selection of free timetables.
● **Heptonstall**
W. Yorks. PO, tel, stores. An extraordinary 'textile village', little changed over the centuries, set high on hills overlooking Hebden Bridge. Walk up the Buttress (beyond the packhorse bridge) or take a bus and visit this settlement barely touched by time. In one small area there is a ruined 15th-C church, its early Victorian replacement and the Octagonal Chapel, one of the oldest continually used Methodist churches in the world, dating from 1764. Also a 16th-C cloth market hall, school museum, a dungeon and David Hartley's (the infamous coiner) grave. There is also the grave of Sylvia Plath, American poet and wife of Ted Hughes. The village

BOAT TRIPS
Hebden Bridge Cruises (0966 808717; www.hebdenbridgecruises.com) operate the wide beam boat *Gracie*, on food-themed cruises, pirate trips and on charter, starting from the Stubbings Wharf pub. Telephone or visit the website for further details.

provides one of the most spectacular viewpoints in Calderdale.

Heptonstall Museum Church Yard Bottom, Heptonstall, Hebden Bridge HX7 7PL (01422 843738; www.museums.calderdale.gov.uk/visit/heptonstall-museum). Depicts an old school classroom together with varying local history displays. *Open Sat-Sun & B Hols 11.00-16.00.* Free.

Cloth Hall Heptonstall. Built between 1545 and 1558 as a market for local handloom weavers to sell their cloth to dealers. It is now a *private* house.

Weavers' Square Church Yard Bottom, Heptonstall HX7 7PL. A unique area of stone depicting many types of Yorkshire paving.

● **Mytholmroyd**

W. Yorks. PO, tel, stores, takeaways, fish & chips, delicatessen, off-licence, laundrette, garage. Since the 11th C the ingredients of a farming and weaving community have existed in the area, confined largely to individual settlements above the marshy valley bottom. The site of the present village was initially a fordable crossing of the River Calder and, with the coming of the canal and the railway, developed as a focus for steam-powered textile production. Initially producers of cotton goods (with the canal as both supplier of raw materials and shipper of finished goods) the mills went on to manufacture worsted in the late 19th C, which in turn stimulated the growth of local dyeworks. Infamous as the base for the activities of David Hartley and the 'Coiners', Mytholmroyd was also the birthplace of Ted Hughes, the late Poet Laureate, and home to the annual Dock Pudding championships – *held in May.*

The Coiners of Cragg Vale Coining was the illicit manufacture of coins, often using metal filed or clipped away from the perimeter of genuine coins. This was melted down and cast into new coins with an appropriate design hammered onto the face and reverse sides. A new rim was then hammered onto the adulterated coin. On 10 November 1769 an excise man, William Dighton, who had been sent to curtail the activities of the Cragg Vale coiners, was murdered in Halifax by members of the gang. Loyalty was not a notable feature within coiner circles and the miscreants were quickly betrayed to the authorities in return for an enticing reward.

Dock Pudding Championships Dock Pudding is made from the weed *Polygonum bistorta* (sweet dock) and is not to be confused with the large coarse cow docks. Mixed with other ingredients and cooked to a variety of secret recipes, the finished product, looking not unlike a slimy, spinach concoction, is entered into a competition and judged on its culinary merits. Believed by many locals to be an essential spring medicine, efficacious in the cure of acne and as a cleanser of the blood.

● **Luddenden Foot**

W. Yorks. PO, tel, stores, off-licence, takeaway, library. Centred around more recent lines of communication in the valley bottom, the village once featured the railway station where Branwell Brontë was booking clerk. Passengers arriving on one of the earliest passenger lines to be opened in Britain, were greeted with the cry of 'Foo-it! Foo-it!' as porters sought to differentiate this upstart settlement from the ancient, textile- producing village, perched on the hillside ½ mile above. Gas is available at Springfield Camping (01422 883164; www.springfield-camping.co.uk) south of Station Road Bridge 6.

● **Sowerby Bridge**

W. Yorks. All services. See page 54.

Boatyards

See Calder & Hebble Navigation page 54.

Brontë Boats The Marina, Hebden Bridge HX7 8AD (01706 815103; www.bronteboats.co.uk).

🚽🚿🛒D E Pump out, gas, engine repairs, coal, dry dock, slipway, maintenance, boat fitters, insurance repairs, mobile boat repairs, day hire boats.

Longlees Lock (see *page 188*)

Pubs and Restaurants

See also Calder & Hebble Navigation, page 55.

🍺There is a wide selection of pubs to choose from in Hebden Bridge and its environs, together with an even wider selection of real ales. ✕ The variety and diversity of tearooms, bistros, pizzerias, cafés and restaurants is equally copious!

🍺✕ **The White Lion** Bridge Gate, Hebden Bridge HX7 8EX (01422 842197; www.whitelionhotel. net). A friendly and relaxed family pub with many interesting features set in a 17th-C listed building. An excellent selection of real ales and good food, made using fresh local ingredients, served *daily 12.00-21.00 (Sun 20.00)*. Children's room and riverside garden. Open fires *in winter*. B&B. *Open 11.00.*

These two pubs represents worthwhile walks or bus rides.

🍺**The Hare & Hounds** Lane Ends, Wadsworth, Hebden Bridge HX7 8TN (01422 842671; www. hareandhounds.me.uk). Cosy pub serving real ale and tasty bar meals *L and E, daily (all day Sat, Sun)*. Children welcome. Beer garden with stunning views over the Calder Valley – close to the Pennine Way. Wi-Fi. B&B. *Hourly* Halifax service bus no 593 *during day* or minibus H3 and H7 *evenings and weekends*.

🍺**The White Lion** Town Gate, Heptonstall, Hebden Bridge HX7 7NB (01422 842027). The perfect way to round off a visit to this historic, unspoilt village and its museum. Real ale and real cider are both dispensed in this old stone-built pub in the heart of the community. Dogs welcome, open fires and outside seating. *Open 12.00.*

🍺✕**The Dusty Miller** Burnely Road, Mytholmroyd HX7 5LH (01422 885959; www.dustymillermytholmroyd.co.uk). Once the regular haunt of the Crag Vale Coiners. It is now a restaurant with rooms, serving real ale. Quiz *Wed* and carvery *Sun 12.00-17.30*. Wi-Fi. B&B.

🍺**The Shoulder of Mutton** New Road, Mytholmroyd HX75DZ (01422 883165). Opposite railway station. Award-winning hostelry that takes its beer and food seriously. An excellent selection of both regular and guest real ales are served; there are three cosy eating areas, portions are generous and the prices low. Tasty, home-cooked food available *L and E*. Children and dogs welcome. Streamside garden, sports TV and traditional pub games. *Open Mon-Fri L and E (not Tue L); Sat 11.30 & Sun 12.00.*

🍺**The Old Brandy Wine** Station Road, Luddenden Foot HX2 6AD (01422 886173). Real ales are served in this ex-factory and working-man's club. Child- and dog-friendly, sports TV and traditional pub games. *Open Mon-Fri 16.00 & Sat-Sun 12.00.*

🍺**The Puzzle Hall Inn** 21 Hollins Mill Lane, Sowerby Bridge HX6 2QG (01422 835547). South of canal before Sowerby Long Bridge. A wide cross section of customers gather at this 300-year-old hostelry of great character set between river and canal. Real ale and food (a Thai menu is served *Wed-Thu & Sun 17.00-21.00* and Ukrainian food *alternate weekends 17.00-21.00*) are served in this tiny, two-roomed pub. *Regular* live entertainment. Real cider, open fires and a garden. *Open Mon-Fri 15.00 & Sat-Sun 13.00.*

🍺**The Works** 12 Hollins Mill Lane, Sowerby Bridge HX6 2QG (01422 834 821; www. theworkssowerbybridge.co.uk). Converted from an old joinery workshop, this pub eschews TV and loud music in favour of conversation, real ale and appetising food available *Mon-Fri 12.00-20.00; Sat 12.00-17.00 & Sun 10.30-14.30*. Upstairs comedy venue. Open fires, outside drinking area and Wi-Fi. *Open 12.00 (Sun 10.30.).*

🍺**Jubilee Refreshment Rooms** Station Road, Sowerby Bridge HX6 3AB (01422 648285; www. jubileerefreshmentrooms.co.uk). Created by two railway enthusiast, to represent a refreshment room from the golden days of rail travel, this bright, airy establishment serves real ale and hot and cold snacks *Mon-Sat 09.30-21.30 (Sat 21.00) & Sun 12.00-21.30.* Hot meals available *Mon-Sat 12.00-14.00.* The Whistlestop Window opens *Mon-Fri 06.45-09.30.* Outside seating, real fires and Wi-Fi.

🍺**The Shepherd's Rest** 125 Bolton Brow, Sowerby Bridge HX6 2BD (01422 831937). Cosy pub with a flagged floor – dating from 1877 – with a large brick-arched fireplace, serving real ales. Quiz *Mon*, open fires, traditional pub games and a beer garden. Dogs welcome. *Open Mon-Thu 15.00 & Fri-Sun 12.00.*

NAVIGATIONAL NOTES

1 Tuel Lane Lock is only operated by Canal & River Trust staff. *From mid Mar-mid Nov* a lock keeper is on site *Fri-Mon from 8.30am, with the last passage late afternoon*. Outside these times, contact 0303 040 4040; enquiries.manchesterpennine@canalrivertrust.org.uk and give *24 hours* notice to make a booking.

2 Do not enter Tuel Lane Tunnel whilst boats are in the lock, or when the lock is emptying, as turbulence can cause a serious accident.

SANKEY CANAL

MAXIMUM DIMENSIONS
Length: 72' 0"
Beam: 16' 6½"
Draught: 6' 3" (as built)
Headroom: 21' 6" (as built)

MANAGER:
The three Local Authorities own the sections of canal that pass through their boroughs.
Halton BC (0303 3334300)
Warrington BC (www.warrington.gov.uk)
St.Helens MBC (01744 676 789)
Canal & River Trust (0303 040 4040; enquiries. northwest@canalrivertrust.org.uk) own a short section at Blackbrook.

Sankey Canal Restoration Society
www.scars.org.uk

MILEAGE
WIDNES LOCK junction with the River Mersey to:
Fiddler's Ferry Lock: 3½ miles
Bewsey Lock: 6½ miles
Winwick Lock: 8 miles

Sankey Viaduct (Earlestown): 10½ miles
Old Double Locks (junction with Blackbrook Branch):
13 miles

ST HELENS: 15¼ miles

Although this is a long abandoned and, therefore, un-navigable canal, it has a good towpath throughout with the minimum of diversions. However, the two lengths adjacent to the River Mersey locks at Widnes and Fiddlers Ferry, are dredged and act as moorings.

The Sankey Canal Restoration Society has produced a useful towpath guide, containing additional historical insight into the waterway, available from colin.greenall@btinternet.com. This forms an excellent companion to this guide.

Most bridges (and all the locks) shown on the mapping date from the time before the canal was abandoned. Many have since vanished or, in the case of swing bridges, will have been converted to a fixed structure.

To follow the Sankey Canal is to walk through history and the early annals of the Industrial Revolution, its echoes reverberating off the distant Pennine foothills to this very day. This is a navigation conceived, and for the most part constructed, before the completion Francis Egerton's Bridgewater Canal into the Castlefields district of Manchester in 1765.

On 20th March 1755 an Act was passed authorising 'the making navigable of the Sankey Brook' together with 'three several Branches thereof ...' although, in the face of anticipated landowner opposition, it leaned heavily on a clause shared with the earlier Mersey & Irwell Act, 'to make such new Cuts, Canals, Trenches or Passages for water, in, upon or through the lands or grounds adjoining or near onto the same River or Three Several Branches aforesaid ... as they shall think proper and requisite.'

It was surveyed by Henry Berry (then the Liverpool Dock engineer) at the behest of the Common Council of Liverpool, who recognised the escalating need for coal used in salt refining, sugar boiling, pottery and glass manufacture, brewing and for domestic use. He was assisted by William Taylor, who had recently surveyed the route for the still-born Salford to Worsley and Wigan canal, rejected by Parliament due to pressure applied by affected landowners. Both men would have been perfectly aware that the Sankey Brook was too small for practical navigation and, in the event, only a small portion of its bed was ultimately used.

Work commenced on 5th September 1755, supervised by Berry (who was given two days a week leave by his Liverpool employers) on a line connecting the Mersey at the Sankey Brook outlet, with collieries in the Gerard's Bridge district of St Helens, and the first section opening two years later. By 1762 the line was completed to Blackbrook (including construction of Old Double Locks – the first of their kind in Britain) and by 1772 it had climbed the New Double Locks into the town of St Helens itself.

The Sankey Canal developed in tandem with the River Weaver Navigation, supplying coal for salt production. In symbiotic exchange, salt returned to fuel the burgeoning chemical industry and its alkali-dependant processes. Mixed with silica it also provided the basis for glass manufacture.

Access from the tidal Mersey was greatly helped by the westerly extension to the new Fiddler's Ferry Lock in 1762 and further improved with the opening of a second extension into Widnes Dock in 1833.

Traffic was carried by the, then, ubiquitous Mersey Flat, which could be either bow- or horse-hauled, although the open nature of the terrain (and the reliance on swing bridges at crossing points) meant that sailing was perfectly feasible. Craft were generally in the order of 65' x 16' 6" although by the end of the 19th C, when cargoes included alkali, soap, silicate, river and silver sand, acid, tallow, manure, copper ore, salt and copper itself (but no longer coal) some vessels were as large as 68' x 16' 9" and carried up to 75 tons.

The navigation always enjoyed harmonious relationships with its railway partners and it was the complete absence of traffic that led to closure of the five-mile section above Newton Common Lock in 1931. Raw sugar continued to be carried to the Sankey Sugar Works in Earlestown until 1959 and, with its cessation, the waterway was finally abandoned in 1963.

Fiddler's Ferry

The Sankey Canal joins a large body of tidal water at both Fiddler's Ferry and Widnes and, whilst provide a safe mooring for blue-water boats, the navigation is somewhat divorced from the remainder of the inland canal system. However the Mersey, in its close proximity to the canal, is not without its own form of haunting beauty and, as one heads towards Sankey Bridges, the tandem waterways offer a joint haven to the teeming wildlife, under the sombre gaze of the dominant cooling towers. The boat club, pub and boatyards at Fiddler's Ferry Lock add interest, as does the occasional coal train bent on feeding the hungry maws of the power station. Sankey Bridges marks the parting from the Trans Pennine Trail, with its increased towpath activity, as the canal now swings northwards past what was once an area of busy wharfs. This is also the point where the navigation originally entered the Mersey, before the two extensions westwards were constructed to prevent loaded boats from becoming stranded on a neap tide.

● **Widnes**

Cheshire. All services. The Industrial Revolution was a late arrival in the town (indeed it effectively spawned the town), coming with the opening of John Hutchinson's alkali factory in 1847, which produced soap, borax, soda ash and bleach and was ultimately to become a part of the giant ICI. Iron and copper were also smelted in the town earning it the description, in 1888, as 'the dirtiest, ugliest and most depressing town in England' in which 'the spring never comes hither ... there being no place in which it can manifest itself. The foul gases which, belched forth night and day from the many factories, rot the clothes, the teeth, and, in the end, the bodies of the workers, having killed every tree and every blade of grass for miles around.' Things improved after WWI and again following WWII, although there were still 45 major chemical factories recorded in the town in the late 1950's. Today it is a major multi-modal distribution centre and the chemical industry benefits from streamlined, modern production processes. Salmon are once again to be found in the Mersey.

Catalyst Science Discover Centre Gossage Building, Mersey Road, Widnes WA8 0DF (0151 420 1121; www.catalyst.org.uk). Unique, award-winning museum representing the area's chemical industry. Interactive exhibits and hands-on displays. 'Industry in view' is a computer and video based exhibition 100ft above the Mersey, embracing spectacular river views. Reconstructions and original film footage trace the development of the chemical industry from ancient times to the present day. Café with riverside views. Shop selling educational toys etc and activity guides for home-based experiments. *Open Tue-Sun (& Mon B Hol; daily during school holidays) 10.00-16.00.* Charge.

Moore Nature Reserve Arpley Landfill Site, Forrest Way, Sankey Bridge WA4 6YZ (01925 444689; www.wrg.co.uk/moorenaturereserve). Occupying the land bounded by the Manchester Ship Canal and the River Mersey, the reserve is bisected by the route of the long-abandoned Latchford Canal. Taken in conjunction with Wigg Island (see below) to the east, it is possible to make up an excellent circular walk, travelling out (or vice versa) along the Sankey Canal from Widnes to Sankey Bridges, returning on the river's south bank through these interconnecting reserves, using Forrest Way Bridge and Silver Jubilee Bridge at either end to cross the Mersey.

Reel Cinema The Hive Leisure Park, Unit 4, Earle Road, Widnes WA8 0GU (0151 423 0424; www. widnes.reelcinemas.co.uk). Regular screening of all the latest epics.

Spike Island. Now open parkland, ringed by the canal, with several items of industrial archaeological interest. Acknowledged as the birthplace of the British chemical industry, this long-abandoned wilderness was reclaimed as woodland, wetlands and green space between 1975 and 1982.

199

Moorings at Fiddler's Ferry

Wigg Island Off Astmoor Road, Runcorn WA7 1RR (01928 563803; www.cheshirewildlifetrust.org.uk/nature-reserves/wigg-island-visitor-centre). The Reserve can be accessed *anytime* while the Visitor Centre itself is *open on selected days throughout the year*. Telephone for details. See also walk suggested under Moore Nature Reserve above.

Tourist Information Centre Halton Borough Council, 5th Floor Municipal Building, Widnes WA8 7QF (0151 906 3789; www.visithalton.com).

● **Penketh**

Cheshire. PO, tel, stores, chemist, bank, takeaway, baker, off-licence, garage. Originally a small, rural community, Penketh developed on the back of the Mersey ferry crossing and the coming of the Sankey Canal. Industry was limited to boat building and a tannery. Today the town is dominated by the massive coal-fired, Fiddler's Ferry power station,

which is fed by the railway running parallel to the navigation.

● **Great Sankey**

Cheshire. PO box, tel, stores, chemist, off-licence, fish & chips, station. A predominantly rural community, touched by industrial development along the Sankey Canal to the south and, later, by the construction of RAF Burtonwood to the north. Today it is a residential suburb of Warrington.

Pubs and Restaurants

🍺✖ **The Eight Towers** Weates Close, Widnes WA8
3RH (0151 424 8063; www.eighttowerspub.co.uk).
Friendly, family pub dispensing real ale and food *daily*
12.00-21.00 (Sun 20.00). Sports TV and beer garden.
Open 11.00.

🍺✖ **The Ring O'Bells** Pit Lane, Widnes WA8
9LW (0151 424 6330; www.ringobellswidnes.co.uk).
Popular town pub serving real ale and food *daily
12.00-23.00*. Children welcome. *Regular* live music,
quiz *Sun* and afternoon tea available. Garden, sports
TV, pool and Wi-Fi. *Open 12.00.*

✖♟ **The Spice of India** Cuerdley Cross Inn,
Cuerdley, Widnes Road, Widnes WA5 2XD (0151 424
9942; www.spiceofindiacuerdley.co.uk). Popular
restaurant serving contemporary Indian food with a
garden, children's play area and indoor children's fun
house. Quiz *Sun*. Takeaway service. *Open Mon-Sat
17.00 & Sun 12.00-23.30.*

🍺**The Ferry Tavern** Station Road, Penketh WA5
2UJ (01925 791117; www.theferrytavern.com). First
licensed in 1762 to provide sustenance for travellers
using the nearby Mersey ferry, this
hostelry still serves real ales and
food *Fri E* (bookings only)
& *Sat-Sun L and
E*. Dogs,

cyclists, walkers and families welcome. *Regular* live
music and quiz *Sun*. Riverside garden, open fires and
Wi-Fi. *Open Mon-Fri L and E (not Mon L) & Sat-Sun
and B Hol Mon all day.*

🍺**The Crown & Cushion** 181 Warrington Road,
Penketh WA5 2EN (01925 722146). Large modern
pub serving real ale. Outside seating. *Open 11.30.*

🍺**The Red Lion** 164 Warrington Road, Warrington
(01925 722185; www.all-inns.co.uk/pub/the-red-
lion-penketh). Family pub, complete with indoor
children's funhouse, serving real ale and food *daily
12.00-22.00 (Sun 21.00)*. Beer garden, sports TV and
Wi-Fi. *Open 11.30.*

🍺**The Sloop** Liverpool Old Road, Sankey Bridges
WA5 1EE (01925 634853). Just to east of the canal in
Sankey Bridges, serving real ale. Dogs welcome and
there is a beer garden. *Open 12.00.*

🍺**The Black Horse** 272 Liverpool Old Road, Sankey
Bridges WA5 1DZ (01925 635301). Welcoming
pub, just east of the Sankey Brook (and the canal),
serving real ale. *Open 11.30.*

WALKING & CYCLING

The towpath is most easily joined at Catalyst (see
above) where there is free car parking. It forms the
Sankey Way terminating in St Helens. For walkers
and cyclists following the navigation, wishing to
return by public transport, there are regular local
bus services and railway stations at Warrington,
Earlestown (Newton-le-Willows) and St Helens,
allowing a straightforward return journey to
Widnes.
Construction of the new Mersey Gateway Bridge
will be taking place on the east side of Spike
Island, lasting until autumn 2017. Local towpath
diversions will be in place during this time.
The Mersey Way runs from the Liverpool suburb
of Garston to Rixton, east of Warrington, closely
following the estuary and the north bank of the
Mersey, paralleling two artificial cuts from the
long-forgotten Mersey & Irwell Navigation.
Trans Pennine Trail Trans Pennine Trail Office,
c/o Barnsley Council, PO Box 597, Barnsley S70
9EW (01226 772574; www.transpenninetrail.org.
uk). This coast to coast route makes use of the
towpath from Widnes to Sankey Bridges – for
further details visit the website.

Boatyards

Ⓑ**West Bank Boat Club** Spike Island, Upper Mersey
Road, Widnes WA8 0DE (spikeisland1@yahoo.co.uk;
www.westbankboatclub.com). Moorings.

Ⓑ**Ferry Boatyard Harbour Master** Penketh,
Warrington WA5 2UJ (01925 727519/07876 767484;
www.ferryboatyard.com). ⚓ Short- and long-term
mooring, winter storage, boat sales and repairs, engine
sales and repairs, cranage, slipway, chandlery, marine
engineering. *Emergency call out (40 mile radius).*

Bewsey

Beyond Sankey Bridges the towpath crosses both the navigation and then the busy A57 by footbridges, before re-joining the waterway on its west bank. It is a pleasant walk north through this part of the Sankey Valley Park to the site of the first 'inland' lock at Bewsey, where the path briefly makes use of the east bank of the navigation. This is the point where the canal utilised the Sankey Brook, as witnessed by the arrangement of flood control sluices still visible beside the lock. A pleasant, wooded section leads through picnic and play areas to the point where the Brook is crossed by a footbridge, to the north of which is the clear outline of Hulme Lock. A few hundred yards above the lock is the old Winwick canal maintenance yard and dry dock, while beyond the motorway (having skirted the scrapyard by following the marked path), Winwick Lock is still very much in evidence.

● **Warrington**
Cheshire. All services. Founded by the Romans as an important Mersey crossing point, the market town's subsequent prosperity, in the Middle Ages, was established on textile and tool production. As the river was made navigable with the coming of the Industrial Revolution, so the town flourished with the development of its brewing, tanning, textile and steel wire industries. In the 1960's, the decline of heavy industry coincided with growth in technology, distribution and service industries and, in 1968, Warrington was designated a New Town. There is a useful cycle shop 200yds north of Sankey Bridge No 16 – D & M Cycles 2-4 Hood Lane, Sankey Bridges WA5 1EJ (01925 653606; www.dandmcycles.com).
Gullivers World Old Hall, Shackleton Close, Warrington WA5 9YZ (01925 444888; www.gulliversfun.co.uk/warrington). Over 90 rides, shows and attractions for children aged 2-13, ranging from playing around in the clown school to log flumes and tree top swings. 50% of attractions are under cover. Stage and theatre shows. Picnic area. Five restaurants and a gift shop. B&B. *Open 10.30 most days Apr-Aug; limited opening Sep-Dec. Closing times vary.* Check website for details. Charge.
LA Bowl 10-15 Chetham Court, Winwick Quay, Warrington WA2 8RF (01925 639222; www.labowl.co.uk). Apart from the obvious bowling experience there are also dodgems, lasers and karaoke. Café. *Open daily 10.00-23.00 (Fri-Sat 00.30).* Charge.
Museum and Art Gallery Museum Street, Warrington WA1 1JB (01925 442399; www.warringtonmuseum.co.uk). First opened in 1857, and reputed to be one of the oldest museums in the world, today visitors can view local and social history galleries with displays depicting the industries that

shaped the town, which lays claim to its very own dinosaur. Also exhibits from contemporary artists and a Time Tunnel for younger visitors. *Open Mon-Sat 10.00-16.30 (Sat 16.00); closed B Hols.* Free.
Odeon Cinema 100 Westbrook Centre, Warrington, Cheshire WA5 8UD (01871 224 4007; www.odeon.co.uk/cinemas/warrington/29). Six screens. *Open daily 13.30-22.00 (Sat-Sun 10.30).* Charge.
Warrington Market Bank Street, Warrington WA1 2EN (01925 632571; www.warrington.gov.uk/info/200815/warrington_market). Award winning retail market with 200 stalls, home to 130 independent businesses, all located under one roof.
Tourist Information Centre Warrington Bus Interchange, Horsemarket Street, Warrington WA1 1TF (01925 428585; www.touristinformationcentres.com/Warrington-Cheshire/information.htm).

● **Bewsey**
Cheshire. PO, tel, stores, off-licence. Founded around an estate originally owned by the monks of Titley Abbey, Essex who built a monastic grange known as Beausee – Beautiful Place. In 1264 the Grange came into the ownership of the Boteler family and was subsequently passed on to Robert Dudley, Earl of Leycester, in 1586. Following WWI, Bewsey was chosen for a new housing development and during WWII many Americans were stationed in the area, one family even occupying the Hall itself for a while. It is now flanked by the massive Gemini Retail Park, on its western boundary, home of this country's first IKEA.

Pubs and Restaurants

🍺**The Lower Angel** 27 Buttermarket Street, Warrington Bank Quay, Warrington WA1 2LY (01925 653326; www.lowerangel.co.uk). Opened in 1872 (and built next to what was then the Higher Angel), this traditional two-roomed pub has its own microbrewery and is dedicated to the cause of serving excellent real ales, alongside a fine (and sometimes rare) selection of over 70 malt whiskies. Dogs welcome – but no children. Sports TV and a beer garden. *Open 11.00 (Sun 12.00).*
🍺**The Tavern** 25 Church Street, Warrington WA1 2SS (01925 747463; www.4tsbrewery.co.uk/the-tavern.php). The local 4T's brewery tap, offering an excellent selection of real ales, together with a wide range world bottled beers, malt whiskies, vodkas and brandy. Covered patio area, sports TV, traditional pub games and Wi-Fi. *Open Mon-Thu 14.00 & Fri-Sun 12.00.*
🍺**The Bull's Head** 33 Church Street, Warrington WA1 2SX (01925 635680). A rambling 17th-C pub, converted from a row of cottages, dispensing a rotating selection of real ales, together with real cider. Behind is one of the country's few remaining crown bowling greens. Family-friendly, garden, sports TV and traditional pub games. *Open 12.00.*

🍺**The Maltings** Bewsey Farm Close, Old Hall Road, Warrington WA5 9PB (01925 638201). Once a farmhouse and now enclosed within a new town development, this pub serves real ale and food *daily L and E.* Dog- and family-friendly. Garden, open fires and sports TV. *Regular* live music, traditional pub games and Wi-Fi. *Open 12.00.*
🍺**Chapelford Farm** Santa Rosa Boulevard, Chapelford WA5 3AG (01925 717732; www.farmhouseinns.co.uk/pubs/chapelford-farm). An integral part of the Chapelford urban village, this family pub serves real ale and food *daily 11.00-21.00 (Fri-Sat 22.00).* A carvery is available *from 12.00.* Indoor children's play area, garden and Wi-Fi. Quiz *Tue. Open 11.00.*
🍺**The Seven Woods** Westbrook Crescent, Westbrook WA5 8TE (01925 241036; www.sevenwoodspub.co.uk). Food orientated, newly built pub, serving real ale with food available *daily Mon-Fri 11.00-22.00 & Sat-Sun 09.00-22.00 (Sun 21.00).* Garden and children's play area. Sports TV and Wi-Fi. Quiz *Thu. Open Mon-Fri 11.00 & Sat-Sun 09.00.*
🍺✕**Memphis Belle** Gemini Retail Park, Westbrook WA5 8WF (01925 712173; www.greatbritishcarvery.co.uk/our-pubs/memphis-belle). Buried within a massive retail park, this modern pub serves real ale and food *daily 12.00-22.00 (Sun 21.00).* Garden, sports TV and Wi-Fi. Quiz *Mon. Open 12.00.*
🍺**Hoop & Mallet** Callands Road, Callands, Warrington WA5 9RJ (01925 419182; www.hydesbrewery.co.uk). New, family-friendly pub, serving real ales and food *daily 16.00-20.00 (Sat-Sun 12.00).* Sports TV, garden, traditional pub games and Wi-Fi. Quiz *Thu. Open 12.00.*

> **WALKING & CYCLING**
> The Warrington Ranger Service (01925 571836) maintains a keen interest in the canal and its passage through Sankey Valley Park with an excellent series of interpretation boards.

Newton-le-Willows

A tarmac path winds between arable fields and horse paddocks, more or less following the line of the waterway to the outskirts of Earlestown, where again the navigation becomes very much in evidence. Sleek Pendolino, tilting trains, tear along the West Coast Main Railway Line: a reminder of the importance that this area once played in the building of locomotives and rolling stock. Mucky Mountains, beside Bradley (or Bradleigh) Stone Swing Bridge, bears witness to the chemical works that were once so prevalent along the canal, while the site of the Sankey Sugar factory was on the off side, just south of the Sankey (or Earlestown) Viaduct, beyond which repose the remains of Newton Common Lock. Above Old Double Locks lies the Blackbrook Branch, which is a 'must' to visit: there is lots to see and the interpretation is excellent. The final stretch into St Helens is via the New Double Locks, which were re-gated not so long ago. Beyond, a series of footpaths more or less follow the original line of the canal, into the centre of St Helens, to the point where the navigation was terminated in 1898.

● Burtonwood

Cheshire. PO, tel, stores, fish & chips, takeaway, library. Brewing, mining and flying vie with one another as heralds of the village's reputation. The Burtonwood brewery was established in 1867 and embarked on a joint venture with Thomas Hardy in 1998. Today Brakspear ales compose the main output. The USAF occupied the airfield (the largest base in Europe) from 1942-1958 and coal mining once dominated the area.

● Newton-le-Willows

Merseyside. All services. Technically the area surrounding the canal is Earlestown, with Newton-le-Willows (once known as Newton in Makerfield and still an attractive Georgian town) lying a little way to the east. As growing industrialisation focused around the canal and the important railway junction, so amenities and the administrative centre moved west to their present location, although the station still bears the correct appellation. Both Newton-le-Willows and Earlestown stations lie on the original Liverpool & Manchester Railway line and the original station buildings are the oldest examples of railway architecture in the world. The unfortunate MP for Liverpool – William Huskisson – was fatally injured at nearby Parkside on the inaugural run of George Stephenson's Rocket. A little over 130 years later Parkside Colliery, with an

expected lifespan of around a century, was opened, only to close in 1992.

The impressive Sankey Viaduct, spanning both the canal and Sankey Brook, was the world's first passenger carrying railway viaduct and its eastern approach arches housed the Viaduct Foundry, later to become the London & North Western Railway's principal waggon building works. To the immediate south of the suburb of Wargrave lay the Vulcan Foundry, originally opened as Charles Tayleur & Co Ltd in 1832, building girders and similar ironwork for the newly opened Liverpool & Manchester Railway. As the Vulcan Foundry Ltd, the company went on to build thousands of locomotives before closure in the hands of English Electric and its successors in 2002. In the early days Robert Stevenson held a stake in the company, acknowledging that it was cheaper and easier to build locomotives for the fledgling railway on its doorstep, rather than in distant Newcastle on Tyne – his then, home-base. Over the company's illustrious 170-year history, more than 60% of its locomotive output was shipped abroad, although its contribution to the home market was significant, including construction of the Class 55, Deltic. Some 630 homes are being built on the site, now totally bulldozed, the past work force's Vulcan Village the only clue to the area's faded glory.

The Sankey Sugar Company, situated beside the canal,

WALKING & CYCLING
Between Double Rail Swing Bridge No 33 and Broad Oak Basin the original towpath can, in places, be confused with other paths that radiate out through this area of rough ground. Ensure that you follow the line of the canal to Broad Oak Basin (now almost lost in the undergrowth) and then bear right, picking up the now clearly defined towpath and dry canal bed, leading to Old Double Locks. At the top of the locks it is well worth bearing right along the Blackbrook Branch to visit the Sankey Valley Visitor Centre.
To follow the navigation through to St Helens, turn left along the edge of the playing fields to join Boardman's Lane and then right to its junction with Park Road, where you should turn left. On crossing the Sankey Brook you will again see the canal and towpath, stretching away at right angles to the road on your right.

was another significant local employer, and it was waterborne supplies of raw materials and fuel oil that kept the southern portion of the navigation open until 1959. Today, little industry remains in the area, although Nicholls Foods – manufacturers of the ubiquitous Vimto – are still in full production in the town, their factory clearly visible from the West Coast Main Line.

● **St Helens**
Merseyside. All services. The growth and prosperity of St Helens came about as a result of coal mining and glassmaking during the 18th - and 19th C, together with a thriving cotton and linen industry, kept busy by sail making until the mid-19th C. The town is home to some 170 listed buildings. Amongst the most impressive are St Mary's Lowe House, the red brick Gamble Institute (where the Central Library is based), the Beechams Clock Tower and The Friends Meeting House. Today glass manufacture still dominates the town.
Cineworld Chalon Way West, St Helens, WA10 1BF (0871 200 2000; www.cineworld.co.uk). Eleven screen cinema in the town centre.
Citadel Arts Centre Waterloo Street, St Helens WA10 1PX (01744 735436; www.citadel.org.uk). A rare survivor of the early British music hall and dating from 1861, the Citadel today plays host to a wide range of community and arts events. See the website for programme details.
North West Museum of Road Transport The Old Bus Depot, 51 Hall Street, St Helens WA10 1DU (01744 451681; www.nwmort.co.uk). A unique and extensive collection of vintage buses forms the centrepiece of this recently refurbished museum. Shop. *Open Sat-Sun 12.00-16.00; free vintage bus rides 1st Sun in month.* Charge.
Queens Park Health and Fitness Centre Boundary Road, St Helens WA10 2LT (01744 671717; www.goactive.sthelens.gov.uk/facilities/

queens-park-health-fitness.aspx). *Open Mon-Fri 07.30-21.30 & Sat-Sun 09.00-16.30.* Charge.
Sankey Valley Heritage Visitor Centre Blackbrook Road, St Helens WA11 0AB (01744 677772; www.mysthelens.com/places/Sankey%20Valley/SankeyValley.html). Arguably the industrial heart of the Sankey Canal and its original terminus. Today a team of knowledgeable, helpful and friendly rangers oversee the country park, a series of trails benefiting from excellent interpretation, and a centre packed with useful information. Much work has been carried out in conjunction with the Sankey Canal Restoration Society to uncover the area's rich industrial past, which has exposed, amongst other industries, evidence of the Stanley Iron Slitting Mill. The centre carries an excellent range of publications on the area, most of them free, including information on a variety of fascinating trails and walks.
Smithy Heritage Centre Kiln Lane, St Helens WA10 4RA (01744 730744; www.smithyheritagecentre.org.uk). The Centre hosts temporary exhibitions on a wide range of topics, while the permanent displays are dedicated to the heritage of the building and its place at the heart of the history of Eccleston. The skills of the blacksmith, wheelwright, farrier and farmer are celebrated with original artefacts and images. *Open Easter-Sep, Sat-Sun 13.00-16.00.* Free.
Theatre Royal Corporation Street, St Helens WA10 1LQ (01744 756000; www.sthelenstheatreroyal.com). Vibrant regional

theatre with a varied programme. Bar. Booking office *open Mon-Sat 10.00-17.00 and an hour* before performances.

The World of Glass Chalon Way East, St Helens WA10 1BX (01744 22766; www.worldofglass.com). Watch glass making; join a glass blowing course or step into St Helens' Victorian past. Also a variety of changing exhibitions. Shop and canalside café. *Open Tue-Sat, Mar-Oct 10.00-17.00 & Nov-Feb 10.00-16.00. Closed B Hols. Charge.*

Tourist Information Centre The World of Glass, Chalon Way East, St Helens WA10 1BX (01744 755150; www.visit-sthelens.com).

Pubs and Restaurants

◗✕**Fiddle i' th Bag** Alder Lane, Burtonwood WA5 4BJ (01925 225442). Close to the line of the old towpath, this pub-cum-museum is packed with curiosities, oddities and WWII memorabilia. It also serves real ale and food *daily L and E. Open Mon-Fri L and E & Sat-Sun 12.00.*

◗**The Chapel House** Chapel Lane, Burtonwood WA5 4PT (01925 225607). Serving a rotating selection of real ales, this village local *regularly* hosts live music *at weekends.* Dogs welcome. Outside seating area, traditional pub games and Wi-Fi. *Open 12.00.*

✕**Woody Delicious Sandwich Bar** 5a Clay Lane, Burtonwood WA5 4HH (01925 228998). Serving a tasty selection of takeaway food *Mon-Sat 06.30-14.30 (Sat 07.00) & Sun 08.00-13.00.*

◗**The Wargrave Inn** 448 Wargrave Road, Earlestown, Newton-le-Willows WA12 8RT (01925 221922). Welcoming local, dog- and child-friendly, serving real ale and *open Mon-Fri 13.00 & sat-Sun 12.00.* Sports TV, newspapers, traditional pub games and Wi-Fi. Covered children's play area.

◗**The Victoria Inn** Wargrave Road, Earlestown, Newton-le-Willows WA12 8EP (01925 224493; www.victoriapubnewton.com). Homely pub, benefiting from a recent makeover, serving real ale and freshly cooked, homemade food *daily Mon-Sat L and E & Sun 12.00-20.00.* Family-friendly, garden, sports TV and Wi-Fi. *Open 12.00.*

◗**The Blue Lion** 51 High Street, Newton-le-Willows WA12 9SL (01925 225062). Family owned pub serving real ale and food *daily L and E. Regular weekend* live entertainment. Patio seating, sports TV, traditional pub games, newspapers and Wi-Fi. Dogs and children welcome. *Open 12.00.*

◗✕**The Pied Bull Hotel** 54 High Street, Newton-le-Willows WA12 9SH (01925 224549; www.piedbull.com). Family-orientated pub offering real ale and food *Mon-Fri L and E & Sat-Sun 12.00-21.00 (Sun 19.00).* Garden, patio and Wi-Fi. B&B. *Open 12.00.*

✕♀ **Balti Towers** Earle Street, Earlestown, Newton-le-Willows WA12 9LR (01925 227548; www.balti-towers. co.uk). Friendly Indian restaurant offering *daily* meal deals and an inexpensive *Sun* buffet *15.00-20.00.* Children welcome. Takeaway service. *Open daily 17.00 (Sun 15.00).*

◗**The Ship Inn** 273 Blackbrook Road, Blackbrook, St Helens WA11 0AB (01744 752889). Beside the Sankey Valley Visitor Centre. Handy for the Visitor Centre, this pub serves real ale and food *daily 12.00-20.00.* Children welcome, outside seating and large-screen TV. Quiz *Thu* and live entertainment *at the weekend. Open 12.00.*

✕♀**La Casa Vieja** 6-12 Bickerstaffe Street, St Helens WA10 1DH (01744 454613; www.lacasavieja.co.uk).

Sophisticated, yet relaxed, tapas restaurant and bar serving authentic, affordable Spanish food *Mon-Sat L and E.* Children welcome.

◗**The Phoenix Inn** 34 Canal Street, St Helens WA10 3LL (01744 751890). Built in 1903, this welcoming hostelry has its name picked out in glass mosaic sourced from the nearby Pilkington factory, and serves well-kept, competitively priced real ales and real cider. Outdoor drinking area and traditional pub games. *Open Mon-Thu 14.00 & Fri-Sun 12.00.*

✕♀**Le Frog Bistro** 2 Haydock Street, St Helens WA10 1DD (01744 730060; www.lefrogbistro.com/restaurant/ sthelens). Few people are disappointed by their visit to this quirky, baronial hall of a restaurant which serves modern English and Mediterranean food with a French accent. There is something for everyone on their very varied menu and families are made most welcome. *Open Mon-Sat L and E & Sun 12.00-19.00.*

◗**The Cricketers Arms** Peter Street, St Helens WA10 2EB (01744 361846). Friendly local hostelry, supporting local microbreweries, with at least seven handpumps. Also real cider. *Regular* live entertainment, beer garden, sports TV and traditional pub games. *Open Mon-Thu 14.00 & Fri-Sun 12.00.*

◗✕**The News Room** 89 Duke Street, St Helens WA10 2JG (01744 322129). Family-run café bar with a welcoming, friendly atmosphere, serving the local George Wright draught and bottled beers and appetising food *daily.* Children welcome. Wi-Fi.

◗**The Sefton Arms** 1-7 Baldwin Street, St Helens WA10 1QA (01744 22065). Open for breakfast, morning coffee and ultimately for the sale of real ale and real cider. Excellent value food available *all day*, including *Sun* roasts. Outside seating area, sports TV and live music *Fri & Sat. Open 08.00.*

◗**The Market Tavern** 26-28 Bridge Street, St Helens WA10 1NW (01744 757313). Popular town centre pub serving real ale and real cider. Sports TV and outside drinking area. *Open 09.00 (Sun 10.00).*

◗**The Turks Head** Morley Street, St Helens WA10 2DQ (01744 651289). Brewery Tudor, with etched glass, this hostelry serves a choice of a dozen real ales, real cider and a range of draught and bottled continental beers. Food is available *Wed-Sat*; jazz on *Thu* and a Quiz *Tue.* Open fires, sports TV and traditional pub games. *Open Mon-Fri 14.00 & Sat-Sun 12.00.*

◗**The Glass House** 5 Market Street, St Helens WA10 1NE (01744 762310; www.jdwetherspoon.co.uk/home/ pubs/the-glass-house-st-helens). Within a stone's throw of the World of Glass Museum, this pub serves real ale, real cider and food *from 08.00.* Children welcome, large screen TV, outside seating area and Wi-Fi.

▌TRENT & MERSEY CANAL

MAXIMUM DIMENSIONS

Derwent Mouth to Horninglow Basin, Burton upon Trent
Length: 72' 0"
Beam: 14' 0"
Headroom: 7' 0"
Stenson Lock is very tight for 14ft beam craft and Weston Lock is tight for boats of 72ft length.

Burton upon Trent to south end of Harecastle Tunnel
Length: 72' 0"
Beam: 7' 0"
Headroom: 6' 3"

Harecastle Tunnel
Length: 72' 0"
Beam: 7' 0"
Headroom: 5' 9"

North end of Harecastle Tunnel to Croxton Aqueduct
Length: 72' 0"
Beam: 7' 0"
Headroom: 7' 0"

Croxton Aqueduct to Preston Brook Tunnel
Length: 72' 0"
Beam: 8' 2"
Headroom: 6' 3"

MANAGER:

Derwent Mouth to south portal of Harecastle Tunnel:
0303 040 4040
enquiries.centralshires@canalrivertrust.org.uk
South portal of Harecastle Tunnel to Preston Brook:
0303 040 4040
enquiries.manchesterpennine@canalrivertrust.org.uk

MILEAGE

DERWENT MOUTH to:
Swarkestone Lock: 7 miles
Willington: 12¼ miles
Horninglow Wharf: 16½ miles
Barton Turn: 21¼ miles
Fradley, junction with Coventry Canal: 26¼ miles
Great Haywood, junction with Staffordshire & Worcestershire Canal: 39 miles
Stone: 48½ miles
Stoke Top Lock, junction with Caldon Canal: 58 miles
Harding's Wood, junction with Macclesfield Canal: 63¾ miles
King's Lock, Middlewich, junction with Middlewich Branch: 76¼ miles
Anderton Lift, for River Weaver: 86½ miles

PRESTON BROOK north end of tunnel and Bridgewater Canal: 93½ miles

Locks: 76

This early canal was originally conceived partly as a roundabout link between the ports of Liverpool and Hull, while passing through the busy area of the Potteries and mid-Cheshire, and terminating either in the River Weaver or in the Mersey. Its construction was promoted by Josiah Wedgwood (1730–95), the famous potter, aided by his friends Thomas Bentley and Erasmus Darwin. In 1766 the Trent & Mersey Canal Act was passed by Parliament, authorising the building of a navigation from the River Trent at Shardlow to Runcorn Gap, where it would join the proposed extension of the Bridgewater Canal from Manchester.

The ageing James Brindley was appointed engineer for the canal. Construction began at once and in 1777 the Trent & Mersey Canal was opened. In the total 93 miles between Derwent Mouth and Preston Brook, the Trent & Mersey gained connection with no fewer than nine other canals or significant branches.

By the 1820s the slowly-sinking tunnel at Harecastle had become a serious bottle-neck, so Thomas Telford recommended building a second tunnel beside the old one. His recommendation was eventually accepted by the company and the new tunnel was completed in under three years, in 1827. Although the Trent & Mersey was taken over in 1845 by the new North Staffordshire Railway Company, the canal flourished until World War I.

Look out for the handsome cast iron mileposts, which actually measure the mileage from Shardlow, not Derwent Mouth. There are 59 originals, from the Rougeley and Dixon foundry in Stone, and 34 replacements, bearing the mark of the Trent & Mersey Canal Society – T & MCS 1977.

Harding's Wood Junction

At the north end of Harecastle Tunnel (2926yds long) the navigation passes Kidsgrove station and a coal yard; there is also a *shower* in the facilities block beside the north tunnel portal. Beyond is Harding's Wood and the junction with the Macclesfield Canal, which crosses the T & M on Poole Aqueduct. There are *showers, laundry facilities and toilets* at the CRT yard at Red Bull. The canal continues to fall through a heavily locked stretch sometimes called 'heartbreak hill' but known to the old boatmen as the 'Cheshire Locks'.

Pubs and Restaurants

The Blue Bell 25 Hardingswood, Kidsgrove ST7 1EG (01782 774052; www.bluebellkidsgrove. co.uk). Canalside, at Hardings Wood Junction. Friendly, quiet, one-bar local, winnner of many CAMRA awards. Real ale, plus a range of specialist bottled beers, including many from Belgium, plus real cider and perry. No juke box, pool table or gaming machines. Note the trapdoor in the lounge ceiling. Well-behaved children welcome *until 21.00.* Dogs welcome. Snacks are available *at weekends.* Open *Tue–Fri 19.30–23.00; Sat 13.00–16.00, 19.30–23.00; Sun 12.00–22.30 (all day during summer). Closed Mon.*

The Red Bull Hotel Congleton Road South, Church Lawton ST7 3AJ (01782 782600; www. redbullchurchlawton.robinsonsbrewery.com). By lock 43. Popular pub close to Hardings Wood Junction, serving real ale and bar meals, including fish dishes *L and E,* along with good wine. Children welcome. Canalside seating area. Real fires and moorings. Wi-Fi. *Open all day.*

The Broughton Arms Mill Mead, Rode Heath ST7 3RU (01270 883203; www.broughtonarmspub.co.uk). Canalside at Rode Heath. Friendly family pub, with comfortable bars and canalside seating. Range of real ale. Food available in bar and dining area *L and E.* Children welcome away from the bar. Waterside garden. *Open all day from 12.00.*

The Royal Oak 41 Sandbach Road, Rode Heath ST7 3RW (01270 875670). Spacious, roadside pub, close to the navigation serving a selection of real ales and food *L and E.* Family-friendly with a garden. *Open all day from 11.30 (Sun 11.00).*

Two minor aqueducts are encountered, and most of the locks are narrow pairs – the chambers side by side.

● **Kidsgrove**
Staffs. All services. Originally an iron and coal producing town, Kidsgrove was much helped by the completion of the Trent & Mersey Canal. James Brindley is buried here.

● **Rode Heath**
Cheshire. PO, tel, stores, off-licence, takeaway. A useful shopping area right by bridge 140.
Rode Heath Rise ST7 3QD Once the site of a salt works, it has now been landscaped and restored as a wildflower meadow. Telephone (01260 297237/01625 383777) for further information.

NAVIGATIONAL NOTES

HARECASTLE TUNNEL Do not enter in an unpowered craft. With the complete removal of the towpath, headroom is no longer the problem it once was. A one-way system operates, so follow the instructions of the tunnel keepers. *For updated tunnel opening times, telephone 0303 040 4040.*

Boatyards

ⓑ**David Smithsons Solid Fuel and Caravan Centre** Liverpool Road, Kidsgrove ST7 1EA (01782 787887). Near bridge 132. **D** Calor gas, solid fuel, caravan fittings which can be used as chandlery. Also bicycles and bicycle spares for sale.

ⓑ**Red Bull Services** Red Bull Basin, Congleton Road South, Church Lawton, Stoke-on-Trent ST7 3AJ (01782 779033). Haul out, engine repairs, hull blacking, boat repairs and welding.

see Book 4

WALKING & CYCLING
The towpath is in good condition through to Preston Brook and offers the opportunity to sample a varied landscape, ranging from the beauties of the Dane Valley through to the industry indigenous to this long-established salt-producing area.

209

Wheelock

The canal now descends the Wheelock flight of eight locks, which are the last paired locks one sees when travelling northwards. The countryside continues to be quiet and unspoilt but unspectacular. The pair of locks half-way down the flight is situated in the little settlement of Malkin's Bank, overlooked by terraced houses. The boatman's co-op used to be here, in the small terrace of cottages. The adjoining boatyard now specialises in the restoration of traditional working boats. At the bottom of the flight is the village of Wheelock (*toilets* and *shower*); west of here the navigation curls round the side of a hill before entering the very long-established salt-producing area that is based on Middlewich. The 'wild' brine pumping and rock-salt mining that has gone on hereabouts has resulted in severe local subsidence; the effect on the canal has been to necessitate the constant raising of the banks as lengths of the canal bed sink. This of course means that the affected lengths tend to be much deeper than ordinary canals. Non-swimmers beware of falling overboard. The navigation now begins to lose the rural character it has enjoyed since Kidsgrove. Falling through yet more locks, the canal is joined by a busy main road (useful for *fish & chips*, west of Kings Lock; and *Chinese takeaway*, west of bridge 166) which accompanies it into an increasingly flat and industrialised landscape, past several salt works and into Middlewich, where a branch of the Shropshire Union leads off westwards towards that canal at Barbridge. The first 100yds or so of this branch is the Wardle Canal, claimed to be the shortest canal in the country.

- **Wheelock**
  Cheshire. Tel, stores, off-licence, fish & chips. Busy little main road village on the canal.
- **Sandbach**
  Cheshire. PO, tel, stores, garage, chemist, takeaways, bank, station. 1½ miles north of Wheelock. An old market town that has maintained its charm despite the steady growth of its salt and chemical industries. After walking from the canal you can refresh yourself with a pint of real ale from any of the seven pubs visible from the seat in the market place.
  Ancient Crosses In the cobbled market place on a massive base stand two superb Saxon crosses, believed to commemorate the conversion of the area to Christianity in the 7th C. They suffered

severely in the 17th C when the Puritans broke them up and scattered the fragments for miles. After years of searching for the parts, George Ormerod succeeded in re-erecting the crosses in 1816, with new stone replacing the missing fragments.
St Mary's Church High Street, Sandbach CW11 1AN. A large, 16th C church with a handsome battlemented tower. The most interesting features of the interior are the 17th C carved roof and the fine chancel screen.
The Old Hall Hotel High Street, Sandback CW11 1AL. An outstanding example of Elizabethan half-timbered architecture, which was formerly the home of the lord of the manor, but is now used as an hotel.

Boatyards

ⓑ**Malkins Bank Canal Services** The Boatyard, Betchton Road, Malkins Bank, Sandbach CW11 4XN (01270 764595). Long-term mooring, boat building and historic boat restoration, boat repairs, will help with breakdowns where possible.

ⓑ**The Northwich Boat Company** Moss Bridge Cottage, Sandbach CW11 3PW (01270 760160/760770; www.thenorthwichboat.com). D Pump out, gas, boat repairs, boat building and fitting out, new and used boat sales, boatshare sales and management.

Pubs and Restaurants

The Commercial Hotel 2 Game Street, Wheelock CW113RR (01270 760122). Near bridge 154. Set in a Georgian house with an old-fashioned and spacious feel this pub serves real ale. *Open Mon-Fri 16.00-23.00 & Fri-Sun all day from 12.00.* Children and dogs welcome. Beer garden, snooker room, darts and dominoes.

The Cheshire Cheese 466-468 Crewe Road, Wheelock CW11 3RL (01270 760319). Heavily beamed, canalside pub serving real ale and a range of meals and snacks *L and E, daily*. Children and dogs welcome (dogs in the garden). Large beer garden. Traditonal pub games. Mooring. *Open all day from 12.00.*

✕♀ **The Shampaan** 504 Crewe Road, Wheelock CW11 3RL (01270 753528/753511; www.shampaan.com). Authentic South Asian cuisine to eat in or takeaway. Children welcome. *Open Mon-Sat 17.00-23.00 & Sun 16.00-22.00.*

The Market Tavern 8 The Square, Sandbach CW11 1AT (01270 762099; www.themarkettavern-sandbach.co.uk). Opposite the crosses. Lively, old, traditional town pub, dating from 1680, dispensing a good selection of real ales. Large beer garden. Children welcome. Folk club *Tue* and live bands *Sat*. *Open L and E Sun-Fri & all day Sat*. Food available *Mon-Sat L and E & Sun all day* across the square at **The Crown** 10 Market Square, Sandbach CW11 1AT (01270 762161; www.crownsandbach.robinsonsbrewery.com).

The Lower Chequer Inn Crown Bank, Sandbach CW11 1FW (07932 943977). Delightful 16th-C, timber-framed hostelry serving an excellent range of real ales and real cider. Outdoor drinking area and marquee. *Open all day in summer with restricted hours in winter.*

The Old Hall High Street, Sandbach CW11 1AL (01270 758170; www.brunningandprice.co.uk/oldhall). Microbreweries are well represented in this stunning, Grade 1 listed, timber-framed building recently completely restored to a very high standard, displaying it's wood panelling and Tudor fireplace to perfection. Family-friendly and garden – dogs on a leash welcome. Food *available daily from 12.00. Open all day from 11.30 (Sun 12.00).*

The Fox Inn London Road, Elworth CW11 3BF (01270 747022). ½ mile north east of Elton Moss Bridge 160. Welcoming roadside pub serving real ale and food *L and E*. Real fire and pool table. *Open all day*. Takeaway nearby.

Middlewich

The Trent & Mersey skirts the centre of the town, passing lots of moored narrowboats and through three consecutive narrow locks, arriving at a wide (14ft) lock (which has suffered from subsidence) with a pub beside it. This used to represent the beginning of a wide, almost lock-free navigation right through to Preston Brook, Manchester and Wigan (very convenient for the salt industry when it shipped most of its goods by boat), but Croxton Aqueduct had to be replaced many years ago, and is now a steel structure only 8ft 2in wide. The aqueduct crosses the River Dane, which flows alongside the navigation as both water courses leave industrial Middlewich and move out into fine open country. Initially, this is a stretch of canal as beautiful as any in the country. Often overhung by trees, the navigation winds along the side of a hill as it follows the delightful valley of the River Dane. There are pleasant *moorings* with *picnic tables and barbecue facilities*, created by the Broken Cross Boating Club in old clay pits, just north of bridge 176, on the off-side. The parkland on the other side of the valley encompasses Bostock Hall, a Georgian house rebuilt in 1775 to a design thought to have been by Samuel Wyatt: it has now been converted into apartments. At Whatcroft Hall (privately owned), the canal circles around to the east, passing under a railway bridge before heading for the industrial outskirts of Northwich and shedding its beauty and solitude once again.

NAVIGATIONAL NOTES

There are several privately owned wide 'lagoons' caused by subsidence along this section of the Trent & Mersey, in some of which repose the hulks of abandoned barges and narrowboats, lately being salvaged. Navigators should be wary of straying off the main line, since the off-side canal bank is often submerged and invisible just below the water level.

Boatyards

ⓑ**Kings Lock Chandlery** Booth Lane, Middlewich CW10 OJJ (01606 737564; www.kingslock.co.uk). D Gas, overnight mooring, long-term mooring, slipway, engine sales and repairs, boat repairs, Webasto dealer, chandlery (including mail order), books, maps, gifts, solid fuel, Vetus dealer.
ⓑ**Andersen Boats** Wych House, St Anne's Road, Middlewich CW10 9BQ (01606 833668/07771 693981; www.andersenboats.com). Pump out, gas, narrowboat hire, books and maps. Useful DIY shop nearby.

ⓑ**Middlewich Narrowboats** Canal Terrace, Middlewich CW10 9BD (01606 832460; www.middlewichboats.co.uk). D Pump out *(not Fri-Sat)*, gas, narrowboat hire, overnight mooring *(not Fri)*, dry dock, boat building, chandlery, books and maps, engine repairs, laundry service *(not Fri-Sat)*, grit blasting, boat painting, hull blacking. *Emergency call out.* Useful tool hire shop next door.

Pubs and Restaurants

The Badger Inn Cross Lane, Church Minshull CW5 6DY (01270 522348; www.badgerinn.co.uk). Heavily-beamed, 18th-C hostelry once a favourite location for bare-knuckle fighting but now given over to the more genteel pastimes of fine dining and the quaffing of real ale. Food is available *all day* and the pub is open *daily from 11.30 (Sun 12.00)*. Garden. Children eating in the restaurant are welcome *until 18.00*. B&B.

The Golden Lion 61 Chester Road, Middlewich CW10 9ET (01606 737163; www.goldenlionmiddlewich.co.uk). *Open all day* – at the top of the town at the junction between Chester Road and Newton Bank. Now a free house, dispensing real ale and traditional pub food *L and E*. Children welcome, garden. Real fires and sports TV. B&B. *Open all day from 12.00*.

The Boars Head Kinderton Street, Middlewich CW10 0JE (01606 833191; www.theboarsheadhotel.com). Large rambling pub and restaurant offering real ale and food *L and E, daily*. Pool room. Patio. Live music *Sat*. B&B.

The Cheshire Cheese Lewin Street, Middlewich CW10 9AX (01606 832097). Friendly, traditional establishment serving real ales. Children welcome. Landscaped garden with large patio and marquee. *Weekly* karaoke and *occasional* live bands. with large patio. *Open all day*.

The Newton Brewery Inn 68 Webb Lane, Middlewich CW10 9DN (01606 832335). ¹/₄ mile south of the Big Lock pub. Small friendly pub with attractive garden running down to the towpath. Real ale served. Children welcome. *Open all day from 14.00 (Thu-Sat 12.00)*.

The Big Lock Webbs Lane, Middlewich CW10 9DN (01606 833489; www.thebiglock.com). Canalside. Variously a bottle-making factory and canal-horse stables, this pub now serves real ale and a large menu of popular pub food. Freshly prepared meals available *Mon-Fri L and E & Sat-Sun all day*. Children and dogs welcome. Canalside seating.

● **Middlewich**
Cheshire. PO, tel, stores, bank, chemist, off-licence, fish & chips, takeaways, library, garage. A town that since Roman times has been dedicated to salt extraction. Most of the salt produced here goes to various chemical industries. Subsidence from salt extraction has prevented redevelopment for many years, but a big renewal scheme is now in progress. The canalside area is a haven of peace below the busy streets. There is an interesting town trail depicting Roman Middlewich as a Romano-British saltworks settlement in the period 150-250 AD. Interpretation boards can be found on the towpath north of Bridge 172 and beside the Newton Brewery Inn.

St Michael's Church High Town, Middlewich CW10 9AN (01606 738005). A handsome medieval church which was a place of refuge for the Royalists during the Civil War. It has a fine interior with richly carved woodwork.

Anderton Lift

The outlying canal settlement of Broken Cross acts as a buffer between the beauty and solitude of the Dane Valley and the industrial ravages around Northwich. Beyond is another length in which salt mining has determined the nature of the scenery.

Part of it is heavily industrial, with enormous Tata Chemical works dominating the scene; much of it is devastated but rural (just), some of it is nondescript, and some of it is superb countryside. Donkey engines can still be seen in surrounding fields pumping brine. Leaving the vicinity of Lostock Gralam and the outskirts of Northwich, one passes Marston and Wincham (*PO, tel, late-opening stores*). Just west of the village, one travels along a 1/2-mile stretch of canal that was only cut in 1958, as the old route was about to collapse into – needless to say – underground salt workings. Beyond the woods of Marbury Country Park (attractive short-stay *moorings*) and before Bridge 198, there are a full range of facilities including *toilets and showers*, followed by Anderton – the short entrance canal to the famous boat lift down into the Weaver Navigation is on the left. *Gas* is available 100yds south of Bridge 200. The main line continues westwards, winding along what is now a steep hill and into Barnton Tunnel. There is a useful *range of shops*, up the hill from the east end of the tunnel, including a *PO, tel, stores, chemist, butcher, takeaway, off-licence and laundrette*. You then emerge onto a hillside overlooking the River Weaver, with a marvellous view straight down the huge Saltersford Locks. Now Saltersford Tunnel is entered: beyond it you are in completely open country again. There are good moorings in the basins to the east of both tunnels.

NAVIGATIONAL NOTES

1 Saltersford Tunnel is crooked, affording only a brief glimpse of the other end. It is subject to timed passage. Northbound, on the hour to 20 min past; southbound half past the hour to 10 mins to the hour. Two boats cannot pass in this or Barnton Tunnel, so make sure they are clear before proceeding.

2 *See* notes on page 177 covering use of the Anderton Boat Lift.

● **Marston**

Cheshire. Tel. A salt-producing village, suffering badly from its own industry. The numerous gaps in this village are caused by the demolition or collapse of houses affected by subsidence. Waste ground abounds.

The Lion Salt Works Offershaw Lane, Marston CW9 6ES (01606 41823; www.lionsaltworks.org). Beside the canal at bridge 193. The Thompson family established an open pan salt works in Marston in 1842, producing fishery salt, bay salt, crystal salt and lump salt. The salt was pumped as wild brine from 45yds beneath the works and evaporated in a large iron pan. The crystals thus formed were raked into tubs to form blocks, and subsequently dried in brick stove houses, before being exported (with the first part of the journey by canal) to India, Canada and West Africa. The Works closed in 1986 and after many ups and downs is finally scheduled

see Book 4

Map labels: Lane-ends Farm, Leigh Farm, Whalebone Farm, Higher Marston, Marston Hall, Marston Lodge Farm, MARSTON CP, Cheshire Ring Canal Walk, Big Wood, Resr, Fields Farm, Ollershaw Lane, School Farm, Cemetery, Manor Farm, Rose Farm, Bank Farm, WITTON FLASHES, LION SALT WORKS, MARSTON, NEUMANN'S FLASHES, Works, Keepers Wood, Lodge Wood, WINCHAM, Wincham Hall Hotel, Witton Brook, Ashton's Flashes, Village Farm, Witton Mill Bridge, Wks, BOAT TRIPS, Basin Bridge, ROMAN ROAD, NORTHWICH, Springbank Farm, Co Const Bdy, Anderton, Middlewich 5m 4L, BROKEN CROSS, Cook's Lane, High House, Melvin Holme, RUDHEATH, Bakery, Higher Shurlach, RUDHEATH CP, Penny's, Park Farm, Cheshire Ring Canal Walk, Pipe Bridges, Marshall's Gorse, Billinge Green Farm, Gadbrook Farm, Davenham Road, Billinge Green Flash, Yew Tree Farm, Higginsmine Farm, Kingstree

Bridge/distance markers: 196, 193, 192, 191, 190, 189, 188, 187A, 186, 185, 184, 183, 182A, 182, 181, 212

5¼m 0L Anderton / Middlewich 5m 4L

Trent & Mersey Canal Anderton Lift

215

to re-open to the public during spring 2015, having been the subject of an £8 million restoration project. Therefore telephone for details of opening times or visit the website for a progress report. **Marbury Country Park** Comberbach CW9 6AT (01606 77741; www.northwichwoodlands.org.uk). Two-hundred-acre park occupying the landscaped gardens of the former Marbury Hall and estate, once the home of the Barry and Smith-Barry families. Overlooking Budworth Mere, the house was demolished in 1968 and the much-neglected gardens restored to their former glory by Cheshire County Heritage and Recreation service. The Information Centre (½ mile north of bridge 196) houses a display of Marbury's wildlife and history, including its use as a POW camp during World War II. Visitor's moorings and picnic area.

● **Anderton Lift**
Lift Lane, Anderton CW9 6FW (01606 786777; www.andertonboatlift.co.uk). An amazing and enormous piece of machinery built in 1875 by Leader Williams (later engineer of the Manchester Ship Canal) to connect the Trent & Mersey to the flourishing Weaver Navigation, 50ft below. As built, the lift consisted of two water-filled tanks counterbalancing each other in a vertical slide, resting on massive hydraulic rams. It worked on the very straightforward principle that making the ascending tank slightly lighter – by pumping a little water out – would assist the hydraulic rams (which were operated by a steam engine and pump) in moving both tanks, with boats in them, up or down their respective slide. In 1908 the lift had to have major repairs, so it was modernised at the same time. The troublesome hydraulic rams were done away with; from then on each tank – which contained 250 tons of water – had its own counterweights and was independent of the other tank. Electricity replaced steam as the motive power. One of the most fascinating individual features of the canal system, it draws thousands of sightseers every year. Restoration to full working order is now complete, following the original 1875 hydraulic design, using oil as the motive force rather than the chemically contaminated water that was the cause of the 1908 failure. The more recent counter balance weights, together with their ungainly supporting structure, have been retained to demonstrate the engineering development of the lift.

● **Northwich**
Cheshire. All services. Regular buses from Barnton.

A rather attractive town at the junction of the Rivers Weaver and Dane. (The latter brings large quantities of sand down into the Weaver Navigation, necessitating a heavy expenditure on dredging.) As in every other town in this area, salt has for centuries been responsible for the continued prosperity of Northwich. The Weaver Navigation has of course been another very prominent factor in the town's history, and the building and repairing of barges, narrowboats, and small seagoing ships has been carried on here for over 200 years. Nowadays this industry has been almost forced out of business by foreign competition, and the last private shipyard on the river closed down in 1971. (This yard – Isaac Pimblott's – used to be between Hunt's Locks and Hartford Bridge. Their last contract was a tug for Aden.) However, the big CRT yard in the town continues to thrive; some very large maintenance craft are built and repaired here. The wharves by Town Bridge are empty, and are an excellent temporary mooring site for anyone wishing to visit the place. The town centre is very close; much of it has been completely rebuilt however, signs of decay are already beginning to creep in. There is now an extensive shopping precinct. Although the large number of pubs has been whittled down in the rebuilding process, there are still some pleasant old streets. The Weaver and the big swing bridges across it remain a dominant part of the background. **Tourist Information Centre** 1 The Arcade, Northwich CW9 5AS (0300 123 8123; www.cheshirewestandchester.gov.uk). *Open Mon-Fri 08.30-17.00.*
Dock Road Edwardian Pumping Station Weir Street, Northwich CW9 5HL (07970 207941; www. dockroad.org). Intriguing listed building housing unique pumps and gas-powered engines fully restored to working order. Building open and engines working *Easter–Sep Sun and B Hols 14.00– 17.00, groups by arrangement.* Donations.
Weaver Hall Museum and Workhouse 162 London Road, Weaver Hall, London Road, Northwich CW9 8AB (01606 271640; www.weaverhallmuseum. org.uk). The history of the salt industry from Roman times to the present day, housed in the town's former workhouse. Look out for the remarkable model ship, made from salt of course. Shop and coffee shop. *Open Jan-Oct Tue-Fri; B Hols and during school holidays, 10.00-17.00 & Nov-Dec 10.00-16.00. Sat-Sun, Jan-Oct 14.00-17.00 & Nov-Dec 13.00-16.00.* Charge.

NAVIGATIONAL NOTES

1 The Anderton Boat Lift is available for use *7 days a week and pre-booked passage is essential* by telephoning 01606 786777. Visit the website (www.andertonboatlift.co.uk) for more information.
2 Boaters should differentiate between the holding moorings at the top and bottom of the lift, which are solely for lift use, and the visitor moorings.

Boatyards

Ⓑ**Orchard Marina** School Road, Gadbrook Park, Rudheath, Northwich CW9 7RG (01606 42082; www. orchardmarina.com). Beside bridge 182. 🛈🛈⚓ Gas, overnight and long-term mooring, dry dock, boat and engine repairs, boat fitting out, boat and engine sales, DIY facilities, books, maps, solid fuel, toilets, showers, laundrette. *Emergency call out.*

Ⓑ**Colliery Narrowboat Co** Wincham Wharf, 220 Manchester Road, Lostock Gralam, Northwich CW9 7NT (01606 44672). Overnight and long-term mooring, crane, winter storage, boat building, boat sales, boat and engine repairs, wet dock, DIY facilities, toilets.

Ⓑ**Olympus Narrow Boats** Wincham Wharf, 220 Manchester Road, Lostock Gralam, Northwich CW9 7NT (01606 43048). ⚓ D Gas, narrowboat fitting out, boat repairs, dry dock, wet dock.

Ⓑ**ABC Leisure Group** Anderton Marina, Uplands Road, Anderton CW9 6AJ (01606 79642; www. ukboathire.com). Services are on the canal. 🛈🛈⚓D Pump out, gas, narrowboat hire, overnight mooring, long-term mooring, slipway, boat sales, engine sales and repairs, boat painting, covered wet docks for hire, chandlery, gifts, restaurant, telephone, toilets.

Ⓑpy**Uplands Marina** Uplands Road, Anderton CW9 6AQ (01606 782986/07931 323747; www. uplandsmarina.co.uk). ⚓ D Overnight and long-term mooring, boat sales and repairs, boat fitting out, winter storage, slipway, wet dock, gas, coal, chandlery.

BIRD LIFE

The *Kingfisher* is a dazzlingly attractive bird, but its colours often appear muted when the bird is seen sitting in shade or vegetation. It has orange-red underparts and mainly blue upperparts; the electric blue back is seen to the best effect when the bird is observed in low-level flight speeding along a river. It is invariably seen near water and uses overhanging branches to watch for fish. When a feeding opportunity arises, the Kingfisher plunges headlong into the water, catching its prey in its bill: the fish is swallowed whole. Kingfishers nest in holes excavated in the river bank.

Pubs and Restaurants

✕ **The Crusty Cob Café** ¼ mile west of Bridge 192. Chapel Street, Marston CW9 6GJ (07976 936766/07770 821715). Breakfast, snacks, filled rolls, sandwiches, hot and cold drinks. Eat in or takeaway. *Open Mon-Fri 08.00-14.00 & Sat 08.30-13.00.*

🍺**The Salt Barge** Ollershaw Lane, Marston CW9 6ES (01606 43064; www.thesaltbarge.co.uk). Opposite the Lion Salt Works, beside bridge 193. Deceptively large pub with a friendly atmosphere, neatly divided into cosy areas, and with an inviting family room. Real ales and good Food available *Mon-Fri L and E & Sat-Sun all day*. Children's menu and *Sunday* lunch. Garden. Entertainment *Fri.*

🍺**The Old Broken Cross** Broken Cross Place, Middlewich Road, Rudheath CW9 7EB (01606 333111). Beside Bridge 184. Once a row of canalside cottages, this establishment now serves real ale and food *Sun-Fri L and E (not Sun E) & Sat all day*. Family- and dog-friendly. Garden and patio. Open fires and traditional pub games. Sports TV and Wi-Fi. Mooring. *Open all day from 12.00.*

🍺**Nectars Bar** Wincham Wharf, 216 Manchester Road, Lostock Gralam CW9 7NT (01606 333723; www.nectarswinebar.co.uk). Beside Bridge 189. A converted mill, still with its original water wheel, serving real ale and food *L and E*. Canalside seating

and mooring. Sports TV and real fires. Children and dogs welcome. *Regular* live music and traditional pub games. WI-Fi. *Open Mon-Fri L and E and Sat-Sun all day.*

✕♀ **The Moorings** Anderton Marina, Uplands Road, Anderton CW9 6AJ (01606 79789; www. mooringsrestaurant.co.uk). Canalside seating. Boaters please moor outside the basin. Small, independent restaurant and bar overlooking Anderton Marina and the Trent & Mersey Canal. *Closed 17.00-18.30.* Wide variety of food with emphasis on fresh fish and fresh produce, served *L and E (not Mon E or Tue all day)*. Children and dogs welcome. Patio and terrace.

✕ **Anderton Boat Lift Café** Lift Lane, Anderton, Northwich CW9 6FW (01606 786777; www.andertonboatlift.co.uk). Café inside the Lift Operations Centre serving tea, coffee, hot and cold snacks, ice creams, etc. Children welcome. *Open as per the Lift Centre.*

🍺✕**The Stanley Arms** Old Road, Anderton CW9 6AG (01606 75059; www.stanleyarmsnorthwich. co.uk). Canalside, right opposite the Anderton Lift. Friendly real ale pub where children and dogs are welcome. Bar food served *all day, every day*. Outside seating and children's play area. Traditional pub games and open fires.

Dutton

This, the northernmost stretch of the Trent & Mersey, is a very pleasant one and delightfully rural. Most of the way the navigation follows the south side of the hills that overlook the River Weaver. From about 60ft up, one is often rewarded with excellent views of this splendid valley and the very occasional large vessels that ply up and down it. At one point one can see the elegant Dutton railway viaduct in the distance; then the two waterways diverge as the Trent & Mersey enters the woods preceding Preston Brook Tunnel. There is a stop lock south of the tunnel just beyond a pretty covered dry dock; there are often fine examples of restored working boats moored here. At the north end of the tunnel a notice announces that from here onwards one is on the Bridgewater Canal (*see Nicholson North West & the Pennines – Guide 5*). There are good moorings north of bridge 213, and to the south of Dutton stop lock.

NAVIGATIONAL NOTES

1 Access to Preston Brook Tunnel is restricted to *northbound on the hour to 10 minutes past the hour; southbound on the 1/2 hour to 20 mins to the hour.*
2 North of Preston Brook Tunnel you are on the Bridgewater Canal, which is owned by the Manchester Ship Canal Company, and is described in detail in *Nicholson North West & the Pennines*.
3 A Canal & River Trust licence is valid for seven consecutive days on this canal.

Pubs and Restaurants

🍺✕**The Leigh Arms** Warrington Road, Little Leigh, Northwich CW8 4QT (01606 853327; www. leigharms.co.uk). ¼ mile south of bridge 208, overlooking the Weaver and Acton Swing Bridge. Attractive old coaching inn with large restaurant area serving real ales and an extensive menu of home-made food *Mon-Fri L and E & Sat-Sun all day (until 17.00 Sun)*. Children and dogs welcome. Patio and garden seating, children's play area. Moorings nearby.

🍺✕**The Hollybush** Warrington Road, Little Leigh, Northwich CW8 4QY (01606 853196; www. thehollybush.net). ¼ mile north of bridge 209. Listed, timber-framed building, one of the oldest farmhouse pubs in the country, with unique charm and character. Wide range of interesting, home-cooked food served in bar and restaurant *Mon-Sat L and E & Sun all day*. Children welcome. Garden with children's play area, including bouncy castle. Traditional pub games. Quiz night *Sun*. B&B.

🍺✕**The Tunnel Top** Northwich Road, Dutton, Warrington WA4 4JY (01928 718181). Family pub serving real ale and excellent food *L and E*. Children welcome, dogs in large garden only. *Open all day*.

Boatyards

Ⓑ**Black Prince Holidays** Bartington Wharf, Acton Bridge, Northwich CW8 4QU (01606 852945; www.black-prince.com). 🚿♿D E Pump out, gas, narrowboat hire, day-hire mooring, long-term mooring, engine repairs, books, maps and gifts, coal, ice cream.

Ⓑ**Dutton Dry Dock** 3 Tunnel End, Dutton, Warrington WA4 4LA (01928 716701; duttondock1@btconnect.com). Dry dock, historic boat repairs, boat blacking, boat repairs, engineering and machine shop, vintage engine repairs.

● **Preston Brook**
Tunnel 1239yds long and forbidden to unpowered craft. It is crooked, like Barnton and Saltersford tunnels, and there is no towpath.

● **Dutton**
Cheshire. PO box, tel. Small settlement on top of Preston Brook Tunnel, at the end of the lane uphill from the south end of the tunnel.

INDEX

Abbey House Museum 141
Adelphi Mill 150
Aden 217
Adlington 108, 109
Aickman, Robert 57
Aintree 86, 92
Aintree Race Course 92
Aire & Calder Navigation 15–26, 46, 85, 138
Aire, River 15, 16, 20, 124, 126, 132 138
Aire Valley 136, 138
Airedale 126, 130
Albert Dock 86
All Saints Church, Daresbury 28
All Saints Church, Wigan 102
Allerton Bywater 21, 22
Altofts 21, 22
Altofts Lock 22
Altrincham 35
Ancient Crosses 210
Ancoats Mills 184
Anderton 214
Anderton Lift 207, 214–216, 218
Anson Engine Museum 152
Apperley Bridge 85, 92, 136, 137
Appley Bridge 102
Appley Lock 98
Apsley Basin 47, 66
Arrow Mill 187
Art Gallery, Huddersfield 67
Ashton 56, 167
Ashton Basin 70
Ashton Canal 27, 37, 56, 167–179
Ashton Canals Festival 174
Ashton Memorial 80
Ashton upon Mersey 35
Ashton-under-Lyne Junction 56, 174
Ashurst's Beacon 99
Astbury 145
Astley 40
Astley Cheetham Art Gallery 174
Astley Green 42
Astley Green Colliery Museum 42
Astley Hall 11

Baildon 135
Bancroft Mill Engine Trust 122
Bank Hall 100
Bank Newton Locks 116
Bankfield Museum 48
Barbridge 210
Barden Mill 110
Barnoldswick 114, 115
Barnton 209
Barnton Tunnel 214, 211
Barrowford 113
Barrowford Locks 112
Barrowford Reservoir 112
Barton 30, 38
Barton Aqueduct 36
Barton Swing Aqueduct 21, 34
Barton upon Irwell 41

Battyeford 45
Bay Horse Station 70
Beatles, The 86
Bentley, Thomas 207
Beswick Flight 171, 176
Bewsey 202, 203
Billinge Hall 113
Bilsborrow 72, 73
Bingley 132–135
Bingley Five Rise 85, 132, 135, 140
Birkwood Lock 24
Birmingham & Liverpool Junction Canal 141
Blackbrook 204
Blackburn 85, 112–114
Blackburn Cathedral 113
Black Pig's Dyke 27
Black Pit Aqueduct 190
Bluecoat Arts Centre 88
Bluecoat Display Centre 88
Bollington 32, 141, 148, 150
Bollin, River 32
Bolton 162
Bolton-le-Sands 82, 83
Borwick 84
Borwick Hall 84
Bosley 141
Bosley Locks 144–146
Bosley Top Lock 141
Bostock Hall 212
Botany Bay Village 111
Bradford 85
Bradley 126
Brearley 194
Bredbury 173
Bridge Street, Manchester 184
Bridgewater Canal 27–45, 85, 102, 104, 1113, 176, 179, 182, 207, 218
Brierfield 118
Brighouse 47, 52, 53
Brighouse Locks 52
Brindley, James 27, 146, 207, 211
British Oak Colliery 48
Broad Cut Low Lock 48
Broadbottom Lock 194
Broadoak Park 40
Broadreach Flood Lock 24
Broadreach Lock 15
Brock, River 70
Brodrick, Cuthbert 18
Broken Cross 214
Brookfoot Lock 52
Brownhill Countryside Centre 60
Budworth Mere 216
Burnley 85, 114, 116, 118, 119
Burnley Wharf 118
Burscough 85, 96–98
Burtonwood 204
Bury 165
Bury Art Museum 165
Bury Castle 165
Buttress 196
Buxworth 167, 168, 170

Buxworth Basin 154, 173
Byron, Lord 187

Calder & Hebble Navigation 15, 24, 46–55, 66, 176, 174
Calder Aqueduct 74
Calder Valley 53, 114, 116, 194
Calder, River 21, 46, 48, 50, 190, 194, 196
Callis Lock 190
Cambridgeshire 94
Canal Terminus 68
Canalside Craft Centre 79
Capernwray 82
Capernwray Arm 84
Carlisle 83, 124
Carnforth 82, 83
Caroline Bridge 22
Carr, John 26
Carroll, Lewis 28
Castle Hill and Jubilee Tower 67
Castlefield 27, 37, 182
Castlefield Junction 27, 36, 176
Castleford 15, 20–23, 138
Castleford Lock 15
Castleford Museum 22
Castleford Weir 21
Castleton 179, 186, 187
Catalyst Science Discovery Centre 199
Catforth 70
Catterall Basin 74
Central Manchester 36–39, 180–183
Chantry College 182
Chapel Milton 170
Chapel-en-le-Frith 170
Chat Moss 42
Cherry Tree 112
Cheshire 150, 207
Cheshire Locks 209
Cheshire Plain 143
Cheshire Ring 141, 174, 176
Chinese Arch 88
Chorley 68, 108, 109
Chorlton Street Lock 37
Church 114
City Art Gallery, Leeds 18
City of Manchester Stadium 182
City of Mary Immaculate Church, Barton upon Irwell 41
Clarence Dock 18
Clarence Mill 148
Claughton Castle 74
Clayton 68
Clayton Junction 176
Clegg Hall 186
Cliffe Castle 131
Clifton Country Park 158
Clifton Junction 160
Cloth Hall 196
Cloud, The 144
Coach House Heritage Centre 188

Cockerham Sands 74
Colne Lock 63
Colne Valley 56, 57, 62
Colne Valley Museum 67
Conder Valley 78
Congleton 142, 144, 145
Congleton Wharf 141
Conservation Centre 86
Cooper Bridge 46, 50, 51
Cooper Bridge Lock 66
Corn Exchange, Leeds 18
Cottage Museum 80
Courtaulds Factory 188
Cowling Bridge 108
Crag Bank 83
Craven Museum 129
Crayfish 68
Cromford & High Peak Railway
    167, 168, 170
Cromford Canal 167, 170
Cross Keys 124
Cross Stone Church 190
Croxteth Hall & Country Park 88
Croxton Aqueduct 212

Damart Mill 132
Dane, River 144, 212, 217
Dane Valley 214
Danes Moss 146
Daresbury 28
Darnside 80
Darwin, Erasmus 207
Dean Locks 102
Deep Cutting Bridge 78
Delph, The 60
Depot, The 114
Derwent Mouth 207
Dewsbury 48, 49
Dewsbury Arm 48, 49
Diggle 56, 60
Disley 168, 170
Disley Railway Tunnel 154
Dixon 207
Dobcross 60
Dobson Locks 136
Dock Pudding Championships
    196
Dock Road Edwardian Pumping
    Station 217
Dodgson, Charles Lutwidge 28
Doodfield Stores 154
Double Bridge 78
Douglas Navigation 99
Douglas, River 85, 98, 100–101
Douglas Valley 98, 102, 103
Doveholes 154, 167, 170, 173
Dover Lock Inn 104
Dowley Gap 132
Droylsden 176–178
Ducie Street Basin 180
Ducie Street Junction 27, 176
Duke's Wharf 42
Dukinfield Junction 167, 174
Dunham Massey Hall 32
Dunham Park 32
Dunham Town 32
Dunham Town Bridge 32
Dunham Underbridge 32

Dunkenhalgh Estate 114
Dunkenhalgh Hall 114
Dutton 218–219
Dutton Stop Lock 218

Eanam Wharf 114
East Lancashire Railway 166, 182
East Marton 124
East Riddlesden Hall 135
Eastham 39
Eccles 42
Edinburgh 75
Egerton, Francis 27
Eldonian Village 86
Ell Meadow 102
Elland 53
Elland Basin 52
Ellel Grange 78
Ellel Ministries 78
Ellenroad Engine House 187
Elmley Moor 48
Embassy and Bolton Abbey Steam
    Railway 129
Eureka Museum for
    Children 54
Eye on the Aire 16

Failsworth 179, 180, 184
Fairfield 178
Fairfield Junction 37, 176, 178
Fairies Lock 22
Fall Ing Lock 15, 24, 46, 52
Farnhill Hall 130
Farnworth 160
Field Locks 136
Fields, Gracie 187
Figure of Three Locks 48
Fishpond Lock 17
Fleet Bridge 21
Fleet Lock 21
Foulridge 120
Foulridge Tunnel 120, 121
Furness Vale 168, 170
Fusilier Museum 166
Fylde, The 74

Galgate 79
Gannow Tunnel 116
Gargrave 85, 114, 124, 125, 132
Garstang 68, 74, 75
Garstang Basin 74
Gathurst 99
Gawsworth 146
Gawsworth Hall 146
Gilbert, John 27, 42
Glasson 79
Glasson Basin 78
Glasson Branch 69, 78, 79
Glasson Dock 69, 78, 80
Goole 15, 21, 24
Goyt Mill 154
Goyt, River 168, 172, 173
Goyt Valley 154, 168, 170, 172
Gracie Fields Theatre 187
Grand Theatre, The 18
Grappenhall 30, 31
Great George Street, Leeds 18
Great Sankey 200

Great Tit 151
Greater Manchester 174
Greenberfield Top Lock 122
Greenfield 56, 60
Greenhalgh Castle 74, 75
Greens Bridge 148
Greenwood Flood Gates 50
Greenwood Lock 50
Grocers Warehouse 36
Gurnett Aqueduct 146

Hag Footbridge 152
Haigh Hall 107
Halifax 54, 196
Hall Green 141, 142
Hall Green Branch 141
Hall Green Stop Lock 141
Hall i'th' Wood 162
Halsall 95
Hapton 116, 117
Hardcastle Crags 195
Hardings Wood 142, 143,
    207, 208
Hardings Wood Junction 141, 142,
    208, 209
Harecastle 207
Harecastle Tunnel 209
Harris Museum &
    Art Gallery 71
Hartford Bridge 217
Haskayne 94, 95
Haslam Park 70
Hassall Green 209
Headingley 18
Heath Hall 26
Heath Old Hall 24
Heath Village 26
Hebden Bridge Alternative
    Technology Centre 195
Hebden Bridge 179, 190,
    194–197
Hebden, River 190
Henry Moore Institute 18
Heptonstall 195
Heptonstall Museum 196
Hepworth, Barbara 26
Hepworth Wakefield 26
Heron, Grey 76
Hest Bank 80, 82
High Lane 154, 168
High Lane Arm 154
Higher Boarshaw 185
Higher Poynton 152, 153
Higher Walton 30
Hirst Lock 132
Holme Mill Bridge 69
Holmfirth Tourist Information
    Centre 69
Holy Trinity Church,
    Skipton 132
Hopwood Hall, Middleton 187
Horbury 49
Horbury Bridge 48, 49
Houghton Tower 113
Houghton, Stanley 35
Hovis Mill 148
Huddersfield 49, 56, 62, 66,
    67, 174

Huddersfield Broad Canal 46, 51, 56, 65
Huddersfield Canals 56–68
Huddersfield Narrow Canal 46, 47, 56, 174
Hughes, Ted 196
Hull 21, 207
Hulme Lock Branch 36, 104
Humber 179
Hunt's Locks 217
Huron Basin 39
Hyde 174, 175
Hyde Bank Tunnel 172

Imperial War Museum North 39
Irk, River 185
Irwell, River 27, 42, 106, 157, 171
Irwell Sculpture Trail 164, 166

Johnson's Hill Flight 104
Johnson's Hill Locks 85, 111
Joule, James Prescott 35

Keckwick Bridge 28
Keer Aqueduct 84
Keer, River 82
Keighley & Worth Valley Railway 131
Keighley 130, 131
Kellet's Bridge 70
Kellingley Colliery 15
Kendal 69, 84
Kent Green 142, 143
Kerridge Bridge 148
Kershaw, Walter 36
Kettlethorpe 24
Kidsgrove 141, 209, 210
Kidsgrove Station 208
Kildwick 130, 131
King George's Hall 113
Kingfisher 216
King's Lock 207, 210
King's Road Lock 22
Kippax Lock 21
Kirklees Hall 50, 106
Kirklees Light Railway 67
Kirklees Park 50, 51
Kirkstall Abbey 138, 147
Kirkstall Power Station 138
Knostrop Flood Lock 17
Knostrop Lock 15

Lady Lever Art Gallery 86
Lake District 82
Lancashire 92, 192
Lancashire Coalfields 179
Lancaster 69, 78–81
Lancaster Canal 69–84, 98, 100, 106, 111
Lancaster Castle 80
Lancaster City Museum 80
Lancaster Pool 108
Lancaster Priory & Parish Church 80
Larfarge's Whitwood Terminal 15
Leeds & Liverpool Canal 17, 18, 27, 36, 40, 44, 78, 85–140

Leeds 15–19, 82, 83, 85, 122, 124, 126, 132, 136, 138–140
Leeds Bridge 18
Leeds Industrial Museum 18, 138, 147
Leeds Lock 15, 16, 18
Leeds Oil Terminal 17
Leeds Playhouse Repertory Theatre 18
Leigh 36, 44, 45, 85, 104, 105
Leigh Branch 27, 85, 102, 104, 106
Lemonroyd Lock 15, 16, 21
Library Lock 14
Library Theatre 183
Lincolnshire 94
Linthwaite 56, 63
Lion Salt Works, The 215
Litherland 92
Little Clegg 186
Little Lever 165
Little Moreton Hall 143
Littleborough 179, 186, 188, 189
Liverpool 27, 85–87, 96, 207
Liverpool Canal Link 86, 87
Liverpool Cathedral 88
Liverpool Docks 87, 86
Liverpool Football Club 86
Liverpool Heritage Walk 89
Liverpool, Pier Head 90
Liverpool Tate Art Gallery 86, 90
Liverpool Tideway 27
Lobb Mill 190
London 75
London Bridge 30
Longleat Lock 188
Lostock Gralam 214
Lough Neagh 27
Lower Peak Forest 158
Lowry, L S 41
Lowry Pier, The 41, 158
Luddenden Foot 196
Ludworth Moor 154
Lune Aqueduct 82
Lune Estuary 80
Lune, River 82
Lune Valley 82
Lune, The 69
Lydiate 94
Lyme Park 152, 171
Lymm 27, 32, 33
Lymm Cross 32

Macclesfield 141, 142, 146, 150–151, 154
Macclesfield Canal 141–158, 172, 207, 208
Macclesfield Forest 150
Maggoty's Wood 146
Maghull 92, 93
Malkin's Bank 210
Mallard duck 42
Manchester 27, 28, 31, 35–37, 39, 41, 54, 60, 96, 104, 141, 152, 167, 170, 170, 176, 178, 179, 182, 207, 212
Manchester Art Gallery 183
Manchester Cathedral 182
Manchester City Football Club 182

Manchester Jewish Museum 182
Manchester Museum 183
Manchester Ship Canal 28, 30, 32, 36, 38–40, 42, 178, 216
Manchester United Football Club 183
Marbury Country Park 214, 216
Marbury Hall 216
Maritime Museum 80
Marple 133, 142, 154, 167, 173
Marple Aqueduct 172, 173
Marple Junction 141, 154–167, 172, 173
Marple Locks 154, 172, 173
Marple Yard 172
Marsden 56, 62, 63
Marsden Mechanics Institute 63
Marston 214, 215
Martin Mere 89
Melling 93
Mendips & 20 Forthlin Road 89
Merchants' Warehouse 36
Mersey Ferries 89
Mersey, River 28, 34, 39, 179, 207
Merseyside Maritime Museum 89
Metropolitan Cathedral 89
Mickletown 22
Middleton Colliery 18
Middlewich 210, 212, 213
Middlewich Branch 207
Midlands, The 28, 141
Miles Platting 180
Mills Hill 185
Milnrow 187
Mirfield 50
Montague Burton 18
Moons Bridge 72
Moore 28
Moore, Henry 18, 22, 26
Moore Nature Reserve 199
Moorhen 72
Morecambe 124
Morecambe Bay 82
Morris, William 187
Moses Gate 160, 163
Moss Locks 186
Mossley 56, 60
Mossley Industrial Heritage Centre 60
Mow Cop 142, 143
Mow Cop Castle 143
Museum & Art Gallery, Blackburn 205
Museum of Liverpool Life 89
Museum of Science and Industry 153
Mytholmroyd 194, 196

National Coal Mining Museum for England 49
Nelson 120, 121
New Junction Canal 15
New Mills 168, 170
New Mills Heritage Centre 170
Newry Canal 27
New Springs 107
Newton Heath 180, 184
Newton-le-Willows 204

Nob End 164
Norris, John 32
North West Museum 205
Northwich 212, 214, 217
Norton Priory 28
Nuthatch 192

Oakgrove 146, 147
Octagonal Chapel 196
Office Lock 18
Old Mill 184
Oldham 158
Opie's Museum of Memories 102
Ordsall Hall 158
Outram, Benjamin 56, 57, 173
Oxford Street Bridge 37

Pagefield Locks 102
Paradise Mill 150
Paradise Wharf 176
Paragon Mill 184
Parbold 85
Parbold 98, 99
Park Nook Lock 52
Patricroft 42
Peak District 167, 170
Peak Forest Canal 56, 141, 154,
    167–178
Peak Forest Tramway 170
Pendle Heritage Centre 121
Pendle Hill 116, 118
Penketh 200, 201
Pennine Chain, The 144
Pennine Cycleway 125
Pennine Way 122
Pennines, The 32, 54, 56, 58, 60,
    72, 74, 86, 108, 141, 146, 158,
    174, 176, 180, 185, 194
Pennington Flash Country Park
    105
Piccadilly Village 176
Plank Lane 104, 105
Pomona Lock 36, 39
Poole Aqueduct 142, 208
Portland Basin 58, 174
Portland Basin Social & Industrial
    History Museum 174
Possett Bridge 172
Potteries, The 167, 207
Potters Brook 76, 77
Potters Brook Bridge 76
Preston 69, 70, 71, 96, 100, 101
Preston Brook 27–29, 102, 104,
    207, 212
Preston Brook Tunnel 28, 218, 219
Preston, William 76
Prince's Road Synagogue 89

Queen Street Mill Musum 118
Quickworth Church 60

Radcliffe 165
Rain Hall Rock Branch 122
Ramsden's Swing Bridge 24
Red Bull Aqueduct 142, 208
Rennie, John 74, 80
Ribble Estuary 85, 98, 99
Ribble Link 69, 70, 100, 101

Ribble, River 99, 100, 111
Ringley 160
Rishton 114, 116
River Lock 17, 85
Robert Bolt Theatre 34, 35
Rochdale 36, 186–188
Rochdale Canal 27, 36, 37, 54,
    158, 176, 179–198
Rochdale Canal Corridor
    Regeneration 184
Rochdale Pioneers Museum 187
Rode Heath 209
Rode Heath Rise 209
Romiley 173
Rose Bridge Colliery 107
Rose Grove 116
Rose Hill Tunnel 172
Rougeley 207
Rourkes Forge 118
Royal Armouries Museum 17, 18
Royal Assent 27
Royal Exchange Theatre 184
Royal Mill 184
Rufford 98–100
Rufford Branch 85, 96, 98, 99
Rufford Church 100
Rufford Hall 100
Rufford Old Hall 100
Runcorn 27, 28, 31, 102
Runcorn Gap 207

Saddleworth 60, 61
Saddleworth Bank 60
Saddleworth Moor 60
Saddleworth Museum & Art
    Gallery 60
St Aidens Open-Cast Mine 15, 21
St Andrew's Church, Maghull 93
St Chad's Parish Church, Rochdale
    187
St Cuthbert's Church, Halsall 96
St Helens 205
St Helens Canal 27
St Hilda's Church, Bilsborrow 73
St James' Church, Church 114
St John's Church, Galgate 80
St Laurence's Church,
    Chorley 119
St Martin's Church, Sales 35
St Mary's Chantry Chapel,
    Wakefield 26
St Mary's Church, Astbury 145
St Mary's Church, Eccles 42
St Mary's Church, Ellel Grange 76
St Mary's Church, Leigh 105
St Mary's Church, Sandbach 210
St Michael's Church, Ashton-
    under-Lyme 16
St Michael's Church, Macclesfield
    150
St Michael's Church, Middlewich
    213
St Oswald's Church, Warton 84
St Peter's Square, Manchester
    37, 178
St Walburge's Church, Preston 71
St Wilfred's Church, Grappenhall
    31

Sale 34, 35
Salford 41, 158, 159
Salford Art Gallery and Museum
    41, 158, 159
Salford Quays 36, 38, 41, 178
Salt Museum 217
Salts Mill 132, 135
Saltaire 135
Salterforth 122
Salterhebble 14, 36
Salterhebble Basin 52
Salterhebble Branch 52
Salterhebble Locks 52
Saltersford Locks 214
Saltersford Tunnel 214, 101
Sandal Castle 26
Sandbach 210
Sankey Brook Canal 27
Sankey Canal 198, 205
Sankey Valley Heritage Centre
    205
Savile Town Basin 48, 49
Scarisbrick Hall 96
Scholar Green 145
Scout Tunnel 60
Seal 34
Seamons Moss Bridge 36
Sefton Park Palm House 90
Seized 88
Selby 15
Settle 124
Shardlow 207
Sheffield 21
Shibden Hall Folk Museum 54
Ship Canal 27, 28, 30, 31, 36, 39
Shipley 85, 132–136
Shropshire Union Canal 39, 141,
    210
Silk Museum 150
Silsden 130, 131
Simpson's Bridge 114
Skipton 83, 85, 124, 126–129
Skipton Castle 129
Skipton Woods 129
Slaithwaite 56, 63
Slattock Locks 185, 193
Slattocks 185
Smeaton, John 46
Smith Art Gallery 52
Smithill's Hall 162 184
Smithy Bridge 187, 188
Snake Bridge 146
South Locks 185
Southport 96
Sowerby Bridge 22, 46, 52, 54, 55,
    176, 179, 194
Sowerby Bridge Basin 54
Sparth Reservoir 62
Speke Hall 90
Springs Branch 85, 86, 118, 126,
Stables Centre 107
Staffordshire Arm 36
Stalybridge 56, 58–60
Stalybridge Library 174
Standedge Interpretation Centre
    63
Standedge Tunnel 56, 57, 63
Stanley Ferry 24

Steanor Bottom Toll House 188, 189
Stevens, Alexander 80
Stockport 154
Stockport Branch 176
Stockton Heath 30,
Stockton Quay 30
Stoke 143
Stoneclough 160
Stoodley Pike 194
Stretford 34
Strines 168, 170
Stubbing Locks 190
Sudley House 90
Sutton 141
Sutton Lane Ends 146
Sutton Reservoir 146
Swellands Reservoir 56
Swillbrook Bridge 70
Swillington Bridge 22

Tame, River 60, 174
Tame Valley 56
Tarleton 85, 100, 101
Tarleton Lock 100
Tate Liverpool 89
Taylor, Enoch 63
Telford, Thomas 56, 141, 207
Temple Newsam Farm 22
Temple Newsam House and Garden 22
Tewitfield 69, 84
Thackray Museum 18
Theatre Royal & Opera House, The 26
Thelwall 30, 31
Thelwall Underbridge 30, 31
Thelwall Viaduct 30
Thompson Park 118
Thornes Flood Lock 48
Thornes Lock 48
Thornhill 50
Thornhill Double Locks 48, 49
Thornhill Power Station 46, 48, 60
Thornsett Road Bridge 170
Three Sisters Recreation Area 105
Throstle Nest Footbridge 36, 43
Thwaite Mills Industrial Museum 16, 19, 23
Toddbrook Reservoir 170
Todmorden 179, 188-193, 198
Todmorden Locks 178, 192

Tolson Museum 67
Torrs Gorge 170
Town Bridge 217
Towneley Hall 118
Trencherfield Mill 102
Trent & Mersey Canal 27, 104, 141, 142, 207-219
Trent, River 21, 207
Tropical World and Roundhay Park 19
Tuel Lane Lock 179
Tuel Lane Tunnel 179
Turnbridge Loco Liftbridge 66
Turnpike Gallery 105

Upper Peak Forest 168-171
Uppermill 60

Vale Royal 216
Velodrome 178
Victoria Bridge 18
Victoria Gallery and Museum 90
Victoria Mill 180
Victoria Square, Leeds 18

Wainhouse Tower 54
Wakefield 15, 22, 24-26, 46, 49, 138
Wakefield Flood Lock 24
Wakefield Lock 15
Wakefield Museum 26
Walker, The 90
Walkley's Canalside Mill 194, 195
Walsden 189
Walton Hall 30
Walton Summit Branch 85, 110, 116
Wardle Canal 210
Warrington 30, 202, 203
Waterside Arts Centre 34, 35
Waters Meeting 27, 36-39, 42
Waterways Gardens 102
Watery Lane Aqueduct 144
Weaver Navigation 39, 214, 216, 99
Weaver, River 207, 214, 217, 218
Weavers' Square 196
Weavers' Triangle 118
Wedgwood, Josiah 207
West Park Museum 150
West Parkgate 152
West Summit Lock 188

Western Approaches Museum 90
Whaley Bridge 167, 170,
Whaley Bridge Branch 168
Whatcroft Hall 124
Wheelock 210, 211
Wheelock Flight 210
Wheelton 111
White Horse Bridge 72
White Nancy Monument 148
Whitwood 21
Whitworth Art Gallery 184
Whitworth, Robert 56
Widnes 199
Wigan 44, 85, 86, 92, 94, 96, 100, 102-104, 106, 114, 212
Wigan Coalfield 99
Wigan Flight 106
Wigan Lane 105
Wigan Locks 106, 107, 140
Wigan Pier 102
Wigan Pier Complex 102
Wigan Top Lock 85, 111
Wigg Island 200
Wilkinsons Farm 124
Williamson Tunnels Heritage Centre 90
Wincham 214
Winterburn Reservoir 122
Withnell Fold 110, 111
Witton Country Park 113
Wood Row 22
Woodlesford 19, 20
Woodley 173
Woodnook Lock 15, 22
Woodpecker, Green 76
Working Class Movement Library 159
World of Glass, The 206
World Museum 90
Worsley 27, 40-44
Worsley Delph 27, 40, 42
Worsley Old Hall 42
Wyre, River 74

York 21
Yorkshire 18, 46, 192
Yorkshire Coalfield 15
Yorkshire Dales National Park 124, 125
Yorkshire Sculpture Park, Bretton Hall 26